The Age of Anomaly

Spotting Financial Storms in a Sea of Uncertainty

Andrei Polgar

Contents

Chapter 1: Outsmarted by Frogs 1

Chapter 2: What This Book Is and Isn't About................................ 5

Chapter 3: Anomalies, Then and Now 9

    Chapter 3.1: Then.. 11
    Chapter 3.1.1 The Tulip Mania 13
    Chapter 3.1.2 The South Sea Bubble 23
    Chapter 3.1.3 The Mississippi "Bubble" 32
    Chapter 3.1.4: The Panic of 1825 42
    Chapter 3.1.5 The British Railway Mania(s).......................... 47
    Chapter 3.1.6: The German (Weimar Republic) Hyperinflation 54
    Chapter 3.1.7: The Florida Real Estate Boom of the 1920s 60
    Chapter 3.1.8: The Great Depression of 1929 66
    Chapter 3.2: Now.. 72
    Chapter 3.2.1: The End of Bretton Woods and the Gold/Silver Bubble of 1977-1980 73
    Chapter 3.2.2: The Black Monday Stock Market Crash of 1987 80
    Chapter 3.2.3: The Japanese Bubble of the 1980s 86
    Chapter 3.2.4: The Asian Financial Crisis of 1997................ 92
    Chapter 3.2.5: The 1998 Collapse of Long-Term Capital Management 99
    Chapter 3.2.6: The Dot-Com Bubble 104
    Chapter 3.2.7: The Great Recession of 2007-2008.............. 110
    Chapter 3.2.8: The Short Domain Mania of 2015-2016 117

Chapter 4: Spotting Financial Storms 125

    Chapter 4.1: A Sea of Uncertainty... 127
    Chapter 4.2: Dosage and Context.. 136
    Chapter 4.3: Accepting Your Limitations 138
    Chapter 4.4: Canaries in the Coal Mine 141

Chapter 4.4.1: Looking Over Your Shoulder 142
Chapter 4.4.2: Improving Your Reaction Time 144
Chapter 4.4.3: False Positives... 148
Chapter 4.4.4: Mainstream Media vs. Alternative Media.................. 150
Chapter 4.5: The 11 Storm-Causing Deadly Sins 156
Chapter 4.6: Polgar's Prudence Principles 167

Chapter 5: Becoming Resilient...177

Chapter 5.1: Landing on Your Feet as a Way of Life 179
Chapter 5.2: Financial Resilience... 182
Chapter 5.2.1: My (In)Famous Personalized Portfolio Principle 184
Chapter 5.2.2: What Should You Invest In?.. 189
Chapter 5.2.3: Status Quo Assets 192
Chapter 5.2.3.1: Fair-Weather Status Quo Assets 194
Chapter 5.2.3.2: Life Jacket Status Quo Assets................................... 217
Chapter 5.2.3.3: Sentiment-Neutral Status Quo Assets...................... 235
Chapter 5.2.4: Trailblazer Assets 250
Chapter 5.2.4.1: Fair-Weather Trailblazer Assets 253
Chapter 5.2.4.2: Life Jacket Trailblazer Assets................................... 273
Chapter 5.2.4.3: Sentiment-Neutral Trailblazer Assets 283
Chapter 5.3: Other Types of Resilience 292
Chapter 5.3.1: Professional Resilience (Investing in Yourself).......... 294
Chapter 5.3.2: Mental Resilience 300
Chapter 5.3.2.1: Making Decisions Under Pressure........................... 301
Chapter 5.3.2.2: Coping With Financial Losses 304
Chapter 5.3.2.3: Thinking Outside the Box....................................... 308
Chapter 5.3.2.4: Relationships.. 310
Chapter 5.3.2.5: The Medical Dimension 313
Chapter 5.3.3: Physical Resilience 314
Chapter 5.3.4: SHTF Resilience... 319
Chapter 5.3.4.1: General Disaster Preparedness................................. 320
Chapter 5.3.4.2: What If You Have to Bug Out or Relocate?........... 328
Chapter 5.3.4.3: Can You Prepare for Everything?............................ 335
Chapter 5.4: Conclusions... 337

Chapter 6: How I See Things 341

Chapter 6.1: Why So Serious? 343
Chapter 6.2: We're Doomed 348
Chapter 6.3: Keynesian? Libertarian? Socialist? Capitalist? 356
Chapter 6.4: [Insert Prefix Here] + Flation 358
Chapter 6.4.1: Inflation 359
Chapter 6.4.2: Deflation... 363
Chapter 6.4.3: Stagflation... 366
Chapter 6.5: Central Banking Shenanigans 368
Chapter 6.6: Facts vs. Opinions vs. Conclusions..................... 374
Chapter 6.7: The Big Reset.. 379
Chapter 6.8: What Happens After the Big Reset? 386

Conclusions?..391

Bibliography 407

Chapter 1: Outsmarted by Frogs

You've probably heard the reasonably famous story about how if you place a frog in cold water and gradually increase the water's temperature, the frog won't notice it's being boiled alive. Well, that is just a myth. Frogs are apparently smarter than we give them credit for and as University of Oklahoma's Dr. Victor Hutchinson and others[1] pointed out, they'd simply escape in such a scenario.

For humans, however, the metaphor fits like a glove.

But what's this metaphor all about anyway? Simply put, it tells us our reactions to gradually unfolding threats is slow or even non-existent. If you see a man carrying a gun running toward you, running away seems like the natural thing to do. But if the gunman goes about it in a less obvious manner, the likelihood of you running away decreases. If he's really good, he might even manipulate and befriend you, thereby getting close to a victim who welcomes him with open arms.

In his *The Black Swan* book, Nassim Taleb[2] gives an eloquent example:

"A turkey is fed for 1,000 days by a butcher, and every day confirms to the turkey and the turkey's economics department and the turkey's risk management department and the turkey's analytical department that the butcher loves turkeys, and every day brings more confidence to the statement. But on day 1,001, there will be a surprise for the turkey…"

… but what does all of this have to do with my book?

The Age of Anomaly has one purpose and one purpose only: enabling readers to prepare for future financial calamities by helping them become better and better at spotting anomalies on the one hand and on the other hand, helping

---

[1] Whit Gibbons. "The Legend of the Boiling Frog Is Just a Legend." *Ecoviews.* November 18, 2002. http://srel.uga.edu/outreach/ecoviews/ecoview021118.htm.
[2] Nassim N. Taleb. *The Black Swan: The Impact of the Highly Improbable.* London: Penguin Books, 2007.

them be more resilient in general. Contrary to popular belief, you don't have to be brilliant to land on your feet after a financial crisis, you merely need to stop being outsmarted by frogs. The most frustrating aspect (to me, at least) about what I like to call economic anomalies is that they're anything but subtle. In hindsight, they seem blatantly obvious but what exactly about them is it that makes otherwise rational individuals ignore clear warning signals?

In my opinion, it all revolves around an extremely effective numbing mechanism. We don't notice blatantly obvious anomalies mostly because we don't want to. And since we don't want to notice them, we perhaps subconsciously choose not to. I'll kill two birds with one stone by making an analogy to a "relative" of the turkey through yet another myth: that ostriches bury their heads in the sand in a reality-defying attempt at hiding from predators.

Hint: they don't[3] but we do.

Whenever we're in a situation which seems too good to be true (because it is) but are in one way or another either beneficiaries or potential beneficiaries, us humans (unlike our feathered counterparts) choose to ignore reality and bury our heads in the proverbial sand. We don't want the party to end, we want anomalies to go on forever because just thinking about the benefits makes us feel all warm and fuzzy inside.

Of course tech stocks can go up forever. As can bitcoin. Or real estate… or anything else for that matter. We see how rich other people got from something which is clearly an anomaly (a dramatic and unsustainable asset price evolution, for example) and naturally project the same scenario onto our own lives. Of course huge price spikes can't last forever but we want them to, we desperately want them to.

As such, we won't let something as mundane as the blatantly obvious stand in the way of our dreams. We just won't! I want to make it clear that if you're the type of person who proudly states he's unwilling to change his mind, you should stop reading this book right now. Being willing and able to change

---

[3] Hannah Keyser. "Why Do Ostriches Stick Their Heads in the Sand?" *Mental Floss*. April 15, 2014. http://mentalfloss.com/article/56176/why-do-ostriches-stick-their-heads-sand.

your mind when every fiber of your being dictates otherwise is crucial but fortunately learnable.

Through the following chapters, we'll roll up our sleeves and do just that.

Chapter 2: What This Book Is and Isn't About

… so, why have I decided to study financial anomalies and write this book?

Because, quite frankly, this is the elephant in the room. As I'm writing this, our world is changing dramatically right before our eyes and not for the better. The United Kingdom has voted to leave the European Union. An isolationist candidate won the presidency of the United States. The European Union is disintegrating, as rich countries become sick and tired of bailing out poorer ones and poorer countries are fed up with the austerity programs that have been shoved down their throats. China is a massive bubble ready to pop, with gross asset misallocations having taken place over the years, from ghost cities to ultra-speculative investments in anything from stocks to domain names and cryptocurrencies.

The list could go on and on. Calling this a huge mess would be the understatement of the century. The average individual is starting to notice that "something" is just not right. Now most of them cannot accurately pinpoint what the problem is but they do have this spooky feeling deep down inside that something is just waiting to blow. If you start educating yourself in an attempt to find out what's happening, you'll quickly realize there's an overwhelming amount of information to digest. Most of it noise.

When confronted with problems so complex that they make you feel small and inadequate, your first instincts tell you to just look the other way. To move on, live your life and hope for the best. An awful strategy, if you ask me. If ignoring problems would make them go away, I'd be all for it. Unfortunately, it doesn't work that way. In my opinion, systemic disruptions of epic proportions will take place over our lifetimes and I suspect there will be far more losers than winners.

Those caught off guard might see their entire wealth evaporate before their eyes. They'll ask themselves what they did to deserve this. Well, nothing really. It certainly won't be their fault but all of that won't matter. Once a financial tsunami hits, it's too late to start asking yourself questions. The best time to prepare for such cataclysms is right now. If you're reading this book thinking I'm going to give you an exact timetable or something along those lines, you'll be bitterly disappointed.

I firmly believe nobody can predict the future in an accurate and consistent manner. As such, I won't make a fool of myself by telling you a financial calamity will hit in x days or y months. At the end of the day, nobody knows precisely when the proverbial you know what will hit the fan. Sure, there are plenty of gurus who tell you they do but they're charlatans and nothing more. Trust them at your own peril.

Alright, what should people do then?

The only thing you can do is keep your eyes open and develop the habit of being early rather than late to the party. I'd much rather start preparing for a financial crisis that I think is coming one year too early than a day too late. Always add a generous margin of error to the mix. Remember, you're preparing for destiny-altering calamities here, now is not the time for laser precision. Throughout this book, I'll be analyzing various financial calamities one by one and drawing conclusions each time. Does understanding the past make it possible for us to accurately predict the future? No, I wouldn't go so far as to state that. However, the more you read about what happened in the past, the better you will end up being at keeping your eyes open and enabling you to do that will be one of this book's top goals.

Aside from helping you learn from the past, I'll also do my best to help you become better at preparing for the unexpected in general. I for one have studied anomalies extensively but despite the massive amount of information I've gathered over the years, the next cataclysmic event may very well end up taking me by surprise as well. As such, I do my best to always be prepared for the unexpected and through this book, I'll try to help you do the same. From lifestyle changes to investments in assets which thrive when others plummet (antifragile[4] assets, as Nassim Taleb calls them), there are quite a few things one can do, as you will be about to find out.

I don't want *The Age of Anomaly* to be full of fluff and introductions, so we'll get right down to business as of the next chapter and start analyzing past and present anomalies one by one.

---

[4] Nassim N. Taleb. *Antifragile: Things That Gain From Disorder*. New York City: Random House, 2012.

Chapter 3: Anomalies, Then and Now

This chapter has two primary goals: analyzing past anomalies in order to draw conclusions on the one hand and on the other hand, putting today's anomalies under the microscope so as to once again draw but also compare conclusions. The chapter's title therefore speaks for itself and the structure of chapter 3 should be obvious:

1. **Chapter 3.1 (Then)**, through which I will analyze the financial anomalies of the past in chronological order, starting with the very first documented asset bubble, the tulip mania
2. **Chapter 3.2 (Now)**, through which I'll be referring to the anomalies I've identified closer to the present

I've spent copious amounts of time researching so that you don't have to. Rather than invest two weeks of your time reading books and material about the tulip mania, you can simply read chapter 3.1.1 (the tulip mania subchapter) in about fifteen minutes. I've done everything humanly possible to identify the most important facts and figures associated with each anomaly and put them at your disposal in an easy-to-digest form.

By all means, feel free to take things further and read the material I'm referring to in the footnotes but for most readers, that will probably not be necessary. I tried to help you genuinely and meaningfully understand each phenomenon that's been covered. My main goal isn't getting you to robotically memorize some numbers and information, it's enabling you to see each anomaly from the perspective of those who have experienced it.

Make no mistake, you will eventually be in their shoes.

When I share information about anomalies which seem blatantly obvious now but were hard to spot by those who actually experienced them first-hand, you're most likely tempted to raise an eyebrow. To tell yourself you'll be smarter. And more alert. Unfortunately, no matter how much time you dedicate to informing and preparing yourself, I can pretty much assure you that throughout your existence, you'll end up being taken by surprise on more than one occasion.

The sense of superiority we tend to feel when reading about past calamities is misguided at best. Let's try to understand how anomalies work, why they're sometimes ridiculously hard to spot and why those who didn't manage to notice them aren't in any way inferior. They're just, well… human!

Chapter 3.1: Then

A lot of people claim they can accurately predict the future by analyzing the past. They refer to themselves as trend forecasters or something along those lines, using fairly "sciency" terminology that makes them sound legitimate and a lot of gullible individuals fall for it. Perhaps because they have some kind of attraction toward mysticism, I don't know. The bottom line is that all of the people I've come across who've claimed to be able to accurately predict the future have proven to be liars.

I'll even go so far as to say that whenever someone tells me he's able to predict the future by analyzing the past, I raise an eyebrow and adopt a "guilty until proven innocent" attitude rather than the other way around. When you've come across charlatan after charlatan, you can't help but become more prudent. Call my attitude politically incorrect if you'd like to, I for one tend to think of it as a defense mechanism.

But by all means, try to prove me wrong.

If you think one of the gurus you see on TV or on the Internet is actually the real deal, there's an easy way to find out if that's actually the case. I will assume the person you're thinking about is at least moderately well-known, so you should be able to find at least a few past interviews in which the person in question made predictions. Read those interviews one by one and put together a list of predictions made by that guru.

Then start finding out how many of those have panned out. I for one have yet to come across someone with a stellar track record and in fact, some of the gurus I've been keeping track of have proven to be remarkably bad at what they do. You would have been better off flipping a coin than taking their advice. Don't take my word for it though, feel free to always do your own research.

Do I think it's possible to predict the future by analyzing the past?

No.

Then why on Earth am I dedicating a huge section of this book to studying the past? It may seem I'm out of my mind and I might be for other reasons but definitely not this one. While I do very strongly believe the past doesn't tell you exactly what's going to happen in the future, I firmly believe it tells you almost everything else. I warm-heartedly agree with those who say history doesn't repeat itself but it rhymes.

By studying history, you're essentially studying human action or simply put, studying history means studying humans. By analyzing the events which have in one way or another shaped humanity, you end up learning quite a bit about what makes us humans tick. Few endeavors out there tell you more about human nature than studying history. Of course, things change and events have to be put in context, which is precisely what I plan to do through this section of *The Age of Anomaly*.

I haven't written this section with the intention of merely listing events in chronological order. My goal isn't just telling you to memorize information so as to appear smart during dinner conversations. I genuinely believe quite a few pieces of information are worth memorizing if you want to extract as much value as possible from this book and will point them out when the time comes. However, I also believe understanding "why" people did something is even more important than knowing "what" they did.

I'll be analyzing some of the most important economic anomalies in history, starting with the tulip mania, which is the first recorded asset bubble and breathtakingly fascinating at that. Through the next subchapters, I'll do my best to help you see the world through the eyes of the people who have experienced these anomalies first-hand. We don't intend to judge these people, we want to understand them.

Let's take a deep breath and approach the next subchapters with an open mind!

Chapter 3.1.1 The Tulip Mania

As the oldest documented asset bubble out there, the tulip mania tends to be surrounded by an aura of mysticism and unfortunately also one of disinformation. Through this subchapter, I'll do my best to analyze the tulip mania in a rational manner so as to draw the proper conclusions. My main goal should be easy enough to predict: figuring out what anomalies we've witnessed during the tulip mania and what lessons we ought to learn.

A lot of authors have written about the tulip mania but while there's a quite a bit of literature about it, there isn't as much actual, verifiable information. For example, one of the most popular books in which this mania was discussed is one written by Charles Mackay all the way back in 1841[5]. Unfortunately, while it's a great asset from the perspective of literature and features some genuinely superb archaic English, it's not very historically accurate. That's the problem with most of the tulip mania-related literature out there, it approaches the phenomenon as more of a myth than a historical event and that's just plain wrong.

If you want to read a genuinely detailed as well as historically accurate depiction of the tulip mania, I'd highly recommend the work of Mike Dash[6]. Of course, this is only a recommendation for history buffs. For everyone else, the information I'll be sharing throughout this subchapter should be more than enough. I've tried to separate facts from noise so as to put a balanced rather than mythical view on the table.

Let me start with something that seems an anomaly but actually isn't.

I'm referring to the idea that something like a tulip bulb can be worth a lot of money. Some might be tempted to consider this the #1 anomaly associated with the tulip mania but as I'm about to explain, it isn't even an anomaly. Like many other asset bubbles, the tulip mania started out with reasonable

---

[5] Charles Mackay. *Extraordinary Popular Delusions and the Madness of Crowds*. London: Richard Bentley, 1841.
[6] Mike Dash. *Tulipomania*. New York City: Broadway Books, 2001.

"fundamentals" and it's important to get a few facts straight before moving on with our analysis:

1. At the beginning of the madness, people only paid a premium for very rare tulip types. The Semper Augustus was the most desirable tulip out there and rightfully so, with only about twelve (yes, twelve) of them available. It was the epitome of rarity if you will and this is the first argument I want to get across, that the tulips which were initially considered desirable and as such commanded high prices were very, very rare

2. Aside from being rare, tulips were also somewhat of a novelty from the East. They've most likely started making their way from Istanbul (Ottoman Empire) to Antwerpen in the autumn of 1562. In the Ottoman Empire, the tulip was considered sacred. In the 14th century for example, even its then-ruler (Bayezid) wore a shirt on which a tulip was depicted under his armor. His great-grandson Mehmed then conquered Constantinople (now known as Istanbul) and the city ended up becoming the most important one in the empire by far, with vast tulip-filled gardens reflecting the way in which they perceived this flower. As the empire grew, European territories all the way to Vienna were conquered during the reign of Suleiman, the great-great-grandson of Mehmed. This state of affairs made a cultural exchange between the European and Ottoman civilizations inevitable and among other things, brought tulips to the Dutch Empire

3. Let's not eliminate the beauty of the tulip from the equation. Do keep in mind that someone living in the Dutch Republic back in the 17th century had considerably fewer means of entertainment at his disposal than someone living in the Netherlands today. This is especially true for the wealthiest members of society, who regarded gardening as one of the few available hobbies back in the days of the tulip mania

This much is certain: tulips were rare, new and beautiful.

It should therefore come as no surprise that people, especially wealthy individuals, were willing to pay a premium for such flowers. Think about the present and ask yourself: would it really be that much of a big deal to see a billionaire pay a lot of money for a flower such as the Semper Augustus, knowing that only a handful of them exist? Of course not and for this reason, it should be clear that the initial popularity of tulips was not an anomaly. It was simply the consequence of supply and demand. You had a new and beautiful flower for which there was quite a bit of demand and which was available in limited supply. Economics 101.

To understand why anomalies appeared, we have to understand the Dutch.

The Dutch Republic only existed since 1590 and, quite surprisingly, ended up becoming Europe's richest country by far. It didn't possess impressive natural resources and on the contrary, we can call the Dutch Republic a fairly inhospitable place. Politically speaking, things were also anything but easy, especially due to the country's conflictual relationship with Spain. Seemingly despite all odds though, the Dutch Republic managed to do very well, especially thanks to its prosperous trading activities.

In contrast to the economic prestige of the country, the life of the average Dutch was abundant in tales of hardship. The currency of the Dutch Republic was the guilder and it was maintained until 2002, when it was replaced with the Euro. The Dutch transacted in guilders and stuivers, with one guilder being worth 20 stuivers. Let's take a minute to see how the Dutch lived in the 17th century.

The average skilled Dutch worker (a carpenter, for example) earned about one guilder per day. Less skilled laborers such as those who worked in bleaching facilities earned over two times less, only 8 stuivers daily. To put things into perspective, the less skilled laborer's daily wage was enough to buy a large 5.5 kg (12 lb) bread but that's about it. Rents were high and items were expensive, with a rather uncomfortable low-quality bed costing 10-15 guilders and a modern one a whopping 100 guilders.

Dutch workers were usually paid by the hour and during the longer days of the year, willingly put in overtime so as to accumulate enough money to last them for the winter, when the shorter days put a ceiling on their earning potential. To survive back then, you literally had no choice but to be frugal and hard-working, two very strong characteristics associated with Dutch workers. As you surely suspect, frugal people who worked all day just to get by had little interest in admiring flowers.

By 1620, the tulip did end up becoming quite popular in the Dutch Republic but only among society's elites. If you were a dinner guest of one of your city's most influential families, you might have had the privilege of being close to a tulip but that's pretty much it. An average tradesman, who earned a very respectable 6 guilders per day, wouldn't have been able to get his hands on one of the sought-after tulips at that point. Not even a successful tradesman who earned two times more would have had that privilege, simply because those tulips were so rare around 1620 that even if you had money to spend on them, you couldn't buy any.

This imbalance persisted until the following decade.

As of 1623, we start discovering records of premium offers that were made for tulips, initially 1,200 guilders for a highly sought-after Semper Augustus bulb (an offer which was refused), then 2,000 and even 3,000 the very next summer. Those offers weren't accepted either. It was clear that for the most sought-after tulips, the demand far exceeded the supply of bulbs. The star of the show was clearly the Semper Augustus, the most beautiful tulip of the Rosen category. Next on the podium was the Viceroy, the best tulip of the Violetten category and on position number three, we had the "Red and Yellow of Leiden," the star of the Bizarden tulip category.

Strangely enough, the "uniqueness" of the most sought-after tulips was actually a disease. Therefore, as peculiar as it may sound, diseased tulips were far more popular than healthy ones (simple, monochrome tulips). In fact, for a very long time, most tulips didn't even have a market value. The best of the best fetched impressive amounts, whereas most of the other tulips weren't considered investment grade. Only at the very height of the tulip mania did this change, since the best tulips ended up becoming prohibitively expensive and the poorer market participants were forced to trade lower quality bulbs among one another.

In the 1630s, the buying and selling of bulbs came closer to becoming mainstream. Since the stars of the show became prohibitively expensive, investors ended up settling for less rare alternatives but still, the tulips in question were quite spectacular. As time passed, investing in bulbs became a reality for more and more people. It was no longer something limited to a handful of elites. Prices kept going up, initially at a fairly slow pace. As of 1634 however, the pace changed significantly. This rapid evolution continued through 1635 and all the way until the winter of 1636. Prices could double in a little over a week and people wouldn't be surprised.

The height of the tulip mania was reached in December 1636 and January 1637.

Over that two-month period, the prices of several tulip types genuinely exploded and went up roughly ten times. A 1,000% return could have been generated in two months and do keep in mind that even the "old" price was already insanely high. At that point, logic flew out the window and insanity ensued. Everyone wanted a piece of the action. Even the average craftsman wanted in.

But how was that possible? How did people who barely made one guilder after a full working day afford to participate in this madness? Simple, they borrowed money. An eloquent example is represented by the fact that weavers were the very first "middle class" representatives. This is because the expensive looms they used were viable collateral and as such, lenders were willing to offer them money. Money that they, of course, used to speculate on the tulip market. Sanity was a thing of the past.

Aside from credit-funded speculation, another explanation as to how the average Joe could participate is represented by the fact that the "standards" kept becoming more and more lenient as well in the world of tulips. In January 1637, a Semper Augustus fetched 10,000 guilders. An amount a weaver would make after 10,000 full days of work. Or on the 5th of February 1937, a Viceroy bulb fetched 4,200 guilders at an auction held in Alkmaar. Obviously amounts out of reach for the average speculator. The same way, the other "best of the best" tulips were also prohibitively expensive. It should therefore come as no surprise that the previously mentioned standards all but disappeared. Lower value tulips appreciated even more dramatically than established ones. In fact, lots of tulips went from being worthless to being worth a lot of money.

It's fairly safe to say we've identified four anomalies thus far:

1. The fact that tulip bulbs ended up selling for staggering amounts, even as much as 10,000 guilders. An amount a carpenter or weaver would make in 40 years, assuming a year has 250 working days.

Under the same assumption, a lower skilled laborer who works in a bleaching facility would make that much in 100 years. As explained earlier in this subchapter, the fact that certain desirable tulips sell for a premium isn't an anomaly but when prices reach the equivalent of 100 years of labor, we've most definitely ventured in anomaly territory

2. The fact that tulips which were anything but desirable before the mania (they weren't nearly as rare, nor was their beauty appreciated as much) ended up being worth a lot of money as well. The explanation is simple and the irrationality of it all obvious. The explanation merely revolves around the fact that lower-income individuals desperately wanted a piece of the action. This made them head into the realm of irrationality by creating a market for assets which should have never been considered investment grade

3. The fact that the average Joe thought he too could become a successful speculator, despite having pretty much no idea what he was doing. He wasn't passionate about the asset in question (in our case tulips), he wasn't knowledgeable either and quite frankly, he could care less about that asset… the average Joe was in it for the money and nothing else

4. The fact that people got into debt so that they could speculate, something that should always be considered a huge warning signal. From weavers who used their looms as collateral to tradesmen who leveraged their connections to obtain additional capital, people became greedy and obsessed with speculation. Nothing, including capital shortages, could stand between them and their desire to speculate

By 1634[7], the tulip market became wider. A bulb can produce 2-3 offsets yearly, which become flowering bulbs themselves within one to three years. Eventually, people started trading these as well rather than just bulbs. In fact, it represented the first step toward making tulip trading a permanent rather than seasonal endeavor. Bulbs were normally only traded for about 4 out of

---

[7] James Grout. "Tulipmania." *Encyclopaedia Romana*. April 17, 1997.
http://penelope.uchicago.edu/~grout/encyclopaedia_romana/aconite/tulipomania.html.

12 months and since the previously mentioned offsets need years to mature, this made it possible to transact throughout the year.

However, these transactions came with their own risks, as for example nobody could guarantee that the offsets would make it to maturity successfully. But since people were more and more willing to take risks at that point, such layers of risk weren't an obstacle one couldn't overcome. Imagine the average Dutch tulip investor as a gambling addict. It should come as no surprise that such a person will jump at any opportunity to turn a 4-month gambling spree into something permanent.

Things however didn't end there.

As the insanity progressed, bulbs started to be traded based on their weight. That weight was measured in asen, with one asen representing 5% of a gram or 0.17% of an ounce. A fair and logical development if you think about it, as a heavier bulb should obviously be worth more than a smaller, immature one. However, this made it possible for a whole new layer of speculation to be added to the mix.

A bulb you plant in September will be significantly heavier when you take it out of the ground the following June. Therefore, even if the price of tulips didn't go up over that timeframe, your bulb would be worth 3-5 times more money after those 9 months. If tulip prices went down, this acted as a hedge but if prices went up (which they did at that point), it was a "dream come true" situation for speculators.

But why bother physically exchanging bulbs?

At the very beginning, only those who were genuinely passionate about tulips bought and sold bulbs. But as prices kept going up, more and more "amateurs" entered the scene. They could care less about the beauty of tulips or the technical aspects of growing them. They were just in it for the money. Therefore, as of the fall of 1635, you could buy bulbs which were still in the ground. Next to the bulb that was in the ground, there was a small sign on which the name of the bulb, its weight and the name of the owner were displayed. The owner had a piece of paper which contained details about the bulb as well as the date at which it was to be dug out and it's precisely those pieces of paper that ended up being traded instead of bulbs.

By the fall of 1636, the market was literally flooded with beginners, who in order to get in on the action had to either settle for tulips which were utterly worthless a couple of years ago or team up so as to have enough capital for better tulips. Thanks to those from the first category, the prices of the lowest quality inventory out there ended up frequently outperforming the market in general. These tulips were sold by the pound rather than as individual bulbs.

For example, a pound of the cheapest such tulips (Gheele Croon) was worth 20 guilders in September to October 1636 and by the end of January 1637, the price shot up all the way to 1,200 guilders. The better quality Switser tulips also did well, increasing from 60 guilders per pound in the fall of 1636 to 120 guilders by the 15th of January 1637, to 385 guilders on the 23rd, to a whopping 1,400 guilders on the 1st of February!

The period between the beginning of the last week of January and the end of the first week of February are considered the culmination of the tulip mania. The famous Alkmaar auction, which generated 90,000 guilders in sales at the beginning of February 1637, tends to be considered the most popular event associated with the height of the craziness. Most people thought the good times would last forever but there were however a few prudent souls who decided it was time to take money off the table.

In the same month of February, things went terribly wrong elsewhere in the Republic.

Specifically in Haarlem, on the very first Tuesday of February. People gathered to trade tulips, as they usually did. The event started with someone offering a pound of the cheapest tulips, specifically Gheele Croon and Switser, at a fair market price. Normally, several buyers would have jumped on them but this time, nobody did. After some initial murmur, the price was reduced but to no avail. It was reduced yet again but it was as if everyone turned to stone.

A short while after this scene, transactions were halted for the day altogether. It was definitely the beginning of the end. Those who participated rushed to tell their friends what happened and panic gradually set in. Do keep in mind that information propagated much slower back then but still, a couple of days had proven to be more than enough for the news to travel across the entire Dutch Republic.

There was no longer a market for tulips.

Speculators quickly realized that for example the pound of Gheele Croon tulips they had paid 1,200 for was pretty much unsellable. Almost nobody wanted to touch those tulips at that point. While it is true that some people did their best to continue conducting business as usual, it was just not possible anymore. The tulip bubble had burst and a different kind of insanity was just about to start in the Dutch Republic.

Why? Simply because as mentioned previously, tulip transactions ended up becoming extremely complex. Investors took on debt to fund acquisitions. They then bought pieces of paper rather than actual bulbs, keeping some but offering some as collateral to fund other purchases and so on. Figuring out who owed what ended up becoming quite a challenge. Fortunes disappeared pretty much overnight.

The Dutch ended up realizing what "paper wealth" meant. A lot of times, things were even more dramatic than realizing you are a lot less wealthy. Some people went from being rich on paper to being in extreme debt, words can't begin to describe the shock such individuals went through. Naturally, all types of litigation abounded and initially, the authorities wanted to stay away.

They wanted speculators to sort these things out among themselves but that didn't exactly work. Some of the losers expressed extreme outrage and wanted to find someone to blame. Conspiracy theories started popping up, such as one about how the top 20-30 players manipulated and controlled the market. People desperately wanted to find scapegoats and hatred starting to rear its ugly head. Minorities such as Jews and Mennonites ended up being blamed as well and the list could go on and on.

Eventually, compromises were reached such as buyers paying growers 3.5% of the acquisition price so as to absolve themselves of any further obligations and the growers taking possession of the bulbs. The tulip market started crashing in February 1637 but it took until the beginning of 1639 for things to sort themselves out. At that point, despite the tulip mania not affecting the Dutch economy in a meaningful manner, the average Dutch developed quite an aversion toward tulips in general.

We've already identified 4 anomalies earlier on in this subchapter, time for two more:

5. The fact that people were willing to take on additional layers of risk. From investing in bulb offsets which might never make it to maturity to investing in a piece of paper rather than the actual bulb. Do keep in mind that we're talking about the 1630s, when something like this wasn't entirely uncommon but it was certainly a lot less common than it is today

6. The fact that after the bubble burst, people didn't just accept their losses. You'd think someone who invests in ultra-speculative assets such as tulips realizes money can be lost as well. That certainly didn't happen. On the contrary, they ended up blaming anyone but themselves. Conspiracy theories abounded, as did discrimination against minorities. The average sore loser desperately wanted to find a scapegoat

All in all, the tulip mania certainly tells us a thing or two about human nature. But now's not the time to draw conclusions about anomalies in general, we will be doing this after analyzing many more events such as the tulip mania. In each case, anomalies will be identified, anomalies like the six we've found for the tulip mania. Eventually, some patterns will surely become obvious but our journey is just beginning!

Chapter 3.1.2 The South Sea Bubble

Before 1707, England and Scotland were separate countries, legally speaking. Each had its own parliament until the 1st of May 1707, when each parliament decided that the two entities would form a single kingdom with a single parliament called Great Britain. Throughout this entire subchapter, I will be using the term "Great Britain" exclusively for convenience purposes but do keep in mind that some of the events took place before 1707.

Just like it's important to study the atmosphere in the Dutch Republic to understand the tulip mania, it's vital to understand how things stood in Great Britain before moving on to the specifics of the South Sea bubble. The British, quite frankly, were at war with pretty much everyone at that point, from their 17th-century civil war to ongoing conflicts with other European countries.

Back then, just like today, wars were extremely expensive. As such, ridiculously high levels of debt had been accumulated and realistically speaking, the British weren't even sure how much. As of August 1710, Robert Harley was appointed Chancellor of the Exchequer and became the man in charge of Great Britain's finances. He was determined to figure out just how much the kingdom owed and by January 1711, a committee was appointed to conduct detailed investigations. The findings were downright shocking.

The conclusion was Great Britain owed a whopping £9,000,000 and nobody knew how to actually pay it. Harley's main short-term concern however was obtaining the £300,000 needed to cover the expenses of the British army for the next quarter. The central bank of Great Britain, called the Bank of England, was operating a lottery on behalf of the government at that point to raise money. However, it wasn't exactly successful in 1710 and therefore, Harley allowed a questionable but remarkably creative fellow called John Blunt to take over. Blunt turned the lottery into a smashing hit and from the 3rd to the 7th of March 1711, the tickets were completely sold out.

He then organized a larger lottery with very good terms for the participants. A ticket cost £100 and you could win up to £20,000, with a guarantee that each ticket would bring you at least 10% of the cost. These weren't great terms for the lottery itself but there was a catch: winners wouldn't receive their money right away and instead, received payments over a period of several years. In other words, this scheme was basically a way for the government to borrow money but, well… it worked.

Mr. Blunt proved to be quite talented at coming up with such schemes but while the lottery helped Harley cover short-term expenses such as the £300,000 one, it was clear something bigger was needed to tackle the entire debt. As such, the South Sea Company was formed in 1711, a company which initially had one purpose and one purpose only: helping Great Britain pay its huge debt.

How? Simple, by convincing people to whom Great Britain owed money to accept South Sea Company shares instead. The company took on parts of Great Britain's debt and was paid roughly 6% yearly in interest, less than what Great Britain was currently paying its lenders. The people Great Britain owed money to were allowed to trade their debt for South Sea Company shares. For example, let's assume one South Sea Company share was worth £10 and Michael was owed £1,000, receiving 8% in yearly interest. Michael was allowed to turn his debt into 100 South Sea Company shares.

In other words, as of that point, Great Britain would no longer owe Michael any money and instead, Michael now owned 100 shares in the newly formed company. That company received roughly 6% yearly in interest and distributed that interest to shareholders as dividends. Something now becomes blatantly obvious: Michael would receive less "interest" than before. Which begs the question: why would he do it?

Why would Michael choose to stop receiving 8% yearly from Great Britain just so he could own some shares and receive let's say 6% yearly instead? Why exactly should people like him accept such a deal? As strange as it may sound, people considered the deal quite good and if we try seeing things from their perspective, we'll realize they had perfectly rational reasons to see things that way.

By owning shares, people would own a piece of a company with seemingly a lot going for it:

1. The South Sea Company had a monopoly over trading in the South Seas (back then, the South Seas were considered the region around Central and South America)

2. A similar company, the Honourable East India Company (HEIC), had a great reputation and its shareholders were very happy. People thought the South Sea Company would follow a similar path

3. The elites and opinion formers had only positive things to say about the bright future of the South Sea Company. From officials to even people like Daniel Defoe (who wrote the famous *Robinson Crusoe* novel in 1719), everyone seemed to praise the South Sea Company. I'd highly recommend reading Daniel Defoe's 1712 essay[8] to see what the elites had to say about the South Sea Company

At the end of the day, it should come as no surprise that people were excited. Sure, you'd earn less through dividends than through the interest you'd have received as a holder of Great Britain's debt but if the price of your shares doubles for example... who cares about that paltry interest? Investors thought South Sea Company share values would surely go up and as such, were pleased with the deal they were getting.

There's now good as well as bad news for these people.

The bad news is that they were, quite frankly, being lied to. The South Sea bubble is considered the first recorded market manipulation in history. In other words, we can safely consider it a scam. Was it a well-orchestrated scam? Yes. Was it a scam backed by officials and with a legitimacy aura? Most definitely. But no matter how hard you try to put lipstick on a pig, a scam is a scam because:

1. While the South Sea Company did in fact have a monopoly over trading in the South Seas, it never really traded much. Why? Well, mainly because the ports were all controlled by Spain, with whom Great Britain was at war. Eventually, a peace treaty was signed under great political pressure, the Utrecht treaty of 1713[9]. Harley and Blunt desperately pushed for a deal and pulled quite a few strings to make

---

[8] Daniel Defoe. *An Essay on the South-Sea Trade.* London: J. Baker, 1712.
[9] George Chalmers. *A Collection of Treaties Between Great Britain and Other Powers.* London: John Stockdale, 1790.

it happen. Unfortunately, since Great Britain got this deal independently and earlier than its allies, it wasn't a particularly good one for them. Specifically, the South Sea company was only allowed to send one ship per year to trade with the Spanish colonies. One per year, that's it. Needless to say, the South Sea Company didn't exactly end up trading all that much

2. The Honourable East India Company was a much, much better business. Mainly because it actually was a business, sending entire fleets of ships each month to trade in its areas. Comparatively, calling the South Sea Company a business would be a huge overstatement because again, it didn't conduct that much business in the first place. It's fairly safe to consider it a scam and nothing more

3. A lot of the people who gave it glowing reviews were either operating on false information or had a vested interest in the company. Lots of officials had been downright bribed and as such, were anything but a credible source of information

… yet despite all of this insanity, the good news is that things initially went well.

How on Earth did things do well, you might ask? Simple. As any half-decent manipulator can confirm, it doesn't matter how things really stand. As long as people perceive a certain company as legitimate, everything will be all fine and dandy. Accurate information about the South Sea Company was hard to come by in Great Britain, so it shouldn't surprise us that the average person had great confidence in it.

Initially, King George I appointed his son as the governor of the South Sea Company back in 1715. By doing this, the credibility of the company in the eyes of the public skyrocketed. And as of 1718, he became the governor himself. Again, we have to see things from the perspective of the average person. If the king himself becomes the governor of a certain company, an almost impenetrable aura of confidence ends up surrounding it. ·

Were there warning signals?

Of course there were but just think about how easy it is to manipulate people in the present. It should come as no surprise that with so many people vouching for the South Sea Company, the average individual didn't even dare imagine all of this could be a scam. Especially since again, the South Sea bubble is the first recorded example of market manipulation. There wasn't even a recorded precedent for what happened.

Share prices were doing great, experiencing a growth rate which seemed more than robust. They went from £100 to £114 in 1719 and in January 1720, were at £128. Not bad at all, wouldn't you agree? This however was only the beginning because from January to February 1720, prices went all the way up to £175. Then to £330 from February to March and to a whopping £550 by the end of May.

You're most likely aware of the "Don't steal, the government hates competition!" joke but in 18th century Great Britain, it actually wasn't a joke. Given the huge success of the South Sea Company, lots and lots of other companies popped up and offered shares. Some of them were legitimate but a lot weren't, with some of the most peculiar ones promising that they'd develop flying machines or cubic cannon balls. According to Charles Mackay[10] (take this with a grain of salt though because as mentioned in the previous subchapter, his book is splendid as literature but not always accurate), one such "business" referred to itself as "a company for carrying out an undertaking of great advantage, but nobody to know what it is" and leaving the accuracy aspect aside, I think it describes the year 1720 remarkably well (a crazy year in which bubbles manifested themselves all over the place, not just in Great Britain).

Blunt hated this competition.

To defend the South Sea bubble, the Bubble Act was passed in June 1720, which stated that all joint-stock companies needed a royal charter. The South Sea Company obviously received its royal charter, yet another vote of confidence in the eyes of the masses. As a result of the act, lots of businesses went belly-up and this created some short-term difficulties for the South Sea Company as well. Why? Simply because quite a few of the people involved in them were also South Sea Company shareholders and they had to liquidate shares to generate capital. All in all though, the Bubble Act was a net positive

---

[10] Charles Mackay. *Extraordinary Popular Delusions and the Madness of Crowds*. London: Richard Bentley, 1841.

event for the South Sea Company and helped the stock price soar all the way to its peak of £1,050 by the end of June.

To understand just how much £1,050 was, let's take a quick look at wages and expenses.

As we all know, the currency of Great Britain was the pound, just like today, but most of the transactions were conducted in shillings and pence. One shilling was worth 12 pence and one pound was worth 20 shillings. Therefore, obviously, a pound was worth 240 pence back then. This lasted until the decimalisation of 1971, when things were simplified and a pound ended up being worth 100 pence.

That being stated, let's start with the wages. In the 18th century, the average wage of a maid, for example, wouldn't exceed £2-3 yearly but of course, the person in question would also receive food and accommodation. For the sake of our example, let's assume a maid earned an average of £2.5 per year. This means that to afford just one South Sea Company share at the end of June 1720, ten maids would have to work 42 years each and save all of their money in one big piggy bank.

What about agriculture wages[11]? Well, these varied by season. During the winter season, the wages were obviously lower. On a summer day, a worker would earn 1.11 times more whereas during specific periods, wages went up further. Hay wages were 1.28 times higher than winter wages, whereas harvest wages were 1.73 times higher. Over the period we're interested in (the South Sea bubble period), the average winter farm wage was around 10 pence per day. In other words, it would take a worker 24 such days just to receive one pound or 25,200 days of work to buy one South Sea Company share at its peak. You can calculate the daily wages during the other periods by simply multiplying 10 by the previously mentioned numbers (1.11, 1.28 and 1.73).

What about expenses? Well, let's see how much people paid to rent a cottage for example: we're looking at roughly 1.35 pounds per year from 1700 to 1719 and 1.40 yearly from 1720 to 1739. In other words, the £1,050 could be used

---

[11] Gregory Clark. "The Long March of History: Farm Wages, Population, and Economic Growth, England 1209-1869." *Economic History Review.* February 10, 2007.
http://faculty.econ.ucdavis.edu/faculty/gclark/papers/farm_wages_&_living_standards.pdf.

to cover the housing costs of 15 families for 50 years each. It should therefore be obvious just how unaffordable these share prices ended up becoming by June.

Do keep in mind though that there were bumps along the way.

As impressive as the price evolution may seem, there was downward pressure as well at various points. However, Blunt seemed to always have something up his sleeve. For example, when share prices went down from the end of March to early April, he devised a scheme which allowed people to buy stocks by only paying 20% upfront. The remaining amount was payable in instalments, once every two months. This obviously made it possible for investors to buy more shares than they could normally afford and interest in the South Sea Company spiked because of this. When share prices were once again under pressure, Blunt decided to actually lend people up to £3,000 so that they could buy shares. Indeed, he basically paid people to buy his stocks and… well, it worked.

However, nothing lasts forever.

Let's once again look at how things stood at the end of June 1720, when prices were at the record-breaking £1,050 level. As peachy as everything seemed, the situation was rotten beneath the surface. Just like during the tulip mania, a lot of those who held shares were over-leveraged. Therefore, disaster would strike if prices were to drop. What would those who barely afforded to pay 20% upfront do? What about, worse yet, those who borrowed money to afford paying 20% in the first place?

The South Sea Company investors would soon learn a lesson their Dutch counterparts learned the hard way: when the party ends, it ends abruptly. The bursting of the South Sea bubble would soon begin and it wouldn't be pretty. As of early July, something broke. No matter how hard Blunt tried to once again come up with a new scheme, he wasn't a magician and financial reality would soon end up rearing its ugly head.

By early July, prices started to drop and by the end of August, they retreated to below £800. In September, prices fell even more dramatically to a mere £175 and by the end of the year, to the £100 region. Needless to say, lots of bankruptcies followed and suicide rates soared. Just like after the tulip mania, people were desperately looking for scapegoats and the main problem was that corruption climbed all the way to the top.

The credibility of King George I was damaged quite a bit, several people were impeached and imprisoned. But again, most of the elites were guilty in one way or another. Robert Walpole branded himself as one of those who were there to defend the public against corruption and became the first de facto Prime Minister of Great Britain. While it is true that he was no fan of Blunt, he was a net beneficiary of the bubble and actually helped hide a lot of aspects related to it.

Had the public known everything, the likelihood of a revolution would have been high.

Ultimately, things got back on track under Walpole. The South Sea Company stock ended up being divided between the East India Company and the Bank of England, the possessions of the directors were confiscated and used to help the victims. It took time but eventually, the mess the South Sea bubble left behind was cleaned up. After drawing the line, it's time to look at things objectively and identify the anomalies:

1. The fact that people invested in something they didn't understand, an anomaly similar to #3 from the tulip mania subchapter. Just like more and more people bought tulips despite knowing pretty much nothing about them in the Dutch Republic, the average individual bought South Sea Company shares in Great Britain without understanding what he's investing in and frankly, without caring. Getting rich was the name of the game, everything else paled in comparison

2. The fact that people speculated with borrowed money, something similar to anomaly #4 from the tulip mania section. Investors quickly took advantage of each scheme Blunt threw at them. Pay 20% upfront and the rest later on? Sure! Borrow up to £3,000 to speculate? Sure! People didn't care for a very, very long time. Eventually, at the end of it all when the bubble ran out of steam, such schemes stopped working but while the frenzy was on, people threw reason out of the window

3. The fact that regulators closed their eyes. And this isn't limited to just some small-time directors, not at all. Even the King was guilty of this, as were all the Chancellors of the Exchequer, as were those who were supposed to pass laws in favor of the average citizen and so on. Some were downright bribed, whereas others simply had a vested interest due to their own investments in South Sea Company shares

4. Not caring about warning signals. At the beginning, we can give people the benefit of the doubt but as the years passed and nobody asked some much-needed hard questions, one cannot help but wonder how much of this is willful ignorance. When you hear everyone talking about the South Sea Company's amazing deals yet never see physical evidence, you should at the very least ask yourself a few fundamental questions. Yet pretty much nobody did that

5. Recklessly taking on additional layers of risk, an anomaly similar to #5 from the tulip mania. In the "year of the bubble" 1720, people spent fortunes investing in stocks issued by companies that made outlandish claims. Claims which would make even Blunt blush. Eventually, it took legislative action for this to stop, otherwise the British would have most likely continued throwing money at schemes even more ludicrous than the South Sea Company

6. Looking for scapegoats after the bubble burst, just like the Dutch (anomaly #6 from the tulip mania subchapter). Instead of looking in the mirror and laughing at themselves for the (now) obviously foolish mistakes they've made, the British preferred considering themselves blameless victims. Now sure, there's a case to be made as to why they fit the profile of a victim better than the average tulip mania investor (because after all, there was a lot of manipulation involved) but blameless victims? Definitely not!

Chapter 3.1.3 The Mississippi "Bubble"

A quick clarification before starting: please note that I'm rather tongue in cheekily referring to it as a "bubble" because quite frankly, it's more of a monetary phenomenon than anything else. Still, people mostly use the term "Mississippi bubble" because one can indeed identify several bubble-type particularities. Furthermore, the Mississippi bubble that took place in France occurred at pretty much the same time as the South Sea bubble that took place in Great Britain, definitely a "bubbly" historical period.

That being stated, let's start by understanding how things stood in France back then.

Just like Great Britain, France was pretty much insolvent before the Mississippi bubble craziness started. During the long reign of Louis XIV, wars and overall recklessness had taken their toll on the economy of France. It was hard to envision a way out, especially since taxes were already high but there was a silver lining: the fact that France controlled the colony of Louisiana in North America, which included the Mississippi Gulf Coast region[12].

The territory France controlled in North America was vaster in size than France itself, stretching from the mouth of the Mississippi River all the way to parts of modern day Canada. However, not a lot was known about it. If this territory would prove to be rich in resources, France's problems would all of a sudden seem fixable. But let's not discuss these riches just yet and instead, go back to France for a moment.

This much was certain: it seemed as if the country needed a miracle.

And, eventually, it looked like a fellow by the name of John Law had this much-needed miracle solution. Law was definitely an interesting individual, a Scottish "economist" born in Edinburgh, described as a physically appealing character who had a weakness for women and gambling. His first weakness

---

[12] Jon Moen. "John Law and the Mississippi Bubble: 1718-1720." *Mississippi History Now*. October 01, 2001. http://mshistorynow.mdah.state.ms.us/index.php?id=70.

is what eventually forced him to flee to another country and made him land in France. Law had killed a man in a duel over the affections of Elizabeth Villiers, was initially sentenced to death but that sentence ended up being commuted to a prison sentence.

He ultimately escaped from prison and fled to continental Europe in 1694, settling in Amsterdam and educating himself on matters of finance. In 1705, he returned home and started writing about the economic views he had developed, even a book[13] through which he advocated the idea of increasing the amount of currency in circulation. He firmly believed trading via paper money was better than trading through less flexible gold and silver-backed "sound" money.

By 1714, he ended up in France and was quite respected by the Duke of Orleans, the nephew of King Louis XIV. This duke would ultimately propel Law to the very top of France's government. Since the previous king died in 1715 and the current heir to the throne (Louis XV) was still a minor, someone had to serve as a ruler on his behalf. And guess who that was? Exactly, the Duke of Orleans.

Back then, France was somewhat of a sovereign paradox. On the one hand, it had become the most powerful European country but on the other hand, it was crippled by the huge debt it had accumulated during the long reign of Louis XIV (over 72 years, the longest reign of a major European monarch). So crippled, in fact, that we can safely consider it insolvent. Something had to be done.

The Duke of Orleans knew this and set two goals:

1. Making the public debt manageable
2. Developing the North American territories France controlled

To reach these goals, he sought the council of Law, who came up with a scheme that enabled France to kill two birds with one stone. Law realized the problems of France were, among other things, also caused by the fact that France didn't really have a developed financial system like let's say Holland

---

[13] John Law. *Money and Trade Considered, with a Proposal for Supplying the Nation with Money.* Edinburgh: Heirs and Successors of Andrew Anderson, 1705.

or Great Britain. He decided it was about time France had its own central bank but it would be a central bank with a twist, so to speak.

He wanted to create the ultimate monopoly-type situation by:

1. Establishing a central bank with a monopoly on national finance
2. Establishing a state commerce company with a monopoly on trade

Law definitely had views which would be considered Keynesian today and his ideas were music to the Duke's ears. In 1716, Law was allowed to open the Banque Generale, which was authorized to issue paper money. That money was redeemable in gold and silver, which made it quite respected and this was taken to the next level later on, when all public funds ended up being deposited there. Even more importantly, people were allowed to pay taxes using the notes issued by Banque Generale and the fact that it ended up being renamed Banque Royale spoke for itself. Just like the South Sea Company, one can easily say that the French monarchy itself "vouched" for the Banque Royale.

In 1717, Law was granted permission to establish the so-called Compagnie d'Occident (Company of the West) and through an exclusive lease, exploit and develop the French territories in the Mississippi region. The Compagnie d'Occident gradually absorbed other companies and by 1719 ended up effectively controlling French colonial trade (rather than just North American trade). It was ultimately renamed the Compagnie des Indes but was more commonly referred to as the Mississippi Company.

For the sake of convenience, we'll be calling it the Mississippi Company from now on.

As can be seen, it wouldn't be an understatement to say that John Law effectively controlled a huge part of France's economy. People considered him a genius and... why not? For a significant amount of time, it seemed as if absolutely everything he touched turned to gold. France seemed to be on the right path, paper currency was all the rage, sunshine and rainbows everywhere.

But, unfortunately, the entire system was nothing more than a house of cards because:

1. As demand for paper money grew, the bank kept issuing bank notes. Law didn't anticipate the inflationary effect something like this could ultimately have. Bank notes worth a total of 2,696,000,000 livres (the so-called "livres tournois" was the unit of account in France, just like the pound sterling in Great Britain) had been created, two times more than the money that had been in circulation prior to the appearance of Law's bank.

    Now do keep in mind that this paper money was convertible to gold or silver. As long as people had confidence in paper money and Law's schemes in general though, everything was perfect because the French didn't want to convert their paper money to precious metals. One important question arose however: what would happen if for some reason people's confidence vanishes and hordes of French paper money holders would suddenly demand precious metals? There was obviously nowhere near enough gold and silver to meet such a demand, so a proverbial bank run was the number one threat by far

2. Mississippi Company share prices did well. Too well, in fact, with prices skyrocketing from 500 to 10,000 livres within months. Why? Mainly because an amazingly effective marketing campaign convinced the French that the regions France controlled were incredibly rich in resources. The potential seemed endless. People imagined these regions as big piles of furs, silver and gold. Who wouldn't want to invest in something like this?

In January 1720, the company issued a huge dividend (40%) which made the price soar to 18,000 livres. A 36-fold increase, from 500 livres all the way to 18,000 over a very short timeframe. A lot of people became wealthy and the word "millionaire" was born. But these huge prices were based on the perception that the territories the French controlled contained mountains of riches rather than inhospitable swampland

As can be seen, the perfect storm was just around the corner. It should also be noted that just like with the South Sea bubble, actually even more so, people were buying shares on credit. Right from the beginning, it was possible to purchase these shares with a down payment of only 10%. It seems Law was more aggressive in this respect than the South Sea Company mastermind John Blunt because he made it possible for people to buy shares on credit right from day one, whereas Mr. Blunt waited until share prices needed a boost.

We can easily identify a lethal mix of ingredients which makes it clear just how big of a powder keg the scheme was sitting on:

1. Paper money was issued without enough precious metals to back it up
2. The French invested in a company based on rumors and dreams, not facts
3. Not only that, most of them invested with borrowed money

Without this deadly mix of ingredients, prices would have most certainly not risen as dramatically. The smartest and/or luckiest investors made out like bandits. Let's assume you wanted to invest 10,000 livres of your own money when prices were at 500 livres per share. Furthermore, you also took advantage of the "only 10% down" offer and ended up buying 200 shares instead of the 20 you would have normally afforded.

We'll also assume you sold at the very peak, when prices were at 18,000. Congratulations, you're now 3,600,000 livres richer. Just the type of person the term "millionaire" was coined to describe. However, to take full advantage of everything, you should have also been inspired enough to immediately exchange your 3,600,000 livres of paper money into gold and silver so as not to be affected by the monetary drama that was about to follow.

Realistically speaking, those who profited wildly were a minority because:

1. Their timing (when buying as well as when selling) would have had to be perfect
2. They should have also had the foresight to convert their paper money to precious metals

Yes, there are indeed people who managed to do this but again, we're talking about a ridiculously small percentage. As with any other asset bubble, there were more losers than winners. And speaking of winners, guess what happened in early 1720? Naturally, some of these winners decided it was time to cash out, sold their shares and wanted to secure their profits by demanding gold. Enough people did this, in fact, to generate downward pressure on Mississippi Company shares on the one hand and on the other hand, to put the resilience of Law's paper money system to the test.

Law did his best to tackle this issue, for example by creating more paper money and limiting gold payments to 100 livres. But to no avail. Once the perfect storm manifests itself, damage control becomes a Herculean endeavor. Murphy's laws began to kick in and everything that could go wrong ended up going wrong. Stock prices collapsed just as quickly as they went up. And if only it were just that but no: people didn't just want to turn their stocks into paper money, they demanded "old school" gold and silver.

Perhaps the biggest mistake of John Law was not realizing that issuing too much paper money would result in inflation. When times were good, everyone wanted paper money. But guess what happened once people lost confidence in this paper money? Let's assume Joe the baker was more than willing to accept paper money for his products throughout 1719. After all, why wouldn't he? The Mississippi Company seemed like the best thing since sliced bread (see what I did there?) and paper money was all the rage.

But as of 1720, that changed. All of a sudden, shares and paper money went from being "must-haves" to becoming hot potatoes that everyone wants to get rid of. I don't know about you but if I were in Joe the baker's position, I wouldn't touch paper money with a ten-foot pole. And lots of people like Joe didn't. The result should be easy enough to anticipate for someone living in the 21st century: inflation, with food prices soaring as much as 60%[14].

John Law was overwhelmed.

Once the snowball effect kicks in, there's little you can do. By September of 1921, prices had fallen to their pre-bubble levels and, naturally, people wanted Law's head. Fleeing was his only option, which is precisely what he did. In 1721, John Law allegedly fled France in disguise. Disguised as a woman,

---

[14] James Narron and David Skeie. "Crisis Chronicles: The Mississippi Bubble of 1720 and the European Debt Crisis." *Federal Reserve Bank of New York.* January 10, 2014. http://libertystreeteconomics.newyorkfed.org/2014/01/crisis-chronicles-the-mississippi-bubble-of-1720-and-the-european-debt-crisis.html.

according to some sources. A few years later, specifically in 1729, he died of pneumonia in Venice.

The person who pretty much controlled France's economy at one point ended up dirt-poor, John Law's story unfortunately had a very sad ending. Realistically speaking, the man was a financial genius. Perhaps if the excitement surrounding Mississippi Company shares and paper money had been toned down a notch (or two, or three), John Law would have managed to ultimately become a hero. But alas, things spiralled out of control and the rest, as they say, is history.

The Mississippi bubble definitely had a strong impact on France, primarily by generating a deep distrust of paper money among the French. In fact, paper money only started circulating again as of the start of the French Revolution in 1789. Just like with the tulip mania and the South Sea Company, it makes sense to see things from the perspective of the average French citizen so as to understand the magnitude of it all.

Let's take a look at some average wages[15] in 18th-century France.

A foreman made roughly 84-90 livres per year, an ox driver 30-36 livres, a stable boy 60 to 66 livres and a female servant 24-33 livres. Realistically speaking, even when share prices were only at 500 livres each, the average French wouldn't have been able to afford one. However, in light of the fact that you could only pay 10% upfront and the rest later on, shares all of a sudden became considerably more affordable.

Still, we're obviously talking about an asset you'd expect affluent individuals to acquire rather than the average French worker. But just like with the previous two bubbles we've analyzed, the profit potential was so appealing that in the end, everyone wanted a piece of the action. If you earned let's say 50 livres yearly, you would have had to pay 360 times more for just one share at the height of the bubble, when prices were at 18,000 livres.

The average French citizen would have needed multiple lifetimes to afford even one share and in hindsight, this seems downright ridiculous. When

---

[15] Henri Eugène Sée. *Economic and Social Conditions in France During the Eighteenth Century*. New York City: A. A. Kopf, 1927.

you're in the middle of it all though, you tend to spend so much of your time thinking about the potential profits that you fail to factor in the cons as well. Again, it's easy for us to laugh at those who lost fortunes during bubbles but when you're surrounded by euphoria, it's far harder to remain lucid than you would expect.

And make no mistake, reasons to be euphoric abounded.

There are various anecdotes[16] about those who had gone from rags (sometimes literally) to riches thanks to the Mississippi bubble. About the waiter who made 30,000,000 livres. The chimney sweep who made 40,000,000. The footman who made 50,000,000. The shopkeeper who generated a whopping 127,000,000 livres. Or the servant who was sent to sell 250 shares at 8,000 livres each but who, since prices were already at 10,000 by the time he arrived, pocketed the difference of 500,000 livres and turned it into two million within days by reinvesting.

These are precisely the types of people for which the term "millionaire" was coined. Let's not even talk about even more peculiar tales, such as the hunchback who became rich by "renting" his back to those who needed to sign paperwork quickly during the Mississippi Company insanity. Don't make the mistake of underestimating how hard it is to remain lucid when everyone around you has gone mad.

We however can, with a clear head, draw the line and identify the top anomalies (#1 to #4 are identical to their South Sea Company equivalents, whereas #5 is identical to #6 from the South Sea bubble subchapter):

1. The fact that people invested in something they didn't understand. The average French wasn't exactly educated back then and let's face it, most of those who invested in shares using paper money didn't exactly know basic economics. They invested in something they didn't understand (the Mississippi Company) based on claims they couldn't verify (the alleged riches that were just around the corner), with a medium of exchange they've never used before (paper

---

[16] John E. Sandrock. "John Law's Banque Royale and the Mississippi Bubble." *The Currency Collector.* August 28, 2008.
http://www.thecurrencycollector.com/pdfs/John_Laws_Banque_Royale.pdf.

money). But none of this mattered. People saw their neighbor get rich and wanted a piece of the action

2. The fact that people speculated with borrowed money. Law was even more aggressive than his counterpart from Great Britain by making it possible to buy shares with an upfront payment of just 10% right from the beginning

3. The fact that regulators closed their eyes. Some of them didn't know better, whereas others might have had their doubts but were blinded by the newly found prosperity. One might expect those who make the rules to be extraordinarily prudent but at the end of the day, the French "elites" had proven that they're humans, just like everyone else

4. Not caring about warning signals. Law's scheme might have actually worked if more prudence would have been added to the mix. Perhaps it would have been possible to make paper money somehow "stick" in the early 1700s if things wouldn't have ended up in bubble territory. Yes, the Mississippi Company wasn't exactly the best thing since sliced bread but again, at least the concept of paper money might have worked a lot better if Law and his acolytes would have exercised more caution

5. Looking for scapegoats after the bubble burst. Make no mistake, John Law was the most hated man in France after the bubble burst. There are anecdotes circulating about how it would have even been enough to point at someone and say "Look, it's John Law!" for a mob to form and start chasing the poor fellow. Now sure, such an attitude is understandable to a certain extent but most of this energy should have been used to blame themselves. For believing outlandish claims. For investing more than they could afford to lose. For not acting on their doubts and so on

6. Thinking you can print your way to prosperity. Paper money definitely had its merits back then, just like today. But Law and those in charge of France's finances got carried away and thought they could simply print themselves into prosperity. It's a mistake that gets made time and time again throughout history. In fact, currency

devaluation has been around longer than paper money, for example the idea of minting coins with less precious metal content. But the Mississippi bubble is the first documented example of this phenomenon affecting paper money, which makes it one of the most interesting case studies in the world of economics

Chapter 3.1.4: The Panic of 1825

This panic primarily involved Latin America and the United Kingdom. It tends to be considered the world's first international crisis, the world's first emerging market crisis as well as the start of modern economic cycles. But perhaps more than anything else, it's remembered as a crisis in which what some consider the most fantastic financial swindle[17] of all time took place. A swindle involving the mythical nation of Poyais, an entirely made-up Central American principality. I kid you not.

But let's take a step back and take a look at the context of it all.

In our world of "Monetary Easy Street" where interest rates are even negative in some cases and where everyone accepts the fact that money is no longer backed by something tangible, it might seem peculiar to hear that after the 1815 end of the Napoleonic wars, the Bank of England embraced tight monetary policy with the intent of resuming the pre-conflict convertibility.

You see, back then, the authorities introduced temporary/extraordinary measures during conflicts but actually eliminated them after the end of the conflict in a lot of cases. These days, "temporary" measures tend to pretty much become permanent and a lot of aspects which would have been considered outrageous in the 19th century are now widely accepted as the status quo. For example, the complete elimination of anything even resembling a gold standard in 1971.

The monetary policy of the Bank of England obviously had deflationary effects but its ultimate convertibility resumption goal was reached in 1821. As of that point, the financial environment became more and more relaxed. The average investor was, needless to say, more optimistic as well. And what do investors do when they become more optimistic?

---

[17] Don Morgan and James Narron. "Crisis Chronicles: The Panic of 1825 and the Most Fantastic Financial Swindle of All Time." *Liberty Street Economics, Federal Reserve Bank of New York.* April 10, 2015. http://libertystreeteconomics.newyorkfed.org/2015/04/crisis-chronicles-the-panic-of-1825-and-the-most-fantastic-financial-swindle-of-all-time-.html.

They reach for yield.

During times of turbulence, investors obviously prefer staying away from risky investments. As such, they run toward safe haven assets such as government bonds. But when there seem to no longer be storm clouds on the horizon, they do the exact opposite. They go from defense mode to offense mode and are willing to take on more risk.

Needless to say, they frequently get carried away and this ended up happening in our case as well. Especially since the perfect opportunity to speculate presented itself in light of the fact that Spain lost control over South America. Several independent states appeared such as Argentina, Mexico, Chile and so on.

These countries needed capital and lots of it.

So... what do you think happened? On the one hand, you had lots of South American countries in dire need of cash and on the other hand, you had UK investors with cash to burn... I mean invest, of course. Predictably, two important investment options appeared, a sovereign one and a private one:

1. The sovereign one was fairly straightforward, as the nations themselves simply issued bonds. Investors jumped on this opportunity despite the fact that it was unclear just how these countries are going to ultimately pay them back. They were new countries with an improper tax collection infrastructure, not exactly the most creditworthy borrowers

2. The private one involved the creation of all sorts of mining companies, which issued shares and gave people the opportunity to own a slice of a company that would soon be busy exploiting the countless mineral riches of South America

... this pretty much describes the 1820s.

What was the problem, you might ask? Well, primarily the fact that people were speculating without having enough information at their disposal to make educated decisions. Even if the weather conditions were ideal, it took half a year to get from London to South America and then return. As you can imagine, information had a much harder time circulating than today.

Also, the companies and South American countries themselves were for the most part poorly organized. Understandable because, well, what they were doing worked. Had investors been more skeptical and thorough, companies as well as nations would have been forced to adopt a more professional attitude. But since that was hardly the case and on the contrary, investors accepted pretty much anything that promised a high yield, hilarity and downright fraud ensued.

The most popular example of this was provided by Gregor MacGregor, who had fought for Venezuela in its war of independence against Spain and returned to England covered in glory. He then used his capital of trust to pitch an "amazing" investment opportunity to England's wealthy elite: bonds issued by the 100% fictional principality of Poyais. Believe it or not, these bonds were issued on the London Stock Exchange in 1822 and not only that but the "glorious" principality of Poyais was able to borrow money at rates similar to those of countries that you know, actually existed.

This climate of insanity continued until the panic of April 1825.

In some cases, a financial panic is caused by an external (exogenous) event. For example, let's say things have been on an unsustainable path for 5 years and the market is just about ready to crash. An exogenous event such as a natural disaster can tip the market over the edge and "cause" the crash. Think of that event as the final drop of water which fills an almost-full glass.

In other cases however, a panic is not caused by a traceable event. It just happens, which is precisely how things unfolded with the stock and bond market crash of April 1825. By the summer of the same year, South American bond prices collapsed by roughly 50%. Naturally, banks were highly loaded with such debt and as depositors went from raising eyebrows to panicking, winter came… both figuratively and literally.

One out of ten banks ended up failing and the ramifications of all this manifested themselves in the real economy as well. Bankruptcies, unemployment, you name it. Initially, the central bank (the Bank of England) didn't take action in the form of monetary relaxation. On the contrary, it even increased rates toward the end of 1825, as the bank run was in full swing.

Eventually however, it was forced to act as a lender of last resort and a lot of economists used this situation as a reference point when trying to explain what exactly "lender of last resort" is supposed to mean and generally speaking, what a central bank should do during times of financial calamity.

Did the panic of 1825 end up crippling the economy? No, it definitely did not[18]. On the contrary, the British funded debt continued to decline throughout the century, its income remained on the high side (well above expenditures) and all in all, it was able to borrow money at the lowest rates of any other government over the 19th century.

It's important to realize that not all panics result in complete economic annihilation. In fact, more often than not, their effects are temporary. But I can say they always give us a fascinating glimpse into the human mind and each financial cataclysm helps us learn a little bit more about who we are as well as what makes us tick.

Let's do just that by identifying the anomalies of the 1825 panic:

1. The fact that people invested in something they didn't understand. From the average investor who was anything but financially sophisticated yet still speculated wildly to the so-called elites who fell for MacGregor's scam, it was clear people invested in assets they didn't understand at all

2. The fact that regulators closed their eyes. Quite frankly, regulators themselves didn't know better for the most part because as mentioned earlier on, information was hard to come by. I would argue that precisely for this reason, they should have added at least another layer of prudence to their strategy but alas, this didn't happen. Yet again, regulators failed to be one step ahead

3. Not caring about warning signals. When a country nobody even knew about such as the principality of Poyais (hint: because it didn't even exist) can borrow money at rates similar to those countries that actually exist borrow at, even moderately sophisticated investors should raise an eyebrow. Unfortunately, that didn't happen

---

[18] Larry Neal. "The Financial Crisis of 1825 and the Restructuring of the British Financial System." *Federal Reserve Bank of St. Louis Review.* May 01, 1998.
https://files.stlouisfed.org/files/htdocs/publications/review/98/05/9805ln.pdf.

4. Thinking something new is automatically worth investing in. A lot of times, people lose money due to an unexplainable desire to be on the cutting edge as an investor. Now sure, investing in new assets can end up being a tremendously profitable endeavor but only if that investment passes other tests as well. Being new and hot just isn't enough of an argument I'm afraid

5. Letting overall euphoria cloud your judgement. Put yourself in the position of the average British investor and it's easy to understand the overall exuberance of the market. Not only was their country well-positioned after the end of the Napoleonic wars in 1815 but even more so, it seemed that after the convertibility resumption of 1821, the good times would never end. This euphoria made people considerably more risk-tolerant than they should have been and we all know how that ended

6. Looking for scapegoats after the bubble burst. Initially, a significant wave of hatred was channeled toward bankers, primarily those from small countries. It was believed that the crisis was caused to a large degree by their reckless speculation. Later on, as the dust settled, people realized the problems were much more complex and were caused by all sorts of issues, from the transition from a wartime to a peacetime economy to overall recklessness (not just that of bankers)

Chapter 3.1.5 The British Railway Mania(s)

There was more than one British railway mania in the 19th century, however the big one that I will be primarily focusing on is the bubble which took place in the 1840s. This subchapter will be a bit peculiar because when describing the mania, I won't be focusing on individual stock prices or index levels. Instead, I'll focus on things like the number of miles built because most of the anomalies we'll identify revolve around the gross misallocation of capital in the direction of the railway industry.

Simply put, the British got carried away when it came to railways.

Now to clear confusion right from the beginning, please note that I'll be using the term "United Kingdom" throughout this subchapter rather than "Great Britain," which I've used in the South Sea bubble section. This is because as of 1801, the Kingdom of Great Britain merged with the Kingdom of Ireland to form the United Kingdom of Great Britain and Ireland. Since the railway mania took place in the 19th century, this is the name that interests us.

To simplify things, I'll use the term "United Kingdom" but please note that the current name of the UK is the "United Kingdom of Great Britain and Northern Ireland." So Northern Ireland rather than just Ireland due to the fact that in 1922, 5/6 of Ireland seceded from the UK. For convenience purposes, I'll use the term "United Kingdom" to describe the "United Kingdom of Great Britain and Ireland" in this subchapter and later on in the book, I'll use the same term to describe the "United Kingdom of Great Britain and Northern Ireland."

To clarify things through a quick history lesson:

- 1707: England + Scotland = Great Britain (as we've learned in the South Sea bubble subchapter)
- 1801: Great Britain + Ireland = The United Kingdom of Great Britain and Ireland (the United Kingdom we'll be talking about in this subchapter)

- 1922: The United Kingdom of Great Britain and Ireland - 5/6 Ireland = The United Kingdom of Great Britain and NORTHERN Ireland (today's United Kingdom)

Sorry for going off-topic a bit but I wanted to make this clarification right from the beginning.

Going back to the railway mania, the bottom line is that the British overestimated the actual demand for railway transportation services and made ridiculously high investments in railway infrastructure. Compared to the four other calamities I've covered thus far, this one has a very interesting particularity: shareholders lost but the United Kingdom itself won. In other words, for the UK, the railway mania was most likely a net positive because after drawing the line, it was left with the most modern railway transportation system in the world.

In the United Kingdom, railway construction capital primarily came from private investors, unlike most places in the world (including the US), where they were government funded. By the end of 1850, British investors had poured about half their country's GDP into railways, roughly £250 million[19]. It's as if US investors would put $9 trillion of today's dollars on the line. Ultimately, the endeavor resulted in a net loss of roughly £80 million for private investors but again, the UK itself was a net beneficiary.

The railway mania of the 1840s was preceded by a smaller mania in the mid-1830s. Between them, there was a devastating depression, from 1837 to 1843. In the UK, you needed approval from the Parliament to build railway tracks and actually, the approval numbers themselves represent fascinating metrics. In the still-depression year of 1843, just 91 miles had received approval. However, in 1844 which we can consider the start of the big railway mania, a staggering 805 miles of railway tracks had been approved. One year later, the Parliament approved 2,700 miles, then 4,538 miles in 1846, followed by 1,354 miles in 1847 and 371 in 1838.

About 12,000 miles between 1844 and 1848, in a country which had just 2,000 miles of railway tracks before the big mania. Out of those, roughly 60% ended

---

[19] Andrew Odlyzko. "Collective Hallucinations and Inefficient Markets: The British Railway Mania of the 1840s." *School of Mathematics and Digital Technology Center, University of Minnesota.* January 15, 2010. http://www.dtc.umn.edu/~odlyzko/doc/hallucinations.pdf.

up actually being built and again, the tracks themselves proved to be profitable for the most part. However, they weren't nearly profitable enough to make shareholders happy, who were counting on a 10%-ish yearly dividend which was definitely out of reach.

Let's try to see things from the perspective of the average investor.

The British were dividend-hungry investors and at a certain point, railway companies were generating a healthy 5-6% yearly dividend, even 10% in a few cases. Those 10% case studies wound up receiving quite a bit of exposure and needless to say, they piqued investors' interest. At that point, one would have earned roughly 3% yearly via government bonds and about the same by investing in agricultural land. Lending to a business would have maybe gotten you an extra percent, whereas the average share dividend was around the 5% zone.

The idea of earning two times more than those who invest in other share types seemed quite appealing, as did the idea of investing in a technological breakthrough. Make no mistake, it would be an unfair understatement to call railway technology a breakthrough. It revolutionized quite a few industries, from agriculture (by enabling farmers to effectively ship goods to various cities) to lifestyle-related ones. The average UK citizen could, in most cases for the first time ever, venture outside his surroundings and for example vacation by the seaside.

What about the UK itself, how was the country doing? Well, it was definitely the superpower we all know it to be on the one hand but on the other hand, it was highly indebted, with a debt to GDP ratio of about 160%. Even by today's more than lenient standards, 160% is quite high. The United Kingdom desperately needed a break, so to speak, and the railway industry seemed like the perfect candidate for the job. A revolution like this one had been long overdue.

As can be seen, we have more than enough ingredients for a perfect storm.

What happened next should come as no surprise, especially after reading the previous subchapters. Simply put, people got greedy. On the one hand, they had this new technology which generated a business model that worked. You had sound companies, providing a much-needed transportation service to people who were grateful and more than ready to reach for their wallets.

Obviously, such a business model deserves to be scaled. But what happens when you get carried away? Well, supply and demand 101. If you're the only person in town who sells apples, you'll do great. If someone else copies your business model, no problem, there's plenty of room in the market for both of you. But if 1,000 people start doing the exact same thing, they'll quickly realize there isn't unlimited demand for apples.

The same principle is valid in the railway industry. You had 2,000 miles of railway tracks before 1844 and the railway business was booming. There was obviously room for growth. Great. But what happens if you add 50% more miles to the mix? You'd probably realize there's still enough demand, so good for you. But if you add five times more miles and bring the grand total to 12,000, you shouldn't be surprised if the market punishes you.

Euphoria made people vastly overestimate the demand for railway transportation.

Now sure, it is true that inaccurate information sources played a role as well. A lot of investors blamed the so-called traffic takers. These people had a great reputation due to the fact that the demand predictions they've made during the first bubble (the one that took place during the mid-1830s) were shockingly accurate. And when these traffic takers made very optimistic demand predictions during the second bubble, pretty much everyone took them seriously.

After all, their track record had been perfect, so why not? Unfortunately, their predictions were embarrassingly inaccurate the second time around and those who relied on them ended up bitterly disappointed. Also, the number of railway industry publications soared during the bubble, as did the exposure on existing newspapers. Everyone was talking about the booming railway industry.

But was literally everyone optimistic?

Actually no, not really. The railway mania actually had a lot more vocal skeptics than the previous bubbles we've taken a look at. From very popular newspapers such as *The Times* to respected newcomers like *The Economist* and even to personalities such as James Morrison, perhaps the richest person in the world at that point. If you have just a little bit of spare time, I'd strongly encourage you to read the *Glenmutchkin Railway* satire by William E. Aytoun[20]. It's splendid literature and helps you understand what the atmosphere was like among investors back then, even if it isn't always terribly reliable.

The skeptics were vocal but unfortunately not always coherent.

In fact, some of their complaints actually made investors even more excited about the railway industry. For example, they complained that things are evolving too quickly and that the railway industry is sucking the energy out of other sectors of the economy. Now put yourself in the position of an investor in railway shares. You'd be delighted to hear that your industry is putting everything else to shame and if anything, you'd treat this warning signal as a pat on the back. If you were someone who was thinking about investing then again, such attitudes could turn greed into greed on steroids.

Therefore, despite the healthier dose of public skepticism compared to past bubbles, the railway mania had proven to be a beast too strong for its opponents. People kept investing and dreaming big. Until they didn't… or in other words, until something snapped. As time passed, investors understood that making money in the railway industry isn't as easy as they thought. Projects take more time to finalize than expected. The profit margins aren't as impressive as they hoped they'd be and so on.

Also, the Bank of England increased interest rates, making investments in government bonds more appealing. After drawing the line, another perfect storm started to manifest itself, this time in the opposite direction. Prices initially stopped growing at a fast pace, then stagnated and ultimately fell. Railroad companies all of a sudden found themselves in a financial predicament and action had to be taken.

To make matters worse, people were allowed to buy shares with just 10% down.

You might be asking yourself when the remaining 90% had to be paid and this brings us to a "problematic" clause which stipulated that at any point, the railroad company was legally allowed to demand the rest of the payment.

---

[20] William E. Aytoun. "How We Got Up the Glenmutchkin Railway, and How We Got Out of It." *Blackwood's Edinburgh Magazine*. October 1, 1845.
http://www.dtc.umn.edu/~odlyzko/rrsources/glen6.pdf.

When capital was plentiful and times were good, few people paid attention to this but once railroad companies found themselves in a bit of a pickle, they started asking shareholders to make the rest of the payment.

And since the average investor was over-leveraged, a nasty chain of events occurred. Small companies became insolvent, easy prey for giants such as Great Western Railway or Midland, who bought them up at a fraction of their value. New players disappeared and big players had a field day. Remember the Bubble Act of 1720 that was mentioned in the South Sea Company section? The act in question came as a result of the fact that lots of questionable companies appeared during the South Sea bubble period and was meant to protect potential investors by making it very hard for such companies to appear and issue shares. Well, that act had been repealed in 1825 and as such, it was a lot easier for all sorts of new companies to pop up. These new companies attracted quite a bit of funding and again, it's the shareholders who ended up footing the bill.

Needless to say, these shareholders were devastated and it seemed as if they just couldn't catch a break. The construction costs ended up being higher than initially anticipated, the operational expenses as well and revenues were, as per Murphy's Laws, lower than they had hoped. Let's not even dwell on stock prices too much, which by the end of 1849 had fallen roughly 60% from the July 1845 peak.

We'll now take a deep breath and start identifying some anomalies:

1. The fact that people speculated with borrowed money, an anomaly we've identified in the previous sections as well. People were allowed, right from the very beginning, to buy shares by only paying 10% upfront, with the notable mention that the companies reserved the right to ask for the remaining amount at any point. Which they ultimately did, to the despair of the average shareholder. Without the possibility of buying more shares than you can afford to pay for upfront, prices would have most likely had a harder time shooting up

2. The fact that when times were good, being pragmatic was considered unimportant. Compared to the previous bubbles we've analyzed, there was a lot more public skepticism when it came to the railroad mania. Perhaps the critics weren't as articulate as they should have

been and no, they have indeed not always done a good job identifying the risks but still, negative voices existed. However, the average investor either didn't take them into consideration or, as mentioned earlier in this subchapter, actually felt encouraged by what the "naysayers" had to say

3. The fact that regulators didn't do their job. As with the previously analyzed bubbles, it seems regulators were asleep at the wheel. Even more so, the 1825 repeal of the 1720 Bubble Act was one of the main drivers of the railroad mania

4. Not caring about warning signals. Once again, a mistake which seems to be common among bubble participants, ignoring warning signals until they become so obvious that it's too late to take decisive action. It should have been clear right for the beginning that 10% dividends were more of an outlier than the norm, yet people set expectations based on such examples. Their optimistic expectations (when it comes to costs, revenue and pretty much everything else) were gradually going down but again, it's too late to take decisive action if you wait until your mistakes become blatantly obvious

5. Looking for scapegoats after the bubble burst, another common denominator in the world of bubbles it seems, so far at least. Some Brits blamed the so-called traffic takers who made overly optimistic demand-related predictions which didn't pan out. Others blamed the so-called "bears" which were basically short-sellers for manipulating markets or even orchestrating the disaster. Anyone but the person they looked at in the mirror each day

Chapter 3.1.6: The German (Weimar Republic) Hyperinflation

The Weimar Republic is what people refer to when describing Germany between 1919 and 1933. The official name of Germany however remained unchanged since 1871. The "Weimar Republic" name stems from the fact that on the 11th of August 1919, the new constitution of the state was written and adopted in Weimar.

Throughout its short history, the Weimar Republic has been through all sorts of turmoil. Hyperinflation, left-wing as well as right-wing revolutions and the list could go on and on. We will be focusing of course on the hyperinflation dimension throughout this section.

Like pretty much all countries, Germany had suspended its gold standard during World War I so as to make funding the war easier. Its line of thinking was that if they win the war, they'd easily be able to get back on track by annexing productive nearby regions, making other countries pay high war reparations and so on.

However, the exact opposite happened.

Through the armistice signed on the 11th of November 1918, which effectively ended World War I, the Germans agreed to withdraw their troops and retreat to their pre-World War I borders. Then, on June 28 1919, the Treaty of Versailles imposed debilitating conditions on them.

At the end of the day, the Treaty of Versailles didn't really please anyone. Needless to say, the Germans found it offensively destructive. Countries such as France and Italy however would have wanted even harsher terms, they would have wanted even greater compensation for the debilitating damage the war with Germany had done. Through president Woodrow Wilson, the United States was much more lenient and willing to find a solution which would ensure long-term peace and the same way, the British proved to be very flexible.

At the end of the day, as we all know, the treaty ended up proving to be a miserable failure.

In 1921, an amount was set which needed to be paid by Germany and that amount was the equivalent of 132 billion gold marks. However, Germany was not allowed to pay the war reparations in its own currency which was off the gold standard and instead, had to pay either in accepted international currencies or in nature, by sending commodities, goods and so on.

The equivalent of 132 billion gold marks in 1921 was approximately $31.5 billion and in today's dollars, that amount would represent an astronomical $392 billion. The experts of the allies knew all too well that there was just no way Germany could pay the full 132 billion gold marks. As such, right from the beginning, this figure was only meant to keep the general public happy because let's face it, the average person found the fact that Germany would pay huge reparations reassuring and fair.

In reality, Germany only had to pay 50 out of those 132 billion gold marks. The remaining 82 billion were basically fictional debt that did appear on paper but that amount would in fact not actually have to be paid. Still, those 50 billion gold marks represented roughly $11.9 billion and in today's dollars, we'd be looking at approximately $148.5 billion. Needless to say, it was an amount that crippled the German economy.

As mentioned previously, Germany abandoned the gold standard as well as printed money to fund World War I and initially, the currency depreciation level wasn't something you could label hyperinflation. Before World War I, you would have needed 4.2 marks to buy one US dollar. Shortly after the war, about 7.9 marks would have been required to buy a dollar.

The Treaty of Versailles however took its toll on the mark and by the end of 1919, you would've needed 48 marks to buy one dollar. The mark continued depreciating and ended up stabilizing at roughly 90 marks per dollar in early 1921. However, things became tricky once it was decided in 1921 that Germany had to pay the previously mentioned 50 billion gold marks. It was supposed to do so in annual instalments and the first payment was due in June 1921.

The Germans had to exchange marks for foreign currency and naturally, their currency suffered, dropping dramatically to 330 marks per US dollar. By early

1922, prices pretty much stabilized around the 320 marks per dollar zone. But with the mark losing so much of its value, Germany found itself in a bit of a predicament.

A huge predicament, actually.

Simply put, it could not afford to buy the gold and foreign currencies it took to meet its payment obligations and as such, toward the end of 1922, Germany just didn't pay. These continuous missed payments ultimately made the French and Belgians decide to occupy the highly industrialized Ruhr region in January 1923. They thought that by doing so, they could strong-arm Germany into making its payments.

Their plan didn't exactly work.

They were met with increased resistance and the workers of the Ruhr region decided to go on a general strike as a form of resistance. The German authorities supported this general strike and helped finance it but of course, doing so took its toll on their already weakened currency. Also, remember, the Ruhr was the industrial heart of Germany. The strike did indeed make the life of the French hard but it had an even greater effect on Germany's already crippled economy.

Germany basically found itself without an engine able to sustain any kind of meaningful economic growth and on the other hand, they had to keep printing currency to meet their various obligations and among other things of course fund the Ruhr strike and resistance. The situation became the final nail in the coffin of the mark and by November 1923, one US dollar was worth 4.2 trillion marks. No, this is not a typo.

Trillion!

The average German was literally speechless. A loaf of bread he could've bought with 250 marks at the beginning of 1923 now had a whopping 200-billion-mark price tag. It became clear that a new currency had to be created. However, implementing a new gold standard would have of course proven to be impossible due to a severe lack of… well, gold.

As such, the new currency ended up being called the Rentenmark and was backed not by gold but by land used for agriculture and business. That currency was introduced at a rate of one Rentenmark to 1 trillion of the old paper marks and the exchange rate compared to the US dollar was 4.2 Rentenmarks to one dollar. It was basically the pre-war exchange rate, as you can notice.

On the 30th of August 1924, the Reichsmark became the new official legal tender of Germany and was equal in value to the Rentenmark. That Reichsmark was then put on the gold standard and again, it was worth the prewar $4.2 per unit of currency. As we can see, it's a transition from a paper currency to ultimately a gold-backed currency with the help of a currency backed by real estate which made it all possible.

The Weimar hyperinflation and the overall weakening of the German economy were due in large part to the debilitating war reparations which were requested. All of this contributed to the ascent to power of Adolf Hitler and ultimately the start of World War II. It was not the German hyperinflation in and of itself that caused World War II but it was without a doubt one of the leading causes and for this reason, we can safely consider it one of the financial storms with the most devastating effects in history, right alongside the Great Depression of 1929.

Let's take a step back and analyze the anomalies we've witnessed:

1. Placing confidence in something you do not meaningfully understand. On the one hand, it is somewhat logical that countries which were financially devastated after World War I such as France were relying on war compensations to rebuild their economies. Their most crucial mistake however was not understanding the instrument in which they had so much confidence. It's easy to say that you'll just make the loser of the war pay but in reality, there are millions of upon millions of lives involved and the true ramifications of the Versailles treaty were never understood properly. While in a different way compared to other financial storms, it has once again been proven that humans are far too willing to place confidence in something they don't truly understand

2. Thinking you can print yourself out of a mess. John Law did this back in the days of the Mississippi bubble of the 1720s and time and time again, people as well as governments don't learn. This is

especially valid in the case of severely weakened countries such as Germany after World War I. A strong country with a robust economy can of course get away with trying to print itself to prosperity for a very long time in some cases but when you have a weakened nation such as Germany, it doesn't take a lot to blow your currency to smithereens. Which is precisely what happened

3. Desperately trying to find scapegoats. This is something that both parties have been guilty of. Whenever the average person experiences a standard of living reduction after something like a war, he or she demands answers and most importantly, wants to know who is to blame. Telling them that the world is complex and that something like a world war is triggered by causes that revolve around the guilt of pretty much everyone... let's just say that's not going to be a popular option. It's always much easier to blame the other side after a conflict, which is precisely what people did after the end of World War I and the consequences have been devastating

4. Ignoring obvious warning signals. While it is true that on a historic scale, we can say events unfolded rather quickly in Weimar Germany, the pace was still slow enough for people to have noticed that something was fundamentally wrong with the way in which they were approaching the problem. Perhaps the Allies would have been wise to tone their demands down a notch for let's say at least a decade or so, give Germany ample time to recover and ultimately work out a manageable repayment framework. Especially when they noticed how after the war, the mark dropped in value dramatically, even before an official repayment amount was set in 1921. But people and politicians alike preferred to go after short-term gratification and ended up missing the big picture completely

5. Not seeing things from the perspective of others. It's easy to think of Germany as just one big evil country that ruined your life but by doing that, you'd be overlooking the fact that millions upon millions of innocent Germans lived there as well. People who, just like you, want to live their lives in peace and had absolutely no intention of destroying anyone's life. By only seeing things from their own

perspective, the Allies overlooked the huge social costs of the measures they were imposing

6. The authorities were overwhelmed. This is especially true when it comes to the German authorities who quite frankly ended up losing control. However, the Allies were anything but perfect in this respect as well because as the authorities usually tend to do, they were laser-focused on the immediate future and failed to meaningfully take the long-term implications of their actions into consideration. A perfect storm of political incompetence as well as frequently bad faith

Chapter 3.1.7: The Florida Real Estate Boom of the 1920s

The United States entered World War I as a debtor nation but after the conflict, it emerged as the world's best-positioned country by far. The conflict had devastated Europe, which was focusing a lot of its economic energy on its efforts to rebuild itself, whereas the United States was experiencing a boom.

The average citizen of the United States ended up having more and more money at his disposal and a financially potent middle class emerged. From pensioners to new members of the middle class, quite a few people now found themselves with more money to spend than ever. On top of it all, the growing popularity of the automobile made it possible for an increasing number of US citizens to vacation throughout the country. One of their favorite destinations was of course the state of Florida, with a tempting climate and tourist-friendly surroundings.

As can be seen, you had all the ingredients necessary to generate a real estate bubble. And boy did one end up being generated! From 1920 until 1925, so in just five short years, the population of Florida had grown by 30%. That was just ridiculous and it's easy to determine just what kind of an effect all of this had on real estate prices.

Aside from the fact that people simply had more money to spend than before, other aspects contributed to the growing popularity of Florida real estate. For example, the state authorities did everything in their power to make Florida seem more appealing to those who want to re-locate. Among other things, they did this by eliminating the state income and inheritance taxes in Florida.

Yet another reason for individuals, especially wealthy people, to consider moving to Florida. Some Americans wanted to simply buy a vacation home. Others wanted to move to a more tax-friendly state and so on. Quite a few people even bought real estate in Florida without having any intention whatsoever of moving there, they did it exclusively because it was going up in value so quickly.

In the end, a huge real estate bubble was in full swing, affecting not just the Miami area but also other places such as Boca Raton[21] and let's say pretty much the entire state of Florida. It seemed as though Florida was a paradise on Earth and a wealthy investor by the name of Carl G. Fisher even purchased a huge "It's June in Miami!" ad in Times Square to make a tongue-in-cheek reference as to how great the weather was in Florida compared to New York City. Again, all the ingredients were there.

Eventually, the speculation reached such levels that even people who had no intention of setting foot in Florida wanted a piece of the action. For example, some individuals even made money without actually paying for the land they ended up selling. This was possible because it was a common practice to seal the deal by paying a binder, which was a non-refundable payment that people made upfront and within 30 days, they had to pony up the rest.

A lot of speculators simply paid the binder and then went on to look for other buyers, with the intention of re-selling the property before having to pay for it as a result of the fact that the 30 days had passed. Essentially, all you needed was the binder payment to make money in such a transaction. Or should I say, the only thing aside from the fact that real estate prices had to go up!

As more investors wanted a piece of the action, even those who didn't even have the binder payment set aside wanted to speculate. Believe it or not, some people speculated by borrowing money to even pay that initial binder. In the absence of such extreme types of borrowing, it would have been hard for the bubble to reach truly epic proportions.

To give you a quick glimpse into how crazy things actually were, it should be noted that at a certain point, most Florida real estate was sold by mail to people who had never even visited the state. As another anecdote, the *Miami Herald* became the most massive newspaper in the United States (as in literally heavy), due to the impressive number of advertisements it ended up containing.

Florida itself or the authorities in other words got involved as well. This is because they obviously had to accommodate the huge number of people who

---

[21] Donald W. Curl. "Boca Raton and the Florida Land Book of the 1920s." *Tequesta*. March 01, 1986. http://digitalcollections.fiu.edu/tequesta/files/1986/86_1_02.pdf.

were coming to Florida. As such, ridiculously high amounts of money were borrowed to finance all sorts of public investments such as infrastructure spending. Literally everyone was involved.

Another aspect of the bubble was represented by the fact that due to all sorts of construction-related activities taking place, there was an insanely high demand for commodities. After all, the house doesn't exactly build itself and let's not even talk about all sorts of grandiose structures built during the height of the craziness.

Logistically speaking, getting all of the building materials to Florida was a nightmare and in a lot of cases, railroad freight cars were stranded across the state, pretty much choking all of the other types of railroad traffic. To put it differently, the rail system was clogged by the numerous building supplies that had to be shipped to Florida. So much in fact that the three largest railroad companies ultimately placed an embargo and only allowed certain types of goods to be transported.

Just like pretty much every other real estate bubble however, the Florida bubble collapsed under its own weight. This happened while the rest of the United States was still deeply entrenched in a period of euphoric prosperity and capital misallocation called "The Roaring 20s." For the rest of the United States, the roaring 20s continued but for the Florida region, the times of prosperity stopped in 1925.

As it usually happens with financial bubbles, there comes a point when the levels of speculation become so extreme that people decide to book their profits. At the height of the bubble, real estate prices quadrupled within one year, which is extremely hard to achieve when you think about the fact that we're dealing with expensive assets.

"Rags to riches" stories abounded, such as the anecdote about the guy who invested $1700, which was his last remaining wealth, in a Florida property and his sons had him committed to a sanitorium because they thought he was crazy to do that. Its value however soared to, believe it or not, $300,000 by 1925. The person in question ended up getting released and suing his sons… this was the level of insanity at which things were.

It should come as no surprise that some investors wanted to lock in their profits because even in the midst of all that madness, there were still reasonable individuals who took a step back and asked themselves whether or not realistically speaking, there was still room for prices to go up. It turns out that the answer was no, it was time for the bubble to collapse under its own weight.

Aside from the simple effect of people selling their real estate to book profits, more and more negative media coverage about Florida appeared. Authoritative publications such as *Forbes* criticized Florida real estate as an investment opportunity and all in all, more and more negative forces drove the price of Florida real estate down.

And don't forget that a lot of investors were depending on prices going up. This was because they took on debt to invest in Florida real estate and if prices didn't continuously go up, they'd be underwater. Let's not even talk about those who could barely afford the binder payment and had to take out loans just for that.

Just like a domino structure collapses, the Florida real estate bubble fizzled. The snowball became bigger and bigger. People either decided to cut their losses and sell or were simply forced out of their positions regardless of what they wanted due to a shortage of capital. As if all of this wasn't enough, a devastating hurricane affected South Florida in the autumn of 1926, a hurricane which caused 415 deaths and over 13,000 homes were destroyed. Another hurricane came in 1928, then came the crash of 1929 and aside from that, the Mediterranean fruit fly destroyed the citrus industry on which Florida was counting.

All of these things combined put the Florida land the boom of the 1920s to a complete end. People's dreams were shattered, Florida had proven to not exactly be the paradise everyone wanted it to become and it would take until the end of World War II for things to get back on a sustainable path for Florida.

As usual, it's time to draw conclusions by identifying the anomalies of the Florida real estate boom:

1. People invested in assets they didn't understand. It's amazing to think about just how many people bought real estate in Florida by mail despite the fact that they had never, not even once, set foot in

the state. Investors were desperate to get in on the action and nothing else mattered

2. Speculating with borrowed money. Things started with people simply taking out mortgages (which were easy to obtain) so as to be able to afford a property and were taken to the next level when speculators were borrowing money just so they could afford the initial small down payment called the binder and then have 30 days to find another buyer. It was ridiculously easy for people to finance these purchases and as a result, this acted as a jetpack for the bubble on the way up but on the way down, it gave it one of its biggest blows

3. The authorities were overwhelmed. Not only did they not take measures to ensure that the real estate market would not overheat, they did the exact opposite. Legislation was passed which turned Florida into an extremely tax-friendly place and furthermore, the state took on very high levels of debt to accommodate all of the people who were all of a sudden moving to Florida

4. Not caring about the warning signals. Even if hindsight is 20/20, it's still hard to explain how people missed the ridiculously obvious warning signals of the 1920s Florida real estate boom. When prices go from $1,700 to $300,000 and you have people investing in Florida homes or land despite having literally never been there, what can be said? Time and time again, it is proven that greed and the desire to have a piece of the pie affect people's better judgment and all their fears are rationalized away

5. The fact that people were willing to take on additional layers of risk. Investing in real estate with money you already have is one thing. Borrowing money so as to invest in real estate by getting a mortgage is still on the acceptable end. But when you borrow money just so you can make the initial down payment and are then forced to quickly find a buyer, knowing that you would lose out if prices go down… I'm sorry but there must be some kind of a limit when it comes to your willingness to take on additional layers of risk

6. Seeing reality with rose-colored glasses due to your desire to make money. The state of Florida definitely had its advantages but as the

land boom of the 1920s made clear, people embraced an idealistic view of the state, as if it were the number one place in the universe. People forgot about the vast areas of swampland, the occasional extreme weather conditions and so on

These are the anomalies I for one have noticed and this much is certain: in Florida, the roaring 20s ended sooner than in the rest of the United States due to the real estate boom of the 1920s. It should come as no surprise that in the next section, I will be covering the Great Depression of 1929, which affected not just the United States but the rest of the world as well.

Chapter 3.1.8: The Great Depression of 1929

The US had emerged victorious after WW1 and optimism was in the air, as everyone else was exhausted after the war. In the 1920s, the day-to-day lives of average Americans were transformed by electrification and let's say technology in general. An era of prosperity seemed to have begun.

People wanted everything technology had to offer and they were encouraged to become good consumers by the fact that those items could be bought in installments. For the first time, the idea of buying on debt became mainstream. People wanted instant gratification. The Liberty Bonds the US used to borrow from its citizens during the war practically gave most Americans the first contact with the idea of being an investor.

Wall Street stepped in and took advantage of people's growing appetite for investing by marketing other investment instruments to them. Before this period, stocks carried a stigma of being too dangerous but that changed. Brokerages were opened all over the country. Through telegraphic ticketing machines, stock price fluctuations could be printed and reach the average investor within minutes. The market became more and more a part of people's day to day lives.

An era of speculation had begun.

By the mid-20s, around three million people became involved in the market, many of whom had a "get rich quick" mindset, a mindset the media was happy to reinforce. Even celebrities such as Charlie Chaplin or Groucho Marx became investors and shared their positive experiences with others. And on the opposite end, some of Wall Street's most influential players became celebrities. Joseph Kennedy, for example.

More and more people bought shares with borrowed money, an approach known as buying on margin. They only put down a part of the money and brokers funded the rest. By the end of the 20s, 90% of the average stock purchase was made with borrowed money. To give you an idea of just how widely spread this was, over 40% of the money that was lent in the US during the late 20s was lent for stocks.

Needless to say, the demand for stocks skyrocketed.

In 1928, the market went up by 50% in just 12 months. As prices rose, naturally, more people borrowed even more money. Politicians gladly stayed out of the way and enjoyed the prosperity. Politicians such as President Calvin Coolidge, an investor himself. Wall Street's influence, wealth and connections grew. Government regulation was kept to a minimal level and insider trading was very frequent.

From a lot of perspectives, Wall Street seemed like a rigged casino, with pump and dump schemes being quite common. In March of 1929, Herbert Hoover was inaugurated as president and behind the scenes, he was skeptical of Wall Street and the economy. He however remained passive on margin speculation and everything else. Even Wall Street insiders such as Paul Warburg issued warnings.

But everyone was busy making money, so warning signals were disregarded and between May and September 1929, 60 new companies appeared on the NYSE, with over 100 million shares being added. Some pros were astute enough to get out soon. Such as Joseph Kennedy, who (anecdote has it) became convinced the market top was there when a shoe-shine boy[22] was giving him stock tips.

The president became more and more concerned but he was reassured by the bankers.

On the end of Wednesday, the 23rd of October 1929, shares started plummeting on the New York Stock Exchange. In about an hour, roughly 2.5 million shares had been sold. The next day, the downward spiral continued and crowds of regular people gathered on Wall Street to see for themselves what was going on. Some people consider the 24th of October the start of the Great Depression.

Investors thought to themselves that this cannot be real. Winston Churchill happened to be in New York at that exact point in time and recalled how the traders themselves were surprisingly calm, zombie-like if you will. It seemed

---

[22] Jerry W. Markham. *A Financial History of the United States, Volume II*. Armonk, New York: M.E. Sharpe, 2002.

that in slow motion, they were offering each other vast quantities of stocks but nobody wanted any. Not even at a huge discount. Churchill himself lost a fortune at that point.

Confidence was lost.

Leading bankers tried to find a way out and bankers representing $6 billion in assets gathered to see what could be done to support the stock market. They decided to pool together $250,000,000 and use that money to support some selected stocks. They thought that would restore confidence and carried out their plan.

Did it work? Yes.

Stocks started to go up for a while and some believed the crash was over. President Hoover tried to reassure investors as well. On Monday, October 28th, it became clear how dangerous buying with borrowed money was and how losses are magnified on a downturn. People who borrowed to buy stocks were asked by their brokers to put more collateral on the table or their stocks would be sold. Needless to say, most people didn't have that much additional money. As such, the 28th of October (Monday) was a worse trading day than the 24th.

On Tuesday morning (the 29th of October), also called "Black Tuesday," a tidal wave of selling came and no amount of intervention could stop it. By that evening, all stocks were worth around 22% less than when the market opened on Monday. In other words, 22% evaporated in just 36 hours or so.

The president was of a non-interventionist belief, thinking that the market would sort itself out, so nothing was done. By the end of these trading days, 25 billion in personal wealth had vanished. The effects were felt outside the stock market, as people's faith in the banking system sank. One year after the 1929 crash, about 800 banks had failed and 9 million savings accounts had been wiped out. In 1931, approximately 2,000 banks failed[23]. There were no deposit guarantees, nothing at all. People simply lost their money and a ripple effect was generated.

---

[23] Gary Richardson. "Bank Distress During the Great Depression: The Illiquidity-Insolvency Debate Revisited." NBER *Working Paper*. December 1, 2006.
http://www.nber.org/papers/w12717.pdf.

So, can we say that the crash of 1929 brought about the Great Depression?

No, not the crash itself but it generated a sequence of events which caused the depression. Bankruptcies abounded and there was a huge liquidity crunch. Even otherwise viable businesses failed because they couldn't even secure enough money for basic expenses. Even one of the symbols of US prosperity and industrial strength, US Steel, was brought to its knees, as it ended up firing all its full-time workers within 3 years (around 225,000 workers).

People were unprepared and in some cases even took money from the piggy banks of their children, as again, they had nothing set aside and were completely vulnerable. One out of two home mortgages ended up being in default and in 1930, four million US families had no means of support.

To make matters worse, 25,000 miles of land literally turned to dust (the infamous Dust Bowl) and many were forced to flee by heading West. Former bankers, college professors and other highly educated people rode freight trains across the country, looking for a second chance.

Strikes and protests were spreading as well as becoming more violent. President Hoover feared a revolution and movements like communism seemed to be gaining traction. And speaking of the president, he famously limited himself to pretty much just standing by initially. Believe it or not, roughly 100,000 Americans moved to the Soviet Union due to work being available there, it's the only time in history when more people were leaving America than coming to it.

As time passed, the Great Depression spread far beyond the US borders. In Germany, the depression made the already harsh Versailles conditions even worse, generating massive desperation and unrest. The Nazi movement saw Germany's suffering as their biggest opportunity and in 1932, the Nazi Party secured a 37% score in the elections. Not a majority but better than all the other parties and on the 30th of January 1933, Hitler's ascent to power was celebrated through a massive march with torch lights which aroused the masses to such degrees that reason was abandoned and hardship seemed far easier to deal with.

In the same year (1932), it was election time in the United States as well. Herbert Hoover campaigned for re-election but he didn't exactly have the best reputation in the world. Improvised "towns" of unemployed men were called Hoovervilles, newspapers were called Hoover blankets and so on. It was an easy win for his opponent, then-governor of New York Franklin Delano Roosevelt, who implemented his "New Deal" campaign promise.

It was definitely a challenging time for a new president, who in 1933 had to deal not with 4 million unemployed as was the case in 1930 but with 16 million of them, 25% of the American workforce. He recapitalized the banks, guaranteed deposits and regulated the financial system. A 3-year investigation which ruined the reputation of Wall Street was launched by the Senate Banking Committee and revealed quite a few skeletons that were lying in various closets. People desperately wanted to find scapegoats.

Furthermore, FDR pumped new money into the economy in the most massive intervention up until that point. While some of his choices such as attacking the Gold Standard were controversial, he did manage to put lots and lots of people to work and was ultimately re-elected at the greatest margin in US history. The depression however was not overcome completely and would last until the outbreak of World War II.

In Germany on the other hand, a recovery occurred because pretty much everyone was working… unfortunately to a large degree on re-arming the country and getting it ready for war. We all know how that ended. Needless to say, the Great Depression was definitely a phenomenon with long-term worldwide ramifications (perhaps the number one financial calamity in history), something that literally devastated humanity.

We cannot afford not to analyze the anomalies that took place and draw conclusions:

1. People invested in assets they didn't understand. Let's face it, the average US stock investor was anything but money-savvy. In fact, before gaining mainstream popularity, stocks were considered somewhat of a boogeyman due to the volatility and risks they came with. However, none of that mattered once the average investor smelled money and became addicted to stocks

2. Speculating with borrowed money. As if #1 was not enough, investors began speculating on margin. Or in other words, they only

ponied up a certain percentage of the amount and their broker covered the rest. Trading on margin enabled many individuals to experience exponential profit growth while the bull market was in full swing but the same type of trading was their downfall when prices collapsed and their brokers demanded more collateral. Collateral which, needless to say, pretty much nobody was able to put on the table on short notice if at all

3. The authorities were overwhelmed. President Hoover was a non-interventionist who despite having his doubts, decided it's better to just stay away and let the market do its thing. His friends and advisors from the investment world reinforced these beliefs and this attitude would end up costing Hoover dearly

4. Not caring about the warning signals. The Joseph Kennedy situation (realizing that even the shoe-shine boy was giving stock advice) was by no means an isolated incident. It seemed everyone and his dog was all of a sudden a stock expert. After all, they saw just how great their picks were when everything was going up and assumed their profits were a result of financial brilliance. Of course, that was not the case

5. The fact that people were willing to take on additional layers of risk. Speculating with your own money when you clearly don't know what you're doing is bad enough as it is. Taking on debilitating levels of debt to do it is just plain foolish. But people didn't care because as long as prices went up, there was absolutely nothing to worry about

6. Seeing reality with rose-colored glasses due to your desire to make money. As more and more people became "wealthy," an overall sense of prosperity prevailed. Unfortunately, all of this was nothing more than paper wealth. For example, someone who traded on margin might have seemed very wealthy on paper one day before prices started collapsing, yet after that, his positions would be wiped out

7. Going all-in. After all, why diversify if what you're currently doing is working so well, right? Well… no, not really. When all your wealth is tied to the performance of an asset class, on margin to top it all off, you're just one financial calamity away from losing it all. Like many have

Chapter 3.2: Now

Up until this point, we've covered events which have taken place in the (relatively) distant past, starting with the tulip mania which peaked in 1636-1637 and ending with the Great Depression of 1929. The patterns we're seeing in terms of anomalies are so obvious that I feel little need to highlight them.

Are events unfolding in a 100% identical manner?

Of course not. However, you don't exactly have to be a nit-picky observer to notice that (financial) history does indeed rhyme. That humans do tend to kind-of-sort-of make the same mistakes time and time again. The exact manifestations differ of course but fundamentally speaking, the common denominators are literally screaming at us.

But perhaps things have changed.

Maybe the modern-day person is more financially sophisticated, less prone to making the embarrassing errors of the past. I believe that's a fair dilemma to have and therefore, this section will be dedicated to putting more recent events and anomalies under the microscope. The analysis framework will remain intact and for each case study, I'll do my best to help you see things from the perspective of those who have been there and done that so that at the end, conclusions can be drawn and of course, anomalies can be identified.

I urge you not to start reading this section with your mind completely made up. Allow your beliefs to be questioned and perhaps most importantly, don't feel pressured into adopting my way of thinking or accepting my conclusions. Derive value from this section however you see fit and in an unbiased as well as non-judgmental manner, let history act as an open book about human nature.

Chapter 3.2.1: The End of Bretton Woods and the Gold/Silver Bubble of 1977-1980

In 1944, a new international monetary system called the Bretton Woods system was created. However, it only became fully functional as of 1958 and through that system, countries basically settled their international trade dealings in dollars, knowing those dollars were convertible to gold at a fixed rate of $35 per ounce.

In other words, central banks had the right to exchange their US dollars for gold at a price of $35 per ounce whenever they deemed it appropriate. For a while, the system seemed to be working well. But as of a certain point, the United States used its monetary privileges to fund various projects such as Lyndon Johnson's Great Society, its debt kept growing for this reason and also due to the conflicts it was engaged in, primarily the Vietnam War.

All in all, the dollar was obviously overvalued.

Other countries started becoming skeptical and decided to take advantage of the fact that they could convert their dollar holdings to physical gold. The president of France, Charles de Gaulle, was the first official who decided to do this in February 1965 and various countries followed suit.

After World War II, the United States held 2/3 of the world's gold, something that enabled it to be the center of the Bretton Woods system in the first place. Needless to say, that gradually changed[24] and as countries started demanding gold in exchange for dollars, the gold holdings of the United States kept decreasing.

In 1966, the United States ended up having $13.2 billion in gold reserves, whereas other central banks held $14 billion. By 1968, there was 20 times more paper money in existence compared to gold. In other words, only 5% of the currency was backed by gold. In contrast, that figure was 20% in 1950.

---

[24] Peter M. Garber. "The Collapse of the Bretton Woods Fixed Exchange Rate System." *National Bureau of Economic Research.* January 15, 1993.
http://www.nber.org/chapters/c6876.pdf.

As the money supply was being increased, countries gradually decided to leave the Bretton Woods system. West Germany left the Bretton Woods system in May 1971, Switzerland did the same in August 1971 and the US authorities were obviously worried or perhaps even downright desperate.

On the 15th of August 1971, Nixon effectively killed the Bretton Woods system through what he said was a temporary suspension of the convertibility of the dollar to gold. As we all know, that convertibility suspension ended up being permanent. We can say that the entire process was finalized by March 1973, when the world moved to a floating exchange rate system.

The main implication of what Nixon did which interests us in this subchapter is the fact that by eliminating the Bretton Woods system, the official monetary role of gold was effectively over. Now of course, central banks all around the world still to this day have impressive gold reserves but again, gold no longer has a monetary role in that currencies aren't linked to it and as such, it is freely traded internationally just like any other commodity.

As far as the average person is concerned, things are a bit tricky. As of April 5, 1933, an executive order signed by President Franklin D. Roosevelt forbad the average citizen to invest in gold by as they put it "hoarding" gold coins, gold bullion and gold certificates within the United States. It wasn't until December 31, 1974, that President Ford, the successor of Richard Nixon, signed a bill which allowed the average citizen to invest in gold.

At that point, gold was worth approximately $184 per ounce. Needless to say, this was quite an increase from $35 per ounce. Gold ended the crucial year of 1971 being worth $43.5 per ounce, and then moved up to $63.9 per ounce at the end of 1972. By the end of 1973, its value had climbed to $106.7 per ounce.

Since regular individuals were allowed to invest in gold freely as of the end of 1974, some would have expected the price to jump even more impressively in 1975. And indeed, some people did invest in gold to protect themselves against inflation but not enough to make the price jump. In fact, prices declined fairly significantly in 1975, from about $176 in January to just $139 in December. 1976 was a year of gold price stagnation and even slight decline, with prices around the $134 zone toward end of that year.

It's interesting that despite there being a huge uptick in the US inflation rate around 1975, with inflation moving all the way up to 12%, gold prices did not skyrocket. They did however start growing as of 1977, ending that year at roughly $160 despite inflation being considerably lower than in 1975. 1978 was another year of consistent but not huge increases, with gold ending the year at roughly $208 per ounce and this price evolution continued in the first half of 1979.

As we move toward the end of 1979 however, a deadly mix of circumstances brought about a significant upshot of the gold price. You see, when referring to the high of gold in 1980, people overlook the fact that it was an extremely fast up-and-down move, with gold only staying above $700 an ounce for a couple of weeks.

So, what exactly triggered the spike in gold prices during December 1979 and January 1980?

It's never possible to determine with 100% accuracy what makes a market tick but my best guess is that this time, the dose of fear was high enough, fear primarily induced by geopolitical shocks coupled with once again very high levels of inflation. The geopolitical shocks I am referring to primarily revolve around the Iran hostage crisis which started in November 1979, followed by a much more serious invasion of Afghanistan by the USSR one month later. As far as the inflation rate was concerned, a new peak of 14 to 15% was reached.

We saw in 1975 that inflation in and of itself was not enough to move the gold price upwards. Back then, the inflation rate was hovering around the 12% mark, only marginally lower than the inflation rate of late 1979 to early 1980. I am therefore tempted to believe that fear generated by geopolitical shocks was in this case the primary driver of gold and of course silver prices.

In hindsight, knowing that the USSR collapsed in 1991, it's probably hard for us to figure out what Americans were so afraid of. Do keep in mind however that the Cold War was in full swing back then and an outright invasion of another country by the USSR was seen as a potentially catastrophic event. This, coupled with the dwindling confidence that people had in the Carter administration, generated a bit of a "perfect storm" situation.

After reaching its peak of $850 on the 21st of January 1980, gold prices subsided quite a bit, ending the month at around $653. The month of February was a month of price stagnation and in the following months, volatility picked up, with prices frequently touching sub-$500 levels. The rest of 1980 was pretty much a period of precious metal price stagnation, with occasional volatility spikes sprinkled in.

Unfortunately for gold and silver investors, what followed in 1981 and beyond was a multi-year or even multi-decade bear market in precious metals. Americans were confident in the ability of the new Reagan Administration and of course in the central bank (led by Paul Volcker) to keep inflation under control. Reaganomics seemed to be working, Volcker's determination to keep inflation in check through aggressive policy worked as well and as geopolitical fears subsided, the arguments for investing in precious metals became weaker and weaker.

The analysis I've just shared tends to reinforce my belief that precious metals should be seen not so much as a hedge against inflation but rather as a hedge against chaos and uncertainty. The US had high inflation in 1975 but not only did precious metal prices refuse to go up, they actually went down. It's only when high inflation was coupled with serious geopolitical concerns that prices finally skyrocketed.

What about silver?

As usual, the price action of silver tends to move in the same direction as that of gold, just with even more volatility. To give you a general idea, silver prices moved from roughly $6 on the 1st of January 1979 all the way to a high of $49.45 on the 18th of January 1980, so three days before the $850 high was hit by gold.

As you can see, the price of silver increased by a whopping 700% in only about a year or so. A lot of people talk about the price manipulation of the Hunt brothers and it is indeed true that they traded vast enough quantities of silver to be able to move markets but at the end of the day, it's pretty much impossible for any single market participant to meaningfully alter the long-term trend.

The Hunt brothers did indeed manipulate silver prices frequently but we are talking about shorter-term manipulations and definitely not something that could've altered the meaningful long-term trend of silver. The debates about manipulations are a bit too heated for my taste in the world of precious metals and as such, I would strongly recommend taking them with a grain of salt.

Within any market, there are players with large enough bankrolls to manipulate prices in the short run but they tend to trade within the long-term trend and don't possess the power to alter it. The same principle is valid when it comes to gold, silver or any other asset for that matter. However, I do believe it's fairly safe to say that without the Hunt brothers and their efforts, prices would have probably not risen as much. The Hunt brothers engaged in quite a bit of leveraged trading and it's precisely leverage that ended up hurting them when they were met with a margin call for $100 million that they were not able to honor. And since they were large enough players for the financial world to worry that if they go down, their creditors go down as well, they were ultimately bailed out through a line of credit of $1.1 billion provided by several US banks.

So, should what happened to precious metals be considered a bubble?

A lot of people are going to hate me but yes, the kind of market behavior exhibited with gold and silver, especially toward the end of 1979 and the beginning of 1980, to me at least seems perfectly consistent with the type of behavior we've been used to with bubbles in general.

When the perfect cocktail of ingredients presented itself in very late 1979, the rollercoaster ride of gold and silver reached its peak. People were genuinely worried about what was happening in the world geopolitically at that point, inflation was high, the price itself had been on an upward path for a decent amount of time, more and more people were paying attention to this asset class as a result and all in all, again: we have a "perfect storm" situation.

Prices were so high that not even the (relatively) recent top of 2011 matched that of January 1984 when adjusted for inflation. Nominally speaking, the price of gold was in fact higher in 2011 but if you adjust that value by the rate of inflation, the 1980 peak was not reached. When it comes to silver, the situation is even more dramatic, with the 2011 high barely reaching that of 1980 in nominal terms. If we adjust for inflation, we realize that in 2011, silver was far, far away from the 1980 high.

I have nothing against gold and silver, I actually believe there's room in each portfolio for precious metals. What I do think however is that most investors fail to understand what these assets are meant to help you do. In January 1980, many people thought it was in fact even possible to get rich by trading gold and silver. Quite a few believed the same thing in 2011.

And sure, it's possible to get rich trading just about anything if you get the timing right but this doesn't mean that the asset class in question is supposed to make you rich. The primary goal of gold and silver investors should be wealth preservation and hedging against disaster. Not even inflation, as the correlation is in some cases just not there, but rather disasters. Again, I think there is room for precious metals in each portfolio, just don't make the mistake people made in late 1979 to early 1980.

That being stated, let's identify the anomalies associated with the gold and silver bubble:

1. The fact that people invested in something they didn't truly understand. Even today, a lot of investors are still struggling to understand what gold and silver are supposed to help you do. Back then, we do have to take the fact into consideration that people were investing in an asset without much of a track record. After all, Nixon had just decided to suspend the convertibility of US dollars to gold in 1971 and it wasn't until December of 1974 that the average individual was allowed to trade gold and silver freely. So while it is understandable that investors didn't exactly have much of a track record to go by, the fact remains that quite a few of them decided to jump in without meaningfully understanding what they're getting into

2. Letting emotion rather than reason dictate your actions. In the case of gold and silver, investors were driven by two let's call them primal emotions: fear on the one hand, especially geopolitical fears, and greed on the other, especially toward the peak when people saw the price movement and wanted a piece of the action

3. Speculating with borrowed money. While speculative trading on leverage such as what the Hunt brothers did hasn't altered the overall trend, it has most definitely exacerbated its manifestations. Even

more so, without the bailout they've ultimately received, their speculation might have ended up becoming systemically risky as well

4. Trying to find scapegoats. Even today, blaming the Hunt brothers is something gold and silver enthusiasts frequently do. And while sure, some degree of blame should definitely be placed on them, people shouldn't do this just so they can rationalize their own mistakes away. If you invested in gold thinking you're going to get rich in let's say January 1980 and then ended up losing money, I'm sorry but you have to look in the mirror to find out who's to blame rather than simply pin it on the Hunt brothers

5. Seeing an asset class through rose-colored glasses. Now sure, people did in fact have valid reasons to be concerned toward the end of 1979 but a lot of them have made the mistake of only listening to arguments in favor of gold and silver. Back then, just like now, it's easy to come up with verifiable, logical and coherent arguments in favor of pretty much any asset, which is precisely why it's important to always listen to the other side as well

Chapter 3.2.2: The Black Monday Stock Market Crash of 1987

In the 80s, the success of Reaganomics[25] created a wealth effect which undoubtedly ended up clouding people's judgment and affecting their capital allocation decisions. To envision the investment mindset status quo of the 80s, it's enough to simply imagine Gordon Gecko telling everyone that greed is good.

Needed to say, the stock market was doing remarkably well. Stockbrokers themselves were very happy because with the huge amount of transactions taking place, they made a killing. As of the mid-1980s when computers were added to the mix, we can safely say the trading industry was revolutionized.

All of a sudden, it became possible for the top traders (with enough money to have access to cutting-edge technology) to make or break markets by simply pressing a button. While it tends to be an industry adage that in the long run the market is bigger than any individual participant, computers did make it remarkably easier to influence or if you will even manipulate the market in the short term.

When the market is moving up, technology can help accelerate the up-move and everything seems great. But in a downturn, it tends to have the exact opposite effect, exposing the weaknesses of any system and exacerbating a crash. Especially in an environment in which a major technological breakthrough occurred very recently.

On the 25th of August 1987 however, few people thought about the latter. The Dow reached its peak of 2722 and it seemed like sunshine and rainbows were everywhere. Companies enjoyed low taxes, the inflation rate was declining. What more could you possibly ask for if you were involved in the financial industry?

---

[25] Joe Holley. "Beloved Radio Broadcaster Paul Harvey Dies at 90." *The Washington Post*. March 1, 2009. http://www.washingtonpost.com/wp-dyn/content/article/2009/02/28/AR2009022802096_2.html.

On Friday (October 16, 1987), the Dow crashes by 108 points. A remarkable crash without a doubt but many believed things would end there. On Monday (October 19) the market is overwhelmed by the sheer number of sell orders. So much for the crash being over on Friday! $500 million worth of stocks were sold as soon as the market opened and do keep in mind that this was back in 1987, when dollars were "worth" quite a bit more than today's US dollars. The market opened 10% lower compared to the close on Friday and things got downright spectacular.

It should be noted that even with technology evolving, trading was still mostly "manual" back then. Trades had to be executed from the New York Stock Exchange, the CBOE (Chicago) and so on. It's not like today, when everything is handled through servers and individual people can execute trades from the comfort of their own homes.

In fact, let's take a moment to analyze how the average customer used to transact back in 1987:

1. First of all, that customer needed to pick up the phone and call his stockbroker
2. The broker would receive the request and then hand it over to the trading desk of the brokerage in question
3. The trading desk people then picked up the phone themselves and called a booth clerk who was physically present at the exchange at which the trading was being done. Again, the New York Stock Exchange or the CBOE, for example
4. The booth clerk used to actually write down the order and then pass it on to the company's floor broker
5. That floor broker then went to the actual trading post where that company's stocks were traded and finally met a specialist, who executed the order

There was quite a discrepancy between how people with access to trading technology executed orders and how the regular investor did it. If you had the expensive technology it took to develop an edge, then you could of course execute trades by simply clicking on a couple of buttons. And as you can imagine, thousands of computers were executing sell orders like there was no tomorrow at that point.

Let's not get too side-tracked and instead, go back to Monday, the 19th of October 1987. People were selling pretty much all their assets. On Friday, gold was considered a safe haven asset but by Monday, it ended up being sold as well. By 10 in the morning, the sale order volume reached a whopping $1 billion.

It was a full-fledged panic and disaster, Murphy's Laws at their best. It was a true pandemonium on the so-called pits where the previously mentioned physical trading took place, electronic systems were overwhelmed as well and it was pretty much chaos all around. At the end of the trading day, after seven hours of pure and utter horror, the Dow closed an unbelievable 508 points lower. Five times greater than on Friday!

There you have it: Black Monday of 1987 definitely deserves its reputation.

The market lost 22.6% in just one day, the largest single-day market crash in history by far, almost two times greater than the previous record, set by the Great Depression of 1929. Black Tuesday of 1929 (October 29, 1929) saw a crash of "only" 12.82%. This is where the similarities end however, as the 1929 crash ended up, of course, having much more dramatic long-term consequences than the 1987 one.

But enough about 1929, time to get back to 1987.

People were worried about the future, they feared that another Great Depression was just around the corner. For the generation which was too young to remember the Great Depression of 1929, Black Monday of 1987 ended up becoming the most significant day in their "financial" memory. Fortunes have been lost but then again, there have also been winners, like Paul Tudor Jones, who made his investors very happy and earned a pretty penny (low 9 figures, to be more precise) himself.

With so much wealth being lost, the financial system was clearly under pressure. Market makers lost ridiculously high amounts of money and there was a real risk that the entire system would simply cease functioning due to inadequate levels of liquidity. For this reason, the Federal Reserve stepped in as a lender of last resort so as to give these entities the liquidity they needed to survive.

The effects of this were felt as markets opened on Tuesday (October 20), with prices going up at the beginning of the day. However, things were chaotic and a lot of stocks were simply not open for trading. A lot of specialists refuse to execute orders because despite having access to liquidity thanks to the Federal Reserve, they were panicked... there was just no bottom in sight.

They were afraid to buy the stocks that others were lining up to sell them because they thought prices would keep going down and knew the money from the Federal Reserve would have to eventually be paid back with interest. Therefore, despite the initial bump on Tuesday, the Federal Reserve's plan for the most part failed.

Eventually, trading was halted at several venues. The main problem was the fact that there seemed to be no buyers. With specialists having bought everything they could afford or were willing to buy, it just seemed that if you wanted to sell something, there was just no liquidity for you.

At that point, the only index that was still trading was the MMI, with one point in the MMI being worth five times more than one point in the Dow. Fortunately however, as of a certain point, the MMI started spiking up, dramatically so in fact. Suddenly, traders started seeing opportunity and this pretty much jumpstarted the activity of the entire system and made markets reopen elsewhere as well.

All of a sudden, buyers appeared.

Traders saw opportunities to make money, companies started announcing buybacks in a massive manner as well. By the time Tuesday was over, the Dow had gained an impressive 102 points. Desperation ended up being replaced with a general feeling of euphoria. For the rest of the week, markets rallied and the crash of 1987 was over. The main lesson people learned after 1987 was the fact that the financial system can prove to be ridiculously fragile in situations which involve mass panic. People started taking volatility much more seriously and did their best to implement systems which make trading safer, if you will. The extent to which they succeeded is of course highly debatable.

So, what were the main anomalies associated with the crash of 1987?

Let's start identifying them:

1. People, including professionals, invested in a market environment they didn't truly understand. In hindsight, perhaps it seems perfectly natural and logical for the market to occasionally crash, even if it's by as much as 22.6%. But if you judge what happened by the reaction of most people and I'm especially referring to financial industry professionals, it becomes abundantly clear those market participants hadn't even considered the possibility of such a scenario taking place

2. Seeing life through rose-colored glasses. When it seemed that everyone and their dog was making money in the stock market, few people bothered to pay attention to skeptics or think about scenarios in which something would go wrong. Human beings tend to only look at the positives during times of prosperity but by seeing things through rose-colored glasses, you'll be caught unprepared when you're eventually forced to take them off

3. Ignoring the warning signals. The system itself was at that point quite prone to disasters for the simple reason that two worlds were for the first time in financial trading history being interwoven. Earlier on in the subchapter, I've explained just how much of a discrepancy there was between how the average individual traded and how those who had access to expensive technology did it. This in and of itself should have been considered a warning signal that is just looking you in the eye, yet people ignored it

4. The fact that the authorities were one step behind. They were, as usual, reactive rather than proactive. The Federal Reserve did step in as a lender of last resort and the authorities were both willing and able to step in after the fact but again, they reacted to events that unfolded rather than proving they're able to be one step ahead

5. Letting emotional thinking overcome reason. Even at the absolute top of the financial industry, knowledgeable and experienced individuals ultimately allowed themselves to be the prisoners of two of our most basic driving forces: first greed and then fear

6. Ignoring the lessons of history. Make no mistake, these people studied panics of the past. They had all the knowledge and resources one could ask for at their disposal to learn from the numerous lessons history teaches us. Did they? No

Chapter 3.2.3: The Japanese Bubble of the 1980s

After Japan's surrender at the end of World War II, Japanese banks were obviously in trouble. After all, the assets they held had deteriorated dramatically since Japan lost World War II and as such, the banking system itself was on the brink of collapse. It was the first situation in modern Japanese history in which their central bank would end up intervening. The first of many, I might add.

As far as the economy of Japan was concerned, capitalism was implemented and a large number of people became land owners. As ironic as it may seem, after the 1951 amnesty for war criminals, Japan's newly-found democracy and capitalism were implemented by many of the same bureaucrats who got Japan into the war in the first place.

It's important to understand the context however.

The Americans wanted to avoid the type of rural protests and unrest which China was facing and they did that by taking land from the major landowners and giving it to the tenants. Action was initially taken against many of the pre-war elites because they were accused of making the war possible in the first place. However, again, as ironic as it may seem, democracy was implemented by several of the exact same fascists of the 30s. Of course, as often is the case in politics, many started branding themselves as defenders of democracy after the war but their pasts were so murky that no amount of water and soap could fix that.

An eloquent example of this is represented by the fact that in 1957, one of the top war crime suspects ended up becoming the prime minister of Japan. Prime Minister Kishi was one of the primary founders of the Liberal Democratic Party of Japan which would end up staying in power until 1993.

Japan was run through a relatively peculiar system in which the economy was to a fairly large degree controlled by the government and the central bank, so it was definitely not what you'd call a textbook free market economy, but its results were good. Japan became an industrial powerhouse.

Its products ended up being embraced by consumers from all over the world and the standard of living of the average Japanese citizen grew exponentially, being surpassed only by that of countries such as the United States and Western European nations. The wartime industrial power of Japan had been improved and obviously directed toward consumer goods. As we all know, it worked and Japan's corporations became extremely competitive on the international front.

Then along came the 1980s.

It was an era in which deregulation abounded and efforts were made by countless countries to ensure the free circulation of capital. Japan didn't represent an exception. Initially, a five-year plan for the liberalization and deregulation of the Japanese economy was created. As of 1986, a ten-year plan was proposed to reform the Japanese economy and improve the lifestyle of the average Japanese.

The primary goal was creating a system based on the free market in Japan, similar to that of the United States. To achieve this goal however, pretty much all dimensions of Japanese life had to be altered: the political dimension, the economic dimension and even the cultural dimension.

The Bank of Japan engaged in all sorts of relaxation measures which resulted in increased lending activity. Lending policies were on the lenient side and ultimately, it became relatively easy for even very young people to buy not their first home but their second or even third on credit. The increased ease at which you could obtain money from banks generated booms across multiple industries. The real estate market benefited, the stock market experienced a boom as well and the list could go on and on.

The stock market for example experienced a growth of 240% from 1985 to 1989. And during that same timeframe, land prices went up by 245%. To give you a glimpse into just how crazy things were, the market value of one out of Tokyo's 13 districts ended up being higher than the market value of all Canadian real estate put together.

But people found all sorts of explanations for this and didn't worry too much. Again, the boom made everyone fat and happy. The labor market was doing so well that companies even experienced a labor shortage. When times are so good, people tend to rationalize their worries away. Even large manufacturing companies became speculators, creating financial divisions and using borrowed money to speculate on the property and stock market. For example, the popular car producer Nissan made more money through its speculation activities than by selling cars.

People found various explanations for the asset price increases. Some economists said that the land price surges were simply caused by the shortage of available land. Others explained the boom away by saying it was simply fueled by rising productivity. Theories abounded. Pretty much nobody realized that Japan was actually in the middle of a giant bubble.

All sectors of the economy were fueled by the fact that credit was so readily available. The Bank of Japan encouraged commercial banks to issue loans and one of the main problems was that there were just not enough low-risk borrowers out there. As such, banks kept loosening their lending requirements, taking on more and more additional layers of risk.

Some people did raise questions as to whether or not all of this activity was in fact caused primarily by easy access to money but the financial elite dismissed these people and claimed that Japan was pretty much in a "new paradigm" situation and that the explanations for the asset value increases were far more complex.

But the effects of the Japanese bubble manifested themselves well outside of Japan as well.

To give you an idea as to the proportions of all this, let's start by saying that in 1980, more money entered Japan that exited it. We economists call this a net inflow and in Japan's case, it was about $2 billion in 1980. In 1986 however, Japan had a net outflow or in other words, more money left Japan than came in.

How much money left Japan in 1986, you might ask? A whopping $132 billion. The Japanese became top bidders for various international assets such as art, expensive international real estate and so on. In 1986, 75% of all bonds auctioned by the United States Treasury were acquired by, you've guessed it, Japanese buyers.

For a decent period of time, the Japanese were able to do this because the markets didn't devalue their currency. More and more loans were issued for activities which did not result in the production of goods and services. For example, they were issued for real estate speculation. Banks felt comfortable accepting highly overvalued real estate as collateral because nobody suspected that prices would downright crash. It should be noted that in 1969, the total private land wealth in Japan was about ¥14.3 trillion. Twenty years later, by 1989, this increased to a whopping ¥2,000 trillion.

Eventually, even the central bank of Japan decided that lending for real estate purposes needed to be restricted. The party was about to end. Seemingly all of a sudden, asset prices started to drop dramatically. In 1990 for example, the stock market dropped by 32%. During this crash, the central bank of Japan stopped giving commercial bankers guidance and these people were left scratching their heads and worrying about what they needed to do next.

Needless to say, bankers panicked and didn't just limit themselves to restricting the flow of credit toward speculative activities but went much further by limiting the lending of money to everyone else as well. The ramifications reached all the way to the "real" Japan rather than the "paper wealth" Japan, as 5 million people wound up losing their jobs. For men aged 20 to 44, suicide became the leading cause of death.

Between 1990 and 2003, the stock market dropped by a whopping 80%. 212,000 companies went bankrupt and land prices fell by up to 84%. Pressure was put on the Bank of Japan to lower interest rates and indeed, they were lowered all the way down to 0.1%. Furthermore, pressure was also exerted so as to devalue the currency and also, many economists advised that improved government spending would help the economy and gradually boost demand. This ultimately happened, with Japan being forced to take on debilitating levels of debt.

The Japanese wanted scapegoats. They wanted to know who was responsible and the Ministry of Finance was considered one of the top culprits. For the first time, in 1998, prosecutors were actually sent to the ministry. Several officials were arrested and imprisoned, some people even committed suicide.

The Bank of Japan however was outside the spotlight of public criticism and even became independent for the first time in 1998. The bursting of the bubble obviously also took its political toll on the Liberal Democratic Party that had been ruling the country for 40 years, with its supremacy which seemed unshakable being shattered. To this day, the Japanese are still worldwide leaders when it comes to let's call it "unorthodox" fiscal and especially monetary policy.

Japan's "lost decades" aren't over but this subchapter is, with it being time to draw conclusions and spot anomalies:

1. People invested in Japanese assets without properly understanding (… in a lot of cases, without even caring all that much) what exactly was fueling the growth. The smell of money was enough of an argument and after all, why bother asking questions or digging deeper when everything is going great?

2. Credit was handed out in an irresponsible manner. The Bank of Japan (cough-cough, wink-wink) convinced lending institutions that credit expansion is the best thing since sliced bread. So what if it doesn't sound sustainable? So what if there aren't enough low-risk borrowers?

3. Not only were the authorities not one step ahead, as authorities should be in an ideal scenario, they were from many perspectives the main culprits. Japan was the star of the show internationally and this tends to be a dream come true if you're holding public office. As such, the powers that be actually facilitated the gross misallocation of capital that kept taking place

4. Ignoring warning signals, even blatantly obvious ones such as one Tokyo district being "worth" more than Canada. Once again, everyone (from elected officials to central bankers, investors and ultimately regular Japanese citizens) was having a great time, certainly not the kind of climate that makes you want to see things with a critical eye

5. Looking for scapegoats after the proverbial you-know-what hits the fan. When things went south in Japan, they went south in a spectacular but at the same time devastating manner. Needless to say, this made a lot of people furious and what's our first instinct when

something goes bad? Looking in the mirror? Of course not, it's finding scapegoats, which is precisely what happened in Japan, with the Ministry of Finance being in the proverbial spotlight

6. Not understanding that excesses, while they may produce paper wealth and a (relatively) short-term environment of euphoria, can have catastrophic long-term consequences. Japan is perhaps the poster boy for this, with its "lost decade" turning into "lost decades" which still aren't over

Chapter 3.2.4: The Asian Financial Crisis of 1997

In the early nineties, money literally poured into Asia, money frequently originating from some of the most sophisticated investors in the world. The same investors panicked like frightened school children in 1997 in what represented (in my opinion) a textbook example of manic-depressive behavior in the big league of investors.

When we have situations such as those we've encountered with the tulip mania, in which various half-drunk speculators lose money by investing in overpriced tulips, everything is a lot easier to understand because the expectations are low. But when capital allocation decisions are made by top CEOs of financial companies and key figures in government, the bar is supposed to be multiple orders of magnitude higher.

Is the Asian crisis of '97 a tale of incompetence? Yes.

Is the Asian crisis of '97 a tale of corruption? Once again, yes.

We can safely consider it tale of a deadly duo, if you will: incompetence on the one hand and widespread corruption on the other. As someone from Eastern Europe, I am unfortunately all too familiar with this type of capital allocation and it sometimes tends to be a perfect storm. On the one hand, greed and incompetence have made even sophisticated players act in a manic-depressive manner (overly euphoric initially and then excessively frightened) and on the other hand, the state didn't restore reason. Due to high levels of corruption, it ended up doing the exact opposite.

Now sure, as you've found out in the previous subchapter, Japan itself suffered the consequences of incompetence as well as borderline corruption or even downright corruption but compared to what happened in other parts of Asia, the situation in Japan can be considered nothing more than child's play or if you will, a warm-up.

To put ourselves in the appropriate mindset, we must see things from the perspective of those who lived in the countries affected by the bubble which ultimately led to the financial crisis of 1997. Someone from Thailand, Malaysia, Indonesia and so on would be able to tell you that initially, the bar was set quite low. In terms of GDP per capita, lifestyle and pretty much any other kind of indicator, these countries were well behind their western counterparts.

In a lot of cases, we were talking about rudimentary agriculture-based economies for the most part. It was clear that these countries desperately needed a change and consumerism seemed to be just what the doctor ordered. To a certain extent, a significant one, the Asian countries started their boom phase by actually catering to consumerism. Consumers from all over the world wanted more and more products and thanks to their cheap labor, Asian countries were able to provide just that and even better so, do it at a price that was hard to beat.

This export boom significantly altered the economies of these countries to the very core. As you can imagine, those who received a job upgrade by being taken from the agriculture sector and moved to manufacturing experienced a bump in lifestyle as well. As time passed, the economies of these countries grew and along with them, a middle class started to emerge.

As more and more investors have noticed the growing prosperity in Asia, they wanted a piece of the action. It became easier and easier for countries to borrow money on the international markets and of course, this enabled companies to borrow at lower costs as well. On the surface, everything seemed great. International creditors had full confidence in the fact that Asian countries would pay them back, banks had confidence in the viability of the loans they were making locally and it all seemed like a virtuous circle.

The main vulnerability was of course the fact that money was borrowed primarily in US dollars rather than in the local currencies. But when times are good, people don't exactly have the tendency of worrying about these aspects. Central banks did their best to maintain the stability of their currencies by implementing pegs to the US dollar or in other words, they would intervene in the market whenever necessary so as to keep the currency on a stable path. If there was downward pressure on the currency, they would intervene as buyers so as to get things back on track.

And when things were going well, central banks didn't exactly have an extremely hard time maintaining the pegs. However, once disaster struck in 1997, there was just so much downward pressure on the Asian currencies that central banks, even after depleting quite a bit of their external reserves, did not manage to maintain the stability of the currencies compared to the dollar.

Simply put, Asian currencies went on a downward spiral once things got nasty. And speaking of nastiness, it's precisely when nastiness ensues that it becomes obvious just how flawed things were under the surface in Asia, especially Southeast Asia. You see, money being borrowed in a different currency was only a part of the problem. The other part was represented by the fact that the money that was borrowed wasn't always spent wisely. In a lot of cases, it was spent downright recklessly and even criminally.

In all the affected countries, companies deeply associated with those in power got access to huge loans despite the fact that they shouldn't have qualified for them based on their fundamentals. Money was frequently lent to people and entities that should normally have not been eligible to receive such financing. Sometimes due to simple incompetence and a lot of times fraudulently, for political reasons.

Corruption and nepotism were deeply entrenched in the political culture of most of these countries, especially countries like Indonesia and Malaysia. When the boom was in full swing, people felt prosperous and were more than willing to tolerate the unorthodox behavior of their leaders. After all, at the end of the day, the system generated great results.

Right?

Well, no, not exactly. For a while sure, the results seemed downward spectacular but as time passed, it became clear that for the most part, the out of the ordinarily high prosperity of Southeast Asia was a bit of a house of cards. The two broad risks-related mental states of investors are risk-on and risk-off. When they are in risk-on mode, investors get excited or even overly excited whenever they hear good news about whatever it is they're investing in and should bad news appear, they're quick to shrug it right off. When investors are in risk-off mode however, they do the exact opposite. They don't pay all that much attention to positive news and blow every piece of negative information that pops up out of proportion.

This is one of the main reasons why people called the crisis the Asian contagion. Once investors found out Thailand is in trouble, they started second-guessing the other countries as well and a vicious circle ensued. To put it differently, they went from risk-on mode to risk-off mode very quickly. You need to understand that central banks only have a limited amount of firepower. If their currency is falling, then they can sell their dollar reserves and buy that currency. In other words, when there isn't enough demand for their currency, they step in and buy it. But that can only work up until a certain point.

Let's start with Thailand.

At the beginning of the nineties, it had experienced what one could call an impressive economic streak, with stable 3.6%-5.7% inflation and a GDP growth rate of 8.08%-8.94% per year[26] (in fact, if we look at data from 1985 to 1996, its average GDP growth rate exceeds 9%). Its currency, the Thai baht, was trading in a very tight 24.91-25.59 per US dollar range, a peg which seemed rock-solid.

But… well, it wasn't.

In early 1997, the baht had to deal with massive speculative attacks and the central bank ended up realizing that it just didn't have enough foreign currency reserves to keep fighting it. As such, it abandoned the peg on the 2nd of July 1997 and let the currency float. The result was that the Thai baht went from 24.5 per US dollar in June 1997 all the way down to 41 per US dollar in July 1998[27]. Its GNP collapsed in a similar manner, from $170 billion in June 1997 to $102 billion in July 1998. In other words, the currency as well as GNP of Thailand collapsed by a whopping 40% in a year or so.

Unfortunately, the damage wasn't just limited to Thailand.

The Asian crisis of 1997 is also called the "Asian Contagion" for the simple reason that investors were spooked by what happened in Thailand and quickly abandoned other Asian countries as well. Kind of like a bank run on a very large scale. Let's see how other countries from Asia fared.

---

[26] Narisa Laplamwanit. "A Good Look at the Thai Financial Crisis in 1997-1998." *Columbia University.* September 1, 1999.
http://www.columbia.edu/cu/thai/html/financial97_98.html.
[27] RJ Cheetham. "Asia Crisis." *School of Advanced International Studies at Johns Hopkins University.* June 7, 1998. https://www.sais-jhu.edu.

Indonesia was the worst-affected one by far, with its currency as well as GNP dropping by over 83% in one year. Needless to say, the financial crisis turned into a humanitarian and ultimately political one as well, forcing president Suharto to step down on the 21ˢᵗ of May 1998, after ruling the country for 30 years.

Malaysia also ended up in worse shape than Thailand, with its currency dropping by 45% from June 1997 to July 1998 and its GNP by almost 39%. Next, we have the Philippines, which fared slightly better than Thailand, experiencing a currency and GNP drop of 37.4% and respectively 37.3%. South Korea fared yet again slightly better (although "better" does seem to be a tad optimistic when describing this state of affairs), with its currency and GNP dropping by a little over 34%. The stronger Hong-Kong was a bit of an outlier, managing to fend off several powerful speculative attacks but still, it had its own wounds to lick.

So… why did this all happen?

I'd say the primary cause was the fact that, as mentioned at the very beginning of the subchapter, the Asian crisis of '97 is a textbook example of manic-depressive or bubble-like behavior on a large scale. Living proof that even big-league players are anything but perfect, from financial sector players to governments.

Like pretty much any bubble, there were some sound fundamentals initially.

The cheap and reasonably productive/educated/flexible workforce of Asia was definitely a force to be reckoned with. Companies invested in these countries based on sound business reasoning and were rewarded. They made a lot of money, workers experienced significant lifestyle upgrades and governments became quite a bit wealthier.

It all seemed like a miracle and in fact, people were quick to label it as such. As time passed and the word spread, everyone and his dog wanted a piece of the action. This is the stage at which gross misallocations of capital become inevitable and it's precisely what happened prior to the crisis of 1997.

All participants were guilty in one way or another:

- International players were way too generous when lending money to Asia. Risk management concerns were largely set aside and quite a few questionable loans were made based on the false belief that everything you invest in will ultimately turn to gold in Asia

- Instead of acting as a wise mediator, governments did the exact opposite and exacerbated all facets of the "mania" mentality. They recklessly invested money in all sorts of more or less financially viable projects and instead of raising an eyebrow whenever something seemed fishy in the financial sector, wanted their share of it all. Lots of politically-connected companies were "helped" to attract ridiculously high levels of financing and needless to say, a lot of those loans flopped

- The average consumer wanted a piece of the action as well. This is especially obvious if we take a look at the evolution of let's say real estate prices. People were wealthier than in the past but unfortunately, they became blinded by their newly-found prosperity and thought they were wealthier than was in fact the case. It would turn out a lot of that prosperity was nothing more than paper wealth

In the end, international institutions such as the International Monetary Fund and the World Bank stepped in. However, their role and decisions were controversial to say the least. Some economists believe they helped set countries on the right track by "encouraging" much-needed structural reform, whereas others criticize them for making the crisis worse by imposing deflationary austerity measures in an already deflationary environment.

However, despite all controversies, Asian countries recovered relatively quickly. Were there political consequences? Most definitely. Did lots of players (from the average person to big-league lenders and official figures) learn lessons the hard way? Yes, they did but fortunately, Asian countries fared relatively well after the initial shock.

Despite the "not as awful as it could have been" ending (because I refuse to say something that started in Thailand had a happy ending, wink-wink), there are lessons to be learned and conclusions to be drawn. Let's do just that by analyzing the anomalies associated with the Asian crisis of 1997 in a balanced and unbiased manner:

1. People and most notably huge players that we could have easily called sophisticated invested in something they didn't understand. They focused so much on seeing the positives that trying to look beneath the surface was considered a secondary endeavor

2. Borrowed money was in a lot of cases grossly misallocated. Examples of politically-connected companies which received staggeringly large loans without actually deserving them abound and when times are good, this behavior may have very well seemed like something one can sweep under the rug. Unfortunately, the proverbial good times ended and we all know what happened next

3. The authorities were either overwhelmed (incompetent) or complicit (corrupt). Instead of being forces that complement and control one another, market forces and government forces ended up jointly adding more and more gasoline to the fire, not realizing that someone with a match would eventually decide to put an end to the party

4. Not caring about the warning signals. Government officials who dared question the status quo tended to be marginalized (or worse) … let's just say the pre-crisis political elites did not exactly appreciate being told that the good times wouldn't last forever or that their country is on an unsustainable path

5. Seeing reality through rose-colored glasses due to your desire to make money. When analyzing the average investor and noticing this type of behavior, I tend to be more lenient. But when big players with access to brainpower and know-how are guilty of the exact same thing, I consider it a facepalm moment

6. Looking for scapegoats. Initially, politicians loved blaming speculators, occult forces and pretty much anyone but themselves. Later on, some considered the IMF and the World Bank the perfect bad guys. Regardless of whether or not the accusations had their merits, it's abundantly clear that people don't exactly have the habit of looking in the mirror when things go wrong. Why go through that discomfort when finding scapegoats is much easier?

Chapter 3.2.5: The 1998 Collapse of Long-Term Capital Management

If I were to describe what happened with Long-Term Capital Management in 1998 using just three words, the title of Roger Lowenstein's book would be perfect: *When Genius Failed*[28]. What was Long-Term Capital Management anyway? Simply put, it was a hedge fund which initially generated impressive profits by using sophisticated mathematical models to take advantage of market pricing inefficiencies.

If there was a company able to pull it off, it had to be them because Long-Term Capital Management seemed like a financial dream team. It was a company run by an amazing team that consisted of traders with immense experience as well as people with academic credentials, including Myron S. Scholes[29] and Robert C. Merton[30] who jointly received the 1997 Nobel prize in economics for putting together an impressive new method to price derivatives, without a doubt one of the biggest challenges of the financial world.

The people who were involved in Long-Term Capital Management as well as those who invested their money through the hedge fund were ridiculously sophisticated financial players. The hedge fund seemed to have all the ingredients it needed to revolutionize trading. It was hard to find a team in any field, anywhere in the world, with a higher average IQ than the people who were running LTCM.

Furthermore, they put their money where their mouth was by investing most of their own capital in the fund. Also, you were only allowed to invest your money in the hedge fund if you yourself were let's say well-funded (to put it

---

[28] Roger Lowenstein. *When Genius Failed*. New York City: Random House, 2000.
[29] Myron S. Scholes and Fisher Black. "The Pricing of Options and Corporate Liabilities." *Journal of Political Economy*. May 02, 1973.
http://www.journals.uchicago.edu/doi/abs/10.1086/260062.
[30] Robert C. Merton. "Theory of Rational Option Pricing." *The Bell Journal of Economics and Management Science*. May 10, 1973.
https://www.jstor.org/stable/3003143?seq=1#page_scan_tab_contents.

mildly). Long-Term Capital Management was basically a dream team of financial experts who invested the money of well-funded and sophisticated investors as well as their own... could anything possibly go wrong?

Initially, it seemed as if the answer was a clear no.

After its first year (1994), the fund generated an impressive return of over 20% after fees. In the following year (1995), it generated over two times more, 43% to be precise. In 1996, its return was similar (41%) and in 1997, only 17% but still, it seemed that everything these people touched turned to gold.

How did Long-Term Capital Management generate these returns?

As previously mentioned, complex mathematical models were used to take advantage of slight pricing inefficiencies and basically, this meant that on each trade, the actual return per dollar invested was very low. However, by borrowing lots and lots of money and basically engaging in high leverage trading, their returns ended up being augmented.

How much money did they borrow?

Well, toward the end of 1997, they were holding about $30 in debt for every dollar of capital. The great thing about leverage is that it enables you to make a lot of money, even on trades which wouldn't have necessarily produced an amazing return per dollar invested otherwise. To simplify things and help you understand how this works, let's assume you want to invest $1000 and decide to invest in something that would give you a 1% return after the trade is finalized.

The problem is that you are only investing $1000 and 1% would mean 10 bucks, which wouldn't even be worth your time. Therefore, you decide to take on leverage just like Long-Term Capital Management did, 30:1. This means that with your $1,000, you're investing the equivalent of $30,000 and all of a sudden, 1% becomes $300.

The main drawback however is that if instead of making a 1% gain you would have incurred a 3.34% loss, then you would have lost all of your money. When only investing your own money (no leverage), a 3.34% loss in our $1,000 scenario of would merely set you back $33.4. At 30:1 leverage however, you would lose all of your money after just that one trade.

A lot of average Joe investors don't exactly understand how leverage works but needless to say, that was not the case with Long-Term Capital Management. When you have some of the brightest people in the world working for you, it's fairly safe to assume they know what the drawbacks of leverage can be and the people who managed Long-Term Capital Management knew that.

They used their combined brainpower and worked extensively to put together models and strategies which they believed would help them avoid such scenarios. The problem with geniuses however is the fact that they frequently engage in a pattern of thinking dictated by overconfidence. They're smarter than everyone else and therefore automatically assume the models they create are good enough to ensure that humiliating scenarios such as seeing your capital wiped out will not materialize.

Unfortunately, it turned out their models were anything but perfect.

In 1998, the Southeast Asian financial crisis we've discussed manifested itself in an intensified manner again and in August, something unexpected happened when Russia suddenly stopped issuing payments on its debt and devalued its currency dramatically. The perfect storm reared its ugly head for Long-Term Capital Management's strategy and in August, the fund lost a whopping 44% of its value.

Needless to say, the fund was in desperate need of capital and the Federal Reserve decided to jump in. Instead of injecting money themselves or finding a solution which involved taxpayer money, the Federal Reserve assumed an interesting role and basically facilitated negotiations between Long-Term Capital Management and other Wall Street firms. In other words, the fund was about to get bailed out by Wall Street.

Initially, Warren Buffett made an offer of buying out the firm's partners for $250 million and then injecting $3.75 billion into the fund but the offer ended up not being accepted for legal reasons. Instead, another deal was ultimately reached through which 14 Wall Street firms injected $3.7 billion into the fund and in exchange, received 90% of Long-Term Capital Management.

The existing team promised to keep running the fund, under the oversight of a committee made up of representatives of the people who bailed out the hedge fund. By the end of 1999, almost all of Long-Term Capital

Management's remaining positions had been closed and the 14 companies got their money back in full.

The main losers were of course the people who were running Long-Term Capital Management and had a lot of their own money invested as well as the pre-bailout investors. At the end of the day though, this is an interesting example of how the moral hazard risk was eliminated. Yes, people lost money but it's not the taxpayer who ended up on the line in one way or another but rather primarily the people who caused the problems in the first place and of course the sophisticated investors who invested their money in LTCM.

In this book, I did my best to hand-pick the most fascinating crash/collapse case studies of the financial world and the Long-Term Capital Management fiasco is definitely one of them. It's time to identify some of the most important anomalies associated with this event so as to see which conclusions can be drawn:

1. Even sophisticated investors frequently invest in things they cannot understand. Let's be honest, even the very sophisticated financial players who put their money on the line by investing in Long-Term Capital Management didn't understand the complex mathematical models the company employed. Maybe they had somewhat of an understanding but more likely than not, they barely scratched the surface yet were still willing to put their money on the line

2. Thinking you can predict the future. Long-Term Capital Management is perhaps the poster boy case study that you can show to those who claim they're smart enough to be able to predict the financial future. The Long-Term Capital Management team consisted of people with a vast experience when it comes to the financial industry and even included two Nobel Prize winners. It doesn't really get any smarter than that but still, it's blatantly obvious to everyone that they failed at predicting the future. Time and time again, it is proven that no matter how complex the methodology may be, humans tend to be pretty bad at predicting the future

3. Speculating with borrowed money. At the end of the day, it's leverage that ultimately killed Long-Term Capital Management. Their mathematical models were supposed to enable them to make low-

return but practically risk-free trades and that, coupled with high levels of leverage, seemed like a recipe for success. Instead, it turned out to be the exact opposite, a recipe for disaster

4. Seeing the world through rose-colored glasses. It seems even the best and the brightest of the world tend to be guilty of that, especially if doing so strokes your ego as well. You know you're smart, everyone else constantly tells you that as well, so why bother being pessimistic? The Long-Term Capital Management situation proves that even some of the smartest individuals in the world are susceptible to basic human folly. It's precisely when you think you're invincible that you tend to become vulnerable

5. Thinking that this time it's different. Time and time again, hedge funds and various players appear on Wall Street and claim that they have a miracle solution or if you will, a universal panacea when it comes to trading. But hey, when some of the smartest people in the world are involved in the project, then maybe they're actually on to something and maybe this time it is indeed different, right? Unfortunately, no, the Long-Term Capital Management fiasco has proven that yet again, it was not different

Chapter 3.2.6: The Dot-Com Bubble

It's fairly safe to say the commercial Internet appeared in the mid-nineties. The technology itself was of course older but the commercial Internet, as in the Internet that was meaningfully used by the average individual, only started to take shape around the 90s and needless to say, it was a revolution… to put it mildly.

Individuals across the globe could seamlessly communicate with one another and exchange information. Just think for example about how huge of a benefit it is that a researcher in Sydney can continuously share progress reports and findings with his friends in London as well as with other contacts in New York. People realized the Internet would end up becoming something truly disruptive and naturally, money started pouring in.

How much was invested in these companies or let's say generally speaking, just how much was poured into the Internet? Over $5 trillion throughout the second half of the 90s. Also keep in mind that one dollar back in let's say 1999 had the purchasing power of $1.5 in today's US Dollars, so we can safely say the equivalent of 7.5 trillion in today's dollars was poured into Internet ventures over the second half of the 90s.

People had a lot of money to invest back then. The United States was going through a very solid economic period, people felt wealthy, capital gains taxes had been reduced two times and all in all, people's risk appetite in general and appetite for startups in particular soared to the moon.

Various well-funded venture capital entities were formed and these companies were willing to throw money around like crazy in the hope that one of their projects or even several of them would end up becoming a market leader and making everyone rich. To put it differently, one success story could pay for several flops.

Frankly, investment rules were turned upside down.

People were desperate to invest in "the next big thing" and indicators such as the P/E ratio (price to earnings) which had represented a staple of mainstream investing were thrown out the window. Instead, individuals invested based on "exotic" variables such as disruption or in other words, the line of reasoning was something along the lines of:

"Okay, this company isn't making any money but the technology is so innovative/disruptive that I've decided to invest based on the growth potential I envision."

… or if you will, we're talking about a transition from valuation methodologies which revolve around economic soundness to ones based on the potential of explosive growth, which would in the end lead to profits. Hopefully. The main problem was, of course, that these "metrics" were far harder to quantify.

Make no mistake, some of the companies people speculated on back in the nineties not only still exist today but are in fact stronger than ever. Just think about Amazon, for example. Most of them however, the overwhelming majority in fact, ended up fizzling out. One of the most popular examples is Pets.com, which went from a market capitalization of around $300,000,000 to $0 in just 268 days.

The name of the game when it comes to understanding the dot-com bubble is making the distinction between genuine potential and ultra-speculative nonsense. On the one hand, it would be a huge mistake to minimize the disruptive nature of the Internet and its potential when it comes to changing the world. From 1990 to 1997, computer ownership skyrocketed from 15% to 35%[31] and let's not even talk about the present, when it's hard to think of an acquaintance under 50 that doesn't own a smartphone.

So yes, the fundamentals were there.

But just like pretty much all bubbles out there, what started out as a phenomenon based on sound fundamentals (the idea of investing in disruptive companies) ended up being taken to the extreme. If you had "Dot Com" as a suffix, it was easy enough to attract financing… even with "head-scratcher" business models.

---

[31] Tom Rubey. "Computer Ownership Up Sharply in the 1990s." *U.S. Department of Labor.* March 4, 1999. https://www.bls.gov/opub/btn/archive/computer-ownership-up-sharply-in-the-1990s.pdf.

When you get a chance to, I'd highly recommend reading a blog post Mark Cuban wrote on his blog back in 2013[32] because it illustrates rather brilliantly how even stock market professionals acted in the nineties. He takes a stroll down memory lane and remembers how in July 1998, he and his partner Todd Wagner took Broadcast.com public with Morgan Stanley.

Like other companies that went public, they went on a so-called "road show" and basically met with a lot of major players in the financial world. Mutual funds, hedge funds, pension funds, you name it. Naturally, they did their best to put together a solid presentation and assumed that seasoned financial industry players would bombard them with difficult questions.

To their surprise, the exact opposite happened.

The people in question were completely clueless. They didn't know all that much about Internet companies and realistically speaking, didn't even care. As a joke, Cuban and his partner ultimately even inserted completely nonsensical sentences into their presentations, just to see if anyone would notice. The result? Every investor they talked to placed the maximum allowed order.

The lesson to be learned is this: if even experienced professionals were in frenzy mode and didn't care about fundamentals at all, what can be said about the average investor? It's shocking to think about these things but the capital allocation mentality back then, just like with most bubbles, was no longer in sanity territory.

Needless to say, prices soared.

From 1995 to 2000, the NASDAQ went from 1,000 all the way to 5,000 and its P/E ratio of 200 was downright ridiculous. So what if you never made any money? Who cares if your business model makes zero financial sense? As long as you were an Internet company and repeated a few buzzwords, investors were more than willing to throw money at you. It seemed the only aspect everyone cared about was growth potential.

---

[32] Mark Cuban. "The Stock Market." *Blog Maverick: The Mark Cuban Weblog.* January 10, 2013.

Companies raised money and used those funds as follows for the most part:

1. Create something disruptive or improve what they already had. Little thought was given to economic viability. Companies were more than willing to offer value for free or at very low price points initially in the hope that their brand would become a household name, the financial viability of products and services wasn't exactly a top concern

2. Promote growth by any means necessary. The name of the game was spreading the word and building awareness. Those running the companies did "kind of, sort of" think about profits but they were expected a long way down the line and it was certainly the status quo to invest massively in advertising first and ask questions later

3. Offer a "rock star" lifestyle to those running the company, from (in)famous product launch parties to ridiculously expensive Herman Miller Aeron chairs for everyone, chairs which were considered a symbol of the dot-com lifestyle

The bubble ended up affecting pretty much all dimensions of the tech world, from Internet businesses themselves to advertising industry companies, telecom equipment providers, ISPs and so on. Resource allocation mistakes were made on a massive scale but nobody seemed to care. Why bother being a downer when it seems the party will never end?

Unfortunately though, that's exactly what happened.

The NASDAQ peak occurred on the 10th of March 2000, when the composite reached its intraday high of 5,132 but within just 30 months, it fell by a whopping 78%. To give you an idea of just how much "wealth" (even if paper wealth) was lost, it's worth noting that the NASDAQ had a market capitalization of $6.6 trillion in March 2000. In other words, over $5 trillion evaporated just like that.

Liquidity was gone and eventually, most companies burned through their cash reserves and quite a few shining stars ended up being acquired at pennies on the dollar once they no longer had adequate levels of capital and access to additional financing. And unfortunately, the effects were not just limited to dot-com companies.

The tangible sector of the economy was affected as well, with for example many telecom companies crashing. These companies expanded way too quickly, thinking that the good times would never end and ultimately had to pay for their mistakes. The dot-com bubble is most definitely an example of a bubble with severe reverberations across all sectors of the economy:

- Roughly one out of two dot-com companies collapsed
- Industries related to the Internet (such as the telecom one) suffered as well
- Individual investors got burned and the "wealth effect" backfired
- Confidence in not just tech stocks but the stock market in general was lost and people went from "risk-on" mode to "risk-off" mode as a result, rushing toward safe haven assets
- To make matters worse, the September 11 attacks affected markets and the economy in general dramatically as well

As strange as it may seem, the effects of the dot-com bubble are still felt today. You see, the situation was so bad that the then-chairman of the Federal Reserve, Alan Greenspan, decided to lower interest rates all the way down to 1%. A dramatic move for sure and on the one hand, it "worked" as in economic activity was indeed generated. On the other hand though, many believe that due to capital being so cheap, Greenspan's decision was the main cause of the real estate bubble which brought us the Great Recession of 2007-2008.

All in all, here are the anomalies one can easily identify after drawing the line:

1. From the average Joe to (as explained by Mark Cuban) sophisticated/experienced financial industry players, people invested in something they didn't meaningfully understand. If we're honest with ourselves, we cannot help but notice that most investors just didn't care about fundamentals, about what happens under the hood and what not. They saw the momentum and wanted a piece of the action, plain and simple

2. Nobody bothered to pay attention to warning signals. It's downright shocking how warning signals we're tempted to consider blatantly obvious (such as P/E ratios of 200) have been shrugged off.

Everyone was so busy having a good time that nobody felt the need to be a party pooper

3. The authorities weren't exactly interested in curbing the "irrational exuberance" (as Alan Greenspan called it) and speaking of Greenspan, he was actually accused of painting an overly-optimistic picture of stocks back when the frenzy was in full gear

4. Easy access to capital. Imagine you're a tech business owner who is literally overwhelmed by the sheer number of people who are willing to throw money at you. The temptation to make reckless decisions with other people's money can be hard to resist, from giving yourself huge bonuses to throwing money around when managing advertising campaigns since, after all… it's not your money that's on the line

5. Taking on more and more risk. There are quite a few anecdotes about people who quit their jobs to become tech stock traders (they thought they were experts because they were making money but as mentioned elsewhere in this book as well, we're all experts in a bull market, when anything we touch turns to gold) and all in all, people were more than willing to take on huge amounts of risk, from the previously mentioned individuals to telecom companies that over-expanded

6. Looking for scapegoats instead of trying to find a mirror. Because after all, if you speculated wildly and lost money, it's not your fault… right? It must be those evil tech company CEOs who misallocated funds? Or the government and central bank that added fuel to the fire? Now sure, all of those parties may very well be guilty but you can never truly understand bubbles if you conveniently overlook the blame that needs to be placed on all individual speculators

Chapter 3.2.7: The Great Recession of 2007-2008

After the dot-com bubble burst, the chairman of the Federal Reserve at that point, Alan Greenspan, decided to do whatever it took to save the economy. And in his view, that meant lowering interest rates all the way down to 1%, which obviously came as quite a shock. However, it seemed as if he achieved his desired results. The economy recovered after the shock but there was a price to be paid.

And the price was higher than most people would have anticipated. You see, Greenspan decided to revive the economy by giving it a dose of "cocaine," artificially low interest rates. Did it work? Yes, it did but the economy escaped the effects of the dot-com bubble, only to end up blowing an even bigger bubble: the real estate one. The fundamental difference between the real estate bubble and its tech counterpart is that pretty much everyone is affected in one way or another by the prices of real estate. As such, a real estate bubble can have even more devastating effects than something like a tech stock implosion.

So, what happened?

Well, stimulated by the artificially low interest rates, a lot of people decided to get a home loan and finally buy a house. After all, at these ridiculously low interest rates, a house all of a sudden became much more affordable. Some people used these low interest rates as an argument in favor of getting a home that puts the house of the Joneses to shame because after all, they can afford it, right?

No, not really.

There's a world of difference between thinking you can afford something and genuinely affording it, as explained countless times throughout this book. Yet the average US consumer didn't care about that. To him, a house he can afford meant a house that banks were willing to lend him money for. And make no mistake, banks became just as reckless as the average consumer. They were willing to hand out loans to people they should've never lent money to and prudence was thrown out the window.

Aside from the idea of actually purchasing a home, people who already owned homes treated them like their very own ATM machines. Due to the fact that home prices went up and the value of their assets was higher than before, they could take on additional loans with their real estate as collateral. Add the low interest rate environment to the mix and there you have it, the perfect consumer boom.

From people who bought homes they couldn't afford to people who owned homes and ended up using them as their personal ATM machines, lots and lots of consumers went on spending sprees as a result of this low interest rate environment. Gradually, interest rates went back up again but by the time that happened, the bubble had reached critical mass and as such, it had legs of its own.

You would have thought however that within a financial system as mature as that of the United States, there would be safeguards in place to prevent this kind of recklessness. However, not only was that not the case, the exact opposite happened. In theory, bankers are supposed to be responsible and only give out loans to people they believe will most likely pay them back.

In the let's call it traditional banking framework, they have every incentive to do so. Traditional banking revolves around the idea of taking out a loan and establishing a "very" long-term relationship with your bank through which that bank makes money by gradually collecting your monthly payments. It's therefore in their best interest to make sure they're lending money to the right person because again, they're establishing a long-term relationship with that individual.

In modern banking however, the incentive system has been turned upside down. Banks gave people loans but then quickly packaged those loans and sold them as investment vehicles to other people on the open market. In other words, the entire dynamic has been changed and all of a sudden, instead of building a long-term relationship with you, the bank simply sells your loan as a financial instrument called the mortgage-backed security on Wall Street.

What does this mean in terms of risk-taking behavior?

You don't have to be a rocket scientist to figure out that all of a sudden, bankers have more and more of an incentive to be more and more risk tolerant. After all, with each loan they hand out, they're going to earn money by selling it on Wall Street and if something goes wrong, well then it's no longer their problem anymore because the loan belongs to someone else.

An entire bonus system was created around this mechanism in the banking world through which all bankers were highly encouraged to give out as many loans as possible. Not financially sound loans, mind you, the financially sound part was eliminated from the equation… they just cared about issuing as many of them as humanly possible.

Risk management became a joke and toward the final stages, pretty much anyone with a pulse could qualify for a loan. Some loans were so bad that they were called NINJA loans, as in "No Income, No Jobs or Assets." In some cases, they didn't even require any proof of income, a written statement was enough.

Some people in the banking industry even took things one step further and engaged in what is called predatory lending, in that they intentionally misled people in order to make them sign up for loans that the bankers knew would be a bad deal. Realistically speaking, it was clear to the bankers in question that eventually, those people would most likely experience difficulties paying them back.

But was genuinely nobody interested in the risk aspect?

Kind of but not really. Let me explain. You see, many of those who bought these mortgage-backed securities also hedged as it is called in the financial world. In other words, they took out insurance on these financial products and that insurance was called a credit default swap. Now I know all of this sounds incredibly complicated but in fact, things are quite simple. Someone who bought a mortgage-backed security which contained many loans bundled up also purchased insurance from companies such as AIG on these loans, which meant that if something went wrong with that financial instrument, the insurer would compensate the investor.

Unfortunately, insurers such as AIG were just as reckless as the bankers and didn't take risk management seriously enough. After all, a lot of these mortgage-backed securities received the highest possible ratings from rating agencies and all in all, insurers ended up getting carried away and selling credit default swaps with a let's call it overly optimistic mindset.

Why would people from a wealthy country such as the United States stop paying their loans back and even more so, what are the odds of lots and lots of people doing it at the same time? Insurers weren't worried about that particular risk and as such, issued credit default swaps like there's no tomorrow despite knowing that given the compensation they promised people, they would surely go bankrupt if mass defaults were to start occurring.

However, as it usually happens in life, Murphy's Law's kicked in and more and more people started having difficulties keeping up with their mortgage payments. Why? Well, in some cases because as previously mentioned, interest rates gradually went up and all of a sudden, borrowers realized they had a much harder time making their payments.

In other cases, other reasons made people unable to keep up with their mortgage payments, reasons such as for example borrowers losing their jobs after the economy slowed down and so on. Simply put, more and more individuals were coming to the realization they had overextended themselves and were unable to meet their financial obligations.

Needless to say, this triggered a chain of events that is relatively simple to understand. First of all, a lot of important financial institutions which were highly exposed to these mortgage-backed securities became pretty much insolvent. We're talking about players such as Bear Stearns, which ended up being bought at pennies on the dollar by other institutions and Lehman Brothers, which was allowed to collapse. The Lehman Brothers collapse made it clear just how fragile the system was and it became evident that if the authorities do not step in, the financial system would crumble.

And let's not forget about other entities that needed to be bailed out such as insurance companies. As mentioned previously, insurers definitely weren't prepared for scenarios in which so many people would no longer be able to pay their mortgages and as such, were caught off-guard when they realized just how much they owed to the investors who bought insurance from them and who now needed to be compensated.

These insurance companies, just like the financial industry companies, employed some of the brightest minds in the world, including rocket scientists and brilliant mathematicians. Frankly, you would be hard-pressed to find a higher percentage of geniuses in any other industry. These people created complex models in which they had absolute confidence. Their egos got the best of them and those models were in no way suggesting that such a shock could take place. Yet it did.

As such, insurance company such as the huge AIG were, just like various financial institutions, practically insolvent. They had to compensate a lot of people and simply did not have enough money to do so.

Predictably, they themselves had to be rescued. It doesn't stop here because the effects of what is now called the Great Recession of 2007-2008 were felt across many industries, including for example the auto industry. The auto giant General Motors itself was on the receiving end of a massive bailout.

Now you might be asking yourself where all this money came from.

Needless to say, simply lowering rates to 1%, which is what Greenspan did after the dot-com bubble, was nowhere near enough. Therefore, the then-chairman of the Federal Reserve (Ben Bernanke) had to on the one hand reduce rates all the way down to zero and on the other hand inject billions upon billions and ultimately trillions of dollars into the financial system.

The Federal Reserve, just like other central banks, pumped money into the system through a program called Quantitative Easing. At its height, $85 billion were "printed" each month or in other words, more money was pumped into the system in one year than had existed after the entire pre-Great Recession history of the United States, from 1913 when the Federal Reserve appeared all the way until 2007. The authorities insist they've done what needed to be done to save the system from a complete collapse. However, this rescue came at a dramatic price.

As can be seen, considerably more had to be done than after the dot-com bubble burst. There's a world of difference between reducing rates to 1% and reducing them to zero and pumping trillions into the system. Furthermore, a rate normalization such as the one after the dot-com bubble didn't occur. Rates were kept at zero percent for an extremely long period of time and when the Federal Reserve did end up increasing them, it only did so in extremely small increments of just 25 basis points.

And the United States, compared to other places, is doing much better. In the European Union and Japan for example, rates had to be brought all the way into negative territory. As can be seen, unprecedentedly high prices had to be say paid to keep the current system afloat. Some economists believe the authorities did what had to be done to save the financial system. Others however consider that the only thing they did was kick the can down the road and make the problem more complicated, economists who are now asking themselves what exactly the authorities are going to do after the next financial crisis.

Since we are still in the middle of it all, it's way too early to have a verdict. Needless to say however, we are in what can easily be described as an economic twilight zone and it's therefore crucial to understand the anomalies that have taken place and draw some preliminary conclusions:

1. Bankers, traders/brokers and insurers alike "invested" in something they didn't truly understand. Complex financial products based on a completely untested banking paradigm and which contained quite a few less-than-optimal loans were placed on the open market and investors pretty much fought over them at a certain point. A "hot" but improperly understood financial instrument… not the best combination in the world

2. Warning signals were blissfully ignored. The manner in which loans were handed out to pretty much anyone with a pulse should have made even novice investors (let's not even talk about sophisticated players) raise an eyebrow but everyone was too busy counting imaginary profits to care

3. As usual, the authorities were reactive rather than proactive. Complicit in some cases. Nobody, from bankers to authorities, was willing to look at the phenomenon as a whole with critical eyes. On the surface, society seems like a solid system that's full of checks and balances. Unfortunately, that tends to hardly be the case when the proverbial party is in full swing

4. Making reckless capital allocation decisions with borrowed money. Had lending standards been more robust or to be blunt, had lending standards meaningfully existed, the entire craziness would have been

easier to contain. But no, false prosperity obtained on credit was just too tempting

5. Gladly taking on additional layers of risk. The capital misallocations weren't just limited to banking, it was a widespread phenomenon which transcended industries. From insurers to auto manufacturers, everyone was happy to take on more and more risk. In some cases, people hid behind their "on-site" geniuses and their "foolproof" models, whereas in other cases, the parties in question simply didn't care

6. Desperately looking for scapegoats. It's easy to blame it all on the bankers but realistically speaking, that's intellectually dishonest. Without, for example, the willingness of borrowers to overextend themselves just so they can impress the Joneses, the "critical mass" element just wouldn't have been there. The same way, it's easy to find guilty parties wherever you look… especially in the mirror

Chapter 3.2.8: The Short Domain Mania of 2015-2016

I do want to make it clear that when talking about short domain names, I'm referring primarily to domain names such as three-letter .com domain names (ABC.com, for example), three-number .com domain names (123.com, for example), four-number .com domain names, four-letter.com domain names and so on. To make things easier, I will mostly be referring to one of the short domain categories which had the most impressive run, four-letter.com domain names.

That being stated, let's take a small step back in time again and focus on the Great Recession period. Back then, the so-called four-letter .com domain the name buyout was finalized. In other words, all the possible combinations of four-letter .com domain names had been registered (from AAAA.com to ZZZZ.com, all of them). Up until that point, those who wanted random four-letter .com domain names could have simply registered them for the normal fee in certain cases. After the buyout was finalized however, people thought values would skyrocket.

But they didn't.

On the contrary, time had proven that domain names were in fact not safe haven assets but rather assets which perform poorly when the market/economy in general isn't doing well. As such, not only did short domain name values not skyrocket as many would have expected, the actual buyout ended up failing.

For those of you who do not know, you have to pay a yearly fee to keep your domain names. For Dot Coms, doing that is possible for less than $10 per year in a lot of places. Still, some people even bought hundreds or thousands of four-letter .com domain names and the yearly fees added up.

For example, if you owned 1,000 four-letter .com domain names, you would've had to pay let's say $8,500 each and every year just to keep them. For some domain investors, especially after the crisis, that was too much and as a result, the owners dropped those domain names and they became

THE AGE OF ANOMALY

available for registration again. This is what I meant when stating that the buyout failed. After it failed, people were able to once again find random four-letter .com domain names at the regular registration fee.

It should be noted however that the best combinations were all taken. Most of the domain names which were available contained letters that were considered non-premium. To put it differently, letters which weren't as widely used as the others in the Western alphabet. Those letters were J, K, Q, W, X, Y and Z. All in all, most of the four-letter domains that were available at the registration fee probably contained at least one such letter.

Okay, so what happened next?

Well, short domains, after dropping in value initially, stagnated for an extended period of time. Three-letter .com domain names could even be purchased for slightly less than mid four figures and we already know that in the case of four-letter .com domain names, it was even possible to buy various random combinations at the regular registration fee.

But as of a certain point, something changed.

And that something revolved around a country with over a billion people which was exploding economically: China. The Chinese, given their newly found prosperity, wanted to invest in all sorts of assets for various reasons. Some because they wanted to make even more money, some because they wanted to move money out of the country and so on. And since we're talking about a country with a genuinely huge population, needless to say, even if a small percentage of its citizens ends up becoming interested in an asset class as small as domain names, it makes a world of difference.

As I'm sure you suspect, the Chinese became interested in short domain names. Why? Simply because due to the language barrier, it makes more sense for Chinese investors to focus on short domain names than for example one or two-word domain names. When it comes to short domain names, they're investing in assets with a value that is easy to determine and in assets which are most importantly not as susceptible to language barriers. It really should come as no surprise that the Chinese were reluctant to invest in types of domains that required them to have a good grasp of the English language but when it comes to short domain names, they were interested.

As time passed, more and more capital from China was invested in domain names and this changed the industry dramatically. Among other things, the rules of investing were changed because the Chinese liked types of domain names that had been neglected by Western investors. This was especially obvious when it comes to the perceived quality of letters.

As mentioned previously, Western investors up until that point considered various letters such as W or X non-premium. The Chinese however love those letters and instead, consider all vowels as well as the letter V undesirable. The Chinese don't like vowels because in pinyin (the Romanization of Chinese characters), not that many words start with vowels and as such, four-letter domain names that contain vowels have less potential as abbreviations. The letter V doesn't exist in pinyin at all, so it should be obvious why it isn't desirable in domains.

The same way, the world of numeric domain names has been affected as well. For example, the number 4 has a very negative connotation in China as such, it is to be avoided in domain names. Again however, I will be focusing on just four-letter .com domains so as to keep things simple, so let's not get side-tracked.

As interest from China grew, a new four-letter .com buyout ended up being finalized and even more so, domain values kept going up and up. And as mentioned previously, the rules have changed when it comes to figuring out how desirable a domain is and something peculiarly interesting happened. All of a sudden, due to the letter preference of the Chinese, domains which were initially considered the worst of the worst ended up becoming the best of the best.

For example, a domain name such as XYWQ.com was considered awful in let's say 2008. In 2015 on the other hand, it was considered a gem. How much of a gem, you might ask? Well, let's just say domains of that type were dropped massively by people in let's say 2009, whereas at the peak of the short domain bubble, they ended up being worth more than $2,000 each. I kid you not, you could have bought such a domain at the regular registration fee of 8 to 9 dollars around 2009 and then sold it for over $2,000 toward the end of 2015.

The domains which were considered the favorites of Chinese investors ended up being called "Chinese premium" domains or more colloquially chips.

Fortunes have been made with these chips but the same way, a lot of money has been lost as well. Since I am also a domain investor, I have witnessed this firsthand. Never before in my Internet career have I been exposed to such a feeding frenzy as with these short domain names.

Initially, people were skeptical. They weren't exactly sure the Chinese model was sustainable. I distinctly remember even having conversations with people who used to specialize in short domain names and in early to mid-2015, these experts would roll their eyes when I asked them what their opinion about Chinese premium domains was. They told me there's just no way they're interested in any of this, that it's just a fad. The same people became some of the biggest buyers of Chinese premium domain names toward the end of the year.

Just like with any other bubble, things develop in somewhat of a "snowball effect" manner. Initially, the Chinese interest was understated by pretty much everyone. Sure, people knew that China would eventually become a player but nobody expected such an impact. Eventually, some very well-funded players from Hong Kong got involved.

It's perhaps as of that point that the "frenzy" mood kicked in. People realized that you could make ridiculously large amounts of money by investing in these domains and it was crazy just how much capital was allocated in this direction. I want to stress yet again that the domain name market is much, much, much (I believe three are enough) smaller than something like the stock market and as a result, it's enough for even the handful of very well-funded players to enter the marketplace for prices to go crazy.

Which is precisely what happened.

Initially, only those who had interest in short domains in general invested in this category. They were highly debated but again, only among connoisseurs, so to speak. But as prices skyrocketed, literally everyone in the domain industry ended up talking about these domains and naturally, even lots of people who had no interest in short domains and no experience whatsoever wanted a piece of the action. Even complete beginners were making money and it seemed that there was no end in sight for this Chinese feeding frenzy.

Like all bubbles however, there was a point as of which something broke.

Initially, people were tempted to just shrug it off as a temporary hiccup and therefore, the beginning of 2016 was tricky. Some investors still firmly believed there was no place to go for these prices but up, whereas others began asking themselves questions.

One of the favorite arguments among short domain enthusiasts was the fact that activity slowed down due to the fact that the Chinese New Year was getting close. These people were firmly convinced that after the Chinese New Year, activity would pick up and it would be business as usual, perhaps even better.

Unfortunately for them, the Chinese New Year came and went but activity did not pick back up as expected. To me at least, the biggest shock was the fact that liquidity levels downright plummeted. During the height of the bubble, you could have simply listed short domains on a forum and after doing that, it was only a matter of minutes until offers would come pouring in.

It was overwhelming, unlike anything I had witnessed before.

When that feeding frenzy came to a standstill however, it was clear to me that something was wrong. Liquidity levels kept going down and prices followed suit in a downright spectacular manner. They ended up at roughly half their peak levels and have been stagnating since.

So, was the short domain bubble a disaster?

Well, it all depends on your perspective. Compared to the peak, prices went down by approximately 50% and that's obviously a lot. Still, it's also true that domains which could've been bought for eight bucks in 2009 can still easily fetch four figures. Those who own domains that they bought very early on are still in amazing shape.

However, those who invested around the top of the bubble aren't exactly thrilled. Some of them lost a lot of money and those who speculated with borrowed funds (especially Chinese investors) were in a particularly bad position. To this day, I find it ridiculous how easy it was for people in China to invest in domains with borrowed money.

They borrowed at very high interest rates in a low interest rate environment, so they obviously took on a significant degree of risk, but they did it believing that prices will keep skyrocketing. Those people ultimately found themselves in a position in which the assets they invested their borrowed money in are worth 40% to 50% less and not only that but they have to pay back the money they've borrowed with interest. High interest, I might add.

What happens next is anyone's guess. Perhaps prices will keep stagnating for a while and then there will be another feeding frenzy. Then again, maybe they'll keep dropping. Nobody can predict the future and this is just as valid when it comes to domains as it is with other asset classes.

After prices crashed, various theories emerged as to how such a bubble occurred in the first place. For example, some believe that the entire narrative of Chinese premium domains was nothing more than manipulation by the wealthy Hong Kong-based investors I've mentioned earlier on. We cannot know anything for sure. What I do know however is that just like with any other bubble, we can identify several anomalies:

1. The fact that people accepted the Chinese premium narrative and the China narrative related to short domains in general and basically ended up investing in assets they didn't meaningfully understand. While I cannot be 100% certain if this entire episode of Chinese craziness was in fact generated to a large degree by manipulation, I do know for a fact that lots and lots of people who did not understand China and short domains jumped in and just like with a lot of the older bubbles, invested in something they didn't understand at all

2. The fact that people grossly overestimated the potential of short domains. While it is true that the "best of the best" in terms of short domains have value and can be considered investment grade assets, it is without a doubt obvious to me that people overestimated the true potential of short domains. To be honest, it's hard to talk about huge long-term potential when you're paying $2,000 for a domain you could've gotten for just eight bucks a couple of years ago. Again, a lot of the domains that were traded definitely have intrinsic value and can be considered investment grade but their potential was greatly overestimated

3. The fact that people also invested in certain domain types, let's call them "head-scratcher" domains, which are downright worthless. Remember the very first bubble we've covered, the tulip mania? It's ironic that back then, in the days of the oldest documented speculative mania, just like with today's frenzies such as the short domain one of 2015-2016, people continuously make the mistake of investing in worthless assets at the end of a bubble.

    During the tulip mania, people ended up also buying so-called Gheele Croon tulips that were for a long time considered worthless. In other words, toward the very end of the tulip mania, prices were so high and people were so desperate to invest despite not affording these high prices that assets which were once considered worthless were perceived as investment grade. With short domain names, the same thing happened. People who couldn't afford four-letter or five-number Dot Com domains for example or who thought that better returns could be generated elsewhere ended up taking things one step further and even buying, believe it or not, six-number and five-letter Dot Com domains.

    If you want to find out more about what constitutes a good domain, there is a section about domain names in the financial resilience part of this book. However, even before reading it, I'm sure you will realize that a random five-letter domain name is obviously not amazing. It's hard to remember, looks awkward on a billboard and the list could go on and on. Yet those who insisted on getting in and wanted to do so at low price points bought such domain names as well and for the most part, these people lost all their money

4. Investing in highly speculative assets with borrowed money. I'm not sure when it comes to Western investors but I do know for a fact that quite a few investors from China speculated in the short domain space using money that they borrowed. At very high interest rates, I might add. Some of these people were practically 100% certain there was no way for prices to go but up and as such, they thought it was perfectly natural to invest in these highly speculative assets using money that they obtained at close to loan shark level interest rates. A disaster waiting to happen

5. Looking for scapegoats to blame after prices crashed. In our case, the scapegoats were the manipulators from Hong Kong or let's say manipulators in general. Now again, I'm not saying there was no manipulation whatsoever. In a lot of markets, there frequently is. But to blame the price crash and the bursting of a bubble on such situations exclusively is downright ludicrous. Yet in the end, just like with many other bubbles, it's ultimately human nature to avoid looking in the mirror and accepting your own mistakes. Understandable but still wrong

6. Toward the very end of the bubble, everyone considered himself an expert. Even complete domain beginners who had just signed up at forums and had almost no posts talked as if they were all of a sudden masters of domain investing. Everyone had advice to give, everyone was an expert. Once again, just like with other bubbles as well, it's a clear warning signal when pretty much everyone is talking about a certain asset class

Chapter 4: Spotting Financial Storms

If you knew you had to fight a monster, what weapon would you bring to the battle if you had to choose between a machine gun and a water pistol? If I were to ask ten people this question, my best guess is that nine out of ten would quickly tell me they'd choose the machine gun. Some might even roll their eyes, insulted by my offensively simple question. I do think that one person wouldn't be as quick to answer. In fact, he wouldn't answer at all and instead, would ask for more details about the monster.

One of this book's main goals is helping you become such a person.

But why? And what does this have to do with my example? To answer both questions, I have to ask another: what if the monster is made of fire? As an economist, I've read up on pretty much all financial bubbles, certainly all of the even moderately important ones. Time and time again, I've noticed just how important critical thinking can be. Questioning the status quo. Not following the herd.

To prolifically spot financial storms, I'll ask you to do something that pretty much goes against human nature: think for yourself. We're herd animals and naturally find great comfort in the predictable. In following others. Or drawing simple conclusions like the "machine gun" one in my example. And this usually works. We can cope with most of the problems life throws our way without distancing ourselves from conventional thinking.

But financial calamities are different. Just like a water pistol is more effective against a monster made of fire than the much more imposing machine gun, the not-so-obvious frequently outperforms the obvious when spotting and battling financial storms. And battling financial storms is what this book is all about. How do you do that? Well, primarily by:

1. Identifying them early on, before they can affect you
2. If #1 is not possible and you've been affected, limiting the damage by being quick to react/adapt
3. Being genuinely resilient (something we'll be talking more about in Chapter 5) and organizing your life in a manner which enables you to land on your feet under a wide range of scenarios

This chapter will help when it comes to #1 and #2. Can I make guarantees? No. I can't promise you'll always be able to spot financial storms early on. In fact, I'd say that's highly unlikely. And while being able to always react/adapt quickly is a lot more likely, I do have to say that again, nothing in this world is 100% certain. Wearing a bulletproof vest can help you survive if someone shoots you in the chest with a gun but if he has a bazooka instead… good luck with that. I can however make the firm promise that you'll be in far, far, far, far, far (yes, five of them) better shape than the average individual.

Chapter 4.1: A Sea of Uncertainty

More and more people keep telling me they're overwhelmed by a sense of urgency that's troubling them. Simply put, they're worried that something is just not right. With the way in which society is organized, with the economy, on a geopolitical level and the list could go on and on. Most of them aren't able to pinpoint an exact cause for concern, all they know is how strong their gut feeling is that something, deep down, is just not right.

I want to make it crystal clear that even when everything around you seems normal, it's hard to spot anomalies. This is primarily because they tend to sneak up on us and gradually become a part of our day-to-day existence. It's not as if they all of a sudden take us by storm, which would make things a lot easier. On the contrary, they sneakily become a part of our day-to-day existence and squeeze themselves into our lives one step at a time. So yes, when everything around you is normal, when society is organized in a clear and coherent manner, it is at the very least easier for you to spot the abnormal. However, there is little point in talking about ideal scenarios all that much given the fact that our situation is currently anything but perfect.

Anomalies are all around us and each day, we are bombarded with issues for which there is no precedent. Never in the history of mankind has the world been so interconnected. Never has it been easier for everyone else to catch a cold when one country sneezes, in other words. Never before has society been affected by so many economic experiments such as monetary easing on a truly global scale, new forms of economic warfare and so on. To make matters even worse, technological advances exacerbate our already complicated situation.

But this is starting to sound too much like a random rant on my part, so I'll try to take a step back and keep things organized. Why have I decided to call this chapter "A Sea of Uncertainty" and not something else? Simple, it's because without understanding how things really stand in the world we live in, you cannot be in a good position to prepare for storms by trying to spot them. Before trying to determine what needs to be done, let's try to realistically assess our current situation and referring to the top uncertainty generators seems like the logical thing to do.

Let's start with the issue of economic uncertainty.

First and foremost, I would like to refer to the extreme levels of intervention that we are currently dealing with. After the dot-com bubble burst, Alan Greenspan lowered interest rates all the way down to 1%[33], in an effort to stimulate the economy. Over a period of several years (from 1999 until 2004, to be precise), he brought down interest rates from 6.5% to the previously mentioned 1%. On the surface, it worked but the main drawback was the fact that another bubble had been facilitated, an even more dangerous one: the real estate bubble.

Compared to what his successors did, 1% with no monetary easing doesn't seem all that extreme but do keep in mind that the 1% interest rates with Greenspan's signature on them had been the lowest since the early fifties. Time passed and interest rates pretty much normalized, hitting 5.25% by the end of 2006, before the (in)famous Global Financial Crisis of 2007-2008, also known as the Great Recession.

This crisis was so serious that lowering interest rates to 1% was no longer enough to stimulate the market properly. Ben Bernanke (Greenspan's successor) therefore chose to bring rates all the way down to zero and not even that was enough. Central banks ended up also flooding the system with liquidity, in the case of the United States up to $85 billion per month: $40 billion in the toxic mortgage-backed securities (MBS) which were to a large degree responsible for the calamity and $45 billion in Treasuries.

In other words, more money was injected into the system in just one year than had existed for the entire year history of the US dollar up until the Great Recession. As can be seen, it seems we are dealing with the start of a very dangerous pattern and the natural question we must ask ourselves is a simple one: what will governments and central banks have to do once the next financial crisis hits?

If the past is an indicator, they will have to resort to measures even more dramatic than last time. The main exception is represented by the fact that while at least interest rates had the chance to normalize prior to the Global

---

[33] Jeff Madrick. *Age of Greed: The Triumph of Finance and the Decline of America*. New York City: Vintage Books, 2011.

Financial Crisis of '07-'08 hitting, the same thing cannot be said about the present, with interest rates at record lows all over the planet. At least the United States can say it stopped injecting money into the system. The European Union however wasn't even able to do that and on the contrary, just like Japan, brought interest rates in negative territory and is easing even more than before. The European Union is "printing" even more than the US in nominal terms and Japan is flooding the system with obscenely high amounts of money relative to its GDP. Under such circumstances, it should come as no surprise that people are worried.

Next, I would say that a lot of uncertainty is generated by the huge discrepancy between Main Street and Wall Street. It's ridiculously hard to get a business off the ground and turn it into something viable, and it appears this type of risk-taking is not rewarded properly compared to Wall Street speculation. It is clear to anyone who cares to listen that at this point, speculation is disproportionately being rewarded compared to other forms of risk-taking. Why go through the trouble of getting a business off the ground from scratch when you can just go to the glorious Wall Street casino and stand a better chance at earning a fortune?

Yet another layer of uncertainty is added by the fact that the developed world is without a doubt in a deep crisis. This crisis manifests itself through declining competitiveness, to overall stagnation when it comes to innovation and the list could go on and on. It is clear that the Western financial status quo is in jeopardy as we speak.

Another anomaly is the preferential treatment that is being given to entities which are considered too big to fail. These businesses, it seems, are governed by a special set of rules based on which when times are good, they simply collect benefits and those behind them get rich. If or should we say when something goes wrong, there is no need to worry: the good old government and central bank is here to save the day.

Under such circumstances, it should come as no surprise that we live in a world of economic anomaly. When speculation is being rewarded more than genuine entrepreneurship, we have a problem. When there's unprecedented interventionism on a global scale, we have a problem. When not everyone is forced to play by the same rules and even more so, the entities which caused a lot of humanity's problems are given the best of the best in terms of treatment, we have a problem. When the Western world is stagnating or even decaying, we have a problem. Do I really need to provide additional evidence as to why we are currently in a climate of economic uncertainty?

Next, it's time to talk about the geopolitical uncertainties which are plaguing society.

Let's start with the fact that voters from all over the world are desperate to change the status quo. The growing popularity of populism (see what I did there?) and extremism worldwide is in my opinion a symptom. The problem, at least as far as I see it, is represented by the fact that people are sick and tired of the political status quo. The average voter perceives politicians as disconnected from reality and deeply corrupt. As such, it should come as no surprise that more and more people are willing to embrace anything that they consider stands a chance at replacing the status quo. It's easy to give into the temptation of considering those who voted for let's say populist candidates as merely gullible individuals who got scammed but I think that by doing that, we'd be missing the big picture. And the big picture primarily revolves around the fact that people are desperate for change.

Secondly, all we have to do is look around and we will realize that more and more conflicts are rearing their ugly heads. The Middle East is a mess and it seems a sustainable long-term solution is out of sight. The European Union is dealing with the biggest crisis since its inception and it is unclear what needs to be done. Outside the European Union, Russia seems to be destabilizing countries such as Ukraine and the Republic of Moldova. In Asia, things aren't exactly great either. China is a huge bubble that seems just about ready to burst. Japan is in a generational decline and the list could go on and on. Wherever we look, it seems we find conflict, conflict and more conflict. And while the things we are dealing with seem mild compared to the two world wars are grandparents and great-grandparents had to fight, it should be obvious that we are in the most turbulent geopolitical situation humanity has witnessed in a long time.

Currency wars first and then trade wars make it clear yet again that things are currently murky worldwide. It started with countries desperately trying to weaken their currencies so as to boost exports and things have degenerated since then, with more and more international players embracing isolationist policies. History has proven that nothing good comes after currency wars and trade wars. This much is certain. The climate we currently live in, from a geopolitical standpoint, is definitely one of uncertainty.

Let's not forget about technological uncertainty.

The industrial revolution which started about 257 years ago (1760) gave birth to lots and lots of jobs. It was resource and labor-intensive, which was great news for the economy. What about today? Well, the good news is that we're going through a revolution that is changing our lives for the better as we speak: the let's call it hi-tech and Internet revolution that gave us computers, smartphones with Internet access and so on.

Without a doubt, humans got quite a lifestyle boost!

Unfortunately, from an economic perspective, things aren't as rosy because this revolution is from certain perspectives the exact opposite of the industrial one. New jobs are indeed appearing but the creative destruction[34] that is taking place through this revolution is rendering more jobs obsolete than it is creating. In other words, while this technological revolution is making our lives easier and generating unprecedented progress, it is putting quite a bit of strain on job creation.

Another issue that generates uncertainty is our unprecedented dependence on technology which in the grand scheme of things is very, very new. Just imagine what would happen to humanity's various Internet-dependent systems if the Web would cease to function properly for whatever reason. Let's not even think about what we'd do without electric power and the chaos such a scenario would generate. Realistically speaking, our dependence on technology is undeniably one of the biggest problems society has to deal with. Cyber-attacks alone could wipe out a country's power grid and there are various international players who would be able to pull something like this off. Just thinking about the various things that can go wrong makes our heads spin and needless to say, we have valid reasons to be concerned.

I could go on and on with various other examples of uncertainty.

At the end of the day though, all you have to do is look around and you'll find countless arguments which reinforce the idea that right now, humans are drowning in a sea of uncertainty. Love it or hate it, that's our current situation

---

[34] Hugo Reinert and Erik S. Reinert. "Creative Destruction in Economics: Nietzsche, Sombart, Schumpeter." *Springer US*. October 1, 2006.
https://link.springer.com/chapter/10.1007%2F978-0-387-32980-2_4.

THE AGE OF ANOMALY

and we have to deal with it. As far as this book is concerned, uncertainty is without a doubt something that makes spotting financial storms multiple of orders of magnitude more difficult. There's little point in whining about it however, so let's roll up our sleeves and figure out what needs to be done!

The various sources of uncertainty I've referred to might have gotten you worried, so the natural question to ask me after reading the previous pages is the following: okay, then what should we do? Just like psychologists tell their patients, the first step is realizing that we have a problem. I remember that when my mother got sick and whenever other things went wrong in my life, my first reaction was to try to find a rock to climb under and somehow hide from reality. That is anything but the ideal solution.

The first step is just is just that, acknowledging the situation. When you're walking through a bad neighborhood, I wouldn't exactly recommend imagining you're in paradise while you stroll through it. On the contrary, I would highly recommend being aware of your surroundings, acknowledging the fact that it's a more dangerous neighborhood and simply being more careful. The same principle is valid when it comes to the world we live in. Imagining it's all sunshine and rainbows isn't going to do anyone any good. Instead, understand that there is quite a bit of uncertainty surrounding us and plan accordingly.

But what does this mean specifically?

It primarily means expecting the unexpected. In fact, I wouldn't even call it "expecting the unexpected" because what those who live in a good neighborhood consider unexpected is something that those who live in worse neighborhoods have come to know as reality. Somebody who lives in a really bad neighborhood would probably not be surprised to see those around him exhibiting aggressive behavior. However, another person who lives in a rich part of town would probably be shocked to witness scenarios of aggression. I would therefore assert that the following preliminary conclusion can be drawn: in the world we find ourselves living in, the unexpected has become the expected. Consider that (expect the unexpected) my first strong recommendation.

My second word of advice revolves around developing the habit of noticing subtle deviations from the norm. Even in a deeply troubled society, some kind of norm tends to be established and while anomalies may seem more obvious in a less hectic environment because they stand out more, they can be spotted in a more "complex" environment as well. Just not as easily. Perhaps the most useful suggestion I have for you is this: keep your eyes wide open and your ears to the ground.

To be more specific, this means following the news, looking around you at all times and being on the lookout for deviations. Of course, I'm not saying this should end up taking over your life. Like all good things, it helps if done in moderation. Please don't take this advice as me telling you to have the news on 24/7 and look out your window once every five minutes, that is definitely not what I'm trying to say. What I am trying to tell you is that you should avoid living in your own bubble, which tends to be what most people do.

Ask ten random friends about current events or things along those lines and several of them will probably tell you they don't watch the news or don't care about the news. I'm telling you that you shouldn't be one of them, this is the message I want to get across. I know it's tempting to just separate yourself from the noise that being exposed to news sometimes pollutes you with and just retreat to your comfort zone but unfortunately, doing that and spotting bubbles just don't go hand in hand.

Next, I would highly recommend doing everything you can to become more flexible and more adaptable. No matter how hard you try to be one step ahead of everyone else, you might not succeed. One of the things which come with the territory when we are living in a sea of uncertainty is the fact that it's more likely to be taken by surprise because given the crazy world we live in, who knows what might happen! This book will help you become multiple orders of magnitude better at spotting anomalies but at the same time, it cannot offer guarantees.

Expect to be sometimes taken by surprise. I'd say it's important to be flexible and adaptable for two simple reasons:

1. Because spotting anomalies is a lot harder in our crazy world than it would have been in a less complicated environment
2. When things seem so off-balance all around us, the likelihood of going through a shock powerful enough to be considered a reset is a lot higher. What I'm trying to say is that financial storms come in

all shapes and sizes. The more troubled society is, the more likely it is to deal with a big reset. Should that happen, then no matter how prepared you are, your flexibility and adaptability will be put to the test

But what can you do to become more flexible and adaptable?

First and foremost, I would recommend having strategies in place which enable you to land on your feet in a wide range of situations. For example, perhaps the next crisis will be a deflationary one, with a huge market collapse and a contraction of the money supply. However, if it's followed by a tidal wave of central bank intervention, things might spiral out of control and deflation could turn into inflation or even hyperinflation.

This is a hypothetical scenario which makes it clear that being prepared for a wide range of scenarios makes sense. This means having some assets which do well under periods of deflation, having other assets which do well when there is inflation and so on and so forth. I firmly believe in smart diversification. Now this doesn't mean I'm suggesting that you spread yourself too thin and invest 1% of your net worth in hundreds of different directions. I am however saying that if you don't have a strategy which enables you to land on your feet in a wide range of scenarios, you're doing it wrong.

I always hate it when I see how sure of themselves some economists are. Some believe they're 100% spot on when saying we'll have deflation. Others are just as eager to explain how sure they are that we're going to go through inflation. I think they're all wrong. For the love of God, stop trying to predict the future and instead, prepare for the unexpected.

One of the most useful habits you can develop to spot financial storms is being on the constant lookout for canaries in the proverbial coal mine. What I mean by this is that if you wait until everyone is panicking, it's too late to land on your feet. As Darwinist as it may sound, the name of the game is being one step ahead. If there's a bank run in progress in your country and you're only realizing it when there are huge queues in front of all ATM machines, then I'm sorry but it's too late.

The key here is being among the first to react when people are panicking. If you wait until there are 50 people in line waiting for their money, you're too late. Instead, react as soon as you see even a hint of a line being formed. This hardly involves rocket science. When going to work or when running errands, you most likely drive or walk past several ATMs. As such, you already know even if you never thought about it this way what "normal" means in terms of the number of people who are waiting for their money. If you walk past an ATM each day and there are never more than two people standing in line, yet at one point you walk past it and notice that eight people are in front of it, it makes sense to start worrying. Now of course, maybe it's just a coincidence that eight people are standing in line, fair enough. But if you're serious when it comes to the idea of being always one step ahead of everyone else, you have to be willing to understand that false alarms will occur and just accept that as something that comes with the territory. Being quick to react as soon as you see even the smallest hint of a warning signal is crucial. Maybe you will be wrong the first three times but if you're right the fourth time and save your wealth by acting quickly, the entire endeavor will prove to be more than worth it.

I could go on and on but I'm sure you now understand the basic mindset you should bring to the table if you're serious about spotting financial storms in a sea of uncertainty. I believe I've made it crystal clear why we are living in an age of anomaly and throughout this chapter, will be covering some of the issues I've mentioned in this subchapter in more detail so as to help you become better and better at spotting these frequently mentioned financial storms.

Chapter 4.2: Dosage and Context

It seems more and more things around me give me an overall sense of unease. Perhaps it's just something that comes with getting older but I seriously doubt it. A more plausible reason is the fact that aspects which wouldn't have worried me all that much in the past are now troubling me can be attributed to two dimensions: dosage and context. In fact, I think it makes more sense to consider them two core components of just one dimension.

Let me give you a quick example.

If I were to find out that yet another election has been won by an authoritarian leader, I would be more worried now that in the past. The idea that every now and then, populist or authoritarian leaders gain popularity is not unheard of. It does happen time and time again at one point or another, in one country or another.

Even in Western European countries such as Austria in 1999, to give you a less current reference point. The event in question (the Freedom Party of Austria getting most of the votes in the 1999 legislative election) was not what I would consider to be a major cause for concern. However, if that same event were to unfold again, this time I would be worried. Why? Dosage and context!

You see, what irritates me about the world around me right now is not the fact that one specific authoritarian leader is gaining power. For example Erdogan, the president of Turkey. It's the dosage of it all, with more and more authoritarian leaders gaining popularity all over the world. This increase in dosage if you will creates the perfect context for something we could consider a perfect storm.

As can be seen, it's the cumulative effect that bothers me more so than individual situations. Due to the growing volume of problematic situations all over the world, I believe we are dangerously close to a perfect storm. Let's assume you have an empty glass that you leave outside and it starts to rain a bit. Walter obviously makes its way into the glass but the rain stops quickly, so the glass is nowhere near full. As time passes, the weather becomes sunny and a lot of that water evaporates. Then it rains again for a bit, then the water evaporates again and so on and so forth.

But what if instead of this succession of rain and sunny weather, we go through a period of persistent rain? In that case, as I notice how the glass is getting fuller and fuller, I'm much more prone to being worried by each subsequent episode of rain. The fuller the glass gets, the more worried I become. And since sunny weather seems to be nowhere in sight, this creates the perfect context for the glass to ultimately end up being completely full and for spillover to occur.

The same principle is valid when it comes to society as a whole. If the occasional turbulence is only episodic in nature rather than systemic, then it's all good. Certainly nothing humanity cannot handle. However, I firmly believe that if what were once considered turbulences started becoming regular occurrences, the dosage and context dimension should make you deeply worried.

Therefore, as someone who keeps his ear to the ground in order to be prepared for financial storms, it's important to never limit yourself to just looking at events in isolation. In the right environment of dosage and context, even seemingly benign individual situations which would have been quickly shrugged off otherwise should worry you. See society as an entire book and try to get a good grasp of the big picture. Don't become so obsessed with each individual page that you forget to take a step back and think about the situation as a whole.

Dosage and context!

Chapter 4.3: Accepting Your Limitations

As an author, I find it frustrating to write a book like this one for the simple reason that I hate not being able to give my readers certainty. If you read a book about making furniture, you know that if you apply the steps outlined in the book in question, you will be able to do just that: make furniture.

The same cannot be said about this book because no matter how hard you try to apply everything that's mentioned in *The Age of Anomaly* and no matter how hard I try to give you the best advice possible, there is no guarantee whatsoever you will be able to spot the next financial crisis before it hits. I try to make it clear time and time again that even I may very well end up being taken by surprise by the next crisis and I'm the person who's actually written a book about financial calamities.

When deciding to learn more about anomalies, bubbles and so on, it's important to do this but also understand that you have limitations. I always try to distance myself from the various self-proclaimed gurus who claim to be able to predict the future. Many of those who will end up reading my book are people concerned about their future, people who want to protect themselves and their families. You probably didn't pick it up because you simply wanted some extra reading material, you did it because you wanted answers.

It would be the easiest thing in the world for me to position myself alongside those gurus and say that sure, I can predict the future as well and all you have to do is blindly listen to me. I refuse to do that however because, quite frankly, I just don't want to lie to people. Chances are that if you're reading this book right now, you've come across your share of let's call them "doom and gloom gurus" who try to shove their predictions down your throat and brand themselves as people who know exactly what's going to happen in the future. Some tell you to back up the truck and buy as much gold and silver as possible. Others take things one step further and tell you to invest most of your wealth in supplies and so-called prepping materials. I strongly believe these people are doing you a great disservice.

After the global financial crisis of 2007-2008, a lot of these people predicted that hyperinflation was just around the corner and advised those who were listening to them and buying their books to invest as much in precious metals as possible. They were pessimistic about pretty much everything else but highly, highly optimistic about gold and silver. In August to September 2011, there were lots of such people who were strongly advising everyone to buy gold while it was at roughly $1900 per ounce.

When you listened to them or read their material, it was clear just how confident these people were in their predictions. Their arguments seemed perfectly logical as well as coherent and this, coupled with their tone and overall demeanor, made a lot of folks believe that these people knew exactly what they were talking about. So they listened to their advice and bought a bunch of gold at $1900 per ounce but unfortunately for them, the scenarios envisioned by those so-called experts didn't materialize and as such, the ones who listened to them found themselves in the hole. Ironically, they bought precious metals to protect themselves and "protected" themselves so well that they ended up losing significant amounts of money.

Let's take a step back and ask ourselves what these people did wrong. Should they have predicted something else instead of inflation? Of course not, the main message I'm trying to get across is that these people shouldn't have predicted anything in the first place and that economists in general needs to stop making predictions in such manners. It saddens me that people tend to think of economists as fortune-tellers to whom they go demanding specific dates, specific predictions and so on. As good as it may sound, it just doesn't work. Economists are humans just like everyone else and I'm sorry but humans tend to be pretty terrible at predicting the future.

I'm human, you are only human as well and as such, shouldn't expect to be able to predict the future after reading this book. Your main objective here should not be looking for a crystal ball but instead, trying to genuinely understand financial bubbles so as to try (with an emphasis on try) to realize when we're in the middle of one or when it seems that one is on the horizon.

It's kind of like with a serious illness. Not even the best doctor in the world can give you a recipe which ensures with 100% certainty that you will never get a certain disease. However, a good doctor will tell you all you need to know about the illness in question so that on the one hand you can do your best to avoid it but on the other hand, should you end up contracting it, you will be able to spot the warning signals soon enough.

I think this is an accurate depiction of my limitations as an economist and ultimately your limitations as well. The last thing I want is for people to put me on a pedestal. As much as I want to, I'm just not able to promise that I'll be able to help you avoid all future financial storms. What I can promise however is that I'll tell you all I know about them and, just like the doctor in my example, will do my best to help you stay away from them altogether. Or if they creep up on you, at least you'll get better at identifying warning signals soon and taking action before it's too late.

The most important limitation of yours is the fact that you cannot and will never be able to predict the future in an accurate and consistent manner. Maybe you can get lucky once or twice (then again, perhaps not) but you or anyone else for that matter are always incapable of genuinely predicting the future.

This is why it's important for me to tell you to never put together a strategy which revolves around you somehow being able to know what's going to happen in the future, either by predicting it yourself or by taking the advice of people who claim to be able to predict it. You should, in my opinion, do the exact opposite by actually embracing your limitations and making them a part of your strategy.

By acknowledging your inability to predict the future, you will be multiple orders of magnitude more prudent than someone who has the arrogance to claim he has superhuman capabilities. Can I guarantee you any kind of perfection? No, I cannot. I can however guarantee that by putting together a strategy which revolves around you embracing your limitations, you will be multiple steps ahead of most people.

Chapter 4.4: Canaries in the Coal Mine

This metaphor stems from the time when miners used to carry canaries with them for one simple reason: if methane or carbon monoxide levels went up, the canaries would die and since canaries die at concentrations that are lower than those at which humans die, the miners could take action and leave the mine before anything bad happened to them.

I love this metaphor because it's perfect for those who want to become better at spotting anomalies. The name of the game is having canaries with you, canaries that die when exposed to various elements so that when one of them dies, you know something is wrong and take action accordingly. Furthermore, perhaps most importantly, you end up taking action before whatever it is that caused the death of one of your canaries affects you as well.

Not only is this the ideal approach, I would say it's the only one. This is because a lot of times, if the proverbial concentrations end up reaching levels that are high enough to affect you, it's probably too late to take action. Having canaries with you sounds ridiculously simple, rudimentary even. But it does make perfect financial sense.

In this section, I will be talking about the importance of looking over your shoulder and gathering information continuously on the one hand and the other hand, about the importance of taking action quickly. Perhaps every once in a while, one of your canaries will die for other reasons that are unrelated to something that might affect you and as such, you end up taking action despite the fact that you shouldn't have done so.

I like to call those "false positive" situations and will definitely be covering them as well later on. Finally, I will not end this section without referring to the two main dimensions of our information world which are mainstream media outlets on the one hand and alternative media on the other. Let's get started, shall we?

Chapter 4.4.1: Looking Over Your Shoulder

Perhaps the most challenging aspect of writing this book has been making the distinction between being prepared (within reason) and making the idea of being prepared the most important dimension of your existence. Specifically, I find it hard to tell people how important it is to be prepared on the one hand but on the other hand, also make it clear that I'm not a prepper and I don't think you should be the type of person who spends his entire day preparing for disasters.

Basically, the most important challenge of mine is helping readers figure out what a healthy dose of preparedness is. Moving on to the actual topic at hand, I want to make it clear right from the beginning that it is impossible to become better at spotting financial storms without always being aware of what's happening around you and in the world.

Spotting financial storms revolves, to a significant degree, on proverbially keeping your ear to the ground. Quite frankly, if you do not keep yourself updated with respect to current events, there's just no way for me to consider you in good shape to spot financial storms. Most people hate politicians, they hate the apparent meaninglessness of day-to-day news and as such, take great pride in not subjecting themselves to that. They willingly create their own little bubble, that bubble ends up becoming their de facto comfort zone and they never venture outside.

Huge, huge mistake.

Don't get me wrong, I do agree that watching the news for example is frequently a frustrating endeavor. Something that makes me lose faith in humanity every once in a while. At the same time though, I understand that there's just no other way. To spot warning signals early on, you just have to keep your ear to the ground. As frustrating as that may be.

Unfortunately, you will not get to synchronize schedules with an upcoming financial crisis. You will not get a call from Mr. Crisis, telling you that he intends to destroy the world's financial system and asking if the timing is okay with you. When a financial crisis hits, it hits. Regardless of whether or not you had enough time to prepare. Regardless of whether or not you've paid attention to the news and so on. Some things in life just have to be done, as frustrating as they can sometimes be. Staying informed is without a doubt one of them.

What I do want to stress however is that there's a huge difference between staying informed and having the news on 24-7, constantly on the lookout for immediate threats. There's a fine line between staying informed and becoming obsessed, I strongly suggest not crossing that line. It's ultimately all a matter of common sense and balance. There's a Japanese saying that even things that are good for us hurt if they're done in excess. That's a good mindset to live by in my opinion and it definitely applies to those who want to stay informed.

Watch the news from time to time, read the news if that's what you prefer and so on but do it within reason. I know it has become a bit of a fad or if you will the cool thing to do to tell people that you don't watch the news because you don't want to subject yourself to brainwashing but again, that's just not right. Balance is the operative word.

Spotting financial crisis situations early on revolves, to a relatively significant degree, on being aware of your surroundings and picking up signals as soon as possible. If you bury your head in the sand, how can you possibly pick up any signals at all? Look over your shoulder, stay informed but don't be paranoid. Fair enough?

Chapter 4.4.2: Improving Your Reaction Time

As mentioned in the previous subchapter, staying informed and looking over your shoulder is paramount. However, it's just as important to take action once you pick up signals which make it clear something is wrong and furthermore, to do so quickly. I don't know about you but I for one would rather be one year early than one day late.

I frequently explain why those who always believe the world will end any day now are not embracing a healthy attitude. But at least they're doing something. If I were to have to choose between being a gold bug and being the average consumer who is blissfully ignorant of anything outside his own bubble, I would choose the former.

Now of course, you're reading my book because you want to reach the best possible compromise, and I'm here to help you do that. However, I do want to stress the fact that even if you over-prepare to the point of being paranoid, it's still better than ignorance. So as unhealthy as being a gold bug may be, I would say that even the most paranoid gold bugs are in a much better position to protect themselves than the average consumer.

Words can't begin to describe how much of difference doing things on time makes. For example, if you pick up clear warning signals which indicate something is just not right with the banking system of your country, you'd better act quickly. If you wait until something bad appears on the news about your country's banking system, it's probably going to be too late. Banks operate on what is called a fractional reserve system and as such, only a fraction of the amounts people have with the bank as deposits is available in liquid cash form. So if you wait until there are endless lines in front of ATM machines, then I'm sorry but it's too late and all of the ridiculously small cash reserves banks hold will be depleted by the time it comes anywhere close to being your turn.

In such moments, you're probably thinking about how much better it would have been to take action even six months earlier, back when you noticed the very first warning signals. Even if that meant venturing outside your comfort zone. Even if that meant being ridiculed by your family. Again, I'd much rather be six months or even a year too early than one day too late.

Improving your reaction time revolves to a great degree on becoming better and better at exiting your comfort zone. Let's be honest, going to your bank and asking them to give you whatever you held with them as a deposit in liquid cash form will be pretty awkward. If you do it well before the panic sets in, the teller will probably give you a bit of a skeptical look, perhaps he will consider you a tad loony. And you know what, you probably will feel weird doing something like that. Definitely well outside your comfort zone.

But there's no other way.

Ask yourself: would you rather feel awkward for half an hour or lose your life savings? That is the only question you need to ask yourself in my opinion and it will be abundantly clear that no amount of awkwardness is worth losing your life savings and jeopardizing the financial security of your family. If you've identified warning signals yet didn't take action because you were ashamed to do so, then I'm sorry but there's no difference between you and the average consumer who never even suspected anything in the first place. Both of you will end up taking action when it's too late, and both of you will probably lose most of your money.

A second word of advice I have for those who are interested in improving their reaction time is having various plans for various scenarios, plans that have been made well ahead of time. When you make a plan, you subconsciously accept the possibility of whichever scenario you had envisioned happening. You're basically preparing your brain for various extreme scenarios but I won't focus on that just yet, that is a topic for another section. What I do want to focus on is the fact that if you want to improve your reaction time, you as well as your family and possibly even friends need to have plans in place.

For example, let's assume that you and your wife keep your savings at two separate banks and both of you have access to both bank accounts. Ideally, you should act well before people are starting to line up in front of ATMs. But it does make sense to have a plan in place just in case you don't manage to do that and end up taking action a little too late. Your plan should involve both of you obviously going to take out all the money you can from one bank account each. If you're at work, then figure out which bank branch is closer to the workplace of each individual and needless to say, you will go to the bank branch that is closer to you and your wife will go to the bank branch that is closer to her. This is an example of a ridiculously simple plan but you really do have to think about these things beforehand because when everyone panics, your decision-making abilities will be greatly impaired.

How many let's call them contingency plan should you have? I'd simply say that you should use your best judgment and apply common sense. Maybe you can combine business with pleasure by taking your wife on a let's say weekend getaway somewhere in nature where both of you can relax and among other things, you should have perhaps a pen and a piece of paper ready so that you can make a few contingency plans. Pick each other's brain, communicate and try to figure out what needs to be done in the scenarios both of you consider most likely. Again, nothing about this is rocket science. If done early on, even the simplest things make a world of difference.

My third word of advice is not being afraid to include those you genuinely trust in your plans. To illustrate this, let me ask you what would happen if the banking system of your country fails exactly when you and your spouse are vacationing in another country? Needless to say, your reaction time would be genuinely awful and by the time you get back, it'll be too late. For this reason, it makes sense to include at least your immediate family members in your plans. This might mean let's say giving your parents access to your bank accounts. If your wife does the same, then you will have four trustworthy people who now have access to your bank accounts and who can take action if/when necessary. Merely including your immediate family in your plans can help tremendously under the right scenarios. This particular tip is extremely easy to implement but let's be honest, who does it? Practically nobody.

The 4th tip I would like to share revolves around the idea of always being logistically ready for action. This is something with ramifications well outside the world of financial storms as well and I think it's a matter of common sense. For example, let's assume that when financial disaster strikes, you're on vacation but fortunately, in your own country and not another one. Still, you realize that the bank branch nearest to you is maybe 100 miles away. It's bad enough as it is and the last thing you want is to also have to realize that your gas tank is almost empty. I'm sure you understand what I'm alluding to.

Just implement simple measures to ensure you are always action-ready. Again, simple things like making sure your gas tank is always adequately filled and other things along those lines. As mentioned earlier on, don't expect your judgment to be 100% perfect when you have to make decisions under great stress. Something as seemingly insignificant as heading over to your local gas station might prove to be quite complicated and set you back more than you realize when you have to deal with it while in financial survival mode.

My final tip is not complicating your life when you don't have to. This means let's say not choosing a bank that doesn't have an ATM near you or anything along those lines. Or if for whatever reason a bank used to have an ATM in your proximity but it no longer has one, I think that's a perfectly valid reason to switch to a bank that fits the criteria in question. Do these things now because again, if you end up taking action later than you should have, you need every edge you can get and the last thing you want is to find yourself stuck in traffic, heading toward an ATM that's way too far away and beating yourself up for not following tip number five sooner.

This list is by no means definitive.

By all means, feel free to add to it because the bottom line is this: do whatever you can to improve your reaction time. You're already multiple steps ahead of most individuals by actually thinking about these things but of course, for the readers of a book such as this one, the bar has to be set much higher. None of the measures I've outlined are extremely complicated to implement and I'm pretty sure most of the things you will end up thinking about are pretty simple and straightforward as well. Just go for it, take action when times are good and when you're running at optimal capacity, unburdened by debilitating stress levels.

Chapter 4.4.3: False Positives

In the introduction of this section, I've explained why, just like miners used to do back in the day, it makes sense to carry various canaries with you at all times. Each canary will die when exposed to certain elements, different elements for each canary obviously. The great thing is you'll be able to identify trouble early on and as such, should one of your canaries die, you will take action before whatever it is that killed it ends up affecting you as well.

I've also mentioned that every once in a while, one of your canaries might simply die for reasons that are unrelated to something that might affect you. You notice that it died, naturally assume that whichever element you know that particular canary is sensitive to killed it and take action accordingly to protect yourself. However, you ultimately find out that nothing happened. Does this mean you were foolish?

Of course not!

No matter how thorough you are and no matter how smart you are, there will occasionally be false positives. They come with the territory. The only way to avoid false positives altogether is to never prepare for anything, which is the worst thing you could possibly do. Don't treat false positives as something that should make you feel ashamed of yourself but rather treat their presence as proof that you are actually taking meaningful action to protect yourself.

Quite frankly, you might've expected an extremely complicated explanation from me, perhaps some words of wisdom. I'm sorry to have to disappoint you but the only word of wisdom I have with respect to false positives is acceptance. Accept them as a natural part of preparedness and understand that it's better to be wrong once or twice but ultimately right than to be caught off-guard by financial storms.

I do however want to point out that if you end up noticing lots and lots of false positives, it should make you think that perhaps your strategy is just not right. In other words, perhaps you're too quick to take action and need to loosen up a bit, so to speak. So sure, a ridiculously high number of false positives should make you think you're doing something wrong. However, if the false positives count is within the realm of reason, simply accept them.

For example, perhaps in one situation you will assume something is wrong with the banking system and take your money out immediately, only to notice that time passes and nothing happens. Perhaps some of the people you tell this to, although I would generally recommend keeping things like banking between you and only the closest people in your life, but regardless, perhaps most of the people you tell about this will judge you. As such, aside from the weird feeling you had when taking your money out of the bank in the first place, described in the previous subchapter, you might also end up feeling shame.

But there's absolutely no shame in getting in getting it wrong every now and then. As mentioned on multiple occasions throughout this book, humans tend to be terrible at predicting the future. I'd much rather be the guy that got it wrong four times but was ultimately right and able to save his wealth than the guy who laughed at the previously mentioned person but later on ended up losing all his money.

You have to understand that people like you and me, who take preparedness seriously, are a minority. And being in the minority obviously involves doing things that others wouldn't have thought about doing and therefore do not understand. Some of these people will judge you and out of those who judge you, many will jump at the opportunity of making fun of you whenever you take action in false positive situations and reality ends up proving that you were wrong. These people don't know better, try not to judge them.

Human nature is what it is, just focus on your own life and accept false positives as a part of it.

Chapter 4.4.4: Mainstream Media vs. Alternative Media

If you're serious about staying informed and being in a good position to spot financial storms early on, gathering information from mainstream media as well as alternative media outlets is a must. As much as people love picking sides and as tempted as you may be to jump on one bandwagon or another, refrain from doing that. Never ever lose sight of the fact that mainstream and alternative media outlets complement one another.

The evolution of the competition between mainstream and alternative media has been nothing short of fascinating. At the beginning of this competition, we were clearly dealing with a "David vs. Goliath" scenario. Mainstream media outlets were these colossal well-funded organizations, whereas alternative media sources were for the most part shoestring budget projects. At this point however, that's just no longer true[35].

Yes, mainstream media is still huge. It still reaches an unbelievably large audience but at this point, so does alternative media. In light of the impressive Internet-induced growth of alternative media, it wouldn't surprise me one bit if a few years from now, we will once again be looking at things from a "David vs. Goliath" perspective but this time, with inversed roles.

Let's refrain from trying to make predictions however and focus on the present. At this point in time, I'd say the competition between mainstream media outlets and alternative media outlets is reasonably balanced. In both cases, we're dealing with a huge audience and in both cases, there are lots and lots of opinion formers who can be considered extremely influential.

Through this subchapter, I'll teach you how to get the best of both worlds.

I'll do this by focusing on two things you should be doing on the one hand and on two you should definitely not be doing on the other. I want to start with the latter and explain why the two mistakes I'll be referring to below

---

[35] Amy Mitchell. "State of the News Media 2015." *Pew Research Center.* April 29, 2015. http://www.journalism.org/files/2015/04/FINAL-STATE-OF-THE-NEWS-MEDIA1.pdf.

should be avoided at all costs. So without further ado, these are the two things you should *not* be doing, no matter which side of the fence you're on:

1. Thinking it *has* to be black or white

I'll start by giving you a quick example of something that always makes me cringe: the expressions "sheep" and variations thereof. By using these expressions, you allow yourself to give in to a false sense of superiority granted to you by the adhesion to one of the two groups. If you trust mainstream media outlets, then everyone who doesn't and trusts alternative media sources is automatically inferior. Or the other way around.

I'm sorry but that's just plain wrong and I'll explain the irony of it all by using this very terminology in an example. Person A loves mainstream media outlets, whereas Person B loves alternative media outlets. Person A considers Person B a sheep and, you've guessed it, Person B feels the same way toward person A. They clearly both see things in black and white. What's the irony of it all, you might ask?

Well, let's take a step back and try to find a definition for the term "sheep/sheeple," shall we? What's the negative trait of sheep in general? You've guessed it, the fact that a sheep tends to always follow the herd and by extrapolating, people consider this bad because critical thinking is eliminated from the equation and brutally replaced with blind trust.

Maybe you'd define the term in a slightly different manner but most likely somewhere along those lines. Let's once again focus on Person A and Person B in order to understand the irony of their behavior. Who is Person A? Someone who blindly trusts mainstream media sources and considers everyone who sees things differently inferior. Who is Person B? Someone who blindly trusts alternative media sources and considers everyone who sees things differently inferior. While Person A might seem the exact opposite of Person B, the two are remarkably similar, fundamentally speaking.

Why?

Because they're guilty of the same type of bad behavior: picking a side/herd and blindly adhering to everything associated with it. This, my friends, is as ironic as it gets. They consider one another sheeple when in fact, they're guilty of the exact same thing. Irony 101, as I'm sure you'll agree. Don't be like them, avoid sweeping generalizations and understand that things are rarely just black or white.

2. It's all a big evil conspiracy

I'm sorry but I refuse to accommodate such displays of paranoid behavior. No, they're not out to get you. Let's be realistic for a moment, there are lots and lots of mainstream media sources which *compete* against one another. Yes, their interests are sometimes aligned but the same way, they're sometimes divergent… to put it mildly.

The same principle is valid when it comes to alternative media sources. There are quite a few types of alternative media approaches: culture jamming, participatory journalism and so on[36]. To think absolutely everyone will join hands in order to enact some kind of an evil conspiracy is irrational. Pure and utter nonsense. Open your eyes and realize "mainstream media" is in no way some kind of homogenous group of players. Not at all. The same way, there are lots and lots of different alternative media outlets with different agendas/goals as well.

This diversity alone should make you more than confident in the fact that the likelihood of a huge conspiracy materializing is slim. Try putting together 100 different people with different desires, goals and agenda. Then follow them for an extended period of time and tell me how likely it is they'll pull something like a grand conspiracy off.

First of all, I doubt they'd be able to start anything in the first place. They would most likely not even be able to agree on all the various details associated with complex conspiracies but let's assume they pull it off. This is just one side of the conspiracy equation, the other (and considerably more complex) one is keeping the conspiracy a conspiracy by avoiding leaks, betrayal and so on.

I for one consider it seriously unlikely they'd be able to get a conspiracy off the ground in the first place. In other words, I'm not even close to being convinced when it comes to the first part of the equation. Add the second

---

[36] Leah Lievrouw. *Alternative and Activist New Media.* Cambridge: Polity Press, 2011.

one to the mix and I'm sorry but you're better off being worried by the perspective of something like an alien invasion.

That being stated, let's move on to the two things you *should* be doing:

1. Keep an open mind

… even if this means accepting information from alternative media sources if you're a mainstream media enthusiast or the other way around. Believe it or not, it's what being a well-rounded individual ultimately all boils down to: letting go of irrational beliefs and embracing a rational way of life instead. This may very well require you to leave your comfort zone but that's just the way it is.

By all means however, feel free to question the information you're shown. Do your own due diligence. It's actually something I encourage throughout this book. But whatever you do, don't make the mistake of dismissing information altogether just because it comes from an alternative media website or just because it comes from a mainstream media source.

Am I saying you shouldn't have preferences?

No, I'm not. You're not perfect, I'm not perfect either. Let's just do our best to keep an open mind, this is all I'm asking of you. If a certain piece of information comes from a source which has repeatedly proven itself then of course, feel free to let your guard down a little bit. The same way, you can be more suspicious if the information comes from a source which hasn't yet proven itself or even more so, from a source with a bad reputation.

2. Be flexible

I'll be asking you to do something which is anything but easy: admitting you were wrong when it's clear that you were. Yes, I know it's hard and I understand all too well how unpleasant it can be but there's just no way of learning to be good at gathering and interpreting signals sent by various canaries without embracing your imperfection and the fact that you will frequently be proven wrong.

By whom?

By another person, by the markets, it doesn't even matter. What really matters is understanding there's just no way to develop a track record of 100% accuracy. Do you honestly think all of your investment decisions will prove to be wise? I can assure you they won't. Fortunately though, being good at spotting financial storms doesn't involve perfection in any way.

As long as you're willing to adjust your strategy or even philosophy and learn from mistakes, you are in a far better position than the average individual to do well. As per a very popular quote (mis)attributed to Albert Einstein, not learning from mistakes (doing the same thing over and over again but expecting different results) is the very definition of insanity.

I hope you're not insane but if you are, I have the cure: flexibility.

By being flexible and embracing your imperfection, you will gradually become better and better at gathering and interpreting signals. Not even geniuses of the investment world such as Warren Buffett get it right 100% of the time, so stop worrying about things like this and instead, simply try to always be on the right track.

Make decisions. Learn from mistakes. Rinse. Repeat.

Sometimes, you may very well end up being proven wrong by an information source you downright despise. Be it from the alternative media world or the mainstream media one. Don't let these personal preferences stand in the way of flexibility. Swallow your pride, admit you were wrong and move on after learning the appropriate lessons.

If you understand the tips I've provided throughout this subchapter and have the maturity or should I say wisdom to put them to good use, I'm genuinely proud of you. Managing your relationship with mainstream as well as alternative media sources isn't all that difficult as long as you follow a few core principles. It's ultimately all a matter of common sense.

Both types of media sources can enable you to stay informed. To learn new things. To be exposed to anything from slightly different to downright exotic viewpoints. Don't let pride stand in the way. Most people make the mistake of never exiting their bubble. Of only gathering information/signals from a few sources and leaving it at that. By choosing this strategy however, they're shooting themselves in the foot and eliminating entire dimensions of information from the equation.

Don't be one of them. Just don't.

If you're serious about becoming better at spotting financial storms in a world full of uncertainties, you need every edge you can get. Information sources play a huge role in all of this. I'll end this subchapter by making one thing perfectly clear: you need (yes, need) mainstream media as well as alternative media sources if you're serious about considering yourself well-informed. Leave whatever prejudice was holding you back aside and take it from there.

Chapter 4.5: The 11 Storm-Causing Deadly Sins

Through Chapter 3, I did my best to present a balanced list of case studies, from the very first recorded asset bubble (the tulip mania) to recent financial calamities (popular ones such as the Great Recession as well as "exotic" examples like the short domain mania). My intention was definitely not referring to each and every financial storm that ever existed, there's little point in overwhelming readers.

Instead, through careful selection, I ended up with a diverse list than widens your horizon but interestingly enough, I'm sure you've observed something rather fascinating: even though the case studies are remarkably different, the similarities or if you will common denominators are literally screaming at us.

Think of financial storms as diverse manifestations of human nature.

On the one hand, the "package" comes in all shapes and sizes. From people investing their life savings in tulips or domain names to calamities involving mainstream assets such as stocks or real estate. However, after analyzing each case study and drawing the line, you cannot help but notice certain patterns.

I've decided to call the most important ones "the 11 storm-causing deadly sins" and will be referring to each below. Before doing that however, an important question arises: why should you care about these deadly sins? More specifically, why am I telling you about them and how can you use this knowledge to your advantage?

In my opinion, the best way to address this issue starts with me explaining what my intention wasn't rather than was. I want to make it crystal clear right from the beginning that yes, there are easy-to-identify patterns but no, these patterns cannot help you predict the future. If you think this subchapter's main goal is explaining how patterns can enable you to predict the future, you can stop reading.

I love saying that history doesn't repeat itself but it does tend to rhyme. To be fair, the statement in question is actually attributed to Mark Twain (it's debatable whether he actually said this, I'm not going down that rabbit hole however) but regardless, it's hard not to observe how much sense it frequently makes.

So no, predicting the future isn't the main goal here. Instead, these 11 deadly sins will:

1. Help you understand financial storms
2. Enable you to be mentally prepared for financial calamities by knowing what to expect

Please note that you will know what to expect but will be unable to accurately determine when this or that will occur. The name of the game is arming yourself with knowledge so as to gain clarity and ensure your brain is accustomed to behavior patterns which are common but not predictable. There's tremendous value in having this information in your arsenal, especially if you internalize it for the right reasons.

With that stated, here are the most important deadly sins I have identified:

1. **Ignorance** or in other words, not understanding what you're investing in or facing. This specific sin has appeared in 15 out of 16 case studies as follows:

- Anomaly #3 of the tulip mania
- Anomaly #1 of the South Sea bubble
- Anomaly #1 of the Mississippi bubble
- Anomaly #1 of the 1825 panic
- Anomaly #1 of the Weimar hyperinflation
- Anomaly #1 of the Florida real estate bubble
- Anomaly #1 of the Great Depression
- Anomaly #1 of the 1977-1980 gold/silver bubble
- Anomaly #1 of the 1987 crash
- Anomaly #1 of the Japanese bubble of the 1980s
- Anomaly #1 of the 1997 Asian financial crisis
- Anomaly #1 of the LTCM collapse
- Anomaly #1 of the dot-com bubble
- Anomaly #1 of the Great Recession
- Anomaly #1 of the short domain mania

As you've surely noticed when reading the case studies, people are frequently willing to invest in assets they don't understand and quite frankly, they could care less about the assets in question. They're in the game for one reason and one reason only: because everyone else seems to be making money and they want a piece of the action.

While there's nothing inherently wrong with investing in something strictly because you want to make money, allocating capital in a herd-like manner is just plain foolish. If you're only in it for the money then fine but for the love of God, always be professional about it.

Absorb at least a reasonable amount of knowledge about the asset(s) in question before even thinking about pulling the trigger. Analyze data, do your due diligence. There's just no way to circumvent this part of the process. Even if everyone seems to be in frenzy mode and you can't stop thinking about the money that may very well be on the table, try to keep your cool because otherwise, you have "victim" written all over you.

2. **Indebtedness** or in other words, speculating with borrowed money, a sin that has appeared in 13 out of 16 case studies as follows:

- Anomaly #4 of the tulip mania
- Anomaly #2 of the South Sea bubble
- Anomaly #2 of the Mississippi bubble
- Anomaly #1 of the British railway mania
- Anomaly #2 of the Florida real estate bubble
- Anomaly #2 of the Great Depression
- Anomaly #3 of the 1977-1980 gold/silver bubble
- Anomaly #2 of the Japanese bubble of the 1980s
- Anomaly #2 of the 1997 Asian financial crisis
- Anomaly #3 of the LTCM collapse
- Anomaly #4 of the dot-com bubble
- Anomaly #4 of the Great Recession
- Anomaly #4 of the short domain mania

Are there situations in which taking on debt so as to speculate can pay off? Sure, there are exceptions to pretty much anything but realistically speaking, it's ridiculously likely that your decision will come back to haunt you.

Especially if, as is frequently the case with bubbles, you do it when your judgment is clouded.

There are indeed professionals who can make debt/leverage work in their favor but even for the elites of the financial world, it can be hit or miss. The average speculator who is hoping to get rich quick is… well, let's just say not in the best position in the world to juggle debt properly when speculating.

So, am I saying you shouldn't take on debt to speculate? Yes, that's precisely what I'd recommend. Leave trading on leverage to professionals. I have nothing against investing in assets that are on a roll and I'm definitely not saying you shouldn't speculate when the right opportunity presents itself. But be smart about it and only risk money you can afford to lose.

3. **Imprudence** or in other words, the fact that when times are good, warning signals tend to be ignored/dismissed. This sin appeared on 13 out of 16 occasions:

- Anomaly #4 of the South Sea bubble
- Anomaly #4 of the Mississippi bubble
- Anomaly #3 of the 1825 panic
- Anomaly #4 of the British railway mania
- Anomaly #4 of the Weimar hyperinflation
- Anomaly #4 of the Florida real estate bubble
- Anomaly #4 of the Great Depression
- Anomaly #3 of the 1987 crash
- Anomaly #4 of the Japanese bubble of the 1980s
- Anomaly #4 of the 1997 Asian financial crisis
- Anomaly #2 of the dot-com bubble
- Anomaly #2 of the Great Recession
- Anomaly #6 of the short domain mania

One of the most dangerous aspects associated with bubbles is the fact that toxic reasoning patterns are being reinforced by the upward price movement. Specifically, things are going so well that you don't want to even accept the possibility of the party somehow coming to an end.

It's easy and quite tempting to judge people for not reacting to what we consider blatantly obvious warning signals but to them, the warning signals are anything but obvious. Think of it as denial on steroids, when every fiber of your body wants an asset to keep doing well.

Humans tend to be quite creative when it comes to rationalization. If we desperately want to believe something, our brain is frequently able to come up with plausible scenarios which reinforce our current beliefs. As such, it should come as no surprise that being oblivious to warning signals represents one of the top common denominators when it comes to financial storms.

4. **Wrath** or in other words, the desire to find a scapegoat whenever things go wrong rather than look in the mirror, an anomaly that appeared in 12 out of 16 situations:

- Anomaly #6 of the tulip mania
- Anomaly #6 of the South Sea bubble
- Anomaly #5 of the Mississippi bubble
- Anomaly #6 of the 1825 panic
- Anomaly #5 of the British railway mania
- Anomaly #3 of the Weimar hyperinflation
- Anomaly #4 of the 1977-1980 gold/silver bubble
- Anomaly #5 of the Japanese bubble of the 1980s
- Anomaly #6 of the 1997 Asian financial crisis
- Anomaly #6 of the dot-com bubble
- Anomaly #6 of the Great Recession
- Anomaly #5 of the short domain mania

Assuming responsibility for your actions and especially failures may be the mature thing to do but it's not exactly something people tend to be very good at. Just think about the Great Recession for a moment, a financial calamity which had lots of negative consequences: job loss, home loss, wealth loss, you name it.

Naturally, a lot of debates about causes followed and unfortunately, most of them turned into a relatively hard to digest (for me, at least) display of hypocrisy. About how it's all the fault of the bankers, regulators, Wall Street traders and so on. Now don't get me wrong, all of these parties are to blame in one way or another.

However, I believe the intellectually honest approach with such debates is starting by mentioning what exactly it is that you, personally, are guilty of.

And by you, I'm referring to the average individual, who I assure you was not an angel in all of this. The average individual who went on a consumerist binge and treated his home as an ATM machine. The average consumer who bought a huge home he in no way needed (nor afforded) just so he could impress the Joneses… I'm sure you get the point.

If you lost money after a financial crisis, I firmly believe the best approach is starting by looking yourself in the mirror and asking what you did wrong. Otherwise, crisis after crisis will come and go, leaving you behind as a poor eternal "victim" who was of course never ever at fault. I'm sorry but with such an attitude, you'll never learn from the mistakes that I can pretty much guarantee you've made.

5. **Incompetence** (of the authorities) or in other words, the fact that regulators tend to very frequently get caught off-guard and be reactive rather than proactive. We've been able to notice incompetence in 11 out of 16 case studies:

- Anomaly #3 of the South Sea bubble
- Anomaly #2 of the 1825 panic
- Anomaly #3 of the British railway mania
- Anomaly #6 of the Weimar hyperinflation
- Anomaly #3 of the Florida real estate bubble
- Anomaly #3 of the Great Depression
- Anomaly #4 of the 1987 crash
- Anomaly #3 of the Japanese bubble of the 1980s
- Anomaly #3 of the 1997 Asian financial crisis
- Anomaly #3 of the dot-com bubble
- Anomaly #3 of the Great Recession

Perhaps we've been hardwired to believe the proverbial "authorities" are these fool-proof entities that can do no wrong and watch over our every step. After all, we're pack animals at the end of the day and blindly believing in leaders arguably comes with the territory.

But make no mistake, those beliefs are for the most part unfounded. Time and time again, scenarios emerge that put authorities to the test and an astute observer will quickly notice the powers that be are usually one step behind.

THE AGE OF ANOMALY

To put it differently, regulators are for the most part reactive rather than what they should be, which is proactive.

Something takes them by surprise (an exogenous shock, for example) and they scramble to find solutions. In an ideal world, they should have done the exact opposite by thinking about various scenarios beforehand and being prepared for the worst. In the real world however, that hardly happens. If you think the authorities will be there to catch you after the next financial crisis hits, you'll be in for a rude awakening in my opinion.

6. **Delirium** or in other words, excessive optimism. If you will, the tendency to see life through rose-colored glasses, an anomaly I've pointed out in 8 out of 16 case studies:

- Anomaly #5 of the 1825 panic
- Anomaly #6 of the Florida real estate bubble
- Anomaly #6 of the Great Depression
- Anomaly #5 of the 1977-1980 gold/silver bubble
- Anomaly #2 of the 1987 crash
- Anomaly #5 of the 1997 Asian financial crisis
- Anomaly #4 of the LTCM collapse
- Anomaly #2 of the short domain mania

I have nothing against people who tell others to look on the bright side, to see the glass as half full rather than half empty and what not. When it comes to almost everything, it's a decent enough life philosophy and it may very well increase your happiness level over the long haul.

The operative word however is "almost" because in the financial world, this principle doesn't apply in my opinion. If you're an optimism-driven investor who sees the world through rose-colored glasses then I'm sorry to have to say this but you'll get slaughtered out there.

As an author, I'm on a continuous quest to reconcile my desire to please people with the fact that being brutally honest is the only feasible way to get the message across. In this case, I'll go ahead and make it crystal clear that when preparing against financial storms, excessive optimism can turn your entire strategy into a miserable failure.

7. **Foolhardiness** or in other words, the willingness to blissfully take on additional layers of risk. Foolhardiness appeared in 6 out of 16 case studies:

- Anomaly #5 of the tulip mania
- Anomaly #5 of the South Sea bubble
- Anomaly #5 of the Florida real estate bubble
- Anomaly #5 of the Great Depression
- Anomaly #5 of the dot-com bubble
- Anomaly #5 of the Great Recession

When you read about the let's say tulip mania while comfortably sitting in your bed, it may seem perplexing that those people didn't just limit themselves to investing in already wildly speculative tulip bulbs. No, they took things one step further by even buying and selling rights to tulip bulbs, among many other things.

Once again, what you fail to realize is that when you're in the middle of a frenzy, everything changes. A mania such as that of the tulip variety can and will turn otherwise reasonable individuals into compulsive gamblers who are willing to do anything to maximize results.

Does that frequently mean taking on debilitatingly high levels of risk? Of course! Throughout this book, I did my best not to limit myself to merely sharing facts and figures. Instead, I've continuously tried to help readers understand the atmosphere in each case.

When analyzing anomalies, laughing about those who lost money due to reckless capital allocation decisions and thinking it could never happen to you is the exact opposite of what you should be doing. Instead, try to be more reasonable about the limitations of others as well as your own because humility will get you far as an investor.

8. **Thoughtlessness** or in other words, what happens when pragmatic thinking is thrown out the window and replaced with various bizarre rationalization mechanisms, something one can notice in 5 out of 16 situations:

- Anomaly #1 of the tulip mania
- Anomaly #4 of the 1825 panic
- Anomaly #2 of the British railway mania
- Anomaly #7 of the Great Depression

- Anomaly #6 of the Japanese bubble of the 1980s

First and foremost, thoughtlessness is characterized by a severe lack of common sense, plain and simple. For example, common sense should dictate that if the price of an asset increases ten-fold over a certain timeframe, you have valid reasons to raise an eyebrow and ask yourself questions about the sustainability of it all.

However, pragmatic thinking isn't exactly popular when the world is in full-fledged bubble mode. In such scenarios, the implausible becomes reasonable and investors are quickly willing to rationalize their worries away.

Or as Voltaire would put it (although people have been saying it since the days of the Roman Empire), common sense is not so common. There are most definitely instances in which previously rational actors become more than willing to say goodbye to pragmatic thinking and make no mistake, this can and will cost them.

9. **Greed-induced delusion** or in other words, being so blinded by your desire to either make money or for another positive outcome to take place that you make completely irrational financial decisions, such as for example investing in assets that used to be considered worthless and rightfully so. We can notice delusion in 4 out of 16 case studies:

- Anomaly #2 of the tulip mania
- Anomaly #6 of the Mississippi bubble
- Anomaly #2 of the Weimar hyperinflation
- Anomaly #3 of the short domain mania

When people think about market crashes and bubbles, they envision events related to "mainstream" asset classes for the most part. Stock market crashes or real estate bubbles, for example. Yet as history has proven, people are frequently willing to stray off the beaten path and invest in downright peculiar assets.

I believe it's self-explanatory that the first ever recorded asset bubble did not involve let's say real estate and instead, involved… well, tulips. Even when it comes to tulips, things got crazier and crazier because at the very beginning, only extremely rare bulbs were bought and sold. Something that does, after all, make sense. Scarcity, supply/demand and all that good stuff.

However, toward the height of the madness, even flowers which were considered worthless up until that point suddenly became desirable. So not only was there greed-induced delusion when it comes to the asset type itself (tulips), there was also greed-induced delusion when it comes to specific assets choices, with the idea of "quality" being thrown out the window and the "investment grade" concept losing its meaningfulness.

10. **Sentimentalism** or in other words, letting emotion rather than reason take over. Sentimentalism appeared in 2 out of our 16 case studies:

- Anomaly #2 of the 1977-1980 gold/silver bubble
- Anomaly #5 of the 1987 crash

Those who make a lot of money "thanks to" a certain asset inevitably become emotionally attached to that asset. It's a way of thinking that might make sense in other sectors of life (the idea of being grateful) but in the world of economics, it's a surefire way to lose the farm.

When it's time to buy, you buy and when the opportunity to sell at a great price presents itself, you pull the trigger. Investing 101. Regardless of whether or not the asset in question has been good to you up until that point. There's little room for emotion in the mind of an investor.

This is especially valid when it comes to ultra-speculative investments such as those in assets that are in bubble territory. More so than with other assets, you need to watch your back in such cases and understand the game you're playing. If you want sentimentalism, watch a romantic movie but when investing, leave all of that behind.

11. **Disregard** or in other words, ignoring the lessons of history and assuming this time everything will be different, something we've noticed in 2 out of 16 case studies:

- Anomaly #6 of the 1987 crash
- Anomaly #5 of the LTCM collapse

Ah, yes… the (in)famous "this time it's different" situation. You might be wondering why "kind of, sort of" similar mistakes keep being made throughout history. After all, you'd expect rational investors to learn from earlier generations or at the very least from their own past mistakes, right?

Unfortunately, that's frequently not the case and the "this time it's different" or "new paradigm" angle represents the most popular rationalization mechanism out there. With each asset, it's easy to think of things that can be considered game-changers and find explanations as to why that particular asset is poised for greatness.

In most cases however, the overwhelming majority in fact, this kind of disregard will cost you dearly. Time and time again, people end up realizing that no, it wasn't different that time and no, the asset in question isn't just surrounded by sunshine and rainbows. Few things in this world are better at giving me goosebumps than hearing someone explain how this time, it's all going to be different. If that's not a warning signal, I don't know what is.

… and there we have it, the 11 storm-causing deadly sins!

Do keep in mind that this is just my interpretation, don't treat the list I've just shared as the be-all and end-all of deadly sins. By all means, feel free to re-read Chapter 3 and come up with your own list. Perhaps in certain cases, you don't agree with my way of seeing things and that's perfectly fine.

The name of the game is:

1. Being armed with facts
2. Doing our best to interpret them

… nothing more, nothing less.

This book's third chapter is going to help you with #1. As far as #2 is concerned, I'd recommend reading what I have to say throughout this book but in the end, drawing conclusions yourself as well. I've never been the type of economist who claims he holds the universal truth, in fact I believe that's a dangerous attitude to have. Instead, I'd much rather be upfront about my limitations and encourage you to extract value from this section in particular or this book in general in whichever manner you see fit!

Chapter 4.6: Polgar's Prudence Principles

What kind of an economist am I? Well, the strange thing about me is that I always have a pretty hard time defining what I do. I'm definitely not a status quo economist, that's for sure. Instead, I like to think of myself as more a philosopher who tries to simplify things and keep the feet of my peers on the ground.

We'll assume I'm on top of a building with an econometrist (the math guy, the quant or whichever term you prefer). He tells me how he has this great plan to get to the bottom of that building by jumping at a precisely calculated speed, at a precisely calculated angle and holding on to precisely identified bricks to survive. I'm the guy who takes a step back and asks him why we don't just take the stairs.

I'll be doing the same in this subchapter.

I firmly believe that all you have to do to become multiple orders of magnitude better at spotting financial storms is embrace sound principles. No fancy schmancy complexoid statistics, no equations, none of that. So if you're looking for the type of information you can memorize robotically so as to sound smart at parties, look elsewhere. If you're interested in internalizing simple-to-follow prudence principles that actually work, read on.

Please keep in mind that it is by no means my intention to make this a definitive list. These are the principles I personally adhere to, I believe in each and every one of them and do my best to make them a part of my life. The best advice I can give you is to put together your own list. We're ultimately all different individuals, with different backgrounds, lives, desires and needs. What's important is taking the time required to put together a list of your own and furthermore, actually making each principle a part of your life.

Perhaps you will embrace all of my principles, that may very well be the case. Then again, perhaps only half of them are valid for a person such as yourself. It's ultimately all up to you. What you have to understand is that in order to meaningfully take control of your preparedness, you have to get to know yourself and decide in which direction you want to take your life. The average individual goes with the flow, he leaves way too much to the arbitrary and that's just plain wrong. Without understanding who and where you are as well as figuring out who you want to be in the future and where you want to go, it is impossible to see fundamental changes.

I don't believe in imposing my perspective on life on other people. Instead, I'd rather just share it and let you extract whatever value out of it you see fit. Let's get started:

1. Prepare when you see storm clouds, don't wait for the first rain drop. In other words, I for one would much rather be one year too early than a day too late. I strongly advise against waiting until the last minute because by the time you feel the first drop of rain, everyone else will start preparing or even panicking as well and that is not a scenario you want to deal with

2. Strategic planning is something you don't outsource or should I say shouldn't outsource. You live with yourself 24-7 and there isn't a single person on this planet who is in better shape than you are to figure out what the best strategy for your specific situation and needs should be. We humans are frequently tempted to delegate responsibility because of course, the thought of somebody else fixing our problems always sounds appealing. That doesn't mean it's the right thing to do

3. Don't expect to be brilliantly lucid during acute phases of a crisis. No matter how much self-control you have or think you have, you're only human. One of the fundamental things that comes with being human is precisely the fact that under significant amounts of stress, our decision-making process tends to be impaired

4. Leave fortune-telling to the charlatans at the local fair. I say this time and time again, human beings tend to be terrible at predicting the future and I for one would strongly recommend never believing that you have this ability. As convenient as the thought that you or anyone else for that matter can predict the future may be, you should definitely raise an eyebrow whenever someone claims he can teach you how to predict the future or that he can predict the future himself

5. Track records speak for themselves. After reading the previous principle, it becomes clear that this one is a natural follow-up. Whenever someone tells me he's able to predict the future, my first and only reaction is to either request indisputable proof or search for that proof myself. Doing this is quite easy because if the person who makes that claim is even moderately popular, simply googling his name will reveal a lot of past predictions made by the person in question. Did they all pan out? I don't know about you but each time I've tried this, the results were not just negative but downright shameful for the so-called forecaster

6. History doesn't repeat itself but it does tend to rhyme. I want to make this distinction perfectly clear because while I firmly believe that humans are unable to accurately and consistently predict the future, I just as firmly believe that history always teaches us important lessons and that the conclusions we draw will definitely help us in the future.

Why do you think I've dedicated so much time and energy to analyzing various anomalies in this book? It is of course because the lessons of the past are of vital importance to those who want to be prepared for whatever the future has in store. The common denominators I've identified tell us quite a bit about human nature and by getting closer to something that even resembles an understanding of human nature, you're obviously positioning yourself a lot better than the average individual with respect to spotting and dealing with the financial storms of the future

7. Be an optimist in life but a pessimist when planning. Far way too many people mistakenly consider those who go through the trouble of actually preparing for financial storms doom and gloomers, the type of people who isolate themselves in the mountains and hide under their beds all day. Or perhaps those loony people with cardboard signs who insist on prowling the streets and telling everyone that the end is near.

That's just plain silly. I for one always tell people to be optimists when it comes to life in general but definitely pessimists when making plans. I think it's ultimately a matter of common sense. If you prepare for the worst, there are two possibilities: the first possibility is that the worst does indeed materialize but at least you'll be prepared, whereas the second possibility is that something less dramatic happens and you'll be even happier. In both of these cases, the outcome is not devastating. However, what if you were an optimist when planning? In that case, then you'd be bitterly disappointed or even financially devastated if anything other than the optimistic scenario you had envisioned materializes. You tell me, doesn't being a pessimist when making plans seem like a logical option?

8. We're all experts in a bull market. Back when the dot-com bubble took place, it was ridiculously easy to make money by buying tech stocks for the simple reason that for a while, pretty much all of them went up. A lot of people, seeing how much money they managed to make, ended up considering themselves experts. After all, it's easy to understand why you'd see yourself as a tech stock expert if you've made a lot of money by just that, picking tech stocks. However, it's all in your head because unfortunately for your ego, we're all experts in a bull market. From weavers who thought they were expert tulip traders in the 17th century to the text stock experts of the dot-com bubble and so on, it is proven time and time again that you shouldn't rate your expertise based on how well your pics performed during a bull market

9. Your ego will be your downfall. Once again, this is a natural follow-up to the previous principle and I've seen it time and time again how an ego can ruin a strategy and ultimately a person's life. The most dangerous thing about your ego is that it tends to give you a delusion of grandeur or if you will, an inaccurately high sense of competence. This naturally makes you leave your guard down and needless to say, this mistake can literally destroy you

10. You don't have to always or even usually be right. Let's assume that for four times in a row, you prepare for something that doesn't happen but the fifth time, you get it right and save your wealth. Next, take a step back and ask yourself what you've lost the first four times.

If you've been smart about it by following the advice given throughout this book, then you probably lost time and a reasonably but not excruciatingly high amount of money. But you ultimately ended up saving the financial future of your family. On the other hand, the average individual probably didn't prepare the first few times and as such didn't lose anything but when disaster struck, the wealth of his family may very well have been wiped away. Don't assume you have to be right 100% of the time, don't even assume you have to be right one out of two times. As long as you don't go overboard and react to ridiculously high amounts of false positives, you should be in good shape

11. The crowd is an indicator, not a role model. Plus, it's frequently wrong. Humans are herd animals, so at the end of the day, following the herd makes perfect sense and it's deeply entrenched in our DNA. Unfortunately, it tends to be an instinct that gets us in trouble and I for one have developed the habit of looking at what everyone else does or the crowd if you will as an indicator, definitely not as a type of behavior I have to mimic. Don't put the crowd on the pedestal because not if but when it goes down in flames, it'll take you with it

12. The assets your friends recommend are probably close to their peak. This reminds me of a funny anecdote of how someone once asked Joseph Kennedy how he managed to sell before the Great Depression of 1929 kicked in. He simply replied by saying that when he saw that the shoeshine boy gave him stock investing advice, he knew something was terribly wrong. At the end of the day, there's only a finite amount of steam in a bull market and once literally everyone is deeply invested in a certain asset class, be it stocks or anything else, it should be treated as a warning signal

13. When something seems too good to be true, run for the hills. Something we frequently see with bubbles, as you've surely noticed by reading the book so far, is that people don't exactly have the habit of embracing this principle. This is understandable to a certain degree because humans are driven by a deep desire to move toward progress. Therefore, whenever something great happens, our brain is tempted to tell us that even better times are ahead.

This is when common sense needs to kick in. Even in the 17th century, we noticed that weavers and other craftsmen abandoned their occupations to invest in tulips, people aren't very tempted to raise an eyebrow when times are good. A weaver or carpenter saw that people were making a lot more money than them without working nearly as hard. Did they raise an eyebrow and say to themselves that is too good to be true? Many unfortunately didn't and in fact, did the exact opposite by abandoning their occupation and investing everything they had in tulips. The same principle has been valid multiple times throughout history. Raising an eyebrow is frequently the healthy thing to do

14. Paradigm shifts don't occur all that frequently. To add to the previous principle, I'd like to remind you how easy it is to notice people's desire to explain things away. When times are good and you don't want these good times to end, then once again your brain will turn from an ally into an enemy. It's remarkable how good our brain tends to be at rationalizing things away. You want the good times to last forever, so your brain concocts all sorts of scenarios as to why whatever it is that happened represents the dawn of a new age. For example, a lot of dot-com tech stock investors believed it's perfectly natural for companies with no profit potential whatsoever to be worth a fortune because hey, we're at the dawn of a new era. This common narrative is exactly what those who stand to profit from the bubble want to hear but unfortunately, it's misleading

15. Financial storms don't call before dropping by. In other words, nobody is going to synchronize schedules with you. Financial storms are something you cannot control and their occurrence is in no way dependent on whatever works best for you. A financial storm won't care that you were too busy at the office to prepare over the past year, that you were going through a rough patch or that you didn't care, it's going to come regardless

16. Don't always expect logic in the world of economics. For example, simple logic would tell us that if a central bank pumps money into the system, the currency might end up being destroyed. It's precisely what people said back when the Japanese started embarking on their

journey of aggressive monetary policy. Some of them for example chose to short Japanese government bonds and do you know what that trade is called now?

It's called the widow maker because a lot of those who made that trade ended up suffering such devastating losses that they took their own lives. If you heard a lot of them on television enumerating the reasons why shorting Japanese government bonds is a no-brainer, you were probably tempted to agree. Everything they said made or seemed to make perfect financial sense. You saw logic and coherence. Yet, needless to say, their predictions failed miserably

17. Ignorance has a price tag. Your bubble isn't an impenetrable shield, it's frequently the exact opposite. You might be tempted to think you're being very smart by not watching the news, by isolating yourself from the mundane and so on. It's tempting to think of your very own bubble as an invincibility shield but in fact, it's your Achilles' heel. You are unfortunately not in a video game in which you control the narrative, you live in a deeply interconnected world filled with factors which affect you in meaningful and oftentimes dramatic ways. Whether you choose to accept it or not!

18. Fire extinguishers don't help during a flood. One of the biggest mistakes I've noticed among those who believe in being prepared is the fact that they are a one-trick pony. They stick to a scenario and prepare for that scenario and nothing else religiously. If they believe humanity is about to be attacked by fire breathing dragons, they fill their homes with fire extinguishers but let me ask you: what happens when they have to deal with a flood instead? Words can't begin to describe how important it is to diversify, within reason of course. Don't be like the gold bugs who think the only solution to all of humanity's potentially life-threatening and ridiculously complicated problems is buying gold. Precious metals can be a part of the solution, you're making a grave mistake if you think they're the entire solution

19. Become a canary trainer. In other words, do just what miners did back in the day and take not one but various proverbial canaries with

you. Needless to say, I'm referring to indicators when mentioning canaries and firmly believe it's important to have flies on as many walls as possible. Gather information from as many sources as possible, mainstream media as well as alternative media ones and for the love of God and all that is holy, never forget to stay informed

20. What went up fast can come down faster. Everyone wants a piece of the action when the price of a certain asset skyrockets but in such cases, remember to fasten your seatbelts and get ready for a potential roller coaster ride. I'm not saying you shouldn't grab a piece of the action, not at all. Just know exactly what you're getting yourself into and realize that no, the only way isn't just up. I remember how from late 2015 to early 2016, the price of short domains shot up exponentially. I was talking to several domain brokers from China and distinctly recall one such conversation in which he was telling me about how people are accumulating debt so that they can buy more domains and so on. I asked him a simple question: what happens if prices come down? I kid you not, he was literally shocked as I asked that and did not have an answer ready

21. You don't have to pick a side. Again, this is another situation in which our desire to be a part of a pack inhibits our optimal decision-making process. Don't make the mistake of believing that if you invest in precious metals, you have to hate stocks or if you invest in stocks, you have to consider precious metals nothing more than shiny rocks. The same principle is valid when it comes to media outlets and pretty much anything else

22. You don't have to be in this alone. Quite frankly, you shouldn't. Lone wolves are a lot more vulnerable than they realize. By not having the sentimental, logistical or even financial support of other human beings, I would say you are automatically starting out with a significant handicap. It's important to me that people realize I will never ever ask you to become hermits in the name of preparedness

23. It's easy to be an armchair warrior online. What I'm trying to say is that when talking to other people on the Internet about preparedness, about what they're going to do when disaster strikes and so on, you shouldn't blindly believe everything you'll be hearing.

When reading forum posts and what not, you're tempted to believe there are professionally trained Navy SEALs behind each computer screen but I assure you, that is hardly the case. A lot of people tend to be let's say overly optimistic compared to reality when posting online, never lose sight of that

24. Have limited confidence in regulators. Once again, the herd animal within us desperately wants to blindly believe a figure of authority. Unfortunately, case study after case study makes it abundantly clear that authorities tend to be reactive rather than proactive. They scramble to find solutions after things went wrong, point fingers at various scapegoats and so on

25. Life's not too short to prepare. A lot of people take the idea of preparing for financial storms as a laughing matter and will frequently give replies in a tongue-in-cheek manner during conversations about preparedness. Many of them will tell you that life's too short to prepare and in the long run, we'll all be dead anyway. So carpe diem, seize the moment… right? Well sure, we're all going to die eventually but for most of us, that will happen quite a long time from now. And hey, it is true that you could be hit by a truck tomorrow but again, that's probably not going to happen. What is however more likely to happen is being dramatically affected by a financial storm you were too arrogant to prepare for

That's pretty much it. These 25 principles are what I'm able to put on the table by leveraging my knowledge as well as experience. Again, I'm not here to spoon-feed anyone information or brand myself as an expert who is never wrong. I highly encourage you to put together your own list of principles but do believe that using mine as a framework would be a good idea. Where you take things from here is entirely up to you.

Chapter 5: Becoming Resilient

I would probably make a lot more money as an author and economist by simply telling people what they want to hear. When reading a book, most people feel the desperate need to know that whatever it is they're reading is guaranteed to help them achieve perfection, 100% of the time. Unfortunately, I'm afraid that is just not possible.

A lot of authors in the sometimes wonderful but occasionally awful world of economics tell people that if they read their books, they're going to be able to spot all asset bubbles from now on and be one step ahead of each and every financial calamity. I'm sorry but that's just fraudulent behavior. I tell people time and time again that even I will probably end up being taken by surprise on quite a few occasions because, as unfortunate as it may be, us humans are just not very good at predicting the future.

Now obviously, someone who reads this book and actually puts my tips to good use will be much, much better-positioned than the average individual (multiple orders of magnitude better, I might add) to spot financial storms but even if you read this book from top to bottom a hundred times, there are no 100% guarantees.

For this reason, my book cannot be complete if I simply provide tips on how to spot financial storms and leave it at that. This is because there is an entire dimension I would be leaving unexplored by only focusing on spotting financial calamities. The dimension I'm referring to is that of resilience. Being resilient, first and foremost, means that you're going to be a lot better at coping with whatever it is life throws at you. From financial calamities to wars and pretty much anything else you can think of.

To make a real-life analogy, it's obvious that all parents want to keep their kids safe and out of trouble. But no matter how paranoid you are as a parent, I'm sorry but that is simply impossible. There's just no way to make sure that you will always be able to keep your child out of harm's way. For this reason, making sure your child is genuinely resilient is a perfectly logical thing to do. Making sure he is physically healthy, ensuring he's mentally stable as well, that he gets enough sleep and so on. A healthy child who is resilient will obviously be in a much better position than a weak child to withstand the occasional hurdles of early life. From small-time diseases to conflictual situations or anything else.

The same principle is valid when it comes to resilience as analyzed by this book. It would be excellent if there were a surefire way to make sure that you will always be far away from trouble. Unfortunately, that's just not possible. It happens to the best of us. Therefore, becoming resilient enough to be able to withstand the effects of financial storms you weren't able to spot is just as important as becoming better at spotting financial storms in general. The two dimensions complement one another nicely and for this reason, I've decided to dedicate an entire chapter to resilience.

Since I'm an economist, I'm sure you're expecting me to focus primarily on financial resilience. And indeed, most of my energy will be initially directed toward tackling the issue of financial resilience. However, I will be spending just as much time and energy focusing on other types of resilience as well, specifically mental resilience, physical resilience and SHTF resilience. As an author, I firmly believe in giving my readers the full picture and to do that, I don't mind venturing outside of my comfort zone and referring to aspects which don't pertain exclusively to economics.

Chapter 5.1: Landing on Your Feet as a Way of Life

Way too many people make the mistake of thinking that being prepared enables them to thrive under all possible negative scenarios. Believe it or not, some individuals are actually looking forward to financial calamities because they've been preparing for so long and they've been preparing so hard that they cannot wait for the moment when they think that all of their hard work will pay off. What they don't realize is that more often than not, even the best-prepared individuals end up with battle scars. There are two main reasons why this happens:

- The first is represented by the fact that there's no such thing as a strategy that enables you to thrive under absolutely all scenarios. If your strategy is working great when times are good, then that same strategy might end up failing miserably during a financial crisis. Or if your strategy would work great under a scenario of inflation, it most likely underperforms in a deflationary environment. As such, landing on your feet is the name of the game because again, there is no such thing as a scenario that helps you always be a clear winner

- The second reason is represented by the fact that some financial storms are so powerful that even if you're lucky enough for them to catch you at the best possible moment and the scenario question is the one you've prepared the most for, its effects are just so devastating that you will still end up badly bruised. That's just how things are

I think it's vital that people set realistic goals right from the beginning and when it comes to financial storms and disaster preparedness in general, you have to understand that landing on your feet is a more than adequate goal. I always find it amusing how for example those who constantly predict the end of the world and try to sell gold do so thinking that those who buy gold now including of course themselves will end up becoming filthy rich after the next crisis.

I think that is a foolish oversimplification. As much as I believe there is room for gold in each and every portfolio, you need to understand that

179

you're buying it as an insurance policy and not as a get-rich-quick scheme, as it is frequently pitched as. It is naïve at best and foolish at worst to assume that in a complicated landscape such as ours, where anomalies abound and where the likelihood of being taken by surprise is extremely high, all you have to do to not only survive but actually get filthy rich is buy a shiny rock. I'm not a gold basher but then again, I'm not a gold bug either. I firmly believe, as you're about to find out later on in this chapter, that before investing in a certain asset class, you should know exactly what you're getting yourself into.

So, what does "landing on your feet" actually mean?

As mentioned earlier on, no matter how well-prepared you are, there are going to be bruises. First and foremost, I would say "landing on your feet" means minimizing the bruises in question. I'm always the type of economist who advises people against for example buying a small car with no airbags and zero safety features. It's obvious that if you own a solid car with great safety enhancements, you are in a much better position to withstand car accidents than someone who drives a very poor vehicle. But this doesn't mean you should hope to get in a car accident as soon as possible so as to test the features of your car, I do believe this much is a matter of common sense. The same way, you should not anxiously await financial calamities because it won't be pleasant no matter how well-prepared you are.

Aside from bruise minimization, being quick to adapt should be another priority. Most people, the overwhelming majority, are knocked out by financial calamities. By landing on your feet, you're obviously not in that specific category and instead, are in a much better position than most individuals to snap out of it, adapt and figure out what needs to be done next.

Finally, I would also argue that landing on your feet should mean being able to move on as quickly as possible. A financial crisis or calamities of other nature are without a doubt disruptive events. It can take some people many years to recover after such situations and landing on your feet in my opinion also means minimizing the recovery time in question. Will dealing with financial calamities be pleasant? Of course not but landing on your feet means accepting that and doing your best to be in a situation which enables you to move on with your life as quickly as possible.

With that being stated, the obvious question that arises is the following: okay, so what should I do to land on my feet? This is precisely what this chapter will help you with. The previous one was all about telling you how to do your best to avoid financial storms or if you will, to avoid getting hit in the first place. This chapter however will teach you all you need to know to become more resilient so that when you do inevitably get hit from time to time, you will most likely land on your feet.

This chapter will continue with two main sections.

The first of the two will be about, of course, financial resilience. At the end of the day, it's obvious why this is the first issue I've chosen to cover given that I'm an economist. The second section however will refer to everything else or in other words, I do my best not to be an economist who simply lives in his bubble all day and is never able to prescribe anything other than what he's learned from his textbooks.

I firmly believe that if you're serious about adopting the proper attitude when it comes to financial storms, landing on your feet should become a way of life to you. Be humble enough to understand you cannot prepare for everything, hard-working enough to understand that becoming more resilient will involve a lot of time as well as energy and finally, wise enough to realize that dealing with financial storms will in no way be pleasant!

Chapter 5.2: Financial Resilience

Study after study proves that the Western consumer is anything but prepared to cope with a financial emergency. For example, only about 1 in 3 Americans[37] would be able to cover a mere $500 car repair bill or a $1,000 emergency room visit from savings. That, my friends, is the exact opposite of being financially resilient.

If you as a consumer can barely afford to cover an emergency auto repair bill or something else along those lines, then I'm sorry but you are extremely financially fragile. Needless to say, these people are the first to suffer whenever financial disaster strikes. They are completely dependent on the status quo and should anything occur that disrupts the normal functioning of our day-to-day systems, these people would be literally devastated.

This section of *The Age of Anomaly* has one purpose and one purpose only: helping readers become more financially resilient or in other words, become financially prepared so that should emergencies arise, they can easily cope with them. One of the main reasons why I've decided to write books and perhaps the main reason why I've decided to start with *Wealth Management 2.0* which is a personal finance book is the fact that the average individual has received absolutely horrible financial education.

It seems downright strange to me to refer to the average consumer and use the term "financial resilience" in the same sentence because these individuals are so far away from anything even resembling financial resilience that it's just laughable. If you have even a basic foundation of financial education coupled with an ounce of common sense, you are light-years ahead of the average consumer.

Through the following subchapters, I will do my best to help you gain control over your finances. I'll be providing practical tips as to how to build a portfolio which includes assets that are good performers when things are great as well as assets which we can consider insurance policies.

---

[37] Claes Bell. "Budgets Can Crumble in Times of Trouble." *Bankrate*. January 7, 2015. http://www.bankrate.com/finance/smart-spending/money-pulse-0115.aspx.

My experience with the One Minute Economics YouTube channel has made it clear that most people don't even understand the basics. Time and time again, I've noticed how impressed people were with me covering the very basics of personal finance for example. This is because the average individual simply doesn't give these things enough thought. This is understandable because let's face it, we all have our own lives. It's actually the main reason why I've chosen the one-minute format for my YouTube channel. I wanted people to know that one minute is more than enough for me to teach them the basics. And it worked.

Through the subchapters you're about to read, I'm going to obviously take things one step further and will analyze pretty much all asset classes that I consider desirable in detail. After reading the financial resilience section of *The Age of Anomaly*, you will in my opinion be in a very good position to put together the best possible portfolio for your specific situation and your specific needs.

I'm not here to spoon-feed all of you the exact same financial resilience strategy because something that works great for my family might not be a great solution for yours. As such, it's much more important for me to give you the tools you need to make your own financial decisions and therefore, I'll be doing just that. The idea of becoming financially resilient may sound complicated but fortunately, if armed with a bit of patience and a healthy dose of common sense, you will surely realize it's more than doable.

Chapter 5.2.1: My (In)Famous Personalized Portfolio Principle

If a 25-year-old bachelor who works in the IT industry asks me for financial tips, I'll obviously suggest a far more aggressive strategy than if his 65-year-old grandmother asks me what she should do. The same way, I'm not going to recommend real estate if you live in a highly politically volatile country from the Middle East because the likelihood of you losing your real estate as a result of socio-political turmoil is high.

… I'm sure it's obvious why offering one-size-fits-all solutions is downright silly.

We're talking about individuals with completely different backgrounds, social situations and so on. Each person has completely different needs and completely different financial expectations. Now let's extrapolate and refer to this book for a moment. In the previous examples, we're only dealing with three people (the bachelor, the grandmother and the person from the Middle East) but realistically speaking, a decent book has thousands upon thousands of readers, so how could I as an author possibly think I can get away with simply providing one-size-fits-all suggestions?

Even if it were possible for me to speak to each and every reader for a few hours in order to create a personalized portfolio on a case by case basis, it would still not exactly be the ideal solution. Why? Well, ask yourself: who is in a better position to create your portfolio, a person like me who only got a chance to speak to you for a few hours (if that) or you, the one living with yourself 24/7?

This is what the Personalized Portfolio Principle, a term I've coined in the *Wealth Management 2.0* book, is all about. One-size-fits-all solutions are like checks. They may look/sound good but it ultimately all depends on whether or not there's enough money in the account in question. This is precisely why I will never be a fan of one-size-fits-all solutions.

Even broad and seemingly harmless advice such as "real estate is worth investing in" can prove to be dangerous to quite a few people. Egypt is just one example of a country which can be considered unstable. There are millions upon millions of people living in similar environments and some of them will be readers of this book. This is precisely why I think not once but dozens of times before giving advice.

Now okay, if I'm 100% positive my advice applies to everyone or pretty much everyone then sure, I'll go ahead and share it. But realistically speaking, this doesn't happen all that frequently, which is why I've decided to recommend the Personalized Portfolio Principle. Therefore, rather than telling you whether or not you should invest in real estate, I'll do something completely different. I will tell you under which circumstances real estate investments make sense as well as under which circumstances they do not so that you can make the final decision yourself.

A reader from the Middle East will figure out for himself why real estate investments might not be a good solution in his case and the same principle is valid for each and every reader. I've given this issue quite a bit of thought and quite frankly, it's the only coherent as well as intellectually honest approach I could come up with. It might not be perfect but it's without a doubt the best I can do.

The Personalized Portfolio Principle isn't particularly hard to understand. It all boils down to acknowledging the fact that deciding what to invest in is your responsibility. Making the initial decisions, reassessing your portfolio and so on, these are things you could but should not outsource. Yes, you could let other people make decisions on your behalf but it would, in my honest opinion at least, be a very bad idea. Ridiculously bad.

Before continuing, let's go ahead and articulate **Rule #1**:

You and you alone should be responsible for all major financial decisions.

Rule #2 should be just as obvious if you've paid attention thus far:

Don't assume you can predict the future. Instead of being ashamed of your limitations, embrace them.

Think about it this way: what would you choose between a strategy which is definitely wrong and one about which you don't know whether or not it will prove to be appropriate? I don't know about you but I for one would choose the second option. As I've explained rather obsessively throughout this book, humans are terrible at predicting the future. They can't. You can't. I can't. Gurus can't. Pundits can't. Therefore, any strategy which revolves around predicting the future is 100% wrong.

Now as far as strategies which revolve around the Personalized Portfolio Principle are concerned, I don't know whether or not yours will do okay. I honestly don't know, nor do I have any kind of control over your actions. What I do know however is you are at least building on a solid foundation by acknowledging and actually embracing your limitations. Believe it or not, this actually gives you an edge over most investors, who prefer to blissfully live in a fantasy world where either they or their guru of choice possess magical powers (or amazingly accurate crystal balls) which enable them to see the future. Don't be ashamed of your limitations, accept them and even more so, make them the foundation of your financial resilience strategy.

That being stated, let's move on to **Rule #3**:

Put together a list of assets you consider desirable and make having exposure to each and every one a priority.

In a perfect society, all asset classes would be desirable. In the real world however, there are multiple variables at play. Again, please keep the Middle Eastern real estate example in mind, it illustrates rather clearly how there are a series of factors based on which certain asset classes should be given less or more weight. To the person from the Middle East we've referred to previously, real estate represents a less attractive asset class than to someone from the United States or Germany for socio-political reasons.

Instead of generalizing, simply put together a list of assets you personally consider desirable. If your country has a great track record of respecting property rights, real estate would be a good choice. If not, well… it wouldn't. The same principle is valid for all of the other asset classes, so it's all a matter of analyzing your current situation and making some decisions.

Time for **Rule #4**:

Is there an asset class you're in a better position to invest in than most people? Then feel free to have a bit more exposure to it.

Don't go overboard by putting all of your eggs in the same basket but leverage your competitive edge if you have one. For example, let's assume you work with Silicon Valley startups for a living. You're in touch with lots and lots of people involved in the tech space and are therefore in a considerably better position to invest in tech stocks than most individuals.

Instead of only relying on whatever research you've conducted online, you'll be able to leverage your own experience and this most certainly constitutes a competitive edge. The same way, you're in a better position to invest in antique coins than most people if you're actually running an antique coin business or hey, even if you're a history teacher. The list of examples could go on and at the end of the day, the fundamental question you should be asking yourself is this: what is the asset class or what are the asset classes about which I have more knowledge than the average investor? Don't let your competitive advantage go to waste.

Okay, let's move on to **Rule #5**

Take the worst deflation scenario you can envision and ask yourself if your current strategy would help you at least remain in reasonably good financial shape. Now take the worst inflation scenario and do the same. Then, proceed in the same manner with a political turmoil/instability scenario.

It's pretty much impossible to put together a strategy which enables you to actually thrive in all three situations, this shouldn't even be your goal. Your strategy should simply enable you to land on your feet, so to speak. These three negative scenarios represent a decent enough starting point. You should have exposure to at the very least some assets which would constitute a safety net in the event of a deflationary scenario, an inflationary scenario and a scenario which involves political turmoil/instability (everything from unrest to conflicts).

Do keep in mind however that an asset class which performs well in an inflationary environment tends to perform rather poorly in a deflationary one, for example. Again, don't make the mistake of assuming your strategy should make it possible to thrive in all three cases. The name of the game is minimizing losses and landing on your feet, don't lose sight of that.

Now it's time for the exact opposite of the previous rule, here's **Rule #6:**

Take the most optimistic scenario you can envision, where overall bullishness abounds and ask yourself if your strategy would make it possible for you to grab a decent enough piece of the pie.

Don't make the mistake of only following Rule #5 and forgetting all about this one. The Personalized Portfolio Principle isn't just about surviving adverse economic conditions, it's also about thriving under good economic ones. If you're always on the defensive, then chances are that whenever society is dealing with ideal or close to ideal economic circumstances, everyone else will be making money while you're still in doom and gloom mode.

We can't have that. Even if you believe society is in for a catastrophic awakening and the world as we know it is about to end, you should still want to make as much money as possible under bullish scenarios. After all, the more money you have at your disposal, the better prepared you'll be when the proverbial you know what hits the fan. See what I did there?

And last but not least, it's time for **Rule #7:**

Every once in a while, question absolutely everything about your strategy and reassess your portfolio.

The most important aspect you need to understand is this: a strategy which worked last year won't necessarily work well now. It might but then again, it might not. The economy can change in a fundamental manner faster than one might think, you cannot afford not to stay informed and with that stated, I hope you now understand what the Personalized Portfolio Principle is all about.

Can I guarantee your results will be amazing? No, I cannot.

What I can however guarantee is that unlike most investors, you'll be building on a solid foundation by acknowledging the limitations us humans have and, dare I say it, actually assuming responsibility for your actions. Without this mindset, I for one don't see how someone could ever become truly financially resilient.

Chapter 5.2.2: What Should You Invest In?

In the world of economics, perhaps more so than in other industries, people love picking sides. A precious metal enthusiast for example will sometimes continuously bash stocks. The same way, stock investors will laugh at those who spend their money on shiny rocks. I prefer a more balanced approach.

Ultimately, I see a little to no benefit in considering one asset class or another the enemy. Each one has its pros as well as cons and throughout the following pages, I will be referring to pretty much all assets I consider worth investing in. And I am pretty generous in that respect. A lot of authors simply throw percentages out there like for example that you should invest x% of your money in stocks, y% in real estate, z% in precious metals and so on. It's an approach I personally don't believe it.

Why? Primarily for two reasons:

- First of all, as mentioned elsewhere as well, you live with yourself 24/7 and are therefore in a much better position to put together a strategy for your needs than I could ever be. You know yourself or should know yourself, you understand your needs and so on. I don't. Other economists don't. It's our role as economists to give you the tools you need to figure these things out yourself. Economists aren't supposed to make life-defining decisions for you and when they do it, they usually do a pretty poor job simply because they'll never be as well-positioned as you to make such decisions

- The second reason is represented by the fact that in our anomaly-filled world, things are extremely fluid. You're reading this book right now but I'm basically planting seeds in your mind that will manifest themselves in the future as well. The words you're reading right now will, in one way or another, affect your future decisions because the information we expose ourselves to does tend to inevitably alter our way of thinking

There's no way for me to know for sure what the future holds and for this reason, I'd much rather help my readers become resilient than try to predict the future and tell them what they should do ahead of time. Just wait for things to unfold and if you're flexible as well as resilient, you'll have no trouble adapting.

That being stated, let's not forget what our main goal is here. The goal of the book in general is teaching readers how to adopt a proper strategy when it comes to financial storms. The goal of this chapter is helping you become more resilient and the goal of this specific section is teaching you everything I know about financial resilience. I'll be analyzing various asset classes as of this point and will be highlighting the pros and cons of each, especially with respect to the financial resilience dimension.

I will start by analyzing let's call them "status quo" assets or in other words, the asset classes everyone or pretty much everyone has heard about, the asset classes we are all used to. The main advantage associated with investing in them is the fact that you are not venturing into the unknown and also, there is no such thing as a portfolio which shouldn't include them. They have their very well-defined role and I firmly believe you should have exposure to such assets. Now some of these status quo assets are what I like to call fair-weather assets or assets which perform well when things are going great. There are however also assets which tend to be good performers during periods of turmoil, I choose to call them life jacket assets. Finally, some assets aren't necessarily always driven by market sentiment and I consider those sentiment-neutral assets.

The second category of assets can be considered "trailblazer assets" for the simple reason that by investing in them, you're blazing trails or at least generally speaking, are investing in something considerably less proven than the status quo assets. The main advantage of these assets is the fact that since we're talking about something new, opportunities abound, considerably more so than in the world of status quo assets. Unfortunately, they come with a higher risk factor as well. Make no mistake, there's no such thing as a portfolio for which these assets don't represent a good choice. Aside from their higher potential of making you money, they also bring some unique advantages in the realm of resilience to the game. Just like with the status quo assets, some of these trailblazer assets perform well when things are great, others are antifragile, whereas certain assets are of course sentiment-neutral.

As an investor, I am and always will be a fan of smart diversification. I don't believe in telling people to spread themselves too thin and grab a bite of absolutely everything but at the same time, I firmly believe that by leveraging the power of smart diversification and owning desirable status quo as well as trailblazer assets, you'll be positioning yourself quite well and will hopefully be on your way to financial resilience.

Chapter 5.2.3: Status Quo Assets

I think it makes sense to start with the assets that pretty much everyone knows about. It's always easier to discuss the familiar, so let's start by doing that. Please note that there's a huge difference between simply knowing an asset class exists and actually understanding it. Needless to say, we'll be focusing on the latter through this section and will be analyzing the following asset classes in detail:

- Stocks
- Real estate
- Precious metals
- Cash and cash equivalents
- Bonds
- Art and antiques

The common denominator is obviously the fact that these are assets pretty much everyone has at least heard about. However, there are quite a few fundamental differences between them and as such, I have decided to separate them into three distinct categories so as to keep things logical and coherent:

1. Fair-weather assets, in other words assets which perform well when the market itself is doing good and I would put real estate and stocks in this category

2. Life jacket assets or assets that do the exact opposite, by performing well when things are gloomy and in this category, I would include cash and cash equivalents as well as, of course, precious metals

3. The final category is represented by assets I like to call sentiment-neutral. This is a trickier asset class because its performance isn't as driven by market sentiment. The two final status quo assets will be included in this category, bonds on the one hand and art & antiques on the other

I believe I've provided an accurate overview of status quo assets and as such, it is now time to dig deeper and analyze each category as well as of course the asset classes within it in detail. Time to roll up our sleeves and get started!

Chapter 5.2.3.1: Fair-Weather Status Quo Assets

A lot of those who bought this book, the overwhelming majority I'd say, have done so because they are worried. About the state of the economy, about the financial future of their families and so on. Their heart is definitely in the right place. Unfortunately, most of them fall into a pattern of making mistakes that I've noticed over the years as an economist.

They invest so much time, money and energy preparing for disasters that may or may not materialize that they end up forgetting about how important it is to also "prepare" for positive scenarios. In fact, even if the pessimistic scenario you envision will ultimately materialize, it might take far more time than you expected and as such, wouldn't it be a good idea to also collect profits when times are good?

A quote famously attributed to Keynes speaks for itself:

"The market can stay irrational longer than you can stay solvent."

A good example is represented by those who were shocked by what happened in 2007-2008. The Great Recession had such a significant impact on them that as of that point, they spent every waking moment preparing for the next crisis. They stayed far away from stocks, raised an eyebrow whenever someone even mentioned the possibility of investing in real estate and so on. They were in 100% crisis mode despite the fact that as of a certain point, there was no longer an actual crisis to speak of.

Now I realize that many of you, if we had a face-to-face conversation, would start telling me about how the authorities through their reactions only prolonged the inevitable and perhaps even made things worse but the thing is, I actually agree with you. I happen to share the opinion that nothing meaningful has changed for the better after the crisis and even more so, that a lot of things are worse. That the "Too Big to Fail" institutions got even bigger and so on.

This doesn't however change the fact that the markets had a great run after the Great Recession or that real estate values went up as well after the crash.

What I'm trying to say is that by continuously being in crisis mode, you're not able to benefit during periods when the market feels differently. Even more so, to continue my example, those who wanted to protect themselves have in a lot of cases been investing very aggressively in gold and silver. However, over the past couple of years, precious metals have underperformed the stock market for example.

As a result, those who were continuously in crisis mode after the Great Recession have not only dealt with opportunity costs or in other words they didn't just miss out on the opportunity to make money but even worse, the investments they did make ended up proving to be poor choices. The main lesson which needs to be learned in my opinion is the fact that even if you're ultimately right, you might end up losing all of your money by the time the scenario you envisioned actually ends up manifesting itself.

This section is here to help you avoid that. Let's analyze the two status quo assets which, as ironic as it may seem to those who know that fundamentally speaking nothing has changed for the better after the crisis, outperformed asset classes such as precious metals: real estate and stocks.

We'll start with real estate.

In my opinion at least, real estate is without a doubt the most romantic asset class. With which other asset class do we have such a deeply ingrained relationship? Since pretty much forever, we humans needed a roof over our heads. The desire to possess said roof is so deeply ingrained in our DNA it's highly unlikely people will ever stop longing after their own home.

Some might argue giving too much importance to real estate is an overly consumerism-influenced view of life. You for example might value experiences more, another person might value something completely different and so on. I'm not saying the status quo on real estate is right or wrong, the situation is what it is and I'm simply trying to illustrate how things stand for most individuals (again, most, what I've said may very well not apply to you).

But enough with the chit-chat.

It's time to move on to the rational dimension and determine whether or not investing in real estate is the right solution in your case. To make things easier to understand, I'll start by referring to the scenarios in which investing in real estate is a bad idea.

Let me just put it this way: if property rights aren't respected the way they should be in your country or you have valid reasons to believe they won't be respected in the future (for political instability-related reasons, for example), don't even think about touching real estate. Stay far, far away and focus on asset classes which make more sense for your specific situation, unless of course you find the idea of having your real estate confiscated appealing. All in all, this much is certain: in all scenarios which revolve around an improper attitude toward property rights… just say no.

But you do need a roof over your head, do you not?

Yes, you do and it is indeed a fair argument. Fortunately though, there are alternatives such as renting for the time being or even indefinitely, continuing to live with your parents for a while and so on. While they might not seem like brilliant solutions, they do put a roof over your head and just think about how many people ruined their lives due to over-extending themselves for real estate-related purposes.

It's ultimately all a matter of figuring out whether the pros outweigh the cons to a decent enough degree to make purchasing a home better than the alternatives you'd have at your disposal. To this effect, I've decided to briefly enumerate the pros as well as cons associated with real estate as an asset class. Feel free to add or remove items from my list, it is by no means definitive and in fact, should represent nothing more than a starting point.

I'll start with the pros:

- You're investing in something durable. Land, for example, has been around for… well, I don't even know where to start. Let's just say it's been around for quite a while and leave it at that. Real estate is something one can pass on to the next generation(s) and you have to admit, it's very hard not to understand why people consider this appealing

- There's no counterparty risk. If you invest in stocks and use a broker, there's always the risk that the brokerage company in question goes bust, on top of the obvious risk which is a stock market slump or the price depreciation of whichever stocks you have exposure to. With real estate, the counterparty risk variable disappears

- The personal dimension of a home purchase cannot be disregarded. The feeling that you own your home is something special and while it's not something one can place a price tag on, it would be unfair not to consider it a pro. You and your family will feel more secure deep down inside, most certainly an important advantage

- In the long run, investing in real estate can be a decent way to protect your wealth. I'll elaborate a bit later on. While the returns probably won't be spectacular over a long timeframe, they have thus far (historically speaking) been enough to at least enable you as a real estate investor to keep up with inflation. Again, think of real estate as more of a way to protect/preserve your wealth than as a get rich quick scheme

… and here are the cons:

- It's impossible to take your real estate with you if something bad happens to your country. You can't exactly put your real estate in a backpack and flee. For example, back when Jews had to leave Germany, they had to give up on all of their real estate. You can take gold with you, you can take cash with you but definitely not real estate

- In a lot of countries, real estate-related expenses tend to be on the high side. What are real estate-related expenses, you might ask? Well, everything which requires you to reach for your wallet. From the transaction costs you incur when buying and/or selling to things like property taxes and various repairs, it definitely adds up

- Getting scammed is not outside the realm of possibility. You can even lose money during a real estate boom if you make uninspired purchases. When buying real estate, be sure to always keep your eyes wide open for more or less hidden flaws or anything negative for that matter. Are your neighbors reasonable? How safe is the neighborhood? The list of questions you should be asking yourself can go on and on

- Selling real estate is not exactly easy in a lot of cases. If you own a stock portfolio and need to free up some cash, all it takes is a few clicks and bam, you sold some stocks and the money you need might even arrive in your bank account the same day. Selling a home is definitely not as easy. You have to list it, wait for buyers, negotiate and then ultimately (hopefully) seal the deal. Under certain market circumstances, it can take multiple months until you manage to actually sell your home

These were the basics, if you will and the next step is (naturally) asking yourself how much you can expect to make as a real estate investor. I'll be referring to US data since we have a lot of information to work with and I'm sure the numbers when it comes to your country (if you're not from the US) won't be identical. This doesn't matter because my main goal is definitely not providing a set-in-stone percentage but rather comparing real estate to the other asset classes in order to help you set realistic return-related expectations.

Preserving wealth is the name of the game.

I want to make this perfectly clear. If you're investing in real estate with the intention of getting rich, you're doing it wrong. Now sure, you might get rich, I'm not saying you can't. And I know, quite a few people got rich through real estate but those are exceptions rather than the norm. In my honest opinion, the mindset you should be approaching real estate with is this:

"I want to preserve my wealth by combining business with pleasure."

You get to have that warm and fuzzy feeling associated with owning your home and preserve your wealth while you're at it. Not a bad deal at all, if you ask me. It's of the utmost importance to understand what real estate investing is and isn't about, to have the proper mindset. I can't stress this enough: don't expect to get rich or even enhance your wealth in a significant manner, preserving it is the name of the game and there's nothing wrong with this state of affairs.

Nobel Prize-winning professor Robert Shiller published the second edition of his *Irrational Exuberance* book[38] back in 2005 (not all that long before the crash of 2007-2008), a book inspired by Alan Greenspan's famous (or infamous, depending on who you ask) "irrational exuberance" quote. It covered the US real estate bubble and managed to address quite a few myths, if you will.

He gave us extremely juicy historical data, going back all the way to 1890 and until 2005, data which made one thing perfectly clear: adjusted for inflation, prices grew by 103% during the 1890-2005 period. In other words, your "real" returns were to the tune of less than 1% per year. Quite frankly, the returns aren't bad if you view them under the paradigm that real estate isn't supposed to make you rich, it's supposed to help you preserve your wealth over long periods of time.

And in the US for example, it did.

You made enough to offset inflation and even a bit more. While these results seemed disappointing to those who read Shiller's book back in 2005 (at close to the height of the real estate bubble, which peaked in 2006) and thought real estate is a surefire way to get filthy rich, they're really not disappointing at all. They simply illustrate the message I'm trying to get across with respect to the expectations one should have.

Again, we're talking about "real" returns, returns adjusted for inflation. One of the most important points Robert Shiller makes is how wrong it is to compare simple rather than inflation-adjusted returns. You might consider inflation something pretty much negligible but it isn't, it all adds up as the years go by. One example he gave was the sale of a home in 2005 for ten times more than the 1945 price. The 900% return may seem impressive but after you also factor in inflation, we're left with the exact same conclusion: the annualized return was under 1%.

For this reason, expecting the same returns as with stocks makes little sense, despite them both being fair-weather status quo assets. We're talking about two entirely different asset classes which should be approached with entirely

---

[38] Robert J. Shiller. *Irrational Exuberance.* Princeton, New Yersey: Princeton University Press, 2005.

different mindsets. You invest in stocks to enhance your wealth, whereas you invest in real estate to preserve it. Fair enough? Historically speaking, even if we were to analyze data from "favorable" periods (before the crash of 2007-2008) and compare our findings to stock market returns, real estate still wouldn't manage to win, as stocks still did better.

Does everyone know about real estate and stocks?

Yes, I therefore consider them status quo assets.

Do both tend to do better when things are going well with the economy?

Yes, which is why we can consider them both fair-weather status quo assets.

But this is where the similarities end.

Fuad Hasanov and Douglas C. Dacy[39] published a paper in *Real Estate Economics* back in 2009 which explains that from 1952 to 2005 (so before the real estate bubble burst, a data selection which let's say favors this asset class), the real return was still a bit lower than that of the S&P 500, 6.9% compared to 7.3%. This is not bad at all, don't get me wrong but after real estate slowed down, stocks had a tricky but ultimately better trajectory so again, the 1952-2005 range tends to put real estate in a good light.

Let's not forget one aspect: the analysis ends in 2005, so before the real estate bubble started bursting. At the end of the year 2005, the Case-Shiller Composite 20 home price index was at the 202.16 level. Six years later, back in October 2011, it was 31% lower, in other words at the 138.56 level. You'd be tempted to say investors lost 31% but if you also factor in inflation (15%, in our case), the real loss was more to the tune of 46%, which is quite spectacular.

This brings us to another aspect I continuously address in this book. Analyzing historical data is great because it gives us yet another argument but don't for a second assume this means you can predict the future by looking at the past. The next 10, 20 or 100 years may very well prove to be completely

---

[39] Fuad Hasanov and Douglas C. Dacy. "Yet Another View on Why a Home Is One's Castle." *Real Estate Economics.* March 1, 2009.
http://papers.ssrn.com/sol3/papers.cfm?abstract_id=1395426.

different. By all means, analyze historical data because it helps paint a clear picture of what happened but don't make the mistake of considering a tool for predicting the future. Nobody can predict the future in an accurate as well as consistent manner in my opinion. Not using technical analysis, not using historical arguments. It's just not possible. All in all, what's important is this: have reasonable expectations.

Next, I'd like to share a few practical tips which I hope you'll find useful:

- The ideal situation would be not having to resort to a loan. In my country, real estate prices aren't low but still, they're not as high as in places such as Canada or Australia, so I managed to purchase my home in an all-cash transaction. Should you do the same? In my opinion yes, this would be the ideal scenario but it doesn't mean I'm against the idea of taking out a mortgage. If the interest rate is reasonable and you're close to 100% sure you can afford the monthly payments even in an absolute-worst-case scenario, go for it.

  But I wasn't kidding with the worst-case scenario part. Way too many people assume that simply because they can *currently* afford the monthly payments, taking out a mortgage is a good idea. It's definitely not because what happens if a few years down the road, the person or family in question suffers an income reduction? All of a sudden, mortgage payments which were reasonably affordable are out of reach. Expect the best but plan for the worst. If you could barely afford the monthly payments now, think twice before signing on the dotted line. Furthermore, if you aren't able to afford at least a decent down-payment, consider it a warning sign

- I'm sure a lot of you have heard the popular saying which encourages you to buy the worst house in the best location. Now on the one hand, it makes sense. In the world of real estate, location is extremely important. However, do take this saying with a grain of salt. For example, some homes might be in such poor condition that they're basically scams and there just isn't a way to realistically and cost-effectively fix them. Unless you can acquire them at pennies on the dollar, look elsewhere.

The fundamental principle behind the previously mentioned saying is this: if you acquire the worst home in the best neighborhood, you can fix it up and the value increases quite a bit. After all, you can fix a house but it's impossible to do anything to change the location. This is a fair enough argument but again, only if the home in question is in reasonably good enough shape for you to at the very least have something to work with

- Speaking of repairs, they're not just a variable in "worst home in the best neighborhood" situations. In a lot of cases, the home you just bought needs at least a bit of work, not just if it's the worst property in the neighborhood. Don't make the mistake of assuming all you have to do is buy the house and move in. Sometimes, it can be the case but more often than not, repairs will be necessary.

Always take all the potential costs into consideration in order to determine whether or not the asking price for a certain property is fair. Think of a worst-case scenario situation, determine roughly how much it would cost you to fix the home, add the purchase price and if you're happy with the number in question, make the purchase. Work with the worst-case scenario situation because on the one hand, you'll be prepared for it and on the other hand, you'll be pleasantly surprised should it not materialize. Either way, you will at the very least not be caught off-guard

- Don't forget to negotiate. You'll never receive a discount unless you ask for one. It's impossible to tell you how significant the margin will be, as this varies from neighborhood to neighborhood, not even merely from city to city, let alone country to country. Regardless, don't be afraid to ask for a discount and make offers which are lower than the asking price. Worst-case scenario? They'll just say no, it's not the end of the world.

However, if you have valid reasons to believe there are other motivated buyers for a specific property, don't wait too long or you might lose a decent deal just because you wanted to haggle for peanuts. Negotiate but don't get carried away. Always ask yourself if the potential savings are tempting enough to offset the risk of losing that property

- Also (and this is, strangely enough, something a lot of people ignore), don't underestimate the importance of… you know, actually liking the home you're about to buy. Yes, you should think about whether or not it's a good deal and yes, you should wear your wealth management hat as well. But don't forget this is the place you'll be living in from now on, possibly for several years.

  Your home is the place where you'll raise your children, for example. It's more than just a number-based purchase. If you don't like the property you're thinking about buying, don't. Not even if it's a good deal. You will eventually find a good deal on a property you actually like, never forget why real estate is (as mentioned at the beginning of this subchapter) the most romantic asset class

- Up until this point, I've mainly referred to investing in real estate as in buying the home you and your family will be living in. But what about buying and then making money by collecting rent? It may sound great and the returns may seem impressive on paper but personally, I'd advise against this approach. Why? Because there can be so much work involved that it's closer to the idea of running a business than to something one could consider reasonably passive.

  You have to find tenants, tend to their needs, repair things once/if they've been broken and so on. Yes, you can make money (although after eliminating expenses from the equation, the returns probably won't be as impressive as you'd expect them to be) but it would be kind of like learning how to master a new profession from scratch. You already have a lucrative occupation (doing whatever it is you currently do to earn a living), do you really want to invest the time/energy it takes to learn something completely different?

- The same principle or okay, almost the same principle, is valid when it comes to the idea of flipping homes. In theory, it sounds great and everything but how viable is this approach really? If you could simply buy a home, hold for a few years and then sell without doing anything else then sure, go for it. However, things are usually a bit more complicated.

If you want decent returns, you'll probably have to buy properties which require work. You'll have to deal with contractors, will probably get fleeced at least at the beginning and all in all, we're right back to the previously mentioned argument: yes, it can be done but there's just way too much time/energy involved for this approach to make sense

- A decent alternative would be having some REIT exposure or in other words, investing in real estate other than your home but without the hassle associated with doing work yourself. Now of course, the returns will obviously be lower than if you were to actually purchase properties yourself but if you factor in the time you would have had to spend and the energy necessary to get things done, I'm sure you'll be willing to give up the extra revenue in question.

    You'd basically be receiving the best of both worlds, so to speak. Now for most individuals, owning their home should be more than enough real estate exposure but if you want to take things to the next level, I firmly believe the REIT approach is considerably better than the idea of buying properties yourself in order to collect rent or flip them

As I hope you now understand, there are basically two dimensions to real estate. On the one hand, it's an asset class which tends to be reasonably effective at helping you preserve wealth and when times are good, even enhance it. The other dimension is the emotional one, therein lies the main difference between real estate and other asset classes: you actually live in the property you invested in, it's not just a piece of paper (stocks), a number on a screen (bank account) or a shiny rock (precious metals). If you keep my advice in mind and make a smart purchase, you can (and I sincerely hope you will) get the best of both worlds.

As a quick recap:

1. Everyone knows about real estate, it's definitely a status quo asset

2. It tends to perform better when times are good, which is why I'd call it a fair-weather asset. However, do keep in mind that this isn't an asset class you invest in if you want to get rich
3. At the very least owning your home is something I'd strongly recommend
4. You can of course also invest in real estate other than your home and collect rent income but this approach is not for everyone

That being stated, it's time to move on to a fair-weather asset which complements real estate nicely.

You've guessed it, <u>stocks</u>!

So far, I've covered the most romantic asset class, real estate. Now it's time to focus on a less romantic but at least historically speaking, a far more profitable one: stocks. If you think about it for a moment, it all makes perfect sense. Fundamentally speaking, of course stocks "should" be more profitable than other assets and I'll try to explain why.

When you invest in gold, not much happens from a "how does the economy benefit?" perspective. You buy a shiny rock and it just sits there. When investing in real estate by purchasing your home, it's kind of 50%-50%: on the one hand, there is definitely economic activity involved in a lot of cases (the people who build/fix your home, the real estate agent and so on) but on the other hand, it's also a purchase you make for yourself, for the comfort of your family.

Stocks, on the other hand, are a "business only" asset class. Staring at a stock certificate or at a computer screen is considerably less fun than looking at a shiny gold coin or at the home you just bought for your family but from an economic perspective, the benefits are greater for all parties involved. For you, the economy of your country, you name it. By investing in stocks, you're basically making it easier for companies to secure funding. If your country has a developed stock market which is doing well, it's definitely an indicator that its economy is on the right track.

Over the past years and especially after the 2007-2008 financial crisis, the stock market has gotten somewhat of a sleazy reputation. It's associated with shady Wall Street-type individuals, with the proverbial 1% and the participation rate among average individuals is not even high when for example the S&P 500 is breaking records. Think of it as a "the rich are getting richer" situation in which the average individual no longer trusts this asset class and therefore, most people simply refuse to participate, leaving the deep-pocketed big boys as the main beneficiaries of stock market upticks.

This just doesn't make sense.

Stocks are not inherently evil, nor are they inherently good. They are what they are. A tool. A way for companies to generate liquidity by giving you a piece of the action. You shouldn't choose to disregard this asset class simply because some wolves of Wall Street are acting in a dishonest manner, just like you shouldn't stop using knives just because murderers use them as well. By not including stocks in your portfolio, you would in my opinion be committing a grave mistake.

Here is a quote worth keeping in mind:

"One dollar invested in stocks in 1802 would have grown to $8.8 million in 2003, in bonds to $16,064, in Treasury Bills to $4,575, and in gold to $19.75."

The statement in question was made by Jeremy J. Siegel, who wrote *Stocks for the Long Run*[40] back in 1994 (the fifth edition was released in 2014). It covers data since as early as 1802, mostly related to the US stock market. He's a buy and hold guy who calculated that over the past 200 years, the average returns adjusted for inflation have been 6.5% - 7%.

Even he however expects returns to be lower over the next years and it's easy to understand why, in a low interest rate environment such as the one we find ourselves in. Please also remember what I've been repeating time and time again. Historical examples are relevant, they represent decent arguments but are by no means indicative of the future. Sure, stocks have performed well over the past century. Historically speaking, this is pretty much undeniable, as I'm sure you'll agree.

Does this mean they'll do well over the next century as well?

---

[40] Jeremy J. Siegel. *Stocks for the Long Run.* New York City: McGraw-Hill Companies, 1994.

Simply put, no. History tells us what happened, not what's going to happen. Plain and simple. Some people believe they can predict the future by analyzing the past. I don't. I simply believe analyzing the past is useful because it helps us draw conclusions which enable us to do well as investors. They help us understand human nature for example but they most certainly do not make it possible for us to develop superpowers and see the future.

Is this historical data a compelling argument for investing in stocks? Yes.

Can we be 100% certain history will repeat itself? No.

Please also note that most of the historical data I'll be referring to will be related to the United States. As far as most of the other countries are concerned, we unfortunately don't have as much historical data one can consider reliable when it comes to their stock markets. Furthermore, you should never lose sight of the fact that the United States stock market was the clear "winner" of the previous century and here's what I mean.

Back in 2002, Elroy Dimson, Paul Marsh and Mike Staunton wrote a paper entitled "Triumph of the Optimists: 101 Years of Global Investment Returns"[41] which covers data from 1900 to 2000 and makes it clear just how much of a winner US equities have been in the previous century. Back in 1990, the US stock market represented 22% of the worldwide stock market whereas in 2000, this percentage increased to 46%.

Other countries also did well. For example Japan, from 4% back in 1900 to 13% in 2000. On the other hand though, there was a clear decline in other cases, for example the UK went from 12% to 8%. In Europe's case, the decline is even more pronounced. In 1900, it was at 25% or 29% if you also include Austria-Hungary and in 2000, it declined to just 13%. The same way, Russia was at 11% in 1900, whereas in 2000, it's pretty much nowhere to be found.

So, should you or shouldn't you include non-US stocks in your portfolio?

To answer this question, I'd like to refer to a Vanguard paper written by

---

[41] Elroy Dimson, Paul Marsh and Mike Staunton. *Triumph of the Optimists: 101 Years of Global Investment Returns.* Princeton, New Yersey: Princeton University Press, 2002.

Christopher B. Philips[42] back in 2012. Unfortunately, most of the data related to developed markets only goes back to 1970 whereas when it comes to emerging markets, it only goes back to 1985. From a diversification perspective I'd say sure, having *some* exposure to international stocks makes sense. For example, international stocks outperformed US stocks back in the mid-90s yet underperformed in the 2000s.

It's important to note we cannot simply call them "international" stocks, the term is far too broad. I'd recommend keeping these two categories in mind when referring to non-US equities: on the one hand, developed countries such as Germany or Japan and on the other hand, emerging markets such as the BRICS nations (Brazil, Russia, India, China and South Africa), Eastern Europe and so on.

Again, we don't have a lot of historical data but based on the post-1985 information (1985-2011 in our case) we can analyze, emerging markets have outperformed, with an average yearly return of 13.1% versus 9.2% for developed economies. Do keep in mind however that the volatility has also been greater (24.4% versus 17.8%) but this should come as no surprise.

All in all, I tend to agree with the conclusion of the Vanguard paper: a 20% allocation (spread across developed as well as emerging markets) would be a decent enough starting point, even all the way up to 40%. If for example you live outside the United States and believe in the viability of your local stock market, it would make sense to bring your level of exposure closer to 40%. For someone living in the US, the incentive to take things all the way to 40% might not be as great.

Thus far, I believe we've established the following:

1. You should most definitely invest in stocks
2. Investing in non-US stocks (20% to 40% of your stock portfolio) makes sense

When it comes to the US vs. non-US stock market exposure dimension (60% - 80% vs. 20 – 40%), I don't mind throwing a percentage out there. Again, I

---

[42] Cristopher B. Philips. "Considerations for Investing in Non-US Equities." *Vanguard.* March 1, 2012. https://personal.vanguard.com/pdf/icriecr.pdf.

tend to agree with Vanguard's approach. However, you might be asking yourself why I'm not telling you which percentage of your net worth you should allocate toward stocks, why am I not giving you a percentage in this case as well?

It's because in this case, I don't believe the "one-size-fits-all" approach is ideal. Please remember what I wrote when comparing developed markets to emerging markets. Yes, returns tend to be higher but the volatility is higher as well. The same principle is valid when comparing stocks to other asset classes. Yes, the returns are higher but you should expect high volatility as well.

What does this mean?

Well, in the long run yes, the returns are amazing. However, stock market crashes are definitely not uncommon, so you can easily see let's say 40% of the capital allocated toward stocks wiped out just like that during a crash. It has happened and will most likely happen again. If you do not like this kind of volatility, you will unfortunately be disappointed.

To do well with stocks, you have to train your stomach, so to speak. If you panic during each and every financial crisis, I'm sorry but your results will most likely be considerably poorer than the benchmark. Always go by the assumption that volatility is a part of the equation which isn't going anywhere. Which percentage of your net worth you should allocate in this direction depends on a few variables such as the three I'll be referring to below:

1. First of all, your age. Young people tend to be considerably less risk-averse than older individuals, so it makes sense to have a higher stock market exposure while you're young. As you grow older, your willingness to participate in the stock market might decrease and you might decide to lower the stock market exposure percentage

2. The other "high volatility" asset classes you have at your disposal. In the past, stocks were pretty much the only game in town for those who wanted to maximize returns. However, we have all sorts of exotic assets to choose from nowadays, from domain names to cryptocurrencies such as bitcoin. They will be covered later on

3. Powerful external events/shocks. The status quo is that yes, stocks generate the highest returns by far, at least when compared to other traditional asset classes (exotic assets are, again, a new variable which will be analyzed later on). However, certain meaningful events (the mother of all crashes, the transition to an entirely different worldwide economic system and so on) may very well shake what is now considered the very core of personal finance. I'm not saying it will without a doubt happen, I'm simply pointing out it might

All in all, you and you alone need to decide which percentage of your net worth you should allocate toward stocks based on your specific socio-economico-political situation, needs and goals. After the 2007-2008 crisis, way too many people have become overly skeptical and decided to disregard the stock market altogether. Don't be one of them, there's room for stocks in each and every portfolio, especially if you're young and not overly volatility-averse.

Fair enough?

Now, let's see how you should invest in stocks. I've put together a list of 20 tips which, if put to good use, will help you get and stay on the right track. Some of them apply to other asset classes as well but in my opinion, they're especially relevant when it comes to stocks. This is by no means a definitive list, feel free to question some of these tips, remove a few altogether and add your own:

1. Choose an index fund. For most people, the overwhelming majority in my opinion, choosing an index fund is much better than picking individual stocks or hiring a professional to do it for you. As research such as that conducted by Miguel A. Ferreira, Aneel Keswani, António F. Miguel and Sofia B. Ramos[43] proves, working with experts isn't generally the ideal choice. In their case, the conclusion was that "mutual funds underperform the market overall" and you'd think this is because fund managers make poor decisions. But no. The problem is represented by the high fees and a lot of times, even

---

[43] Miguel A. Ferreira, Aneel Keswani, António F. Miguel and Sofia B. Ramos. "The Determinants of Mutual Fund Performance: A Cross-Country Study." *Oxford University Press*. April 18, 2012. http://rof.oxfordjournals.org/content/early/2012/04/18/rof.rfs013.

if a certain fund outperformed the let's say S&P 500, you're left with less money in your hands than if you would have simply chosen an index fund which tracks the S&P 500. To put it differently, the main problem here isn't lack of competence but rather the fact that the "experts" aren't competent *enough* to justify their fees. They're good but for the most part, not good enough to leave you with enough money in your pocket after subtracting the fees

2. Don't be a day trader (someone who, as the name suggests, trades each day and is involved in lots of transactions). For the love of God, just don't. If you choose to pick stocks yourself rather than go with the previously mentioned advice of using index funds, fair enough. But don't be the type of person who buys and sells each day because the market will literally eat you alive

3. I fail to see the utility of the "buy low, sell high" advice. Everyone wants to buy low and sell high, this is pretty much obvious. Therefore, the tip in question is nothing more than hot air. It sounds good but lacks utility and applicability. You're better off taking heed of what Peter Lynch had to say: if you consider the price fair, buy. You probably won't be able to time the highs or bottoms in order to (sigh) buy low and sell high, so what? Most people aren't able to do this and those who actually did it probably got lucky

4. Understand what volatility is all about. If you're the type of person who panics the minute you're let's say 5% - 10% in the hole, stocks are not for you. Again, this brings us right back to the Peter Lynch dimension, stocks can go down in price initially and ultimately still prove to be a good deal. If you think the drop in price is only a short-term thing, hang on tight and don't let volatility "convince" you to sell too soon

5. On the other hand though, don't be afraid to sell if there are enough arguments in favor of this decision. Yes, even if it means losing money. Don't hang on to losing trades just because you won't admit to a mistake. Patience means hanging in there if you have valid reasons to believe the price will go up, not because you simply don't want to admit you were wrong. That's not patience, it's just plain stubbornness

6. The "it's far better to buy a wonderful company at a fair price than a fair company at a wonderful price" Warren Buffett quote is timeless in my opinion. Value investing definitely has its merits and I for one would also rather buy stocks in an amazing company at a decent price than in a so-so company at a steeper discount, unless of course we're talking about an absolute bargain basement price you just can't say no to

7. Imagine you'll be becoming the owner of the company/companies you're thinking about investing in, this is another Warren Buffett principle backed by sound logic. Never lose sight of the fact that at the end of the day, this is what investing in stocks ultimately means: you're giving your money to a company in exchange for a slice of the pie

8. If you're good enough at something to have a competitive edge, don't hesitate to put your knowledge to good use by investing in stocks related to the sector in question. Should those of us who earn a living online (to give an example of a category I'd include myself in) be more inclined to invest in tech stocks? Well, let me put it this way: we should be more inclined to look closely at tech stocks. Maybe we'll conclude prices are too high to be worth it, maybe not. Either way, there's no denying that our experience gives us an edge we can take advantage of

9. Understand fear and greed, as these are the human emotions which make most people lose money in the stock market. Think about it for a moment. Fortunes have been lost and will continue to be lost due to panic selling or greed-induced purchase frenzies. This has been happening since pretty much forever and these emotions aren't going anywhere

10. Don't just look at the Dow or even the S&P 500 to gauge the health of the market, also look at broader indexes such as the Russell 5000 which track more companies, as a healthy market is a market in which not just the dominant players do well. I'm not saying a market in which all indexes are doing well is without a doubt healthy (it might be in the mother of all irrational exuberance-induced bubbles), I'm simply pointing out it's an argument worth including in the equation

11. Understand the concept of counterparty risk and only work with reputable brokers. In some countries, investors are protected via government guarantees, perhaps in yours as well. In other words, you'll be reimbursed if your broker disappears. Maybe you will, sure, but just imagine all of the hassle involved. The paperwork, the time it will ultimately take until you're actually paid and so on. You're better off sticking with reputable companies, don't fall for marketing gimmicks or risk choosing a no-name company just so you can save a buck on commissions

12. Don't spend (waste) your money on "signal" services, software and what not. I've stated this time and time again: nobody can predict the future. I've mainly referred to gurus and pundits but this certainly doesn't mean the various signal services and software the Internet is polluted with represent an exception. They don't

13. Avoid penny stocks. I'm not saying you can't make money, money can be made with pretty much anything but to do well with penny stocks, you have to basically learn a new trade, there's just no way to do it in a reasonably passive manner. If you don't agree and think you can simply do it passively by using signal services for example, please re-read the previous tip

14. Don't limit yourself to looking at "fad" companies or markets, as "boring" ones deserve a place in your portfolio as well. Fad assets receive much more attention than their more boring counterparts and what does this mean? As I'm sure you suspect, it means prices will tend to be on the high side, reducing the likelihood of buying at a decent price

15. Don't forget to take money off the table every once in a while. If the market seems too euphoric for your taste, consider taking some money off the table. Don't take things too far however by assuming you shouldn't ride the winners, never be in a rush to sell the minute you're in the profit zone. All I'm saying is this: if you have valid reasons to believe prices are unjustifiably high, it's time to take at least some money off the table

16. Understand that entire business models can change fundamentally in a very short timeframe. Some of you surely remember how popular Nokia was back in the day, in the pre-smartphone era. At one point, if you asked two or three people what kind of a phone they had, at least one was likely to show you his Nokia. Where is Nokia now?

17. Leave your ego aside, you shouldn't invest in stocks to prove something to someone. You're in this to make money. If you've ever talked to "Wall Street types" and analyzed their attitude, you'll understand why an over-inflated ego tends to make you lose touch with reality. You think you're the best thing since sliced bread and assume you can do no wrong until reality rears its sometimes-ugly head

18. A pundit or stock picker's guess is as good as yours. If they really could predict the future, they'd be somewhere on a fancy yacht counting their billions, not being paid peanuts by TV stations to make occasional appearances. Don't get me wrong, I have nothing against those who appear on TV shows, only against those who think they can predict the future and completely lost touch with reality

19. Understand that a soaring stock market isn't necessarily indicative of a very strong "real" economy due to things like for example stock buybacks by companies who have access to cheap financing as a result of a low interest rate environment. It sounds complicated but actually isn't. Companies have access to cheaper financing than ever before, so they take advantage of this by, among other things, buying their own stocks

20. Stocks which are underperforming the market aren't necessarily bargains, there might just be something seriously wrong with their business model. This once again brings us right back to the Nokia example. If a certain stock is getting beaten and then beaten some more, it might be wise to ask yourself if there's a valid reason for its underperformance rather than assume everyone's just panic selling

These tips, in my opinion at least, should act as an anchor between you and reality. If you expected me to provide things like technical analysis advice, it means you haven't paid enough attention thus far. To let the stock market work for you, it's certainly not necessary to be a rocket scientist who uses enormous computing power and TA knowledge to try to predict the future, all you have to do is adhere to a few common-sense principles.

My main goal with this section isn't teaching you a bunch of professions. Technical analysis, real estate flipping and so on, these are all professions and to even understand the basics, a huge investment of time would be required on your part. The day only has 24 hours and by allocating time in this manner, how could you possibly continue being good (and getting better, as you should) at whatever it is you are currently doing to earn a living?

Does this mean you should be a passive investor?

Well, kind of but not really. Not really because there's no such thing as 100% passive investing. You always have to invest at least some time and some energy to make good asset allocation decisions. But, while 100% passive investing doesn't exist, being a reasonably passive investor is certainly possible and throughout this section, I will try to help you become just that.

To be perfectly honest, I think choosing a couple of index funds would be more than enough. Allocate 60% - 80% of your stock market capital toward an index fund which tracks the let's say S&P 500 and the remaining amount toward an index fund which tracks international stocks. Or okay, perhaps one which tracks developed market stocks and one for emerging markets rather than just one fund for international stocks. In my honest opinion, this approach would ultimately put you ahead of most investors, who think they or whichever guru they've chosen to follow can predict the future in an accurate and consistent manner.

If you don't want to follow my advice and decide to pick stocks yourself, no problem. I'm not saying it won't work, I'm simply saying the likelihood of generating below benchmark returns is high. Why complicate your life if you don't have to and if, even more so, there are more than enough valid arguments backed by sound research on why keeping it simple is a better approach?

I believe the approach I've suggested for the two fair-weather assets makes perfect sense.

Real estate and stocks complement one another nicely and I for one believe each and every person should have exposure to these assets. Don't try to become an expert, don't allocate too much energy toward learning the ropes. As I'm sure you've realized, a healthy dose of common sense coupled with the willingness to put the tips I've provided to good use should be more than enough.

Chapter 5.2.3.2: Life Jacket Status Quo Assets

The best time to buy a life jacket is not when you're on a sinking ship. There's a time and a place for everything. If you wait until the ship you're on starts to sink and only then begin to grab your phone or laptop and shop around for life jacket deals, then I'm sorry to have to say this but you're doing it all wrong.

The same principle is valid when protecting yourself against financial storms.

If you don't shop around for assets that protect you when financial disasters strike ahead of time, you might be in for an unpleasant surprise. Perhaps the most important mistake people make with respect to financial calamities is assuming they can simply react quickly and make financial choices after disaster strikes. That's not exactly how things work.

For example, everyone is going to want to buy gold after currencies collapse. The main problem is that if you waited until after the fact, you'd have a hard time finding people who are willing to accept your now-worthless cash and trade in their precious metals. Simply put, it's going to be impossible. Even if you don't wait until things entered the acute phase, it's still always much easier to buy ahead of time, when discounts abound. Maybe currencies start suffering but aren't exactly dead yet and you decide to buy precious metals at that point. You'll probably be able to do that but the price is going to be high and just thinking about how much cheaper you could've gotten precious metals for had you taken action sooner will make your head spin.

The best time to buy life jackets or if you will, the best time to shop around for insurance policies is always the present, when things are not in the acute phase. If you run an auto insurance company and someone comes to you, one day after his car got stolen and says he wants to buy an auto insurance plan with theft protection, you're obviously going to laugh at him. Even if you do accept, you're probably going to charge him more than the car is worth because you're running an insurance company that needs to be profitable, not a charity.

I realize most people are so deeply entrenched in their day-to-day activities that they forget to think about the future. This is understandable but not excusable. At various points throughout your existence, disaster will strike without asking for permission. Without wondering whether or not the timing is convenient for you. I don't know about you but the best way I for one know to be protected against inevitable disasters is preparing for them ahead of time.

By purchasing life jacket assets, you're doing just that.

I have decided to include a pair of assets that complement one another nicely in this category and on the one hand we're talking about cash and cash equivalents which are great at helping you cope with the immediate aftermath of a financial storm. On the other hand, precious metals might not be as good at that and even more so, might even go down in value initially but in the long run, they tend to do a good job of protecting your purchasing power.

Without further ado, let's start with <u>cash and cash equivalents</u>.

As everyone including financial geniuses such as Warren Buffett can determine, cash and cash equivalents are a walking paradox in terms of asset classes. A lot of economists roll their eyes when someone mentions them because they tend to be very poor financial choices most of the time. For example, Warren Buffet himself cannot help but notice that:

"Today, people who hold cash equivalents feel comfortable. They shouldn't. They have opted for a terrible long-term asset, one that pays virtually nothing and is certain to depreciate in value."

… but on the other hand, the same Warren Buffet admits that:

"Cash is like oxygen, you don't notice it 99.9% of the time, but when absent it is the only thing you notice."

At first glance, the quotes above seem downright contradictory. Believe it or not though, both of them make perfect sense and are equally accurate. During times which aren't let's say turbulent, holding on to cash and cash equivalents is a very bad deal. Why? Simply because as Buffett pointed out, this particular asset class pays nothing (cash) or pretty much nothing (cash equivalents), so you're guaranteed to lose purchasing power due to (you've guessed it) inflation.

On the other hand, when financial turbulence rears its ugly head, not having cash nearby can cost you quite a bit and force you to liquidate other assets at fire-sale prices. If you have cash during times of turbulence, the exact opposite is true and you can acquire highly desirable assets at deeply discounted prices. All in all, it should be obvious why cash and cash equivalents definitely have their place in absolutely every portfolio, no exceptions.

Okay, it's obvious what cash is. What about cash equivalents?

Cash equivalents are pretty much cash, in other words they're extremely easily convertible to cash. Short-term government bonds, savings accounts, bank certificates of deposit and so on. The maturity date is so close or they're so easy to convert to cash that one can conclude the volatility risk is extremely low (due to interest rate changes or other variables).

In my opinion, economists tend to include far too many assets in this class and realistically speaking, some of them wouldn't be as easily convertible to cash as you'd think during a severe liquidity crunch. If there's dismal liquidity, selling even the most liquid of assets may prove considerably harder than anticipated. Therefore, I'd recommend being brutally selective when deciding which assets from this particular asset class you will have exposure to.

It's worth noting that from 1995 to 2014, this was the only asset class with which investors encountered no yearly losses. Even bonds (fixed income) had years when losses were generated. For example, a 0.8% loss in 1999 or a 2% loss in 2013. On the other hand though, as you've most likely expected, it also had the lowest overall returns over the 1995-2014 period, it is what it is. The data I've referred to has been provided by BlackRock[44]. When referring to cash, they are actually talking about the ML US Treasury Bill 3 Month Index, based (as the name suggests) on the value of 3-month Treasury Bills.

It should be clear by now what this asset class is all about. Cash and cash equivalents basically have the least possible nominal downside (however, you

[44] BlackRock. "Asset Class Returns. A 20-Year Snapshot." *BlackRock.com*. Retrieved July 1, 2015. https://www.blackrock.com/investing/literature/investor-education/asset-class-returns-one-pager-va-us.pdf.

always lose purchasing power due to inflation, so there's real downside when adjusting for inflation). On the other hand though, they also tend to have the least attractive upside potential. Now let's move on and analyze specific options.

We'll start with bank deposits.

The return is low but in theory at least, your money is extremely safe. In the United States as well as across the European Union for example, your deposits are guaranteed up until a certain threshold. In the United States, the FDIC (Federal Deposit Insurance Corporation) guarantees bank deposits up to $250,000. In the European Union, deposits are also guaranteed but only up to 100,000 EUR.

If you have amounts which exceed 100,000 EUR if you live in the EU or $250,000 if you live in the US, I'd recommend choosing some of the best banks and investing less than 100,000 EUR or $250,000 in each so as to be covered by the deposit insurance scheme. Quite frankly, even if you have let's say 95,000 EUR and live in the European Union, I'd still recommend spreading the amount across a few banks.

Why?

Because the deposit guarantee, while nice to have as a bonus, is by no means foolproof. In the US as well as in the EU, the actual fund set up for such emergencies only contains a small percentage of the total deposit base. In other words, even if one (just one) of the bigger banks were to go bankrupt, the fund in question wouldn't have enough liquidity to cover all deposits and would need an injection of capital.

Now in the United States, which runs its own currency, this wouldn't be amazingly complicated. I'm sure few people doubt that should the need arise to cover deposits, the Federal Reserve would simply "print" the money in question. Therefore, the risk of the United States not living up to its promise is reasonably low, even if the actual fund doesn't contain enough liquidity to withstand a dramatic event. If the need arises, additional liquidity would simply be injected into the system.

If you live in the European Union on the other hand, things are a lot more complicated because EU countries don't have their own central banks.

There's one central bank (the ECB) for the entire Euro Zone and therefore, Spain for example cannot simply print the currency it takes to respect its guarantee promises. It would need approval from the ECB, the usual drama we've been used to when it comes to the EU would ensue in such a scenario and all in all, you'd have a lot more headaches as a depositor in Europe if the guarantee scheme were to actually be put to the test.

In other countries, you might not even have deposit guarantees, so it all depends on your specific situation. For someone in the US, bank deposits are extremely safe. Why? Because we're talking about the world's strongest country, which runs its own printing presses and can make good on its promise to guarantee deposits if the need to do that arises. Having the dollar as the world's reserve currency doesn't exactly hurt either. In the European Union, the risks aren't as low for the reasons I've outlined but still, they're lower than for example in countries with no guarantee scheme whatsoever.

But banks don't just fail, right?

Well, they do actually. We all know about the 2007-2008 financial crisis, so I crunched some numbers for the January 2009 - December 2014 period to be fair. In the United States alone, there were 482 bank failures during this period. I kid you not. The data has been gathered directly from the official Federal Deposit Insurance Corporation[45] website, feel free to double check. Most people tend to view banks and states as invincible, so it should come as no surprise bank deposits tend to be considered the ultimate safe haven assets. But bank defaults occurred in the past, they happen in the present and will continue to be problematic in the future as well most likely.

Does this mean keeping cash under the mattress is the only 100% safe approach?

Well… no, it doesn't. Unfortunately, there's no such thing as a 100% foolproof strategy. Each approach comes with its pros as well as cons and the same principle is valid when it comes to keeping cash under the proverbial mattress. On the one hand sure, there's no counterparty risk whatsoever, it's

---

[45] Federal Deposit Insurance Corporation. "Failed Bank List." *FDIC.gov*. Retrieved June 11, 2015. https://www.fdic.gov/bank/individual/failed/banklist.html.

just you and your money. No bank, no broker, no middle-man entity which can go bankrupt.

On the other hand though, there are other risks you need to be aware of. For example, let's assume thieves steal all of the money from the vaults of the bank branch you just gave your money to. Does this affect you? No, it doesn't. The bank would simply eat the loss, you wouldn't lose one red cent. The same way, nothing would happen to you if the bank branch in question were to burn down or be affected by a flood. It would be the bank's problem, not yours.

When storing money at home however, you have to keep these risks in mind. Someone might steal it. Or maybe instead of a burglary, you'll be dealing with a fire or a flood. These things happen, you most certainly wouldn't be the first person in the world affected by something like this. Failing to acknowledge these risks means, quite frankly, being irresponsible.

An initial word of advice: for the love of God, don't actually keep your money under the mattress. It's an expression, don't take it literally. If you're serious about keeping money at home rather than in the bank, do it right and buy a safe. Fortunately, there are several decent fire as well as waterproof safes out there at reasonable prices, so this purchase shouldn't break the bank.

If you also want a safe one can consider burglary-proof however, things won't be as simple. Finding a safe which is fire and water-resistant but doesn't cost a fortune isn't hard. Unfortunately, those safes are easy targets for even moderately skilled burglars. There are products out there which are actually close to being burglary-proof but those tend to cost a pretty penny.

Furthermore, don't forget another aspect. You might have the best safe in the world but what if a criminal breaks into your home and threatens you with a gun? It would make sense to hide your "real" safe and have a cheaper "fake safe" at home with a relatively small amount of money in it. That way, should your life end up being threatened by such a criminal, you'll simply take money from the safe in question and the burglar will most likely think it's the real one.

For most people, the following approach would be enough in my opinion:

1. Buy a decent fire and water-resistant safe, it probably won't be all that burglary-resistant but that's just the way it is, there's no such thing as a perfect deal. Unless you have literally a truckload of money at your disposal, spending a fortune on a safe just isn't worth it. Therefore, for the average individual, a decent fire/water-resistant safe should be enough, even if it would only prove let's say mediocre in the event of a burglary

2. Hide the safe in question somewhere and don't even think about telling anyone you have one. Not even your closest friends should know and I'm not saying this because I think those friends will devise a plan to rob you as soon as they find out. I'm not paranoid or at least I hope I'm not. But maybe they'll tell some friends by accident, then those friends will let others know and so on. You'd be surprised as to how information like this can travel and how it could reach the wrong ears, if you catch my drift

3. Buy a cheaper safe, put some money in it (not a huge amount but not ten dollars either) and use it as the "fake safe" I've mentioned previously in case you end up being threatened by criminals. In most cases, as long as everything seems reasonably credible, you should be able to trick the burglars in question and get away with it. They threaten you and you give them the money from the fake safe, end of story. But again, everything should be believable. Don't use the cheapest safe you can find and put something like $100 in it, don't underestimate the intelligence of the average burglar

These are some common-sense recommendations with respect to keeping cash at home. Feel free to come up with your own strategy or alter mine. Be creative because at the end of the day, your wealth is on the line. Thus far, we've covered two options: bank deposits on the one hand and keeping cash at home on the other. These are in my opinion the best choices when it comes to this asset class.

But what about the other options?

As mentioned at the beginning of this subchapter, you have to be brutally selective because in the event of a credit crunch, a lot of the so-called cash equivalents would prove to not actually be cash equivalents and to avoid

THE AGE OF ANOMALY

surprises, I'd recommend limiting yourself to cash and bank deposits for this specific asset class. Especially if you don't live in the US.

For those of you who live in the US, short-term government paper is also a safe option, primarily because having its own central bank or in other words, running its own printing presses is a huge advantage for the United States, let's not even talk about the perks associated with being the world's reserve currency.

When it comes to other countries, I'm not quite sure short-term government debt for example can be trusted in the event of a serious financial calamity. And since this asset class is basically an insurance against just that, a serious financial calamity, I fail to see the appeal of assets about which I have doubts concerning how liquid they'd be in the event of a crisis.

Again, money in the bank and cash properly stored at home should be enough.

Which percentage of your net worth should you keep in this manner? It all depends on how worried you are about financial calamities, there's no one-size-fits-all answer. If you live in the US then sure, cash is good to have whenever a financial crisis such as the 2007-2008 one appears but don't go overboard. If however you live in a less developed country, you probably deal with financial calamities on a more frequent basis and therefore, should allocate a larger percentage of your net worth toward this asset class than someone who lives in a "safer" country.

As a general rule, the more potentially financially unpleasant situations you are exposed to (for example because you live in a more economically vulnerable country), the larger the percentage of your net worth allocated toward cash and cash equivalents should be. However, this principle is only valid up until a certain point. What I mean is that if your country can be considered extremely dangerous (as in violence on the street, off the charts criminality and so on) rather than just economically vulnerable, I'm not quite sure the "keep money at home" approach is sound.

To be perfectly honest, let me just put it this way: if you live in a neighborhood, region or country which is violently dangerous, I'm sorry but you're better off moving somewhere else (more information on that will be provided in the section about SHTF resilience). What you need in this case isn't a wealth management strategy but rather a relocation strategy. Come to think of it, relocating would actually be your wealth management strategy under such circumstances.

For most people however (leaving extreme cases such as the one I've mentioned previously aside), the guidelines which have been provided up until this point should be more than enough. Keep enough cash and cash equivalents at hand to land on your feet in the event of a financial calamity (you might even make quite a bit of money down the road if you end up acquiring desirable assets at deeply discounted prices) but be smart about it and don't go overboard.

That being stated, let's move on to precious metals.

Throughout this book, I've made it clear on several occasions that a lot of precious metal investors have lost touch with reality, that they've made perhaps the number one mistake you need to avoid when managing your wealth: they fell in love with the asset class they're investing in.

Bad idea.

However, don't make the mistake of thinking that just because I've criticized such approaches rather aggressively thus far, I hate precious metals in general and gold/silver in particular. I don't. On the contrary, I think each and every person should have at least some exposure to this asset class. If you don't own any precious metals and aren't interested in eventually getting some, you are making a mistake in my opinion. This doesn't mean you should turn into a gold bug, it simply means that not being willing to make this asset class a part of your investment strategy wouldn't be something I'd recommend. Here's why I like precious metals or if you will, here are my top pros:

- Scarcity is among the top selling points of precious metals. For example, three Olympic swimming pools are enough to hold all of the gold that has ever been mined. Yes, ever. Take all of the gold humans have mined throughout their entire history and you'll barely be able to fill the previously mentioned swimming pools

- They have various uses. Gold and silver for example are used for jewelry, for investment purposes, in electronics (their malleability and conductivity make them a great fit for electronics) and so on. This varies from precious metal to precious metal but the bottom line is this: as much as I dislike using the term "intrinsic value", one cannot help but admit that if it were to be used to describe an asset, it would be hard to find something for which it represents a better fit than precious metals

- Throughout history, it's pretty much impossible to think of a time when precious metals weren't desirable. The first gold treasures we've dated are from 4,000-ish BC. They've been found in Eastern Europe, pretty close to home I might add (I live in Romania). Around 560 BC, the first gold coins are believed to have been minted (in Lydia, the western part of today's Turkey) and since then, precious metals have been used as money a lot. In fact, if you think about it for a moment, it hasn't been that long since we stopped using gold as money altogether. This basically happened in 1971, when Nixon took the US and thereby the world off anything even resembling a gold standard for good. And while gold is no longer used as money at this point, it doesn't mean it's no longer desirable, not by a long shot. People still invest in it, it's still used for jewelry as well as in electronics and what not

- Precious metals are the most easy-to-transport forms of tangible wealth. If something bad happens in your country and you have to leave, gold and silver can literally be life-savers. You can easily take your gold jewelry with you, whereas you'd have to leave most of your other possession such as real estate behind. Now again, they're the most easy-to-transport forms of *tangible* wealth, not the most easy-to-transport asset, not anymore. Thanks to the Internet and the emergence of intangible assets such as domains and cryptocurrencies, you can "transport" forms of intangible wealth without carrying anything on your person. All you have to do is remember some login details (your online wallet login details for bitcoin, the login details at the company your domains are registered with and so on) and you'll be good to go. I will be covering digital assets in detail later on

On the other hand though, the cons need to be taken into consideration as well:

- Buying and selling precious metals is reasonably easy in the United States but in other countries… not so much. In my country for example, buying is easy but selling at close to the market value is extremely hard. You can buy gold (bars or coins) from banks but if you need to sell it back to them, you'd take a significant price haircut. There aren't as many gold businesses as in the US (not by a long shot), so obtaining fair value for your precious metals is easier said than done. You basically have two options: you can either sell for whatever you can obtain quickly and get it over with or you can try selling through venues such as online classifieds to get closer to the market value but this will take significantly more time. The bottom line is that while in the US and in a handful of developed countries, precious metals are highly liquid, they are considerably harder to sell at a fair price in other countries

- Precious metals don't generate any revenue. Maybe you own some gold, perhaps some silver. Good for you. They're nice to look at but don't expect them to generate any revenue for you. No dividends, no rent revenue, nothing. This is one of the main reasons why I don't recommend having too much exposure to precious metals, they definitely have a place in your portfolio but precious metals are by no means the Holy Grail of investing

- Not only do they not generate revenue but you have to actually invest money to store precious metals safely. If you like the idea of being able to touch the let's say gold you own (and I do tend to recommend physical over paper gold, it would be a shame to have exposure to this asset class and not be able to hold your precious metals in your hand) and decide to store it at home, I'd at the very least recommend investing in a decent safe. Just like with cash, I'm sure the reasons are obvious

- As technology evolves, expect precious metals to become less and less "safely portable" for lack of a better term. By this I mean that should something like a revolution take place in your country, you might decide to leave and take your precious metals with you. The thing is, you'll have to cross a border to do that. Unfortunately, technology will work against you in such cases because as time passes and technology evolves, it will get easier and easier for let's say border guards to detect your precious metals and take them off your hands

I've shared my top 4 pros and my top 4 cons, so I'll stop here. I could go on and on but I'm sure you understand that just like any other asset class out there, precious metals aren't perfect. This is actually the main problem I have with most of the strategies precious metal enthusiasts end up choosing: they act as if gold or silver are all you need to protect yourself and that's just plain wrong. The name of the game is understanding what precious metals are and what they aren't. They're a very good store of wealth (and have been since pretty much… well, forever) but you know what they aren't? They are most definitely not a "get rich quick"-ish asset class, they really aren't. Now sure, you can get lucky and buy at the precise right time, only to see prices skyrocket afterward, I'm not saying this can't happen. It most definitely can, just like with any other asset class.

For the most part though, you don't buy precious metals to get rich, you buy them to preserve your wealth. Preserve, preserve, preserve. This is the most important word you have to remember with respect to precious metals. They should, in my opinion at least, be treated as a hedge or an insurance policy, if you will. A hedge against what, you might ask? Well, a lot of people treat them as a hedge against inflation but I for one tend to consider precious metals a hedge against the unexpected. The unexpected, in the world of economics, can come in many forms and having exposure to an asset class which has pretty much always been desirable is in my opinion a decent hedge.

As an investor, it's crucial to always know why you're buying a certain asset. You buy let's say stocks for an obvious reason: to enhance your wealth. Everything related to stocks revolves around the idea of enhancing wealth. You look at profits, competitiveness and so on. It's all about deciding whether or not the company you're thinking about investing in can keep making money or, better yet, make more. Precious metals should, in my opinion, not been seen through the same lens. In other words, I don't think it's a good idea to analyze precious metals from an aggressive wealth enhancement perspective because quite frankly, you will most likely end up being bitterly disappointed. Not because there's something wrong with gold or silver (hint: there isn't) but because there's something wrong with your attitude toward them. Don't consider them aggressive wealth enhancement vehicles, analyze them from a wealth preservation or "insurance policy" paradigm and you are much closer to the truth.

A paper published by Robert J. Barro and Sanjay P. Misra[46] back in 2013 gives us some very juicy numbers concerning the returns one should expect from precious metals, findings which reinforce the idea that they're a wealth preservation vehicle more than a wealth enhancement one. From 1836 to 2011, they concluded that the real (inflation-adjusted) rate of return was 1.1% for gold and 1.2% for silver. That's actually not too shabby because precious metals did just what they're supposed to do: enabled those who owned them to keep up with inflation and make a little something extra as well. Nothing earth-shattering by any means but still, you came out ahead. Compared to the 7.4% returns stocks put on the table according to the same paper however, precious metals tend to lose their luster (pun intended). Again: precious metals are what they are, not what you want them to be.

Also, I do want to make it clear, just like I've done throughout this book, that historical data doesn't provide any guarantees with respect to the future. Things may have unfolded in a certain manner for close to 200 years, from 1836 to 2011 for example, but this doesn't mean the next 200 years won't be completely different. If I knew for a fact that the next 200 years would be similar to the previous 200 in terms of returns, I'd recommend not buying any precious metals at all and instead, investing everything in the best performing asset over that timeframe.

But since I know absolutely nothing about the future for a fact, I'd much rather recommend a more balanced approach. Therefore, while I don't suggest investing a huge percentage of your net worth in precious metals, I definitely recommend owning at least some gold and silver. How much, as a percentage of your net worth, you might ask? Well, that depends exclusively on variables related to your life, variables I have no access to.

If you live in a less-than-stable country and thus conclude the likelihood of eventually having to move is on the high side, I'd recommend staying away

---

[46] Robert J. Barro and Sanjay P. Misra. "Gold Returns." *National Bureau of Economic Research.* February 1, 2003. http://www.nber.org/papers/w18759.pdf.

from real estate and instead, investing a considerably bigger percentage of your net worth in portable assets than most individuals. This includes precious metals. Again, I wish there was a way for me to know everything about everyone from behind my computer screen but I just don't. Therefore, have limited to no confidence in my ability to make decisions on your behalf and, instead, believe a lot more in yours.

I do however want to share a few tips I hope you'll find useful:

1. For the most part, I'd recommend limiting yourself to investing in gold and silver. I'm not saying the other precious metals out there aren't worth it but I for one would advise against investing in let's call them "not-as-mainstream" precious metals. If you can, try to own both, as they complement one another nicely in my view. Gold is obviously the king of precious metals. Your returns can be greater with silver though but of course, with greater returns comes higher volatility

2. Buy physical gold and silver. I realize owning "paper gold" and "paper silver" would be a more hassle-free approach but remember that we're dealing with an "insurance policy"-type investment and as such, having it within reach would be recommended. Why? Well, let's just say that should you need to actually cash in your insurance policy, the world might be in pretty bad shape and I'm not sure to which degree you'd be able to turn the gold/silver you have in your trading account into the real thing. You invest in precious metals to prepare for "worst-case scenario"-ish situations and in such situations, having access to physical gold and/or silver would be highly recommended

3. If you live in the United States or another country with a lot of places where you can buy/sell gold coins or bars then sure, buying pure gold (again, coins or bars) makes perfect sense. If however you live in a country such as mine where it isn't as easy to sell this type of gold, you're better off limiting yourself to investing in jewelry. In most countries, gold jewelry for example is more liquid than coins or bars

4. If you end up deciding to buy gold jewelry, then even more so than with coins or bars I'd say, being careful is highly recommended. Buy a cheap gold testing kit and learn to use it, I definitely believe this is a skill worth having and fortunately, this approach will be neither expensive nor time-consuming. Gold testing kits are cheap and learning how to use them shouldn't take more than a few minutes

5. If you keep your gold at home, then for the love of God, don't tell others you have gold. Even if you have a good safe. Keeping your mouth shut is, in my opinion, the best strategy. I know a lot of people love precious metals and would like nothing more than to share their enthusiasm with the rest of the world but that's a really bad idea because it might turn you into a target. If you want to talk about precious metals with others, do it online (anonymously, of course, definitely not with your Facebook friends that you also know offline for example), never tell people from the offline world about your exposure to this asset class

6. Speaking of keeping precious metals at home, the same principle as with cash applies. Invest in a decent safe, hide it properly and have a "fake safe" somewhere around the house with some cash or jewelry in it, just in case you're eventually threatened at gunpoint. Don't keep too much in that safe but don't keep pocket change in it either, the name of the game is making everything believable

7. For most people (the overwhelming majority), gold and silver should be assets that you buy and hold, not trade. The precious metal world is highly volatile and the market will most likely eat you alive if you decide to trade. Don't embrace this occupation, that would be my honest advice. Buy precious metals and only touch them if you absolutely have to

8. Don't fall in love with this asset class. Maybe it's the fact that people have loved gold for thousands upon thousands of years, maybe it's something else but I cannot help but notice that more people tend to be guilty of this mistake with precious metals than with other asset classes. It doesn't even matter all that much why this is the case, what matters is that you don't make this mistake

9. Don't spend too much on an insurance policy. Now again, the percentage of your net worth you should allocate toward precious metals varies depending on your specific situation but if you live in a reasonably developed country and don't think you'll end up having to relocate anytime soon, it would be very hard for me to recommend having more than 10% of your net worth in precious metals, something along the lines of 5% should be more than adequate

10. Make no mistake, you will without a doubt go through periods when precious metal prices will fall dramatically. Don't panic, this is to be expected with such a volatile asset class. It's just something that comes with the territory, be sure to keep this in mind and avoid becoming a panic seller

11. The same way, dramatic price upswings also come with the territory. Don't embrace the other extreme either, don't become overly euphoric and invest everything you have in precious metals whenever there's a short-term upswing. Remain calm and never lose sight of your strategy

12. Don't say no to other forms of portable wealth such as bitcoin or domains just because you happen to like gold and/or silver. You don't have to pick a side and in fact, these forms of wealth complement one another. Easy to transport tangible as well as intangible forms of wealth deserve to have a place in the portfolio of each and every serious investor

13. I have mixed feelings about bank safety deposit boxes. This is because if your country ends up being run by lunatics, these safety deposit boxes may very well end up being confiscated. Think about it: among other things, you also buy precious metals as a hedge against precisely such scenarios, so I for one would think twice before choosing to store precious metals in bank safety deposit boxes

14. You don't have to buy gold and silver at the same time, always pay attention to the gold/silver ratio. Let's assume you want to invest $5,000 in precious metals and decide to go with 50% gold and 50% silver. If at this point, based on the Gold/Silver ratio, silver seems undervalued then buy some silver now and as far as your gold

purchase is concerned, it might be a good idea to wait a bit. Maybe you'll conclude that buying at the same time is the best approach and that's fine, just keep in mind that you don't have to

15. It may seem blatantly obvious but do keep in mind that if you decide to invest a lot of money in precious metals, let's say something along the lines of $100,000 or more, it might be a good idea to invest a considerably higher percentage in gold than in silver. If you go 50% - 50%, you'll quickly realize that even $50,000 buys you an awful lot of ounces of silver. I'm sure I don't have to explain why carrying that much silver with you in a relocation scenario isn't the best idea in the world

16. If you decide to buy gold and/or silver from another country and are traveling via plane, be sure to know your country's legislation as well as the legislation of the country you'll be buying from regarding such situations. The last thing you want is to risk having your precious metals confiscated (and make no mistake, this definitely happens) due to not knowing what, when and where to declare

17. Understand that as strange as the concept may currently seem, there may very well come a time when (due to technological advancements), the market will be hit by a huge supply of gold. Asteroid mining represents an interesting scenario worth analyzing and the bottom line is this: certain things may very well happen that make gold for example considerably less scarce than it currently is

18. Will governments confiscate gold again in the future, something along the lines of what FDR has done in the United States? Well, in my opinion (and it's just that, an opinion, treat it as such), something like this is highly unlikely. Back when FDR decided to confiscate everyone's gold, the United States was on a gold standard and the role gold played in society was completely different. I for one doubt you currently have valid reasons to worry about mass confiscations

19. Just like with any other asset class people can invest in, there can and will be bubbles with precious metals. An eloquent example is represented by the bubble which peaked back in January 1980, when gold reached $850. If you adjust those $850 for inflation, you'll

conclude that even when the high of 2011 was reached, prices still didn't top the January 1980 one when adjusted for inflation. Be very careful when people start believing a certain asset can only go up in value because those who bought back in January 1980 are still in the red (in real terms) as we speak. This tip goes hand in hand with tip #11 (which was about short-term price surges, whereas this one is about longer-term bubble-type price evolutions)

20. There are a lot of self-proclaimed gurus in the world of precious metals, I'd strongly advise against listening to them. How do you identify one? Well, if that person is only capable of making one recommendation (to buy gold/silver) and if he's been doing the exact same thing throughout his entire career, it might be a good idea to run like the wind. Even a broken clock is right two times a day, so these people will without a doubt be on a roll when precious metals occasionally outperform other asset classes by a wide margin. Furthermore, they'll be sure to obsessively remind you they "got it right" but will conveniently overlook to mention the fact that for an insanely long period of time, those who listened to them lost a lot of money

This brings me to the end of the life jacket section and I'm reasonably confident the attitude toward cash and cash equivalents as well as precious metals that I've recommended is a common-sense one. I like both asset classes, I think there's a place for them in each and every portfolio but within reason. There's a lot of hyped up doom and gloom surrounding these assets (especially precious metals) and there are a lot of snake oil salesmen out there, so remember: invest in life jacket assets but do it within reason.

Chapter 5.2.3.3: Sentiment-Neutral Status Quo Assets

The final status quo asset category I would like to refer to is the sentiment-neutral one. You have to understand that not everything in the world of finance moves in a 100% predictable matter, right alongside the current market sentiment. That is the case with the two assets I've decided to include in this category. Bonds on the one hand and art and antiques on the other.

Both asset classes fall into this category but they do it for different reasons.

When it comes to bonds, I consider this asset class as a whole sentiment-neutral for the simple reason that there are various types of bonds which move in completely different ways in various market sentiment scenarios. For example, during periods of calamity, a lot of people rush toward government bonds issued by the world's strongest countries such as the United States or Germany for safety. However, those same people would dump or stay away from bonds issued by weaker countries like for example Vietnam, which are considered junk bonds and are quickly sold during periods of turmoil. As can be seen, the very best government bonds can be considered life jacket assets, whereas the worst government bonds are anything but.

However, during times of economic prosperity or perceived economic prosperity, it's junk bonds that become desirable because people are optimistic when it comes to the worldwide economy in general and as such, much more willing to take risks. Again, there are various different types of bonds, which will be covered later on in more detail. For now, I just wanted to explain why I consider bonds sentiment-neutral.

When it comes to art and antiques, the situation is a bit different. For example, things might be going great almost everywhere in the world but if there is a huge degree of uncertainty in let's say China, then obviously Chinese investors will want to move money out of the country. Among other things, history has proven that they like to do it by investing in art and antiques as well. Therefore, it's safe to say that art and antiques can indeed be influenced by let's call them regional circumstances. The same way, they can be influenced by various different other trends as well and for this reason, it's hard for me to consider them anything but sentiment-neutral.

So, should you invest in bonds? What about art and antiques?

Let's find out and we will start with bonds.

Everyone knows what real estate is, just like everyone knows what stocks are. Therefore, there was little need to define the two terms, it would have been pointless to explain something everyone already knows. However, when it comes to bonds, things are a bit different. A lot of people kind-of-sort-ok know what bonds are but some have no idea, so let's try to define them.

A bond is basically a form of indebtedness which works like this: an entity (the bond issuer) receives a certain amount of money (the principal) from another entity (the bondholder) and has to pay back the amount in question plus interest (the coupon) later on (the maturity date). As I'm sure you'll agree, it doesn't sound all that complicated and it may in fact seem strangely familiar.

As you've probably realized by now, it's basically a loan.

An extremely important aspect worth noting is this: you can sell your bonds to another party on the secondary market, just like you'd sell let's say stocks. Therefore, should you need instant liquidity because an unexpected expense arose, you can sell your bonds to someone else. You might not make everything back and have to sell at a discounted price to entice buyers but then again, there are also market conditions which can influence things in a positive manner.

Let me give you an example. Let's assume you bought bonds issued by the German government back when interest rates were higher, we'll go with 4%. If you wanted to sell back when interest rates were still pretty much at the same level, you would have received a price you probably wouldn't have been satisfied with. If however you decide to sell when interest rates are considerably lower, your bonds (which generate a far better yield) would all of a sudden seem far more attractive to buyers and the likelihood of selling at a satisfactory price increases.

There are multiple types of bonds. The German bonds I've referred to are government bonds. But not just countries themselves can issue bonds, cities for example can issue municipal bonds. The same way, companies can issue corporate bonds and so on. Either way, the same principle remains valid. An entity (maybe a country, perhaps a city or a company) needs money and is willing to pay back the principal plus interest if you're willing to be a lender.

So… is being a lender worth it?

It depends but we won't refer to returns just yet. For now, there is an issue (which I'm even willing to call myth) I'd like to address, the risk factor involved. The main difference between stocks and bonds is represented by the fact that with stocks, you get a piece of the action. You actually own a small part of the company you're investing in and will receive dividends for as long as the company exists and you own the stocks in question.

With bonds, you don't own a portion of the company in question and won't receive dividends but on the other hand, you'll know right off the bat how much money you're supposed to make. Stocks can go up and down in value, whereas things seem much more straightforward when it comes to bonds. You lend $x to an entity and receive your $x back plus interest.

This makes a lot of people consider bonds extremely safe.

Are they? In my opinion no, they're certainly not as safe as people consider them. To illustrate why, I'll take things one step further and analyze the safest type of bonds according to most of the population: government bonds. After all, you're lending money to a huge government, it's not like it can simply take it and run, right?

Well, a country certainly can't take your money and run but on the other hand, it can default. As in not pay. As in goodbye money. It has happened far more frequently than the average individual realizes, frequently enough for me not to be excited about the manner in which bonds are priced at this point. I don't consider the interest rates attractive enough to justify the risks involved and will try to explain why I'm currently not thrilled.

Carmen M. Reinhart and Kenneth S. Rogoff have written some very interesting papers about sovereign defaults over the years and for now, I'd like to refer to the one entitled "Financial and Sovereign Debt Crises: Some

Lessons Learned and Those Forgotten"[47] that has been published in 2013. I will be focusing on the documented defaults from the 1920's to the 1960's.

Now do keep in mind this is the perspective of just these two authors, there are a lot of grey area issues surrounding defaults. Was it actually a default? Was it not? The numbers and conclusions aren't always the same (some authors may consider a certain event a default, others might not) but regardless, this data is a decent enough starting point which makes it clear why sovereign bonds aren't as safe as most people think they are, as I'm sure you'll agree.

Below, you'll find a list of defaults which, as mentioned previously, occurred from the 1920's until the 1960's. We're not talking about multiple centuries, we're not even talking about one. The fact that so many defaults occurred during this period should at the very least make us think about whether or not sovereign debt is as safe as most people consider it.

Here is the list of default episodes, based on the work of Reinhart and Rogoff:

- Australia - 1 episode (1931 - 1932)
- Austria - 6 episodes (1920 - 1922, 1932 - 1933, 1934, 1938, 1940 and 1945)
- Belgium - 1 episode (1934)
- Canada - 1 episode (1935 - the Alberta province defaulted)
- France - 1 episode (1934)
- Germany - 3 episodes (1922 - 1923, 1932 and 1948)
- Greece - 4 episodes (1932, 1932, 1934 and 1941 – 1944)
- Italy - 6 episodes (1920, 1924, 1926, 1934, 1944 and 1946)
- Japan - 3 episodes (1942, 1945 and 1946 - 1952)
- New Zealand - 1 episode (1933)
- Spain - 1 episode (1936 - 1939)
- United Kingdom - 1 episode (1934)
- United States - 1 episode (1933 - yes, the abrogation of the gold clause and the 40% US dollar gold content reduction represented a default)

---

[47] Carmen M. Reinhart and Kenneth S. Rogoff. "Financial and Sovereign Debt Crises: Some Lessons Learned and Those Forgotten." *International Monetary Fund.* December 24, 2013. https://www.imf.org/external/pubs/ft/wp/2013/wp13266.pdf.

All in all, we've had quite a few defaults less than one century ago. And we're not talking about countries perceived as risky, for example African countries or some of the poorer Asian ones, not at all. Just re-read the list and you'll find the world's strongest economies in it. Household names such as the United States, Japan, France, the United Kingdom and so on.

Another paper[48] from the same authors, written back in 2008 refers to the remaining periods. We can notice that during 1970 - 2007, Argentina was one of the biggest culprits, with 3 default episodes (1982, 1989 - 1990 and 2002 - 2005) or how between 1750 and 1920, none other than the United Kingdom was one of the main defaulters, with 4 episodes (1749, 1822, 1834 and 1888 - 1889).

The first ever recorded sovereign default takes us all the way back to the 4th century BC (Greece in 377 BC, to be precise) and as time passed, it has become blatantly obvious that nobody is immune. We've had defaults from all continents, from all cultures and with all this in mind, I think people should definitely not perceive government debt as risk-free.

I'm not saying it should be avoided, just don't consider it risk-free.

With this in mind, let's move on and take a look at returns. Burton Malkiel's *A Random Walk Down Wall Street*[49] book (initially published back in 1973 but with several revised editions, we'll be referring to the 2007 one) gives us some very juicy data when it comes to the historical returns of bonds from 1926 to 2005. Those who invested in long-term corporate bonds saw returns of 6.2%, those who invested in long-term government bonds received returns of 5.5%, whereas those who bought US treasury bills saw returns of 3.8%.

The average inflation rate for the 1926 – 2005 period was 3.1% and all in all, it's clear bonds underperformed stocks, it's not even up for debate. If you take a look at the Vanguard portfolio allocation models (Google is your friend), you'll notice the fundamental difference between bonds and stocks even better, with information ranging from 1926 all the way to the present.

---

[48] Carmen M. Reinhart and Kenneth S. Rogoff. "The Forgotten History of Domestic Debt." *National Bureau of Economic Research*. April 15, 2008.
http://www.nber.org/papers/w13946.
[49] Burton G. Malkiel. *A Random Walk Down Wall Street*. New York City: W. W. Norton & Company, 2007.

Over this timeframe, bonds generated an average annual return of 5.5% according to Vanguard. The best year was 1982, with a return of 32.6%, whereas the worst year was 1969, with a loss of 8.1% All in all, there were 14 out of 89 years when bonds generated losses. Stocks on the other hand did roughly two times better, generating 10.2% over the same timeframe. The best year was 1933, with a return of 54.2%, whereas the worst one was 1931, with a loss of 43.1%. All in all, losses were incurred in 25 out of 89 years with stocks.

Higher risk, higher returns.

As we can observe by analyzing the previously mentioned figures, there's considerably more volatility with stocks. The returns are greater but on the other hand, the losses can be considerably higher as well. Just look at the worst performing year, a 43.1% loss for stocks versus just 8.1% for bonds. Therein lies the fundamental difference between bonds and stocks.

For those who have been willing to accept the increased volatility associated with stocks, the returns have been approximately two times higher between 1926 and 2014 than with bonds. Can you be 100% certain things will continue in this manner? Well no, nothing is certain but the historical arguments analyzed thus far can certainly be considered extremely compelling.

So, should you invest in bonds?

The idea itself definitely has its merits and this asset class is certainly here to stay. On the other hand though, if you ask me if you should invest in bonds in the current low interest rate environment, let me just put it this way: it will be extremely hard (not impossible but extremely hard nonetheless) to find situations in which you will be properly rewarded for risking your capital.

As mentioned previously, investors tend to consider bonds unbelievably safe. Add central bank involvement (through monetary easing) to the mix and you're left with bonds which have returns that are, quite frankly, ridiculously low. As illustrated by the data I've presented throughout this subchapter, government bonds are definitely nowhere close to risk-free. This state of affairs is not just limited to poorer countries, re-read the information I've shared and you'll see pretty much all of the "household" names on the list, from the United States to the United Kingdom, to Japan and all the way to Australia and New Zealand.

Don't get me wrong, I have nothing against risk.

I'm an entrepreneur who understands the importance of taking calculated risks when an opportunity presents itself. I'm also an investor who considers risk a fundamental part of the equation. Again, I have absolutely nothing against risk. What I do have a problem with is not being rewarded properly for the risk I take on and this is precisely what's wrong with bonds at this point in my opinion.

The returns are far too low across the board for this asset class to be considered attractive. My verdict may sound harsh but it's just the way I perceive bonds at the moment of writing. Let me put it this way. When issuing a bond, Country A is basically asking me for a loan. I don't discount the idea of lending money to Country A altogether, I am however expecting to be rewarded for the risk I take on by giving them my money as opposed to allocating it in another manner.

There are basically three questions you should be asking yourself:

1. How likely is a default? It should be clear by how that countries as well as companies can and do default. Go bankrupt. Refuse to pay. Demand a fresh start. Feel free to use any term you deem appropriate for it. The bottom line is you're not getting any more money if something like this happens and therefore, risk assessment from this perspective is crucial

2. How much am I making after factoring in inflation and the currency risk? In a lot of cases, the "real" (inflation-adjusted) returns are actually negative when you're investing in bonds issued by the world's top economies. In other words, the returns you're making aren't even high enough to offset inflation. Other countries however may and frequently do offer returns which, on paper, seem more than enough to offset inflation. But what if you'll end up being paid in the currency of the country in question? Let's assume the inflation rate in your country is 2% and that you earn 5% from a bond issued by another country in another currency. You might think you managed to offset inflation but what if the currency you were paid in for the bond in question depreciated by 7% compared to yours? I'm sure you get the point

3. How does this investment opportunity stack against my alternatives? Perhaps you're thinking about investing in a bond which would generate 5% per year. The third and final question you should be asking yourself is whether or not there are other investments which yield 5% per year (maybe bonds issued by a different country, perhaps other assets) which carry less risk. If there are, why not choose those instead?

If the answer to these three questions isn't satisfactory, move on. For example, bonds issued by one of the world's strongest countries carry little default risk (in other words, the answer to the first question is satisfactory) but the returns are too low for you to even keep up with inflation. In other words, the answer to the second question is not satisfactory.

In our case, the second question represents a deal breaker. Yes, the answer to question number one is reassuring but if the answer to the second one isn't, move on. Each of the three questions constitutes a potential deal breaker. If you're not happy with the answer to one of them (even if you're content with the answers to the other two), it's a valid enough reason to move on.

Again, I for one see few investment opportunities in the bond world at the moment of writing. This may or may not change in the near or distant future, I have no idea and this is precisely why I've shared the three questions as opposed to giving a final verdict now. Aside from those questions, here are a few more tips you should be keeping in mind when it comes to bonds:

- Unless you're positively convinced you're getting an absolutely amazing deal, avoid bonds with very long maturity dates such as 30-year bonds. So much can happen in 30 years that the risks associated with these instruments are very high. An interest rate which seems attractive now may prove to be dismal down the road but, of course, the exact opposite can also be true. This much is certain: bonds with very long maturity dates are extremely risky, be sure to proceed with caution

- Junk bonds are called junk bonds for a reason. In a world with record-low interest rates, investors are scrambling for yield and therefore frequently willing to lend money to borrowers one cannot exactly consider an example of solvency. If you're desperately searching for higher yields, consider other asset classes. Stay away from junk bonds because in most if not all cases, the risk/reward ratio is completely unappealing

- Don't assume a municipal bond associated with one of the top countries in the world is 100% safe. For example, the risk of a sovereign default by the United States or Germany is extremely low. This however doesn't mean the bonds issued by all US or German cities are safe, the risk of certain municipalities defaulting is considerably higher than the sovereign default risk. Once again, don't let yield desperation get the best of you

- If possible, go with English law bonds. If for example you're investing in bonds issued by your own country, it's likely you aren't receiving English law bonds and as such, should a problematic situation arise, the government has a wider scope when it comes to taking action. There are several examples of why the English law bond variable is important, from Greece to Argentina. For example, in the case of Greece, those who owned English law bonds received 100%, whereas Greek law bondholders received a so-called haircut (in other words, less money than they were supposed to)

- Understand that the banking sector of a country and its bonds are extremely closely interlinked. In fact, the same principle is valid when it comes to a certain country's bonds and the banking sector of its neighbors in a lot of cases. Remember the Cyprus banking crisis? It was in no small part (understatement of the century) influenced by the fact that the banks invested heavily in Greek government bonds. So if something bad happens to a country's bond market and you have reasons to believe your bank is exposed to those bonds, it's time to start worrying

- Another aspect worth keeping in mind is this: to partially answer the question as to why, at least historically speaking, stocks outperformed bonds by a reasonably wide margin, it might be a good idea to understand where the money in question goes. When investing in bonds, the money goes to governments which are let's say not always extremely financially responsible. Stocks on the other hand are linked to companies which, while not a prime example of financial excellence by any means, tend to at least manage money better than governments

- To be fair though, I want to make it clear stocks don't *always* outperform bonds in an unbelievably meaningful manner. South Africa is an example. An interesting *Southern African Business Review*[50] paper contains data about stocks as well as bonds from April 1986 (basically when reliable data first became available) and until February 2013. For stocks, the average yearly return was 16.08%, whereas for bonds, it was 15.39%. In other words, a difference of only 0.69 per year

- Nobody can ever know for sure whether in a given year, stocks or bonds will outperform. To illustrate this, I'll once again refer to data published in the previously mentioned South African paper. Based on this data, the authors put together a simulation of what would have happened if you had invested 1,000 Rand (the South African currency), with January 1, 1987 as the start date and December 31, 2012 as the end date. Had you invested everything in South African stocks, you would have had 49,226 at the end of this period. On the other hand, you would have had 42,348 if you invested everything in bonds. There is a difference, of course, but nothing Earth-shattering. However (brace yourself), you would have generated 660,493 Rand if you had superpowers which enabled you to see the future and pick the best performing asset class each year

The only conclusion I can think of is this: bonds are what they are. As long as you understand this asset class, you'll be able to make informed decisions as to whether or not investing in them is worth it. Personally, I'm not thrilled about the risk/reward ratio most bonds put on the table at the moment of writing but this doesn't mean bonds should be eliminated from the equation altogether.

---

[50] Christo Auret and Robert Vivian. "A Comparative Analysis of Returns of Various Financial Asset Classes in South Africa: A Triumph of Bonds?" *Southern African Business Review*. December 9, 2014. http://www.unisa.ac.za/contents/faculties/service_dept/docs/Sabview_18_3_Chap%208.pdf.

Alright then, what about <u>art and antiques</u>?

Well, I'm reasonably confident all of you will agree this is the most glamorous asset class by far. However, while the glamour factor is great and everything, one question and one question only is relevant to our interests: is art worth investing in? At the end of the day, you should be just as brutally rational when it comes to "romantic" asset classes such as art and antiques or real estate as you are with "business only" assets such as stocks or bonds.

Let's start by analyzing some historical returns, shall we?

Now when analyzing the historical returns of stocks for example, there are a bunch of reliable indexes which paint a reasonably clear picture. The S&P 500 for US stocks, the DAX for Germany and so on. There are indexes when it comes to art and antiques as well but unfortunately, they aren't as relevant. In other words, they don't paint an accurate enough picture for the most part, pun intended.

It's hard to draw conclusions when it comes to art and while indexes make perfect sense for other asset classes, one cannot say the same about art. Why? Simply because indexes are based on, obviously, works of art which sold. But what if you bought a painting by an artist who ended up not living up to expectations, so you just keep it in the living room? Well, the index in question doesn't include your painting.

However, if a friend of yours made a better choice (he bought a painting by an artist who did better) and sold his asset on a public venue, it will be included in the index. A paper written by Arthur Korteweg, Roman Kräussl and Patrick Verwijmeren[51] in 2013 makes it clear why art indexes tend to let's say be on the optimistic side, as hopefully illustrated by my example as well.

The main problem is this: we're talking about illiquid assets.

Therefore, take these indexes with a grain of salt. At the end of the day, they're better than nothing but in light of the previously mentioned liquidity issue,

---

[51] Arthur Korteweg, Roman Kräussl, and Patrick Verwijmeren. "Does It Pay to Invest in Art? A Selection-corrected Returns Perspective." *Review of Financial Studies, Forthcoming.* October 15, 2013.
http://som.yale.edu/sites/default/files/files/Roman%20paper.pdf.

you shouldn't make the mistake of placing as much weight on these indexes as you would when it comes to stock market indexes, for example. However, we'll be working with them because again, it's the best data we have for this asset class.

Here's how art performed compared to stocks:

- Over a period of 10 years, art generated 7.25%, whereas you would have made 7.10% with stocks
- Over a period of 15 years, art generated 5.92% compared to the 4.47% stocks would have yielded
- Over a period of 20 years, you would have made 5.32% by investing in art and 8.22% by investing in stocks
- Over a period of 25 years, art once again underperformed significantly, 5.08% versus 9.7%
- Over a period of 50 years, the underperformance of art isn't as obvious, only 8.18% compared to the stock market's 9.8%

The data above comes from an interesting paper by J.P. Morgan[52], which compares art returns (based on the Mei Moses World All Art Index) to the S&P 500, among other things. On the surface, it seems art performed rather well compared to let's say bonds, being remarkably close to the S&P 500 return-wise. It even outperformed it over the 10-year and 15-year timeframe.

But again, for the reasons I've referred to previously, art indexes are misleading. Also, each index has its own particularities you need to be aware of. For example, the Mei Moses Fine Art Index only includes information for works of art which sold more than once. Data is collected from Sotheby's and Christie's but their online sales are not included. Other indexes are completely different. I for one tend to consider these numbers (those illustrated by indexes related to this asset class in general) on the optimistic side but still, art performed reasonably well, even if we tone the optimism down a notch and adjust for illiquidity.

According to the same paper, the art market was in the $56 billion zone in 2012, a six-fold increase in just 20 years. Some people might raise an eyebrow

[52] Kyle Sommer. "The Art of Investing in Art." J.P. Morgan. August 22, 2012. https://www.jpmorgan.com/pages/jpmorgan/is/thought/magazine/3Q2013/art.

and conclude we're dealing with a bit of irrational exuberance, other people might say significant increases when it comes to assets central banks cannot simply print (such as art/antiques or precious metals) are normal in light of the central banking aggressiveness issue we've all noticed.

Draw your own conclusions, I honestly have no idea.

What's relatively clear is this: while art and antiques don't tend to outperform stocks (historically speaking), they did quite well. Therefore, by strictly looking at the numbers and not analyzing the particularities of this asset class, you'd be tempted to be pretty excited about its let's say potential. Therefore, rather than limiting myself to bringing some data to your attention, I'll also be analyzing the pros and cons associated with art and antiques.

I'd like to start with the cons:

- You need to know how things work when it comes to art and antiques or you'll end up making bad purchases. The learning curve involved can be quite problematic. Now if you're passionate about art and/or antiques then fair enough, it will probably be fun. If not however, it will be excruciatingly difficult. You can't just blindly pick a random item, purchase it and bam, you're now an art investor. Not going to happen

- High transaction costs. A large percentage of art transactions take place at auction houses and you should expect to pay double-digit commission percentages. In a lot of situations, both the buyer and the seller have to pay a commission. A very high one, mind you. Compared to something like an index fund or the commissions charged by online brokers, it's an entirely different world in terms of how much middle men charge

- No income is produced, unless you do something like putting together a museum and making money from entry fees. A highly unlikely scenario for most individuals. For the most part, the same principle as with precious metals is valid when it comes to art and antiques. They're pleasant to look like, they make you feel all warm and fuzzy inside but no income whatsoever is being generated. With stocks for example, you own an asset (a stake in a company) but also receive returns on a regular basis (dividends). Real estate is another example of owning an asset (a house, an apartment, land) which can produce revenue (making money by renting your property out)

- Just like you need a safe to keep money at home, you have to take measures of precaution when investing in art. Where are you going to store whatever it is you're thinking about buying? Do you plan to spend money on insurance, for example? All in all, storing art safely tends to be considerably more expensive than storing cash in a safe. Okay, things like antique coins are relatively easy to store but what about some of the bulkier examples of art and antiques such as paintings or sculptures? In such cases, the costs can end up being ridiculously high

- Less than impressive liquidity. Selling art takes time, so in the event of a cash crunch, don't count on the liquidation of your art portfolio as a viable short-term plan. Let's assume an economic crisis rears its ugly head and you need additional capital as soon as possible. In such a situation, art and antiques are some of the harder to liquidate assets

On a more optimistic note, here are the pros:

- Governments can't print art/antiques, they're hard assets and therefore obviously tempting if you're worried about the current central banking policies and their potential effects. In an inflationary environment, art and antiques will most likely perform reasonably well, so it's safe to say this asset class represents a relatively effective hedge against inflation

- It can be a nice way to combine business with pleasure but only for those who are actually passionate about art. Those of you who genuinely like these assets will have a lot of fun researching, making purchase decisions and so on. You'd basically be able to make money by doing something you like, not a bad situation to be in

- In some cases, if a certain artist ends up becoming extremely popular, the returns can be amazing (in exotic asset territory even but more on exotic asset returns in the next section). It all depends on how much risk you're willing to take on. If you only invest in safer "blue chip" art and antique-related assets, you're taking on less risk but will most likely never generate amazingly high returns. On the other hand, if you're willing to be more aggressive and for example buy something from a less popular artist who you think has potential, the upside is considerably juicier

- Art and antiques are relatively easy to transport (for the most part) in case you have to let's say leave the country for politico-economic reasons. You can't take real estate with you if you have to move to a different country but you can definitely take a painting or some coins. Now again, art and antiques are for the most part (as opposed to always) portable, there are however exceptions such as heavy or bulky sculptures

So, should you invest in art?

I'd like to answer this question based on one variable, so I have to ask you a question as well: are you passionate about art and antiques? If you genuinely like this asset class, investing in it will be fun rather than simply potentially lucrative. You won't perceive the research dimension (which is not exactly negligible) as somewhat of a chore and instead, will be glad to read and stay informed. Therefore, you will be considerably more likely to do well than other investors.

If however you don't consider art and antiques all that interesting, it's hard for me to recommend allocating a significant percentage of your net worth toward them. The research curve is quite steep and if you aren't exactly excited about the idea of learning and researching, your results probably won't be amazing. Therefore, if you're not passionate about this asset class, you're better off limiting yourself to "blue chip" assets (rather than taking chances with more obscure artists/assets) and not allocating all that much capital in this direction.

So, are art and antiques desirable assets? In my opinion yes, they definitely are but on the other hand, investing in this asset class is anything but easy if you're serious about doing it right and drawbacks such as liquidity-related issues should not be discounted. It ultimately all depends on whether or not you're willing to invest the time/energy it takes to do a good job.

Chapter 5.2.4: Trailblazer Assets

You won't exactly hear economists talk about trailblazer assets too frequently, simply because a lot of my peers are excessively attached to their comfort zones. Furthermore, the assets I'm about to refer to are deeply connected to the digital world and I do have to say that me being an entrepreneur as well as an investor in digital assets gives me a significant edge over the average economist.

I don't judge the economists who don't refer to digital assets all that much because again, we're talking about something new and from a lot of perspectives unproven, but I do firmly believe that if you aren't serious about adding them to your portfolio, you're making a huge mistake. I will be referring to fewer asset classes than with status quo assets. Four, to be precise:

- Domain names
- Private equity and peer-to-peer lending
- Cryptocurrencies such as bitcoin
- Websites

Just like with the status quo assets, there are three types of trailblazer assets:

1. Fair-weather trailblazer assets, which just like the fair-weather assets of the status quo type, perform well when the market in general is in good shape and poorly otherwise. In this category, I've decided to include domain names as well as private equity and peer-to-peer lending

2. Life jacket assets and again, we're talking about assets which just like the status quo life jacket assets, are solid performers when everything is gloomy. In this category, I will be referring to cryptocurrencies and particularly bitcoin

3. Finally, the sentiment-neutral asset category does not "behave" in a predictable manner along with the overall market sentiment and in this category, I will only be including only, primarily because there

are so many website types out there and they tend to be so diverse that painting them with the same brush of market sentiment makes little sense

As you will be able to find out, trailblazer assets have redefined certain sectors of the financial world. For example, who would have believed that we would eventually have assets that are far, far more portable than precious metals? Yet here we are today, in an age where asset classes exist which don't even require you to physically carry anything on your person. Just remember your login details and you're good to go for the most part.

In fact, all of the trailblazer assets I will be discussing are more "portable" than precious metals. Do you want access to your domains? Then simply remember the login details of your registrar and you can move them from one country to another without carrying anything on your person. The same principle is valid when it comes to using online cryptocurrency wallets and even the more secure offline versions are easier to transport than precious metals. The same way, while there are more login details to remember when it comes to websites, not just domain registrar login details but also hosting login details and everything else, it is still possible to transport this form of wealth easily. Without any kind of tangible element, in other words. The same way, all you have to do is remember a few login details and you're going to have access to your peer-to-peer lending accounts and as such, should the need to do that arise, you will be able to take them with you without any shred of physical evidence that could be confiscated at the border if things deteriorate socio-politically. However, since most of them are country-dependent, things are a bit trickier, as we're about to find out later on.

The younger generation tends to take these things for granted but make no mistake, we are living in truly revolutionary times. For this reason, I think it would be downright foolish to put together a strategy which has the end goal of making you financially resilient without having significant exposure to such assets.

The main drawback however is, of course, the fact that we are dealing with unproven assets and should disruptions occur when it comes to the Internet and other systems, you might be in trouble. I keep telling people that there is no such thing as the perfect investment, there are pros and cons to literally everything. For this reason, I think it's a mistake to be overly conservative by only investing in status quo assets but the same way, I would just as strongly advise against limiting yourself to trailblazer assets.

Let's roll up our sleeves and start by analyzing fair-weather trailblazer assets.

Chapter 5.2.4.1: Fair-Weather Trailblazer Assets

Just like the fair-weather status quo assets, we're dealing with assets that perform well when the overall market sentiment is positive/optimistic and which of course tend to underperform when that's not the case. That being stated, let's move on to the first asset class that I think belongs in this category.

We'll be talking about a favorite of mine, <u>domain names</u>.

The first domains ever registered were Nordu.net and Symbolics.com (in this order) back in 1985 but this was before the beginning of the let's call it commercial Internet, as in the Internet used by regular individuals rather than just a relatively small group of people. Back in 1985, the Internet existed but was far, far away from critical mass territory. The average Joe kind-of-sort-of knew about "this Internet thingy" (after reading an article in the newspaper, hearing about the Internet on the radio or watching a TV show about it) but was definitely not ready to adopt it.

The Internet as we know it was probably established about 10 years later.

You basically had two options if you wanted to visit a website. You could type in its IP address (a numeric string which tends to be extremely hard to remember, for example 123.456.78.90) or type in its domain if one existed, a considerably more user-friendly option (for example domain.com or website.net). As time passed, pretty much all websites ended up having domains for an obvious reason: using them was much more convenient.

Domains gradually ended up establishing themselves as Internet real estate, the online equivalent of having a store or a physical presence. Up until 1995, domains were free but as of 1995, Network Solutions started charging money for them, $100 for two years initially and then $70 as of 1997. As time passed however, competitors started appearing and prices, at this point, are considerably lower.

So, why should one invest in domains?

For the same reason you'd invest in real estate. Imagine you want a physical store in your city, what would be the ideal situation? Having a location in the best neighborhood, obviously. There's just one problem: everyone would love to own real estate in the best neighborhood and as you've probably guessed by now, supply and demand start doing their thing.

The results shouldn't surprise anyone: the better a neighborhood is, the more desirable its real estate is considered and the more you'll ultimately have to pay if you want a store there. The exact same principle is valid when it comes to domains: every car-related business owner for example would love to own Car.com or Cars.com and therefore, supply and demand theories as well as common sense tell us the price of such domains will be higher than that of less desirable alternatives.

What makes a domain desirable, you might ask?

Unlike with real estate, crystal-clear valuation methodology doesn't exist for domains aside from a few notable exceptions. We're still in the "Wild West" stages at this point and as such, domain valuation is more of an art than an exact science. However, a few common-sense principles definitely apply and I'd recommend asking yourself the following three questions to assess the desirability of a domain:

1. Does it pass the radio test or the phone test? In other words, how easy would it be to remember the domain in question if you heard it on the radio for the first time or if a friend told you about it during a phone conversation? To pass the radio test, a domain should be easy to pronounce because otherwise, people might end up being confused.

   Everyone remembers YouTube.com because it's an insanely popular brand at this point but believe it or not, the domain itself doesn't pass the radio/phone test. Why? Well, say it out loud and assume for just one second you'd be telling someone who doesn't know what YouTube is about it. Wouldn't you agree the person in question might believe you said "U" instead of "You" and end up typing in UTube.com instead of YouTube.com?

2. How easy is it to spell? As I'm sure you'll agree, people tend to be embarrassingly bad at spelling and if a domain contains a word which tends to be mistyped frequently, you're going to have a bit of a problem. A good domain should be extremely easy to spell because again, the average Internet user isn't an editor by any means.

   Don't assume your target audience is different, try to keep things simple and go with domains with which there's little to no room for interpretation. The more prone to being misspelled a word your domain contains is, the more likely it will be to create confusion and if there's one thing you don't want when it comes to domains, it's confusion

3. Is it reasonably short? In the domain world, less is more, especially in the age of smartphones, tablets and what not. People don't want to type in an insanely long domain when they are for example surfing the Web on their phone (it's considerably more inconvenient) and therefore, short domains tend to be quite desirable.

   The same way, individuals will most likely want to place a domain on their business card or promotional materials, even a billboard. Imagine you're driving and notice an ad for a car repair shop with the domain RepairYourCarNowItsCheap.com. First of all, it's hard to read when you're driving and need to focus on the road. Secondly, it's highly unlikely you'll remember such a domain

It should now be clear what makes a domain desirable but I don't want to move on without addressing another real estate similarity. Back when a city was still in its infancy stages, people were able to secure real estate at ridiculously low prices. As the city in question began to grow, real estate prices obviously went up as well and those who invested early on were rewarded.

The same way, a city can experience difficulties from time to time. Economic problems, socio-political issues and so on, all of these things make it less attractive and as such, real estate prices tend to go down during times of turbulence. If someone invests when prices are depressed and the city ends up ultimately reverting to its former glory days, the investor in question will obviously do well.

With domains, we're dealing with pretty much the same situations.

Those who bought amazing domains back in the nineties risked quite a bit, just like someone who buys real estate in a newly-established town. The Internet ended up obviously doing very well, so it should come as no surprise fortunes were made among those who had the foresight and courage it took to invest early on. Make no mistake, a lot of people considered them crazy back then.

They invested their hard-earned money in something quite a few individuals considered nothing more than a fad. Even Nobel prize-winning economists such as Paul Krugman or insanely influential tech entrepreneurs such as Bill Gates greatly underestimated the Internet's potential. Paul Krugman assumed the economic impact of the Web would be no greater than that of the fax machine, whereas Bill Gates seriously doubted people would genuinely want to use computers for something other than the offline applications he became famous for offering.

In such an environment, investing in domains seemed downright peculiar.

Yet a handful of people actually did this and they deserve to be rewarded. The same way, those who invested in domains during times of turbulence deserve the same treatment. An interesting story, documented in the book David Kesmodel launched back in 2008[53] as well as in many other sources is Frank Schilling's path. He risked quite a bit by aggressively investing in domains after the dot-com bubble burst, when many people thought the glory days of the Internet were over.

As we all know and as the data shared at the beginning of this chapter proves, those predictions have been proven wrong. After the dot-com bubble burst, the Internet continued to grow at a remarkable pace. The dates of the top 10 documented domain sales speak for themselves and make it clear why people like Frank Schilling ended up doing well to put it mildly:

- Sex.com - $13 million (sold in 2010)
- Hotels.com - $11 million (sold in 2001)

---

[53] David Kesmodel. *The Domain Game: How People Get Rich From Internet Domain Names.* Bloomington, Indiana: Xlibris Corporation, 2008.

- Fund.com - $9,999,950 (sold in 2008)
- Porn.com - $9,500,000 (sold in 2007)
- Porno.com - $8,888,888 (sold in 2015)
- Fb.com - $8,500,000 (sold in 2010)
- Diamond.com - $7,500,000 (sold in 2006)
- Beer.com - $7,000,000 (sold in 2004)
- Z.com - $6,784,000 (sold in 2014)
- Slots.com - $5,500,000 (sold in 2010)

And there are many more juicy sales where these came from. According to Domaining.com, there have been (at the moment of writing) 86 sales of over one million dollars, 180 sales which exceeded $500,000 and 310 sales of over $250,000. If I were to list all of the "four figures and up" sales, I'd probably need another book exclusively for this purpose.

The bottom line is this: those who invest in domains can be considered pioneers. People like Frank Schilling, Rick Schwartz or Mike Mann (the person who, as a fun fact, holds an interesting record after registering 14,962 domains in a single day) risked quite a bit and it paid off. Believe it or not, those who invest in domains now can also be considered pioneers.

Yes, it seems the Internet has been around forever.

It's now such an important part of our day-to-day life we'd be tempted to consider it anything but uncharted territory. But make no mistake, we're still in the early stages of the Internet, we're still pioneers. Alan Dunn wrote an eloquent article for *Business Insider*[54] through which he shared quite a few interesting facts which, in my opinion at least, help put things into perspective.

Think about this for just one moment: a 30-second TV ad costs six figures and a one-month radio spot is easily in 5 figure territory, whereas even as far as newspapers are concerned, a quarter-page New York Times ads will cost you mid 5 figures. For such amounts, business owners could buy an amazing domain and unlike the previously mentioned campaigns which would only

---

[54] Alan Dunn. "Why $10,000 For A Domain Name Is Still Cheap." *Business Insider.* April 11, 2011. http://www.businessinsider.com.au/why-10000-for-a-domain-name-is-still-cheap-2011-4.

have a temporary effect, a domain is yours forever as long as you pay a ridiculously low yearly renewal fee (even single digit renewal fees for Dot Coms or Dot Nets, for example).

Furthermore, a lot of people still underestimate the Internet. Yes, some companies get it (CNN owns Money.com, Intel owns PC.com and so on) but others are still blissfully ignorant when it comes to the true potential of the Internet. The domain world is definitely still in its Wild West phase, prices are all over the place and misconceptions as well as opportunities abound.

As an example of just how much confusion still exists, I'd like to share an interesting anecdote. The domain Cowboys.com was auctioned at the TRAFFIC domain investment conference back in 2007 and a representative of the Dallas Cowboys NFL team came to bid. He ultimately won the auction with a $275,000 bid but guess what? He thought he had bid $275, not $275,000 and ended up not buying it.

I kid you not.

I'm sure you now understand why domains basically represent highly desirable Internet real estate and why we're still in the Wild West stages of domain investing. The next question which arises should be fairly obvious: which types of domains should you invest in? There are in my opinion two main types of domains you should be aware of at this point:

1. Legacy domains or in other words the "traditional" domains which have existed for a very long time. On the one hand, we have the legacy general TLDs (or gTLDs, as they are called) which are Dot Com, Dot Net and Dot Org (also Dot Info or Dot Biz I guess, but those appeared later on and are kind of in limbo, for lack of a better description) and on the other hand, we have country code TLDs (or ccTLDs) such as Dot De for Germany, Dot Fr for France and so on.

   These are the domains pretty much everyone knows exist. Even those who aren't extremely Internet-savvy know about Dot Com (the extension the overwhelming majority of their favorite websites are in), Dot Net (their ISP is most likely using a Dot Net, for example), Dot Org (used by many well-known organizations) and their local ccTLD if they don't live in the United States

2. New domains, called new gTLDs. Lots and lots of domain extensions appeared after the powers that be (ICANN is the organization I'm referring to) decided to expand the namespace. They started going live back in 2014. dotShabaka Registry's شبكة. (which stands for ".shabaka", the Arabic term for Web) was the first new gTLD to see the light of day, followed by 7 new gTLDs ran by the Donuts registry: .guru, .bike, .holdings, .plumbing, .singles, .ventures and .clothing.

    It was only the beginning as at this point, there are hundreds upon hundreds of new gTLDs. More of them were added in just one year (as mentioned previously, 2014 is the year in which new gTLDs started appearing) than in the entire pre-2014 history of the Web. And again, this is just the beginning, as more and more will be added as time passes

So, what should people do?

In my opinion, you're better off limiting yourself to investing in domains from the first category. Figuring out why is by no means a matter of rocket science, just plain old supply and demand. As mentioned when categorizing extensions, most people know about Dot Com, Dot Net, Dot Org and their ccTLD if they're not from the US. But this is where it stops for the most part.

Even legacy extensions such as Dot Info and Dot Biz (which appeared several years before the new gTLD craze of 2014) had a hard time gaining traction. Try an experiment and see for yourself. Ask 20 people to give you five examples of domain extensions such as Dot Com and the conclusions will most likely speak for themselves. You'll quickly realize the average individual barely knows about let's call them tier 2 legacy extensions such as Dot Info and Dot Biz, let alone new gTLDs.

Here are the main reasons why I wouldn't recommend investing in new gTLDs:

- People just don't know they exist. Now as time passes, the awareness when it comes to new gTLDs in general will probably increase (more and more people will know lots of extensions exist) but at that point, there will most likely be thousands rather than hundreds of extensions out there. Therefore, it's hard for me to understand how marketing a website built on a new gTLD or trying to sell such a domain will be anything other than an uphill battle

- In a lot of cases, the registration and renewal fees are higher than for Dot Coms. If you only own a few domains, it isn't a big deal but if you own let's say hundreds or even thousands, the impact on your business model is quite severe

- There's pretty much no investor-to-investor liquidity. Let me explain. If you invest in domains, you have two types of buyers. End users (those who want to use the domain and turn it into a website) and other domain investors. The ideal scenario is selling to an end user but if you need money quickly, selling to other investors can be a great option. However, there aren't all that many domain investors out there, so there's only so much money floating around. Selling a good Dot Com to other investors is relatively easy but when it comes to new gTLDs, all I can say is good luck with that

- The end user demand isn't exactly impressive either. There are lots of similar new gTLDs to choose from, so why would they pay a premium for yours? Some extensions are almost identical to others. For example, there's a Dot Accountant (singular) and a Dot Accountants (plural) new gTLD, which is downright silly. With so many options to choose from, it should come as no surprise end users won't exactly be eager to buy the new gTLD domain you invested in. To give you an extreme example, here's what you can choose from if you're a lawyer (I kid you not) who wants a domain for his "Legal Counseling ABC" firm: LegalCounselingABC.Lawyer, LegalCounselingABC.Lawyers (plural), LegalCounselingABC.Attorney, LegalCounselingABC.Attorneys (plural), LegalCounselingABC.Law, LegalCounselingABC.Legal and LegalCounselingABC.ESQ... that's just plain ridiculous

I could go on and on but again, we're dealing with basic supply and demand economics. New gTLDs aren't highly desirable (limited demand) and there are too many of them (too much supply). One plus one equals two. Am I saying you can't make money by investing in them? No, I'm sure there are examples of domain investors who did well with new gTLDs. What I am saying however it that the risk to reward ratio isn't tempting enough for me to consider new gTLDs worth it.

So, does this mean you should invest in legacy domains (domains from category #1)?

Well, yes but at the same time no because not all legacy domains are created equal. Investing in an amazing one-word Dot Com isn't the same as buying a four-word Dot Net despite the fact that both are legacy domains. The same way, not all Dot Coms are created equal either. At the beginning of this chapter, I've explained what makes a domain desirable, so I won't repeat myself.

Limit yourself to investing in Dot Coms and the best ccTLDs (Dot De, Dot Fr and so on). This is because there's quite a bit of awareness in their case and this is unlikely to change. Dot Com's supremacy as a global TLD cannot be threatened, just like Dot De cannot be threatened in Germany, Dot Fr in France and so on. No Dot Nets, No Dot Orgs and certainly no Dot Info or Dot Biz domains.

You know what?

If you're not willing to become a professional domain investor and invest quite a bit of time educating yourself, you're better off only investing in Dot Coms. Highly liquid and highly desirable Dot Coms. I for one would recommend two categories: one-word Dot Com domains (popular words, not obscure dictionary terms) and short/catchy domains such as three-letter Dot Coms and three number Dot Coms.

The difference between these two categories (one-word domains and short domain) is represented by the liquidity variable and the return potential one. One-word domains aren't as liquid (easy to sell to other investors) as short domains and quite frankly, short Dot Coms are the only domain category for which it's relatively easy to determine the market value at a certain point in time.

This is both a blessing and a curse.

It's a blessing because when buying a short Dot Com, it's relatively easy to make sure you're getting a decent deal and aren't overpaying. It can however also be a curse because everyone else can do the same thing and when selling a domain, it will be very hard to obtain considerably more than the current market value of the domain you invested in.

When it comes to one-word domains, the exact opposite applies. They're harder to appraise than short domains, so this means you have to be more careful as a buyer. On the other hand though, the upside potential can be considerably higher if you do your job right and pick solid domains at good prices. It all depends on your willingness to take chances.

Here are three tips for investing in one-worders:

1. As mentioned previously, not all one-word Dot Com domains are valuable. So if you're excited about the fact that a dictionary word Dot Com is available at a low price or even at the registration fee (in other words, if it is available for hand registration), ask yourself just how popular the word in question is. I'm sorry but obscure one-word keyword Dot Coms are pretty much worthless

2. You should find the right balance between commercial words and brandables. An example of a commercial word domain would be Scissors.com, whereas an example of a brandable domain would be Cool.com. As you can see, commercial word domains basically describe an actual product, whereas brandable domains don't necessarily have blatantly obvious potential uses

3. If the term is extremely strong then sure, two or even three-word Dot Coms can be valuable. For example, MakeMoneyOnline.com is a great domain despite consisting of three words. If the term is strong (lots of search engine results, lots of searches for the keyword and so on) and the price makes sense then by all means, don't say no just because the domain isn't a one-worder

Investing in one-worders can be quite tricky. Domains such as Scissors.com or Cool.com would be very expensive to acquire, so most investors will be unable to afford inventory of such caliber. Therefore, one has to settle for lower quality one-worders and finding the right opportunities isn't exactly easy. A lot of research is required and at the beginning at least, you will probably not make the best decisions.

For people who don't want to research and learn too much, the recommended investment would be short domains, specifically LLL (Letter – Letter – Letter) and NNN (Number– Number – Number) Dot Coms (three-letter Dot Coms and three-number Dot Coms). They are expensive but have a reseller market value which is relatively easy to determine and I consider them the closest thing to a domain market index fund.

Here are three tips for investing in short domains:

1. Not all letters are created equal. Some are more valuable than others, the most valuable ones are called premium letters (A, B, C, D, E, F, G, H, I, L, M, N, O, P, R, S, T). Personally, I'm a bit on the fence about the letter H, it's great but not as good as the others in my opinion. The non-premium letters are J, K, Q, U, V, W, X, Y and Z. However, five of them (J, K, U, V, W) are considered better than the remaining four (Q, X, Y, Z).

   As of 2015 however, things have changed quite a bit when it comes to letters due to surging demand from China. Nowadays, all domains which do NOT contain A, E, I, O, U or V are considered "Chinese Premium" inventory (this is because not that many Chinese words start with vowels and because the letter "v" doesn't exist at all in Pinyin) and as another observation, the letters L, N, P, Q and R (while still considered premium) aren't as sought-after as the others. Whether this is just a short-term fad or a valuation principle that's here to stay remains to be seen

2. As far as numeric domains are concerned, the overwhelming demand originates from Asia and this has a huge impact on perceived number quality as well. For example, the number 4 is considered bad in China and for this reason, domains which contain it tend to sell for less than those which don't. The number 8 however is considered great and so on

3. If you consider three-letter and three-number domains too expensive, you can try four-letter/number domains on for size as well but I'd recommend stopping there. As far as four-letter domains are concerned, CVCV Dot Coms (Consonant – Vowel – Consonant – Vowel) are the best in my opinion and when it comes to numerics, things like repeating numbers would be a major plus

It ultimately all depends on how much time you're willing to invest to learn the ropes. If you want to maximize results and are willing to put in the hours, one-worders could generate amazing returns. However, if you can't invest the time it takes to become a good domainer, three-letter Dot Coms and three-number Dot Coms represent a considerably safer choice. The returns probably won't be as great but it's far harder to screw up royally.

As a final recap, here are the main advantages of domains over other asset classes:

- The potential returns can be considerably higher than with traditional assets
- They're even more portable than precious metals, remember your registrar login details (username + password) and you're good to go
- You can make money when the reseller market in general does well and even if it doesn't, you might generate amazing end user sales (just don't count on that!)
- A ridiculously low renewal fee will be your only holding cost
- You can make money by taking advantage of their existing traffic (domain parking, for example) or generate more traffic by developing them

… and, of course, the main disadvantages:

- The risks are also higher than with traditional asset classes, not just the returns
- Your domains might get stolen if you don't apply proper security measures (strong passwords, two-factor authentication and so on)
- It will be harder for you to find gems than it has been back in the nineties, for example (the more time passes, the harder it will be)

- Type-in traffic is more of a bonus than a sustainable revenue source, treat it as such

All in all though, I do believe every portfolio should contain at least some exposure to domain names. It's up to you to decide in which domain categories you'll be investing. Buying short domains (LLL, NNN and CVCV Dot Coms) might seem like the easiest approach but unfortunately, this short domain category is quite prone to "pump and dump" behavior.

For example, from late 2015 to early 2016, prices went up dramatically and I mean genuinely dramatically, unlike anything I had seen up until that point. Later on in 2016, they collapsed but still, they're a lot higher than they were prior to the craze. As such, tread carefully and make sure you're getting a genuinely good deal.

If English is your first language, I'd suggest focusing on one-word Dot Coms due to the higher upside potential. If not, short domains might represent a better option but again, remember that there's a lot of "pump and dump" behavior in the world of short domains and act accordingly: with trailblazer assets more so than with status quo ones, prudence is the operative word!

Also, please remember that domain names are fair-weather trailblazer assets and as such, they tend to go down in value when the market as a whole performs poorly. Right after the Great Recession of 2007-2008 for example, a lot of domain investors mistakenly thought domain names would somehow be immune… an oasis in the middle of the desert, if you will. That was not the case. Domain values fell abruptly and have been slower to recover than stocks.

Now sure, the occasional end user sale might get you a huge return even in times of turmoil but as mentioned previously, those situations are exceptions rather than the norm. Realistically speaking, understand that if you buy domain names, you're buying fair-weather trailblazer assets which will perform poorly when the market sentiment isn't exactly upbeat.

However, investing is more than just protecting yourself against the effects of financial storms and for this reason, I want to repeat that I believe there's room for domain names in each portfolio. Investing in an asset class as ridiculously new as domain names is a privilege previous generations didn't have. Don't let your desire to protect yourself blind you and make you disregard promising asset classes just because of their fair-weather nature.

That being stated, let's move on to the second and final fair-weather trailblazer asset class, private equity and peer-to-peer lending.

I'd like to start by stating that this much is certain: banking isn't what it used to be. Perhaps banks have lost touch with reality due to being considered "too big to fail" by governments. Maybe greed is the culprit or then again, what about incompetence? Hard to tell, all we know is the traditional banking paradigm (limiting yourself to using money from deposits to issue loans) is long gone.

Nowadays, banks do everything from trading to lobbying… they've spread themselves too thin in my opinion and this leaves a hole in the financial world which needs to be filled. By whom, you might ask? Well, look in the mirror and you might just find the answer. Never in the history of mankind has the average individual been in a better position to act as a bank.

Why shouldn't you make money by lending to others?

The Internet enables you to have all of the information you need right at your fingertips and it should come as no surprise private equity and peer-to-peer lending are on the rise. Think about it for a moment. If you're a saver, putting your money in the bank isn't exactly appealing, with interest rates at ridiculously low levels. If you're a borrower, you probably aren't thrilled about the flexibility traditional lending institutions are capable of putting on the table.

In the world of the Internet, savers and borrowers can seamlessly interact either directly or through user-friendly platforms. Savers can lend directly to borrowers, receiving considerably higher interest rates than by keeping money in the bank. On the other hand, borrowers who wouldn't normally have had access to financing are now able to pursue their dreams by working directly with lenders.

Win-win all the way.

Let's start with the first dimension, private equity (we'll analyze peer-to-peer lending later on). Private equity, as the name suggests, basically revolves around offering financing to companies which are not publicly traded on the stock market in exchange for either interest (a certain agreed-upon percentage) or equity (a piece of the company). There are three types of equity investors:

- Private equity companies
- Venture capital companies
- Angel investors

The last category is relevant to your interests as a reader because yes, even average individuals can have access to this asset class and these individuals are called angel investors. Angel investors are basically people who provide financing for businesses in exchange for either interest or equity. I wish I could speak more from experience (like I do when it comes to domains, websites and cryptocurrencies) but over here in Romania, the idea of being an angel investor is not exactly widely spread.

The United States dominates by far, with 100 times more angel investor capital than the United Kingdom (which is a major player in finance, to put it mildly) for example. I got the numbers for the United States from the Peter T. Paul College of Business and Economics[55], whereas the United Kingdom numbers come from Nesta[56]. As far as other countries are concerned, the discrepancy is even wider than the US – UK one.

But what about the returns?

Robert Wiltbank from Willamette University and Warren Boeker of the University of Washington published the very first study about angel investor returns entitled "Returns to Angel Investors in Groups"[57] back in November 2007. It tracked 539 angel investors with 1137 exits (hold times are long, expect this) from 1990 until 2007 and all in all, the average return was 2.6

---

[55] Jeffrey Sohl. "UNH Center for Venture Research: Angel Investor Market on Solid Path of Recovery in 2011." *Peter T. Paul College of Business and Economics*. April 4, 2012. http://www.unh.edu/news/cj_nr/2012/apr/lw03angel.cfm.

[56] Robert E. Wiltbank. "Siding With the Angels: Business Angel Investing – Promising Outcomes and Effective Strategies." *Nesta.org.uk*. May 15, 2009.https://www.nesta.org.uk/sites/default/files/siding_with_the_angels.pdf.

[57] Robert E. Wiltbank and Warren Boeker. "Returns to Angel Investors in Groups." *SSRN*. November 14, 2007. http://papers.ssrn.com/sol3/papers.cfm?abstract_id=1028592.

times the investment over a period of 3.5 years or an Internal Rate of Return (IRR) of 27%.

This study makes it clear the returns outperform compared to lots of other asset classes but also that:

1. More hours of due diligence correlate to greater returns
2. More experience is correlated with greater returns
3. Involvement of the angel investor (helping with coaching, mentoring, advice and so on) is also correlated with greater returns

So yes, your returns can be higher but there's considerably more work involved. The more research/due diligence you're willing to conduct, the better positioned you will be to make informed decisions. The more experience you have under your belt, the better your results will be and last but not least, it would help a lot if you have something else to put on the table rather than just money. Maybe your experience, perhaps your coaching capabilities, your contact list and so on. As I'm sure you've realized by now, private equity (specifically angel investing) has its pros as well as cons, just like any other asset class.

Let's start with the pros:

1. The returns are quite high, outperforming let's say the S&P 500 for example. Yes, angel investing (if done right, of course, as mentioned when referring to the Wiltbank and Boeker study) can be quite profitable. You are helping the economy by providing financing to companies with potential and have skin in the game (to paraphrase Nassim Taleb, as done on more than one occasion throughout this book), so you deserve to be rewarded

2. If you're willing to be actively involved in the company and have the expertise and/or contacts it takes to help it, your returns can go up dramatically compared to the returns generated by people who prefer a more passive approach. The more time and energy you invest rather than just money, the higher your returns can end up being

3. Taking part in something new is always exciting and definitely a learning experience. You never know when the experience you've

gained as an angel investor or the contacts you've made will prove to be useful. Perhaps when running your own business or maybe in another future situation, just keep an open mind and you'll surely be able to leverage your experience in one way or another down the road

The cons however need to also be taken into consideration:

1. Liquidity issues can definitely cause problems to unprepared and undiversified angel investors. The returns associated with angel investing are indeed on the high side but if you need cash quickly and have no other assets to liquidate, you'll be in a bit of a predicament. I can't stress this enough, always understand the nature of the asset you're investing in

2. Angel investing is definitely not passive, at least not if you're serious about doing it right. If you think it's all going to be as easy as setting up a bank deposit and earning interest, think again. If my interpretation of the Wiltbank and Boeker study doesn't make this clear enough, please read the study in question yourself in full to understand just how much of difference in terms of returns there is between angel investors who prefer a more passive approach and those willing to roll up their sleeves

3. There isn't as much data/information available as with other asset classes. Yes, there are studies such as the Wiltbank and Boeker one but again, it's considerably easier to learn the ropes with other asset classes. Think of yourself as a trail blazer. If anyone could easily be a successful angel investor, lots and lots of other people would be doing it, driving the returns down significantly. Supply and demand 101

All in all, angel investing is a good choice if you're excited about this asset type and are willing to put in the hours it takes to do it right. However, in light of the fact that it's not exactly passive or easy, I'd say it would be a relatively poor choice for most individuals. Do I recommend angel investing? Well, I'd compare it to investing in art and antiques, as strange as it may sound.

Let me explain. If you like the idea of investing in art and antiques and consider it somewhat of a combination between business and pleasure, go for it. If not, don't. The same principle is valid as far as angel investors are concerned. If you like the idea of being involved with new/promising companies and are willing to accept the workload associated with this endeavor, go for it. If not, you're better off staying away.

Peer-to-peer lending would represent a more passive option.

The peer-to-peer lending phenomenon started in the United Kingdom with the March 2005 launch of Zopa and in the United States, when Prosper was launched back in February 2006. LendingClub followed and other players appeared after that. Based on the research Monica Steinisch published in 2012[58], the returns vary pretty wildly, from 5.6% to 35.8%, depending on variables such as terms or borrower risk profile.

If you want to play it safe by lending exclusively to borrowers with a great risk profile, you'll obviously have to settle for lower returns. On the other hand, you can of course choose to chase higher yields but will have to accept the higher risk factor associated with your approach (which in our case manifests itself through a higher default percentage), it's all up to you.

The peer-to-peer lending industry has evolved rather dramatically.

Back in 2012, the two largest companies in the United States (LendingClub and Prosper) issued about $2 billion in loans together: $1.5 billion for LendingClub and $500 million for Prosper. At the moment of writing though, the numbers are remarkably higher, with over 35 billion dollars in loans together: $26 billion for LendingClub and $9 billion for Prosper.

However, things aren't always peachy and in other countries, peer-to-peer lending hasn't been as successful. An obvious example would be United Kingdom-based Quakle, which went live in 2010 and closed down approximately one year later due to a staggering default rate of almost 100%. It may sound like a joke but unfortunately for those who put their money on the line, it's not.

---

[58] Monica Steinisch. "Peer-to-Peer Lending Survey." *Consumer Action.* June 21, 2012. http://www.consumer-action.org/downloads/english/CA_News-Summer_2012.pdf.

There are non-US success stories as well such as Zopa in the UK but for the most part, peer-to-peer lending is still in its infancy, especially internationally-speaking. Just like with everything else in life, there are pros as well as cons when it comes to this asset type. Let's not waste any time and start analyzing the two dimensions in order to draw some conclusions.

The pros would be as follows:

1. The returns are quite high, even if you choose to play it safe by limiting yourself to borrowers with a very solid profile. In a low interest rate environment such as the one we find ourselves in, even 5.6% per year is nothing to sneeze at. Especially for a country such as the United States, where banks pretty much offer no interest

2. Peer-to-peer lending is relatively passive compared to the other asset type presented in this subchapter for example (angel investing). Now of course, it's nowhere near 100% passive and it's still less hassle-free than let's say putting your money in a savings account but from a hassle/ROI perspective, peer-to-peer lending looks more than appealing

3. You can make choices depending on your risk appetite and most importantly, you'll know what you're getting yourself into for the most part. You have enough information about each potential buyer at your disposal to make educated decisions or at least you should if the peer-to-peer lending platform you're using is even half decent

But let's not forget about the cons:

1. The industry hasn't yet fully matured, so default rates can be quite high, especially if you venture into uncharted territory by working with one of the companies which hasn't yet proven itself. Again, the oldest peer-to-peer lending platform out there (UK-based Zopa) barely had its 12th anniversary, this fact alone speaks volumes about the industry

2. At this point at least, international companies have a relatively poor track record. Yes, the top companies have a solid one but if you don't live in the US or let's say maybe the UK and 2-3 other countries, the

risk goes up exponentially. This is why it's hard for me to provide one-size-fits-all answers, as variables such as this one are insanely important

3. Peer-to-peer lending is very dangerous if you're chasing yield rather than limiting yourself to "proven" borrowers and/or platforms but then again, the same statement is true for pretty much all assets. I understand the temptation of aiming for higher returns by lending to riskier borrowers or working with unproven companies which try to win you over with attention-grabbing but possibly misleading promises, we're all only human. Make no mistake however, failing to resist this temptation can have devastating financial consequences

To conclude and keep things simple: if you live in the US or let's say a handful of other countries (which have a proper peer-to-peer lending infrastructure) and are able to work with proven performers such as LendingClub, Prosper or Zopa then sure, allocating at least a small-ish percentage of your net worth in this manner makes sense. If however you don't live in a country which enables you to have access to companies with a proven track record, stay on the sidelines for now.

Also, as far as the issue of portability is concerned, things are once again tricky. On the one hand sure, you can take your "wealth" with you by simply remembering your login details, which can be of great help if you're forced to leave your city due to a natural disaster for example and temporarily re-locate somewhere else within the country's borders. On the other hand, if you have to leave the country, there's a high likelihood that you'll end up losing access to the wealth you have tied up in peer-to-peer lending platforms.

Again, I consider peer-to-peer lending a viable option to those who live in the US or in one of the select few countries that have a proper peer-to-peer lending infrastructure and companies that are proven performers. For everyone else (myself included), let's just say there are far better options out there.

Chapter 5.2.4.2: Life Jacket Trailblazer Assets

Just like with their status quo counterparts, life jacket trailblazer assets can be considered the exact opposite of the previously discussed fair-weather trailblazer assets. Let me ask you, which trailblazer asset class went up sharply after banks closed in Cyprus and capital controls were implemented? Which trailblazer asset class tends to go up in value whenever there's turmoil?

I am of course referring to <u>cryptocurrencies</u>.

Quite frankly, cryptocurrencies are the only life jacket trailblazer assets I'd recommend investing in and as such, won't be mentioning any other asset classes in this section. I will, of course, be primarily referring to bitcoin, unquestionably the king of the cryptocurrency world. Bitcoin alternatives will however be covered as well.

Back in September 2008, a paper entitled "Bitcoin: A Peer-to-Peer Electronic Cash System" was published by Satoshi Nakamoto[59], basically marking the very beginning of the bitcoin phenomenon. Other attempts at creating let's call it e-cash have existed in the past (for example e-gold, which was backed by… you've guessed it, gold) but they pale in comparison.

The first bitcoin transaction took place in January 2009 (when Satoshi Nakamoto sent 100 bitcoins to Hal Finney) and I'd like to share two interesting anecdotes related to the early price of bitcoin. Believe it or not, 10,000 bitcoins were used to buy two pizzas back in the day, a transaction negotiated by two users on a bitcoin forum. And on the same forum, another user tried to sell 10,000 bitcoins for just $50 but wasn't able to find a buyer.

Therefore, it's safe to say that at the very beginning, a bitcoin was worth less than $0.005 ($50 divided by 10,000). The price evolution of bitcoin since then has been volatile to say the least. In June 2010, the price went up ten-fold, from $0.008 to $0.08 and less than a year later (in early 2011), all the way to $1. The price reached $31 in July 2011 and then very briefly fell to just $0.01

---

[59] Satoshi Nakamoto. "Bitcoin: A Peer-to-Peer Electronic Cash System." *Bitcoin.org.* November 1, 2008. https://bitcoin.org/bitcoin.pdf.

(one cent indeed, that was not a typo, the price did in fact touch $0.01 at the absolute low of the flash crash on the now-bankrupt MtGox exchange), ultimately stabilizing at around $2.

Over the next two years, it shot up to a seemingly staggering $266 (April 2013) but by June the same year, it dropped almost four times. Another high was reached in November 2013, $1,250 but by early 2015, the price dropped to the $200-300 level. After a relatively long period of stagnation, prices went back up to the pre-crash zone, a new all-time high of around $1,300 was reached in March 2017 and an insanely impressive bull run followed, with it being too soon to draw conclusions.

Let's just say that the 2017 high was around $20,000 per bitcoin at most exchanges and in some cases (South Korean exchanges, for example), prices climbed even higher.

All in all, bitcoin went from less than $0.005 in 2009 to over a thousand dollars in 2013 and around $20,000 in 2017. In other words, it was worth over 250,000 times more in 2013 than in 2009 and over 4,000,000 times more in 2017 compared to 2009.

Had you invested one hundred dollars back in 2009 and sold in 2013, you would have made $25,000,000 and no, it's definitely not a typo. Nor is it a typo that in 2017, those bitcoins would have been worth $400 million.

Don't lose any sleep over it though.

Realistically speaking, pretty much nobody generated such returns. In theory sure, it would have been possible, just like it's possible to have 50 brilliant stock picks in a row and make just as much or more. There are examples of this nature as well but they are exceptions and most certainly not the norm. Beating yourself up for not timing the top and/or bottom properly is a surefire way to go crazy.

Instead of choosing the destructive approach, go with a constructive one. Let's analyze bitcoin to figure out why and how it became popular in the first place. On the other hand, let's not lose sight of the cons associated with bitcoin and cryptocurrencies in general. My recommendation would be looking at the cryptocurrency phenomenon in a pragmatic manner and drawing some common-sense conclusions about one of the most exotic asset classes in the history of finance.

Let's start with the pros:

- There are indeed quite a few documented case studies of people who did amazingly well. For example, one of the earliest ones is that of a Norwegian called Kristoffe Koch invested approximately $28 in bitcoin and turned his investment into $827,750. In other words, he made almost 30,000 times more than the amount he started out with. For him and several others, bitcoin was the investment vehicle which turned pocket change into life-altering profits

- Bitcoin is far more portable than precious metals. You can store bitcoins on a piece of paper (offline wallet) or if you're using an online wallet service, all you have to do is remember some login details and you're good to go. If things go terribly wrong in your country (capital controls and all that good stuff) and you decide to leave, the customs people will most likely find any precious metals you have on your person and confiscate them. Finding your bitcoins on the other hand would be considerably more complicated (but still possible if you have an offline wallet they can find) or downright impossible (if you have no physical "clues" whatsoever on your person and simply remembered a few login details)

- People can make bitcoin payments at low fees, even with issues such as mempool clogging situations. The fees associated with wire transfers for example may seem low but if you want to make a very large payment, they definitely add up. Large bitcoin transactions on the other hand carry extremely low fees and on more than one occasion, millions of dollars in bitcoin have been traded at "coffee money" fees

- Bitcoin is definitely revolutionary enough to get people excited. A lot of interesting services ran by brilliant individuals have appeared thus far (from obvious ones such as online wallet services, exchanges and payment processors to innovative services such as bitcoin insurance) and there have been a lot of positive vibes in the tech world around it

- It's getting easier and easier to actually spend your bitcoins. At the very beginning of the bitcoin craze, exchanging bitcoins to cash was pretty much your only option. However, as time passed, more and more options started appearing. Aside from the previously mentioned bitcoin-related services (bitcoin vaults, bitcoin insurance and so on), you can also purchase a wide range of other products/services such as domains, hosting or even real estate (there are several documented examples of real estate sellers who were willing to accept payments via bitcoin) and expensive cars. If you're a merchant and are willing to accept bitcoin payments, the community will welcome you with open arms and a lot of publicity can be generated this way, which is why more and more options for those who want to spend bitcoins are appearing

- The holding costs of bitcoin are on the low side. With real estate for example, you have to pay a bunch of taxes, maintain your property if you own buildings as well rather than just land and the list could go on and on. Bitcoin on the other hand can technically even be held without any costs. You just print a paper wallet and there you have it, problem solved. However, paper is fragile and susceptible to theft, fire or water damage, so I'd strongly recommend investing in a decent fire and waterproof safe (just like what you'd do if you were to hold physical cash) if you keep your bitcoins at home. Or, of course, you can use a third-party bitcoin storage service at whichever fee the company in question charges if you'd rather not keep valuable things at home

- Bitcoin is continuously improved by the community and furthermore, a lot of other cryptocurrencies have appeared and will appear. Most of them are just clones which bring pretty much nothing new to the table but some on the other hand do come with improvements. Even if those cryptocurrencies won't gain traction, they set the bar higher and might end up ultimately leading to improvements being made to bitcoin itself

However, it's not all sunshine and butterflies in the bitcoin world. Here are the cons:

- Yes, there are lots of services out there but bitcoin is still without a doubt in its Wild West phase. Even the once-largest exchange (MtGox.com, which as a fun fact used to be a Magic the Gathering platform in the past) ended up going belly-up and this is just one example. Exchanges went bust, online wallets have been hacked and the list of threats could go on and on. The novelty of cryptocurrencies is both a blessing (opportunities) and a curse (pitfalls)

- As mentioned when referring to the pros, there are several documented examples of people making money. However, bitcoin prices are highly volatile, so there are definitely also examples of people who lost a lot of money due to bad timing. Fortunes have been made in the cryptocurrency world but make no mistake, fortunes have also been lost

- Furthermore, you don't just lose money due to price swings. You can also experience losses due to an improper bitcoin storage strategy (losing your offline wallet, not having strong enough online wallet login details and so on) or downright bad luck. For example, in 2013, a man from the United Kingdom called James Howells accidentally threw his hard drive away. His bitcoins were stored on the hard drive in question and James ended up ultimately losing 4.6 million GBP or approximately 7.5 million USD and that's the value of those coins at the time the news went viral. Today, they'd be worth considerably more

- There are a lot of great services built around bitcoin but unfortunately, there are quite a few shady ones as well. Therefore, don't be surprised if your local authorities tend to raise an eyebrow whenever bitcoin is discussed. China for example banned banks from dealing with bitcoin-related activities in December 2013, more drama followed in September 2017 and you never know what might happen in the future. Maybe governments and central banks will tolerate bitcoin but then again, perhaps they won't and this is an extremely important variable

- It's not as hassle-free to buy and sell bitcoins as you might think. There are basically two options. You can either meet someone face to face locally (through platforms such as LocalBitcoins.com) or buy/sell through online exchanges or other platforms. Meeting someone face to face can be complicated or even dangerous and in order to use online exchanges, you pretty much always have to for example submit photos of your government-issued ID to companies one might consider questionable or even downright shady

- There are more than a few other cryptocurrencies (called altcoins) and it's getting easier and easier to launch one. As mentioned when referring to the pros, competition can definitely lead to improvements. On the other hand though, most altcoins are nothing more than pump and dump schemes. If you're a beginner and don't know what you're doing, stay away from altcoins

- Prices are now very high. Now of course, they could go up 100-fold without me being surprised but realistically speaking, it would lead to a bitcoin market cap in the tens of trillions and this would hardly be sustainable. The bitcoin world is maturing and as such, you shouldn't expect returns as high as they were for early adopters

I've referred to seven pros and seven cons, which leads me to the number one dilemma associated with this subchapter: are cryptocurrencies in general and especially bitcoin worth investing in? In light of the amazing returns people could have theoretically generated up until this point, the temptation to simply answer this question with a resounding "yes" has been quite high.

However, I won't give in to this temptation.

Why? Simply because seven words have to be added to the previously mentioned question before we can proceed. The words in question are "at this point and in the future" and they belong at the very end of the question. You see, my main goal shouldn't be limiting myself to strictly analyzing the past but also (or even especially) looking at the present and the future.

Yes, bitcoin has been an amazing investment in the past. Fortunes have been made. But as far as the present and the future are concerned, I owe it to my readers to be intellectually honest by explaining why the likelihood of similar returns being generated in the future is quite low. We'll start with the fact that yes, a bitcoin was worth 250,000 times more than in 2009 at the high of the 2013 bull run. Or if we refer to the next bull move and compare the 2017 high to the 2009 price level, a bitcoin was worth roughly 4,000,000 times more. Four million!

But are such price increases sustainable?

Definitely not.

This is because back in 2009, it would have been hard to sell bitcoins at even $0.005 each. However, the high of 2013 was $1,250 and another 250,000-fold increase would bring the price all the way up to $312,500,000 a pop. Or if we crunch numbers based on the 2017 high, another 4,000,000-fold increase would bring the price to $80,000,000,000 per coin. Not exactly likely, as I'm sure you'll agree. To get at least a rough idea as to how high the price of bitcoin could realistically get, we have to analyze the "market cap" of bitcoin, even with the obvious limitations of this metric.

In other words, how much all of the bitcoins currently in circulation are worth combined. At the moment of writing, there are almost 17,000,000 bitcoins in circulation and based on the bitcoin algorithm, coins are being mined and added to the pool on a regular basis. However, as per the bitcoin protocol, the number of bitcoins in circulation will "never" exceed 21,000,000. Now of course, due to the nature of how bitcoin works, the limit might end up being increased if enough people agree but all in all, it's safe to say there is currently a cap of 21 million.

It will be quite a while until we get close to 21,000,000 however, so let's focus on the current number of bitcoins instead. At the March 2017 high (prices have gone up a lot since then but I'm using this as a reference point because that's when the 2013 high was topped) of $1,300 per bitcoin and the number of bitcoins in circulation back then, the market cap was $21,125,000,000. In other words, around $21 billion… which is kind of a big deal. At end of 2017 (December 31, 2017 to be more precise), the market cap was $221,485,178,979, with the 2017 high being over $325 billion.

Let's see what would happen in a few optimistic to very optimistic scenarios:

- The market cap at the end of 2017 was, as mentioned previously, $221,485,178,979 (more than the GDP of my country, Romania, with a population of roughly 20 million)

- A 10-fold increase would bring the market cap to roughly $2.2 trillion (more than half the GDP of Germany)
- A 100-fold increase would bring the market cap to about $22 trillion (more than the GDP of the United States at the moment of writing and almost as much as the market cap of the entire S&P 500, so the combined market cap of all companies included in the S&P 500 index)
- A 1,000-fold increase would bring the market cap to $221 trillion (about 3 times the GDP of all countries combined)

… and a 250,000-fold increase (just like the one from 2009 to 2013) would bring it all the way up to approximately $55.25 quadrillion. I'll let you calculate where a 4,000,000-fold increase such as the 2009-2017 one would bring us and I'll also let you be the judge of just how realistic such scenarios are. The bottom line is this: a price increase similar to the one from 2009 to 2013 or 2017 is not merely unlikely but downright outside the realm of reason.

But there's absolutely nothing wrong with that.

Sure, your returns probably won't be as amazing as those earlier adopters witnessed but this doesn't mean there isn't money to be made. It just means there isn't *as much* upside on the table. The same principle is valid when it comes to let's say domain names. You can do very well as a domain investor at this point but realistically speaking, your returns will most likely not be as impressive as those generated by the people who had the foresight it took to buy domains in the nineties.

The ride is probably nowhere near over when it comes to cryptocurrencies. It's the newest exotic asset class out there and as such, opportunities abound. On the other hand though, the pitfalls are more plentiful and dangerous than with proven asset classes such as stocks or real estate. Even more established exotic assets such as domains are let's say safer but on the other hand, the return potential tends to be lower as well.

If you do decide to invest in cryptocurrencies, here are a few things to keep in mind:

1. If you're a beginner and aren't willing to treat investing in cryptocurrencies as a full-time occupation, stay far away from

altcoins. Altcoins come and go at an overwhelming pace, which makes them the perfect "newbie trap" for lack of a better name. There's lots of money to be made but certainly not by beginners who aren't willing or able to treat this occupation seriously. If you're a newbie and want investing in cryptocurrencies to be somewhat passive, stick to bitcoin or let's say the top 3 coins. Nothing more

2. Be mentally prepared to deal with steep price drops. If you're quick to panic, investing in cryptocurrencies isn't for you. In 2011 for example, the price went from $31 to a mere $0.01 (albeit briefly) before climbing all the way to $266. Would you have had the stomach it takes to hold during such a drop? If you're a cryptocurrency investor, such price drops come with the territory

3. Don't put all of your eggs in the same basket. Never make the mistake of keeping all your bitcoins on the same exchange or even using the same storage strategy. Keep some coins at exchanges, some in offline wallets, some in online wallets. The likelihood of losing some coins at one point or another is reasonably high, deal with it

4. Take at least some money off the table every once in a while. The temptation to hold, hold and hold some more is high. I understand this. Bitcoin has had an amazing ride but nothing lasts forever. I'm not saying you should liquidate everything after an upswing, I'm simply making a case for smart money management

5. Don't become emotionally attached to the cryptocurrency phenomenon. Yes, the technology is fascinating. Yes, it may very well end up changing the world as we know it. But this doesn't mean you should abandon reason and become a cheerleader. By all means, be optimistic. By all means, voice your excitement. But within reason

A lot of amazing things are happening in the technology world as we speak. Being able to witness all of these first-hand is a huge privilege. Make no mistake, your children and grandchildren will be amazed at the fact that you "were there" and you have a moral obligation toward them to take advantage of at least some of the various opportunities technology has to offer. Cryptocurrencies most certainly qualify.

On the one hand, you're investing in something truly revolutionary by acquiring cryptocurrencies and on the other hand, you're also protecting yourself by investing in a ridiculously "portable" life jacket trailblazer asset. I firmly believe that if you don't allocate at least some of your capital toward cryptocurrencies, you're doing your portfolio a significant disservice.

Chapter 5.2.4.3: Sentiment-Neutral Trailblazer Assets

The sentiment-neutral trailblazer assets, like their sentiment-neutral status quo counterparts, don't necessarily go with the proverbial market sentiment flow. In other words, they tend to have a mind of their own rather than predictably go up or down based on the performance of the overall market.

In this category, I've decided that <u>websites</u> are the only assets worth listing.

Investing in websites may seem similar to investing in domains at first glance but trust me on this, it's not. Therefore, before starting to wonder why I consider websites sentiment-neutral rather than fair-weather trailblazer assets, read on and you'll see there's some method to my madness.

You see, most people tend to lump them together because in their mind, a website is basically a fancier domain. That's hardly the case. We're talking about two fundamentally different assets and the difference between them is pretty much the difference between let's say buying land and buying a home which needs major repairs in order to collect money via rent or flip it.

Investing in land is for the most part strictly a "buy and hold" arrangement. Land just stays there, no work whatsoever is required. When buying a property and repairing it on the other hand, things change quite a bit. You need knowledge, preferably experience as well and let's not forget about the willingness to invest quite a bit of time and energy if you're serious about doing a good job.

The same principle is valid when comparing domains to websites.

Domains are like land. You buy one and no other action will be required on your part. You don't have to work on it and all in all, no other investment aside from money is required. Websites on the other hand need to be maintained, you can't just set it and forget it as people do with domains. Therein lies the fundamental difference between the two assets.

Still, can we consider domains as well as websites Internet real estate? Sure, with one caveat: domains are like land, whereas websites are kind of like developed real estate. While it is possible to lump both in a broad category such as real estate, it's paramount to understand just how fundamentally different these two are in many respects.

The main reason why I've decided to consider websites sentiment-neutral is the fact that there are so many development business models out there that it's just impossible for the entire asset class to move in tandem with the overall market sentiment. For example, let's assume you run a hobby forum about vintage auto restoration and also sell a course with tips & tricks. If a huge financial panic emerges, it's quite likely your forum will experience a dip in activity and that you'll also sell fewer courses. At the end of the day, people who are worried about their immediate future will probably dedicate less time and money to their vintage auto restoration hobby, at least for a little while.

On the other hand, if you run a forum about prepping (preparing for disasters) and sell a prepping course, then not only will a financial panic not negatively affect you, it will probably be good for business. After all, when people are scared, they're more likely to land on your forum, more likely to buy your course and so on.

… I'm sure you get the point.

That being stated, let's take a look at the disadvantages websites have compared to domains:

1. The holding costs can end up being considerably higher. With domains, all you have to do is pay a ridiculously low yearly renewal fee. A Dot Com domain for example can be renewed for under ten dollars per year. As long as you don't forget to pay the renewal fee in question (you can also renew domains for up to ten years in advance), you can keep your domain name.

    With websites, there are all sorts of other costs which need to be factored in. Each website has to be hosted somewhere, there's just no way around this and depending on how much traffic the website has and how it is coded, the hosting costs can range from less than a dollar a month to gazillions of dollars monthly. Then there are license fees if applicable (for the software you're using) and so on, it goes well beyond simply paying a yearly renewal fee

2. With a domain, no work is required, you just buy and hold whereas websites have to be managed. You can buy a domain, renew it for ten years in advance (this should cost you less than $100) and not touch it as of that point. You can take a let's say five-year leave and when you return, the domain in question will still be in your account.

    A website however has to be managed. If it's a blog or let's say an informational website in general, you have to add content (articles and videos, for example) on a regular basis. If it's a community such as a forum, you have to moderate it and the list could go on and on. Don't assume the site can keep doing just as well if you don't continue working on it

3. An additional layer of security concerns is added compared to domains. You have to be careful with domains as well if you don't want to risk having them stolen. However, a few common-sense measures such as having strong as well as unique passwords (unique as in not using the same password for all of your accounts) and possibly two-factor authentication should be enough.

    With websites however, you have more things to worry about. For example, servers frequently end up being hacked and websites can end up dealing with things like denial of service (DDOS) attacks, the list could go on and on. Some of these problems are relatively easy and inexpensive to overcome but in certain cases, ridiculously high investments and a huge number of sleepless nights are required

4. The buying and selling process itself is considerably more complicated with websites than with domains. All you have to do to change the ownership of a domain is push (if you're keeping it at the same registration company) or transfer it (if you want to move the domain to another company). A push takes place instantly and as far as transfers are concerned, we're talking about a few days at most.

    To change the ownership of a website, a lot more work is involved. You have to also transfer the files over rather than just the domain, make sure there aren't bugs (website transfers rarely take place without at the very least a few tweaks being required due to various hiccups), teach the new owner how to run it if necessary and so on

Moving on, let's analyze the advantages of websites:

1. You can generate considerably more revenue than with domains without selling the asset. Now sure, some domains have type-in traffic which can easily be monetized via parking. You simply change the nameservers and you're good to go. However, don't expect the revenue to be amazing. For the most part, it will be anything but impressive.

    With websites on the other hand, it's possible to generate considerably more revenue. Unlike domains, websites are actually sold based on revenue multiples (more on those a bit later), so you'll most likely be earning revenue right off the bat. Some however don't have revenue and are sold exclusively based on future revenue potential, just like domains. However, generally speaking, we're talking about considerably more revenue when it comes to websites

2. If you work hard, your website can do better and better. This is actually the ideal scenario when purchasing one. You find a website you think can easily be optimized, buy it and take it to the next level. The current revenue can definitely be increased if you know what you're doing and it might end up proving to be so good that you decide to just keep the website indefinitely as opposed to selling/flipping it.

    You can improve a website by doing a better job of monetizing its current traffic or, of course, by generating more traffic. Do keep in mind though that these things are easier said than done. If everything were blatantly obvious, the previous owner would have implemented changes a long time ago. Taking a website to the next level often requires time, money and energy

3. Running a website can be fun if you know and love what you're doing. Let's assume you're passionate about surfing (as in actual surfboards, not surfing the Web) and decide to make money by

taking advantage of your experience as a surfer. You buy let's say a forum about surfing and are in a reasonably good position to do well with it because you're actually an avid surfer yourself.

Think of it as getting the best of both worlds. By investing in a website related to something you're knowledgeable in as well as passionate about, you're able to make money off something which used to be merely a hobby. If you love whatever it is your website is about, you automatically have a huge advantage over most competitors

As can be seen, the disadvantages tend to outweigh the advantages. Don't get me wrong, you can get filthy rich by running websites but this is a section on financial resilience in a book read by people who want to protect themselves against financial storms, not Web development. Therefore, I have to see things from the perspective of someone who has a nest egg and wants to invest his money. I always imagine such a person looking me in the eyes and asking whether or not he should invest in whichever asset I'm referring to.

And when it comes to websites, I'm afraid my answer is for the most part negative. Why? Simply because unlike with domains, it's impossible to do well if you're not willing to put in the hours. Without a significant investment of time, it's just not possible to invest in this asset type properly. Therefore, investing in websites is not a good solution for most people.

Most, not all.

There's one scenario which, in my opinion at least, represents a notable exception: investing in a website related to something you're passionate about. In other words, running the website will be somewhat of a hobby, something fun you look forward to doing. You'll basically be combining business with pleasure and for this reason, won't mind investing time.

So by all means, don't say no if the opportunity to buy a great website related to something you're passionate about arises. If however that is not the case, you're better off looking at other assets. If you do however decide to invest in websites, here are a few tips I think you'll find helpful. I've run my share of websites (including an auction platform, an escrow service, development service-related businesses, blogs, forums and so on) and would recommend the following:

1. If possible, invest in websites built on a great domain. Marc Ostrofsky's example with Business.com[60] is quite eloquent. He bought the domain for $150,000 with the intention of turning it into a magazine but the domain was so good he ended up selling after making two buyers bid against one another. He did very well thanks exclusively to the domain.

   Now I'm not saying things will always unfold in such a manner but this much is certain: having a great domain is always a major plus, as it grants you instant credibility. Whether you're talking to potential partners, negotiating with suppliers, reaching out to advertisers or selling the website, having a very good domain helps quite a bit. Again, instant credibility

2. Buy websites which aren't easy to replicate. Most of the websites which are actively being sold are extremely easy to replicate. Buy a domain, put up a website, generate some search engine traffic and then sell the website. This is a business model way too many people use and I'd advise against acquiring such sites, they're just way too easy to replicate.

   Instead, aim for websites with let's say a higher barrier to entry. For example, communities such as forums or complex websites rather than just random WordPress-powered content sites with a bit of organic traffic. If you're interested in owning an informational website, you're better off building it yourself. The difficulty level isn't exactly prohibitive. However, getting a community such as a forum off the ground is multiple orders of magnitude more difficult, therein lies the difference you have to understand

3. Revenue multiples alone aren't a reliable indicator, they're just one of the variables you should be taking into consideration. If someone tells me he's willing to sell a site for "just" eight times its monthly revenue, I don't get all giddy about it right away. It may sound like a bargain but without having more information, I can't tell for sure.

---

[60] Mark Ostrofsky. *Get Rich Click!: The Ultimate Guide to Making Money on the Internet.* New York City: Free Press, 2013.

What if the website is easy to replicate and with traffic having halved month after month over the past x months? All of a sudden, eight times its monthly revenue doesn't seem like such a screaming bargain. Don't get me wrong, the revenue multiple is an important indicator but without detailed stats and a firm understanding of the website's business model, it's impossible to draw proper conclusions

4. Ask yourself why the owner is selling. Is the traffic on a downward spiral? If yes, then why and what are you planning to do about it? Is managing the site too time-intensive? If yes, then why and are you one hundred percent certain you're both willing and able to give the website you're thinking about buying the TLC it demands?

   You can ask the owner directly but don't assume the answer you'll receive will be the truth. Maybe it will be but then again, perhaps the current owner will lie. Aside from asking the owner, do your own due diligence. Analyze the website, put yourself in the position of the current owner and ask yourself why you'd consider selling the site

5. Are you knowledgeable enough to fix bugs, add new features and so on? The technical barrier can frequently be somewhat of a deal breaker. If you're a programmer, you can skip this tip altogether, as I'm sure you're not worried about this aspect. If however you are not, you have to make sure you're in a good position to run the website you're thinking about acquiring.

   Some websites are extremely easy to manage. Blogs built on platforms such as WordPress, forums built on popular platforms and generally speaking, any site built on a user-friendly foundation. If however that is not the case and if you're not exactly unbelievably tech-savvy, then at the very least make sure the previous owner will put you in touch with the person who created the site so you can hire him whenever the need arises

6. Avoid over-reliant websites, sites which depend on just one company for their traffic and/or revenue. Way too many sites rely pretty much exclusively on Google Search for traffic and Google AdSense for revenue. You're just one policy change away from a nightmare

because essentially, your entire business model revolves around just one company: the big G.

I'm not saying sites can't do well with this business model, I'm simply pointing out it's not the ideal choice. After countless algo update horror stories such as Google Panda and Google Penguin, it should be obvious why an over-reliance on a certain company (not necessarily Google, it's simply the most common example) is a bad idea

7. Before even thinking about making a purchase, set short and long-term goals for the website. When it comes to short-term goals, I'm referring to aspects such as whether you want to improve the site (as in generate more traffic and/or revenue) or just keep things as they are. Long-term goals are decisions such as whether you want to ultimately flip the website or hold it for an extended period of time.

To ensure your purchase is a smart one, you need to have clearly-defined expectations right off the bat. Don't just play it by ear in a "bid now, ask questions later" manner, as it would be a surefire way to blow through your budget with not enough to show for it. Know what you're buying as well as why you're making the acquisition

8. The best marketplace for buying and selling websites (by far) is Flippa.com, previously known as the SitePoint marketplace. It's run by some extremely talented and ambitious Australians, definitely the "go-to" destination for those who want to buy and/or sell websites. You can also sell domains via Flippa but it isn't as popular for domain transactions.

There are other marketplaces as well but the turnover rate is quite high. A lot of them are here today and gone tomorrow, so I've decided to only provide Flippa as a specific example. The likelihood of Flippa going anywhere anytime soon is quite low, so I feel comfortable mentioning it in the book. The bottom line is this: marketplaces such as Flippa are excellent platforms for connecting buyers with sellers

9. However, if you want to get even better deals, you're better off contacting website owners directly instead of purchasing through marketplaces. The popularity of a marketplace is both a blessing and a curse. On the one hand sure, it helps buyers find sellers and the other way around. The same way though, with everything "out there" for lack of a better term, it's hard to find an absolute bargain on Flippa and other marketplaces.

   Too many eyeballs, too much competition. If you can, try to acquire sites directly from the owners. Pick a niche, pick a website type and contact a bunch of owners to ask whether or not their site is for sale. It's really not rocket science, all you have to do is send a bunch of emails and negotiate with the people who end up replying

10. Read Murphy's laws. Then read them again. Everything you think "might" go wrong will. Far too many people tend to downplay the hurdles associated with running a website and assume everything will be a walk in the park, Then the same people get their sites hacked or DDOS'ed and end up giving up because reality looks nothing like the picture-perfect world they thought they were about to discover.

    Websites get hacked. Websites get DDOS'ed. It happens more frequently than you could imagine. Acknowledge this reality and do your best to avoid such situations. Keep your plugins updated if you're running websites built on platforms such as WordPress or if your site is custom-coded, be sure to always have the programmer around in case something goes wrong

I think you're now in good enough shape to decide whether or not investing in websites is a solid choice for your specific situation and if so, what you can do to increase the likelihood of doing well. I firmly believe most people are better off staying away from this asset class due to time and energy constraints but if you come across an opportunity to acquire a great site related to something you're passionate about at a bargain basement price then by all means, go for it!

Chapter 5.3: Other Types of Resilience

Since *The Age of Anomaly* is a book about financial calamities, it obviously makes sense to start with and focus primarily on financial resilience. And I have. The previous section of Chapter 5 hopefully helped you understand what it takes to become genuinely financially resilient. The second section however will focus on... well, everything else.

As strange as it may seem, there's more to life than economics.

Furthermore, there's also more to financial calamities than economics. Writing the book would have been a lot easier if I would have simply focused on a "textbook economics" approach and left everything else aside. After all, I'm an economist and as such, should limit myself to focusing on aspects strictly related to economics... right?

Wrong! To be a good economist, you have to embrace a balanced perspective toward life in my opinion. And to do that, you have no choice but to venture outside the world of economics every now and then so as to understand as well as accept the complex nature of our existence. By focusing strictly on economics and ignoring everything else, I'd end up being intellectually dishonest by recommending an approach that I know doesn't represent the best choice.

My editors would love it if I'd make my books shorter. It would be better for business as well but I refuse to do that. Simply put, I only launch a book if I'm certain I've done the best job possible and the same principle is valid when it comes to this chapter. Without talking about investing in yourself, about mental resilience, about physical resilience and about "SHTF" preparedness, I can't put a well-rounded perspective on the table.

So sit back, hang on tight and be prepared for a ride outside the world of economics!

This involves me venturing outside my comfort zone quite a bit but that's fine. In fact, as you'll be able to find out, I'm actually practicing what I preach here because you'll be exposed to the idea of abandoning your comfort zone quite a bit. Without further ado, let's get right down to business and start with the first section of this subchapter, about... you've guessed it, investing in yourself.

Chapter 5.3.1: Professional Resilience (Investing in Yourself)

Few investments out there make you more resilient than those in yourself. Since I'm an entrepreneur, investor as well as economist, I'm sure I don't have to explain why pretty much everyone I know considers me the "money guy" and as such, a lot of people frequently ask me what they should invest in. It's definitely a fair question but unfortunately for them, I rarely if ever have a simple/straightforward answer and I'll try to explain why.

In a lot of cases, the people in question don't manage to put all that much money aside. Sure, we can talk about diversification, asset classes and what not but realistically speaking, such discussions are irrelevant if the person you're talking to doesn't manage to set a decent sum of money aside each month. If someone asks what he should invest the hundred bucks he set aside this month in, it's hard for me to simply pick an asset class and leave it at that.

Quite frankly, such an approach is anything but ideal for small amounts. There's more than one way to become resilient and this book is all about helping you figure out what works best for you. If you're a multi-millionaire then great, it would be the easiest thing in the world for me to tell you to purchase a self-sufficient farm or something along those lines. Realistically speaking though, such people are a minority… to put it mildly.

The average reader wants to become resilient on a budget, so to speak. Fortunately for them, that is definitely possible and I for one cannot think of anything more effective than investing in yourself. Why? Simply because for small amounts such as $100 per month, you'd need insanely high yields to generate decent results. Like for example 1,000% per year. Easier said than done by investing in stocks or other traditional asset classes, wouldn't you agree?

I have two questions for you:

1. Is your budget too low to buy your way to resilience?
2. Are you also interested in high yields rather than just resilience?

If the answer to at least one of those questions is yes, then investing in yourself is the best piece of advice I can offer. First and foremost, you need to understand that investing in yourself is all about spending money on things which enable you to be better at whatever it is you currently do to make money. If you're a photographer, this might mean investing in better equipment. Or photography courses, perhaps a conference and so on. The same principle is valid when it comes to other occupations. By investing in let's say a course now, you will reap rewards for the rest of your life. The course you invest $500 in this month may very well end up helping you generate $100,000 in the long run. Again, such situations are not unheard of.

There's just one caveat: investing in yourself also involves hard work. These investments in yourself (courses, equipment, conferences, you name it) don't work for you in the manner in which for example stock investments do. They do something completely different: they enable you to make more money but for this to happen, hard work needs to be added to the mix.

If you buy Company A stocks then great, your money is technically working for you. Company A produces whatever it is it produces, it generates profits and you as an investor receive dividends. However, for the most part, you shouldn't expect those dividends to be amazing. It's kind of a trade-off. When investing in Company A stocks, you're accepting lower returns in exchange for the higher degree of passivity associated with this capital allocation approach.

When investing in yourself on the other hand, you and you alone are responsible for the work which has to be done to generate "dividends" and therein lies the fundamental difference between this approach and others. A good course can give you the knowledge you need to make more money but if you don't work hard and put this knowledge to good use, it's all in vain.

In my opinion, there are two main approaches:

- Investing in something **specific**, like for example a course or a certain piece of equipment
- Investing in things which affect your **well-being** and enable you to be in optimal shape. Healthy food, a nice home, a safe vehicle and so on

When it comes to the first approach (investing in something specific), you should think of it as running a business: the name of the game is chasing after attractive investments from a cost/benefit perspective. To do this, I'd recommend applying something I like to refer to as the ABC method. In other words, whenever you're thinking about investing in something specific, be it education or equipment, always keep the following three dimensions in mind:

- **A – Analysis**: analyze whatever it is you're thinking about investing in from various perspectives. Ask yourself which goals the investment in question will most likely help you reach and whether or not achieving those goals would be the optimal choice for your career. Don't forget one thing however: in the absence of proper goals, all of your hard work will only help you get to the wrong destination faster.

  When it comes to the "Analysis" step, you shouldn't think about numbers at all. Don't think about how much you'd have to pay, don't think about how much money you'd be able to make. Instead, focus on one thing and one thing only, seeing the big picture and determining whether or not fundamentally speaking, the investment you're thinking about making is in line with your short, mid and long-term career-related goals

- **B – Benefits:** it's now time to throw numbers into the mix. If everything is okay with the "Analysis" dimension, it's now time to ask yourself how much of a financial impact the investment you are considering is likely to make. How much money are you making at this point? How much additional revenue do you think the investment in question will help you generate right away? How much additional revenue will it help you generate in the long run?

  These are just three examples of questions you should be asking yourself at this point. Now of course, I do understand it's impossible to be incredibly precise when it comes to a lot of occupations. Fair enough, your best guess should do. Take the most pessimistic scenario you can envision, then think about the most optimistic one as well. The final outcome will most likely lie somewhere in-between

- **C – Costs:** if you're serious about determining whether or not a certain investment makes sense, you can't just ask yourself how tempting the benefits could prove to be. It's just as important to take the costs into consideration. Let's assume your best guess is a certain investment could help you generate $25,000 over your entire career.

  Sounds great, right? Well, you don't know for sure without also asking yourself what the costs are. If the costs exceed those $25,000, the investment is obviously less than stellar. Even if the costs would lie at exactly $25,000, the deal would still be lousy if you factor in inflation, as the $25,000 you'd gradually end up making would in all likelihood be worth less than the $25,000 you had to spend initially

It's ultimately all a matter of taking the most pessimistic scenario you can think of as well as the most optimistic one and determining whether or not after drawing the line, your investment makes financial sense. Personally, I'd rather work with the pessimistic scenario because if a certain investment makes sense even under the most pessimistic projections, then there are two possibilities. If the pessimistic scenario materializes, you'll still be satisfied with the results of your investment. On the other hand, if it doesn't, you'll obviously end up being even happier.

On the other hand, if you work with the most optimistic scenario instead, things are more complicated and the uncertainties start piling up. If the optimistic scenario does indeed materialize then good for you, plenty of reasons to be pleased. If however it doesn't, the investment in question would prove to have been a bad one, making you an unhappy camper.

I don't know about you guys but the pessimistic scenario method makes way more sense as far as I'm concerned. Why? Because I'll end up satisfied if it materializes and even more satisfied if it doesn't. When it comes to the optimistic scenario method on the other hand, there's a significant likelihood I'll end up disappointed. Common sense 101, no rocket science involved.

Ok, so what about investing in your well-being?

This time around, things aren't as straightforward. On the one hand, the costs are known but on the other hand though, the benefits are hard or even downright impossible to quantify. A high-quality mattress costs $x, this much is easy to determine. It will help you sleep better at night. Sleeping better makes you more productive. If you're more productive, you're more likely to increase your income. Fair enough thus far, right? But let me ask you, how much money will this particular purchase (the mattress) help you make in the long run?

A tough question, wouldn't you agree? Determining exactly to which degree your productivity will increase after the mattress acquisition and how much money this will enable you to make is quite frankly impossible. Even if you were to ask me for a rough estimate, I still wouldn't know where to start. Therein lies the fundamental difference between investing in something specific and investing in something which is likely to affect your well-being in a positive manner.

I for one think asking yourself the following two questions is a decent starting point:

1. Which percentage of my desire to acquire something is strictly related to my belief that my well-being will be affected in a manner which will lead to increased productivity?
2. Which percentage of the previously mentioned desire is related to nothing more than the perfectly natural "it's so awesome, I want to buy it" basic human impulse?

Figuring these things out shouldn't be extremely complicated. For example, what about the mattress we've just referred to as opposed to let's say a home cinema? It should be pretty obvious which of the two is likely to actually have a positive long-term impact on productivity and which would be a purchase based on completely different arguments.

Don't fall into the trap of using the "hey, it affects my well-being, therefore it's a smart buy" statement as an excuse to make purchases which have absolutely nothing to do with productivity. You'd be shooting yourself in the foot, plain and simple. Don't, just don't. Instead, try to focus on acquisitions which enable you to at the very least do one of the following:

1. Improve your health (better health – better productivity)
2. Save time (more free time – more time for potentially lucrative endeavors)
3. Develop a career-related edge (a nice suit, for example)

Don't just limit yourself to these three, my main goal was merely explaining what the difference between an investment you actually need and one you don't is. If you're honest with yourself, figuring these things out shouldn't even remotely be in the realm of rocket science. You'd be amazed as to how useful common sense can be in a wide range of situations. All in all, it should be obvious why investing in yourself can prove to be considerably more lucrative than investing in traditional asset classes. Never however lose sight of the fact that while the returns can be amazing, there's considerably more work involved. Needless to say, the word "passive" should be eliminated from your vocabulary altogether when it comes to such investments.

I don't really believe in the "universal panacea" concept but do have to say that investing in yourself comes pretty close. Someone who invests in himself properly will be in a far better position to face whatever it is this manic-depressive world throws at him. On the one hand, they're generating impressive yields and this can bring financial security within reach. A financially secure individual will always be in a far better position to react and adapt than the average let's call him consumer. On the other hand, they're also continuously working on their physical as well as mental well-being, which is I'd say just as important.

When thinking about someone who embraces the habit of investing in himself, I'm picturing a balanced person. Someone with his feet firm on the ground, someone who is in touch with all dimensions of his existence. I tell people time and time again that I can never make guarantees. I can't guarantee you'll spot the next financial crisis soon enough. Or that my advice will always help you adapt and figure out the perfect strategy. I can however state the following: words can't begin to describe how well-positioned a reader of *The Age of Anomaly* is compared to the average person. Let's not even go there.

The conclusion of this section is therefore simple enough: invest in yourself generously and in an intellectually honest manner. Become better and better at what you currently do for a living and never lose sight of your physical and mental well-being either. Being prepared doesn't mean hiding in your basement surrounded by guns and canned goods. It means, perhaps more than anything else, facing the curveballs life throws your way with dignity and being the best version of yourself that you can be.

Chapter 5.3.2: Mental Resilience

Far too few economists talk and write about the importance of mental resilience. Whether you realize it or not, the bursting of a bubble affects you on a psychological level. As does the idea of losing money for whatever reason and so on. Without paying attention to the mental health dimension, there's just no way we can talk about genuine resilience.

Which is why this section of *The Age of Anomaly* will focus on just that.

We are going to talk about how to make decisions when you are under pressure, how to deal with the inevitable financial losses you'll find yourself facing at one point or another, how to develop the habit of thinking outside the box, how to establish and nurture vital relationships and finally, I'll be referring to the medical aspects of it all as well at the end of this section.

I want to make it clear right from the beginning that this section is about the economic dimension of mental health, if you will. Don't lose sight of the fact that I'm an economist, not a psychologist or psychiatrist. As such, I will obviously focus on aspects which help you become more mentally resilient from an economic perspective.

Fortunately, implementing even seemingly insignificant changes can frequently be more than enough to make huge progress from a mental preparedness and resilience standpoint. Most people, when preparing for financial calamities and calamities of other natures, tend to make the mistake of only focusing on economic issues, logistical issues and so on. Let's face it, how many people genuinely pay attention to the mental health dimension of economics? Practically nobody.

Don't make the same mistake!

I'm not telling you that mental resilience should be your number one priority and that you should expend 90% of your energy in this direction. Not at all. I am however saying that if you don't pay adequate attention to this part of your life, you're doing yourself and those around you a great disservice. I don't intend to let that happen.

Chapter 5.3.2.1: Making Decisions Under Pressure

How much is 35 multiplied by 10? It's obviously 350. How much is 11 multiplied by 11? It's 121. These are fairly straightforward calculations, right? Well sure, they are. But what if someone is pointing a loaded gun at you and asking you to make those calculations? Needless to say, in such situations, even simple decisions or calculations become multiple orders of magnitude more complicated.

I've said this time and time again. It's easy to give in to the temptation of judging those who have lost a lot of money during bubbles, for example. A lot of decisions currently seem blatantly obvious, so we tend to judge those who haven't seen the obvious and thereby lost money. But when you are under great financial and mental pressure, the obvious can sometimes pose dramatically complicated problems.

It's pretty much an axiom that most people can't cope well with pressure. Individuals otherwise capable of making perfectly rational choices end up screwing up royally when they are forced to make decisions under pressure. Fortunately, I like to think of it as a muscle that can be trained. It would've been pretty depressing to simply tell you that, well, some people just aren't capable of working well under stress but I won't limit myself to stating the obvious.

It is true there are lots and lots of personality types out there and some people are obviously better than others at coping with stress but this doesn't mean there isn't room for improvement. I'm not here to tell you that by implementing a few simple tips, you're going to work better under pressure than highly trained Navy SEALs for example. I can however promise that by implementing a few simple tips, you will be able to become a lot better at making decisions under pressure than you currently are.

Here's what I'd recommend:

1. Don't run away from stressful situations. I frequently don't see eye to eye with most motivational speakers and trainers but do have to

say that when they're telling you to face your fears, they have a point. This brings us right back to the analogy with a muscle that can be trained. If you always run away when things get tough and constantly avoid stressful situations, then I'm sorry to say this but how can you possibly be training your mental resilience muscles? Now of course, I'm not telling you to take on extreme sports as of tomorrow. I'd definitely advise against accepting too much stress in your life. That being stated though, I firmly believe that in the right dose, exposure to stressful situations helps

2. Develop the habit of visualizing negative scenarios and your reaction to them every now and then. What would you do if your bank were to go bankrupt tomorrow? What would you do if civil unrest would start to occur? These are just two examples of questions you should be asking yourself as an experiment, if you will. Pick a scenario, imagine it, try to envision all sorts of reactions that you think you might have and do your best to pick the best one. By visualizing such scenarios, you're basically training your brain and you can think of it as a video game. You can expose yourself to various new ideas, and most importantly, you'll do it in a controlled environment. This is great because on the one hand, it helps you from a creativity perspective and broadens your horizons and on the other hand, should you end up actually dealing with a situation that's similar to one you've envisioned, it obviously won't catch you off-guard. So next time you're stuck in a traffic jam or are simply bored, it's perhaps a good idea to try my experiment and take it from there

3. My next suggestion would be working on your ability to make quick decisions. I have to admit, this is something I struggle with as well. I tend to be very good at making strategic long-term decisions but not as good at making short-term ones. Play basketball, enroll in a chess competition, do whatever you can to expose yourself to situations which require you to make quick decisions

4. Don't forget that lifestyle choices matter. There is a world of difference between making decisions after two sleepless nights and making decisions under pressure when you are at least adequately rested, hydrated and nourished. No degree of mental preparedness

can make us rise above the laws of physics unfortunately. We are only flesh and bones at the end of the day, with all limitations that derive from this

5. I'm now going to share a tip that sounds motivational and I guess kind of is: have confidence in yourself. If you develop the habit of continuously second-guessing your decisions and lack self-confidence, you're going to experience difficulties when making decisions under pressure. I realize having more confidence in yourself is easier said than done but that's no excuse. Needless to say, this would help across other areas of your life as well rather than just economics, so treat this step as yet another incentive to develop the habit of having confidence in yourself and in your ability to make decisions

…I'm confident (see what I did there?) you get the point.

As sure as I am that some of you even have nightmares related to scenarios in which you're forced to make decisions under pressure, I have to say you simply have to get better at it. No matter how hard you try to isolate yourself, you will undoubtedly come across at least a handful of such situations and they're sometimes downright life-altering. In quite a few cases, you'll simply have no choice but to make decisions under pressure. Might as well get better at it and I sincerely hope this subchapter helped!

Chapter 5.3.2.2: Coping With Financial Losses

You can re-read this book each month for the rest of your life and I still wouldn't be able to guarantee you will never experience financial losses after the bursting of a bubble, the start of a financial crisis and so on. In fact, I can pretty much guarantee the opposite. Can you minimize losses? Sure. Can you win more than you lose? Of course. What I'm trying to explain however is that financial losses are inevitable. Words can't begin to describe how important it is not to let this affect you. A lot of people find that quite difficult. They get depressed after losing money, their judgment ends up being clouded and naturally, they end up making even more mistakes.

Vicious circles 101.

We're only human, I realize that. But this doesn't change the fact that if you don't get accustomed to the idea of financial losses, the result will ironically be that even more financial losses come your way. There's just no way around that. I'll even go so far as to say you cannot call yourself mentally resilient if you lack the ability to cope with financial losses properly.

As an entrepreneur, I've been involved in lots and lots of industries, so it's fairly safe to say I know more about financial losses than most people. Why? Simply because I've experienced them myself. I've started design businesses, content businesses, a small escrow service, an auction platform, a blog that ended up being popular, three hosting services, a YouTube channel and so on.

As anyone with business experience can confirm, not everything you touch turns into gold. Some projects turn out to have been better ideas than others and sometimes, well, you lose money. It comes with the territory and even more so, is an essential part of being an entrepreneur. If nine out of ten projects end up being failures but the 10th is a smashing hit, the money it will make can prove to be more than worth it.

The secret if you can call it that is keeping yourself in the game.

Not letting losses bring you down and make you give up, in other words. I'm not certain if the Pareto principle[61] applies when it comes to entrepreneurs but I am confident in my statement that there are more people who fail than there are people who succeed. This isn't because those who fail are not smart enough or for other such reasons but rather it's to a very significant degree because these people gave up. They started a project, the project flopped and most people simply said to themselves that being an entrepreneur is not for them and gave up. Again, keeping yourself in the game is where it's at.

When preparing for and dealing with financial storms, the same principle applies but fortunately for you, you'll have to deal with losses less frequently than let's say entrepreneurs. Therefore, the tips I am about to suggest should be more than enough to help you cope with financial losses. Let's get started:

1.   Consider financial losses a certainty. Don't make the mistake of assuming it cannot happen to you because when (not if) it does, you'll end up being devastated. Think of it this way: when playing sports, the occasional bruise is pretty much unavoidable. Just take it as a part of the game and accept this reality

2.   Have proper safety nets. Now this is easier said than done but it's crucial. You'll obviously be much less affected by the occasional financial loss if you're sitting on a decent enough nest egg. If you're living paycheck-to-paycheck however, then that's an entirely different story. I'm sorry to have to say this but there's no way around the idea of working toward financial security. You have to, that's just the way it is

3.   Understand that this too shall pass. When I was a young entrepreneur with more than reasonable savings for someone my age, my mother got sick and getting her the best treatment money could buy in Europe involved taking her to another country. As such, my savings had been 100% depleted after the entire process which involved surgery, multiple rounds of chemotherapy and a long period of radiation therapy. But I'm still here.

---

[61] Vilfredo Pareto. *Manual of Political Economy*. Augustus M. Kelley. New York City: Augustus M. Kelley, 1971.

As much as it sucked and believe me, it did, the experience didn't kill me. Now some motivational speakers like to insist on the idea that what doesn't kill you makes it makes you stronger and perhaps that is true but I for one don't necessarily adhere to the principle 100%. That experience scarred me so much that I for one feel it would be great if I had a button which enabled me to just keep my mom healthy and not have to go through the entire ordeal. But life sometimes throws curveballs at us, c'est la vie. Since then, I've never been in a situation which involved seeing my entire net worth evaporate but I have frequently gone through periods of financial losses. I promise you, it's not going to kill you. Will it suck? Of course it will. But kill you, it will not

4. An important piece of advice I can give you is this: realize that it's simply a matter of winning more than you lose. This has been a bit of an "Aha!" moment for me and it's ridiculous just how much this simple realization can help. Nobody is expecting you to be perfect, in fact it's certain you won't be. Just remember one thing and one thing only, that coming out ahead means simply winning more than you lose. It's how it works in business, it's how it works in the world of investing and ultimately how it works in life

5. Have a strategy in place for the period shortly after a situation in which you experience financial losses. Do whatever you can and whatever works best for you to clear your mind and regain focus. If you're a nature-oriented person, this can mean anything from taking a stroll through the park to taking a day off and exploring a nearby forest. Or perhaps something else works in your case, for example a good book or a nice documentary. Maybe driving for a couple of hours and listening to your favorite music. It's important to have such strategies because it basically means that you have a system in place and know what to do after experiencing financial losses. This in and of itself helps tremendously

6. Not taking things too far and using the idea of clearing your mind as an excuse to procrastinate. I feel the need to make this additional clarification in the form of a stand-alone tip because a lot of people do this. Watching a movie or two after experiencing financial losses

is perfectly fine. However, binging on Netflix shows for an entire month is obviously a bad idea. If you are doing this thinking that it helps you relax or is in any other way effective, you're fooling yourself

By putting the simple and straightforward tips I've provided above to good use, you'll ultimately end up accepting the idea of occasional financial losses as one of life's unfortunate certainties. This isn't a book about sunshine and rainbows. At the end of the day, it's a book about life. Bubbles grow and burst, a financial crisis frequently ruins what seemed like a good run, political calamities pop up and so on. These are all certainties of life. You can accept them or not, they'll take place regardless. I would therefore strongly suggest doing the former and even more so, using my advice to prepare properly.

Chapter 5.3.2.3: Thinking Outside the Box

It's hard for me, as someone who is fairly well-known for thinking outside the box, to write about this topic and try to give advice. This is because thinking outside the box isn't something that can always be taught. Think about it. If I were to give you a detailed guide on how to be original, would you be able to say about yourself that you're original if you were to follow my guide 100%? Of course not, you would simply be adhering to my version of originality, and as such, you'd be the exact opposite of original. I can however most definitely give advice that points you in the right direction and will actually be doing just that.

Without further ado, here's what I'd recommend:

1. The first word of advice I have for you is not putting the status quo on a pedestal. Our current systems are frequently quite awesome but a lot of times, they're deeply flawed. You need to acknowledge this and not consider the norm or everything in the realm of status quo automatically perfect. I assure you, that would be a mistake. Furthermore, it's an attitude that keeps you from reaching your true potential in terms of critical thinking and originality. After all, if things are perfect the way they are, why go through the trouble of thinking critically? It's impossible to beat perfection, so why try in the first place? I'm sure you get the point

2. Develop the habit of experimenting. Whenever you're experiencing difficulties and aren't sure what needs to be done, don't be afraid to simply experiment and see what happens. If you fail, then so be it. You will however get it right from time to time and as such, your brain ends up accepting the idea that original solutions can actually work. I consider this a breakthrough for most people

3. Take part in activities that encourage creativity or original thinking. This can mean anything from playing challenging games to embracing new hobbies, it's all up to you. Just do whatever works

best for you and whatever you feel challenges you in a creative manner

4.   Allow information sources which challenge your beliefs into your life. Don't be like a Republican who only watches Fox News or a Democrat who takes all of his information from MSNBC. In other words, ironically, getting out of your own bubble helps you become better at spotting the bubbles we talk about in this book. Allow yourself to be exposed to various viewpoints, even if this won't be easy at the beginning

5.   Surround yourself, if possible and whenever possible, with creative people or if you will, with others who think outside the box. Being exposed to creativity and original thinking can only help, so why not?

6.   Try to escape your daily routine every once in a while. By taking part in anything that's new to you, by practicing a sport with which you have absolutely no experience and so on. If you allow yourself to be encapsulated by your daily routine, you need to understand that a certain degree of rigidity comes with it. Becoming better at thinking outside the box is a lot easier if you free yourself from such rigidity by occasionally saying no to your daily routine

As can be seen, you will in pretty much all cases have to venture outside your comfort zone. Something that isn't always easy. But if you're serious about developing the ability to think outside the box and becoming better and better at it, you have no choice. Fortunately, developing the habit of occasionally thinking outside the box isn't as difficult as it may seem at first sight. Furthermore, it can and should also be fun.

Chapter 5.3.2.4: Relationships

In your quest toward mental resilience, you need all of the help you can get. Study after study[62] proves that having strong relationships with others helps your overall well-being, your mental well-being and even enables you to live longer. If you're an extrovert, what I'm saying probably sounds fairly straightforward but make no mistake, human beings (whether introverts or extroverts) are after all herd animals and as such, interpersonal relationships play an extremely important role in our lives no matter how diverse we are in terms of personalities.

It's hard to envision any area of our lives that isn't enhanced by fostering quality relationships but I'm choosing to cover this topic in the subchapter about mental resilience because I feel that from a mental health perspective even more so than when it comes to other dimensions, relationships are paramount.

You cannot just clap your hands and expect to have meaningful relationships overnight, these things take time. This is why there's no time like the present to start working on your relationships. If you plant seeds now, you're dramatically improving the likelihood of them turning into plants you can rely on when the time comes... don't wait until it's too late.

Here are a few practical tips to get you started:

1. Eliminate toxic people from your life. If you buy a great piece of land with a really awful property on it, the first step will obviously be getting rid of the highly-deteriorated house in question. The same way, a good first step toward your goal of improving the quality of your relationships is starting a phase of let's call it spring cleaning in your life. Few things are more important than your time, energy and mental health. By not getting rid of all of the toxic relationships you

---

[62] YC Yang, Courtney Boen, Karen Gerken, Ting Li, Kristen Schorpp and Kathleen Mullan Harris. "Social Relationships and Physiological Determinants of Longevity Across the Human Life Span." *Proceedings of the National Academy of Sciences of the United States of America.* January 19, 2016. https://www.ncbi.nlm.nih.gov/pmc/articles/PMC4725506.

can, you're making it multiple orders of magnitude harder for yourself to build on a solid foundation. Of course, you should be delicate about it but at the same time, you need to understand that not only is weeding out toxic people from your life a right you have, I'd even go so far as to call it an obligation

2. Have a clear understanding of what constitutes a quality person. Don't make the mistake of assuming a quality person is someone who thinks like you and acts like you. By only surrounding yourself with people like you, you're practically living in a bubble and that's not exactly healthy. A quality person is first and foremost a good person. A person with whom you have things in common when it comes to core values. And by core values, I mean for example even basic things like not humiliating fellow human beings, especially behind their backs. Other desirable values might be the willingness to be there for your friends and for the people you care for and so on. Of course, defining a quality person is a highly subjective endeavor and therefore, you and you alone are responsible for figuring out what the definition should be in your case

3. Even if you aren't the most social person in the world, do your best to have a reasonably active social life. In our family for example, my wife is an introvert, whereas I am somewhere in the strange region between introvert and extrovert. As such, neither of us are people you would call exuberantly social. Still, we actively try to take care of our social life. By meeting friends, by visiting those who live abroad and so forth.

It's definitely possible, and we can attest to this, to have a reasonably active social life even if you're not a textbook extrovert. Furthermore, it's something you need to work on because building and maintaining relationships takes time. Resist the temptation of being a workaholic to such a degree that it affects your social life because unfortunately, without an active investment of time and energy, your social life will deteriorate without you even realizing that. This is perhaps the most dangerous aspect, the fact that the changes and especially deterioration can take place without you realizing it

4. Develop the habit of giving and helping without asking or expecting anything in return. As a personality type, I am what you would call a giver, so it just comes natural to me. However, even for people like me, the willingness to help without expecting anything in return is what makes the difference between a healthy giver and an unhealthy one. You cannot expect others to be kind and generous toward you without being willing to do the same and even more so I would add, without being able to start the virtuous circle yourself. It might not be easy at the very beginning but it's a habit I highly recommend embracing. Ask others if they need help, be ready to be of assistance and most importantly, do all of this without expecting anything in return

5. Do everything you can to become the best version of yourself possible. If you're facetious, manipulative, a liar and so on, then don't be surprised if people start avoiding you. Do your best to become the type of person others want to have as a friend. Perhaps this is the tip I should have started with because before expecting something of others and judging other people, it might be a good idea to look in the mirror and ask yourself if you are the type of person others would want to have as a friend. If not, it might be a good idea to start by working on that

As can be seen, there are no quick fixes if you're serious about building quality relationships. Think of a good relationship by envisioning a bank account. In other words, think about building relationships as you would about saving money. With each friend, you basically have an account. Each time you do something positive like having a pleasant experience together, helping that person out and so on, you deposit goodwill to that account and each time something negative happens, you obviously withdraw from it. Needless to say, just like it takes time until you have enough saved up to comfortably say that you have a decent nest egg, it will take a long time until you have accounts with other people that are impressive enough for you to say that your life is filled with meaningful relationships.

Chapter 5.3.2.5: The Medical Dimension

I don't want to end this section without making it crystal clear that if you have a mental disorder or anything along those lines, the best course of action is obviously not trying to find solutions in a book written by an economist. In other words, I hope everyone realizes that through this section, I'm referring to the economic dimension of mental health.

I am not a psychologist or a psychiatrist, I'm an economist. Therefore, if you currently have any kind of mental issues or think you might have them, then the number one advice I'm giving to you without thinking twice is this: seek the help of a professional. Through this section, I have had two primary goals:

1. Emphasizing the importance of mental resilience to those who are serious about becoming better at spotting financial storms and dealing with them
2. Providing coherent and easy-to-implement tips which enable you to become more mentally resilient

Please don't give into the temptation of simply skimming through this section without taking it all too seriously because make no mistake, mental resilience can be a huge asset on the one hand and on the other hand, the lack of mental resilience can and most likely will prove to be something that holds you back.

And it would genuinely be a shame because as you've been able to see, the tips I've provided are by no means in the realm of rocket science. Therefore, the conclusion is simple in my view: if you're a person with no mental health issues who wants to work on his mental resilience, putting the tips I've provided to good use will be a huge step forward.

If you have a mental disorder or anything that could be considered a medical health problem on the other hand, then please seek the help of a professional as soon as possible. I believe I've made myself perfectly clear and with that stated, I wish you the best of luck in your journey toward mental resilience!

Chapter 5.3.3: Physical Resilience

As I'm sure you've noticed by now, I'm a pretty peculiar economist. In other words, I frequently tell you things you don't exactly hear from my peers and that is perhaps my main selling point, if you will. This section won't represent an exception and as strange as you may find it initially, I am actually giving you physical health-related advice in a book about economics. However, once you hear me out, I think you'll agree with me that there is (some) method to my madness.

The bursting of a bubble or even worse yet a serious financial crisis can be a truly life-defining moment. There aren't many such moments in our existence and as such, when they do occur, we need every edge we can get. Huge transfers of wealth tend to take place during periods of economic calamity and of course, the average individual is usually on the losing end. But this doesn't have to be a self-fulfilling prophecy.

By going through the trouble of actually reading my book, you are already many steps ahead of most individuals because you've proven that you actually care about these things and are doing your best to position yourself properly. Time and time again, as an economist, I've noticed just how interlinked things are in today's world.

You might think that a crisis affecting oil-producing nations which are far, far away won't impact you but that is a dangerous statement to make because it's not only the direct impact that counts. As such, those who downplay the impact of such events might just be in for quite a surprise at the gas pump, when realizing that no, they aren't 100% shielded from international events. That's just an illusion.

The same principle is valid if you're serious about becoming more resilient. You're most likely reading this book because you want to learn more about financial anomalies and become better at spotting them. Fair enough. You might however be tempted to believe only financial resilience is important if spotting financial storms is your main goal and that's just plain wrong. Everything is interlinked and if you don't pay attention to other types of resilience as well, you're shooting yourself in the foot.

As far as I see it, the situation is fairly straightforward: somebody who is generally healthy and in reasonable shape is in a much better position to cope with anything life throws at him. And believe me, life can throw quite a punch! There's no telling what will ultimately happen to our financial system. Anomalies are all around us and I for one am not ruling anything out. At the risk of sounding like a broken record: you need any edge you can get.

That being stated, here are the tips I'd recommend when it comes to the physical dimension of resilience:

1. Get adequate amounts of sleep and make sure it's high-quality sleep. This is something fewer and fewer people do. Now I'm not going to offer any one-size-fits-all solutions as to how much sleep you need because this varies from person to person. Perhaps you're a morning person who, like my wife, can get up at four or five in the morning and function pretty much perfectly on less sleep than someone like me for example, who needs more rest and relaxation. You might already know how much sleep you need to function properly and if not, feel free to experiment. The bottom line is this: figure out what works best for you when it comes to sleep and implement lifestyle changes accordingly

2. Avoid poisoning your body. If it's one thing I can attest to when it comes to health and wellness based on my experience, it's that sometimes, it is more important what you don't do in terms of your overall health than what you do. In other words, if you smoke two packs of cigarettes per day and eat some broccoli afterward, then I'm sorry but that's just not going to cut it. I do my best to avoid clichés but I do have to say that your body is indeed a temple and perhaps more so than anything else, you treat it with respect by not polluting it

3. Eating and drinking the right things. When deciding how much you spend on food, what you eat and what not, you're practically deciding how to invest in your well-being. It might be a lot cheaper to simply live on noodles and ketchup from now on but in the long run, this might do more harm than good. I don't know about you guys but I would much rather eat the right things now and reduce the likelihood

of contracting all sorts of illnesses than make compromises when it comes to food quality now and be excited about the short-term benefits without thinking about the long-term implications. Do whatever works best for you but I for one don't shy away from spending more money on food if I have valid quality-related arguments

4. Don't forget about fitness. You know, getting in shape if you currently aren't and staying in shape if you currently are. Now again, I'm giving you this advice from the perspective of someone who wants you to become more resilient. I'm definitely not saying you need to become a marathon runner as of this point. I do however strongly, strongly recommend being in shape and a lot of times, seemingly insignificant changes make a huge difference. For example, taking your bike instead of your car to work from now on, of course if that is possible. Or if you live on the eighth floor of a building, taking the stairs from now on instead of using the elevator. Things you can seamlessly turn into habits that make the difference between somebody who is in shape and someone who isn't. Consistency is the operative word here. I'd much rather see you embrace small healthy habits that you can hang on to forever than get a gym membership after reading this book, be excited initially and then abandon everything after a couple of months. Sustainability is paramount

5. Taking care of medical-related aspects early on. For example, if you need dental work done, I would strongly advise against delaying and delaying it like most people do. Now I realize you aren't exactly giddy with excitement about going to the dentist but I for one would much rather get my medical house in order when times are good and nothing is in the acute phase than have to deal with a medical emergency when times are rough. Will it be the most pleasant experience in the world? Probably not but if you take care of things early on, it will certainly be a lot better than if you procrastinate

6. Don't limit yourself to only visiting your doctor if you feel as if you're about to die. Even if you don't have any medical problems that you're aware of like for example the dental issues I've mentioned previously,

it makes sense to get tested regularly and to perhaps go through various screening processes based on the recommendations of your doctor. Again, the sooner you identify and take care of problems, the better

7.   Have emergency cash at hand for medical situations. Maybe you have seemingly rock-solid insurance that you're very happy with, that's awesome. However, do keep in mind that in a systemically devastating financial crash, there are casualties and insurance companies will fairly certainly be among them. As such, you should never make the mistake of relying too much on insurance companies, no matter how great their track record may be or how happy you are with your current relationship

I could go on and on but I'm sure you get the point. Becoming physically resilient is simply a matter of making lifestyle choices in a coherent and sustainable manner. This is a book about spotting financial storms and preparing for them. As such, I'm doing my best to present advice from a primarily economic perspective. Becoming more physically resilient however is obviously something that's going to help across all areas of your existence, its scope is not just limited to the world of economics.

You'd think taking care of your physical health and your mental well-being are things we can consider so straightforward that writing about them seems like overkill. But if we take a step back and analyze our way of living in the 21st century, we realize that is hardly the case. Just think about things from the perspective of let's say the average workaholic. He wakes up after getting way too little sleep, pumps way too much caffeine into his body to get his day started and then even more caffeine to get through it. He grabs a bite to eat here and there, probably not the healthiest things money can buy either because he doesn't have time for that. He's been at the office pretty much the entire day working under constant pressure, only to arrive home after the fall of night, undernourished, over-caffeinated, way too stressed and knowing he's going to start all over again the next day.

Society as a whole is definitely not ready to cope with let's say a real crash of the financial system or generally speaking, a calamity of epic proportions. This is because the average person is just not resilient. We're all living in our own little bubbles, oblivious to the fact that we are ridiculously fragile. For this reason, without genuinely understanding the chapter about resilience, you will in no way be truly equipped to cope with financial storms. Your family isn't, your friends and acquaintances aren't either.

As you can see, the section about physical resilience isn't exactly huge. This is because becoming more physically resilient is possible by implementing a few simple lifestyle and mentality changes. However, I wouldn't have been able to conclude that I've covered this chapter properly without addressing the issue of physical resilience as well. Most people make the mistake of rolling their eyes when someone mentions an aspect as "mundane" as physical resilience. Don't be one of them.

Chapter 5.3.4: SHTF Resilience

Let me just start by making it clear I'm not a prepper. I understand preppers but don't agree with the degree to which they allocate capital toward prepping-related activities. Frankly, I'm convinced most preppers take things too far and invest way too much of their net worth in let's call them insurance policies.

On the other hand though, I do believe it's highly likely that we'll deal with at least one serious "You-know-what Hit The Fan" event throughout our existence. As such, while I wouldn't recommend becoming a prepper, I'd strongly suggest being prepared. The difference between the two is mostly a quantitative one. Throughout this section, I'll provide what I consider to be common-sense SHTF preparedness tips but again, moderation is the operative word.

I'll be analyzing various scenarios, starting with mild disruptions caused by a financial crisis and ending with scenarios in which relocation is your only option. I'll be doing this from the perspective of an economist who firmly believes in being prepared. Some would say I tend to be more prudent or even downright pessimistic when making plans compared to other economists... and they're right.

I'm an optimist in life but when making any kind of plans, I for one prefer to be pessimistic. This attitude keeps me on my toes and usually enables me to avoid overlooking threats. Most of my peers would have chosen not to include an SHTF section in an economics-related book but I think that would have been a mistake. At the end of the day, I believe in giving my readers the full picture when it comes to financial storms and their potential consequences so that they can prepare properly. Over the next few pages, I'll be doing just that.

Chapter 5.3.4.1: General Disaster Preparedness

This book primarily deals with financial disasters such as the bursting of a bubble, a financial crisis and so on. One might be tempted to assume that the effects of such events are, at worst, financial losses. But in worst-case scenarios, financial calamities can degenerate to such a degree that they end up disrupting your day-to-day life significantly.

I'm an economist and, naturally, am supposed to be someone people turn to for answers. But even someone like me has an extremely difficult time picturing what society would look like if the financial system would cease to function for whatever reasons. Perhaps as a result of a significant financial crisis which brings it to its knees, perhaps due to a cyber-attack and so on.

Our day-to-day lives are extremely dependent on the well-functioning of systems which are inherently quite fragile. Let's try to envision such a scenario for a moment and assume banks would stop functioning as of tomorrow. No withdrawals, no bank transfers. Nothing. Since most of the currency we use is in digital rather than physical form, trade in general would be dramatically disrupted. A lot of businesses would probably close up shop the very next day because they just don't have the infrastructure in place to function in such scenarios. And even in the cases in which certain businesses would stay open, it remains to be seen what they would accept in return for the goods or services they're selling.

For example, your local supermarket will obviously not be able to accept credit card payments, so perhaps it will accept cash only. But since the average person in Western societies doesn't exactly hold on to a lot of cash, consumers would experience excruciating difficulties meeting even the most basic of needs.

Not only is the average consumer not resilient, I'll even go so far as to say he is downright spoiled. Spoiled or should I say completely out of touch with anything outside of the bubble he's living in. The average Westerner is used to going to the office each day, getting paid, making payments with credit or debit cards and so on. His entire life revolves around systems which, as previously mentioned, are extremely fragile. If the financial system were to cease functioning, I don't want to beat around the bush: those people would be doomed.

However, don't make the mistake of assuming that if you have a bit of cash under the proverbial mattress, you're all set. The supply chain will be broken in the absence of a functioning financial system and as such, expecting to find the shelves of supermarkets full of food, just waiting for you and your cash would be quite foolish in my opinion. I'm sure you now understand just how fragile the balance we're currently living in is. Now, let's take things one step further and envision various scenarios, starting with scenarios for which preparing is a lot easier and continue with more challenging ones.

I'd say a mild financial disaster would be something like a financial crisis which disrupts your day-to-day life in a relatively mild but still significant manner. For example, a financial crisis which makes the authorities resort to a bank holiday or in other words, a financial crisis which has the immediate result of banks being closed but only for a relatively short period of time.

For such a scenario, I think the term "disaster preparedness" is too drastic because realistically speaking, employing a few common-sense measures would be more than enough. First and foremost, you need to always and I mean always have adequate cash reserves at hand. If your credit card stops working or if banks stop functioning for whatever reasons, you need to know you can always count on the cash reserves you've set aside for precisely such situations.

I for one seriously doubt such disruptions would result in severe food shortages or anything along those lines but still, I firmly believe that even the most optimistic readers of this book should have reasonable food and water supplies at hand. If you don't have a disaster preparedness strategy in place which at the very least makes it possible for you to cope with let's say a couple of difficult weeks or a difficult month, then I'm sorry but you're doing it all wrong.

It's definitely not my intention to turn you into a prepper and make you spend your entire net worth on various survivalist supplies, not at all. Believe me, there are people who actually do this and they're making a huge, huge economic mistake. I am however saying that your basic necessities need to always be covered. Grabbing a bit more rice, a bit of bottled water here and there, some medicine and hygiene items such as toilet paper and so on really shouldn't be all that complicated. Again, having some reasonable cash reserves will most likely be more than enough if we only end up dealing with relatively mild disruptions in the financial system but still, prudence is the operative word, so be sure to have reasonable suppliers set aside as well.

But what about more severe financial disasters?

For example, if we're talking about a financial market meltdown of such proportion that it renders the financial system obsolete for an extended, indefinite amount of time, then things tend to become quite complicated. Chaotic would perhaps be a better word. This is because, without a doubt, some form of commerce will continue being conducted. However, it will look nothing like our current relatively orderly system.

Think about it: if the financial system stops functioning for an extended period, the dynamics of money as we know it would change dramatically. As mentioned in my previous, lighter example, you can forget about using the money you had on your debit card or in your bank account. If you have cash, then you will probably be able to get by, but then again, I'm reasonably confident that some sort of a barter type system would eventually function as well. However, chaos is the operative word because unlike the proven financial transactions system that we have grown accustomed to, whichever new system temporarily replaces it will have a distinct Wild West feel to it.

To prepare for such situations, I would say that there are two broad options: on the one hand, classical preparedness which revolves around you securing various necessities right now so that you can use them when the time comes and another option would be not necessarily having everything at hand but rather having a set of core supplies/assets and then a strategy in place that is flexible and enables you to adapt to the manner in which the disaster unfolds.

The first approach, let's call it "old school preparedness," revolves around securing the following:

1. The basic necessities. So water, food and shelter. Water obviously comes first because while you can survive for a more extended period of time without food and you can put some extra blankets on if it

gets cold, you'll be in trouble far sooner without water. Next comes food, mainly in the form of canned goods as well as food that has an extremely long or even indefinite shelf life if stored properly such as pasta and rice. Then comes the dimension of shelter or in other words, everything you need to live properly, not get cold and so on.

The main problem with all of this is represented by the storage aspect. If you only want to cover your basic necessities for let's say a month, then storage isn't that much of a big deal, even if you aren't living in a huge house. If however you want to be prepared for six months or even a year, things get a lot more complicated. This is especially valid when it comes to storing water because the volume which needs to be deposited would be so great that you truly would require quite a bit of space to pull it off. This is why some people prefer thinking outside the box but I'll get to that when analyzing the next approach. For now, we'll stick to old school preparedness

2. Medical supplies and toiletries. While it might not be the first thing you think about, the hygiene and medical aspect is without a doubt essential to your survival. Have you ever asked yourself why people live so long nowadays compared to the distant past? You might be tempted to think it's because we have various high-tech treatments for complicated diseases but the truth is that the "simple stuff" like antibiotics, cheap vaccines and basic hygiene[63] played the most important role.

    In the distant past, people died from basic infections that pose no problems whatsoever at this point to a much greater degree than you might imagine. But today, the most basic drugs together with basic hygiene conditions make it possible for a lot of the leading death causes of the past to disappear.

    Words can't begin to describe how important having medical supplies and basic toiletries is. Especially the dimension of medical supplies. Think about Murphy's Laws, about how no matter how bad

---

[63] Richard Suzman and John Beard. "Global Health and Aging." *National Institute on Aging.* October 1, 2011. https://www.nia.nih.gov/research/publication/global-health-and-aging/living-longer.

things are now, they're probably going to get worse. Or about how people say that when it rains, it pours. The same way, you might just find yourself in the middle of a catastrophic situation, realizing you have to also battle an infection. Don't forget about the medical and hygiene dimension when times are good because by the time things get worse, what is now simple planning can end up being a lot more difficult

3. Having cash at hand. Now sure, maybe people will lose faith in all types of money altogether when disaster strikes but that's probably not going to happen. In fact, cash will most likely be the first thing people turn to. Therefore, it makes sense to have adequate cash reserves. No matter how well you plan, it's hard for me to believe you'll be able to store absolutely everything you could possibly need for an extended period of time yourself. You need a medium of exchange so as to secure the thing you didn't think about getting and others will be in a similar situation. That medium of exchange is most likely going to be cash, so as bad as cash tends to be as an investment due to inflation and all that, you definitely need it from a disaster preparedness perspective

4. Get some highly desirable and tradable items as well. No matter how confident you are that cash will maintain its value and will be enough to get you out of trouble, you have to accept the possibility that this might not happen. You never know. For this reason, assuming some sort of a barter situation takes place, it makes sense to own items people want and that are easily tradable so that you can use them when necessary. It's hard for me to say what such items will be because it's highly geo-dependent. In the United States, I'm sure ammunition will be in high demand for example. In other places with less of a tradition when it comes to guns, we'll most likely be talking about something else like for example jewelry

There are various other aspects I can refer to, like the importance of having a strong social circle or the importance of mental resilience, but these are things I've covered in other sections of this chapter and as such, there is little point in referring to them again. Instead, let's move on and refer to another type of disaster preparedness, which relies a lot less on storing massive amounts of supplies and much more on ingenuity and flexibility.

We can call it "flexible preparedness" and there are several key differences between it and old school preparedness:

1. Instead of filling your entire basement, garage and even house with gallons upon gallons of water, store a much more reasonable amount, let's say enough to keep you going for a month and aside from that, simply have a smart water acquisition and filtration system in place.

    No matter how big of a financial or geopolitical crisis we're dealing with, it is most likely still going to rain. As such, why not take advantage of what nature has to offer and put together a simple water catching system? Filtering that water is also relatively simple, all you have to do is perform a little bit of research and there you have it: your water needs will be more didn't adequately met and best of all, you don't need all that much storage space

2. When it comes to food, things are a bit more complicated because I won't exactly go so far as to tell you that you can simply learn how to hunt pigeons. I'm a reasonable guy and realize that not everyone can or wants to acquire such skills. This is definitely not a prepping book, I'm not a prepper myself and don't believe in taking things to the extreme. However, this doesn't mean you shouldn't be smart when it comes to your food supply

3. Always realize that the space issue needs to be taken into consideration. As such, as someone who has a limited storage capacity more so than someone who has lots of space at his disposal, you need to be selective when deciding which supplies are worth acquiring and which are not. Just think about why it makes more sense to store let's say canned goods than a bag of Cheetos from the perspective of quality calories gained/volume occupied. Again, common sense. Being flexible is especially important if for example you live in a small apartment and just don't have all that much space at your disposal

4. When it comes to cash, I have to say the modus operandi will be identical to the strategy you should choose for the old school preparedness approach. No matter which strategy you might have, I

for one cannot think of any way to circumvent the need to have a cash stash

5. When it comes to tradable items, the situation is a bit more complicated. For example, everyone needs toilet paper but this doesn't mean it's a good idea to fill your home with rolls of toilet paper in the hope that you can treat them as tradable items. I'm sure you get the point. Some tradable objects represent a better choice than others and those who opt for a more flexible strategy are usually individuals who know that it makes sense to focus on tradable objects which are also highly, highly portable

I'm sure you get the point. Now I for one tend to favor the more flexible approach but this much is certain: both of them will put you multiple steps ahead of the average individual, who is anything but prepared for real financial disasters. But what about more dramatic scenarios, in which not only does the financial system stop functioning but society as a whole deteriorates? I'm talking about situations which also involve civil unrest, social tensions and so on. In this case, compared to the previous situation type, another dimension is added to the mix: that of safety.

I for one tend to be a proactive person rather than a reactive one. In other words, I try to avoid problems in the first place rather than have to deal with them and their effects. This is why, when buying a home, I highly recommend not making compromises when it comes to the location. When times are good, you might be happy about the fact that you're saving a few bucks by purchasing a home in let's say not the best part of town. But if the fiber that holds society together starts to deteriorate, it's precisely those locations that will pose the greatest threat. Whenever people ask me about real estate, the first thing I always tell them to do is focus on buying real estate in the best location possible because location is something you cannot change later on. You can renovate a home, you can make various improvements but its location will remain the same.

But what if you no longer have that luxury? What if things are bad now and you need to decide what to do? In such cases, limiting your exposure to the dangerous environment as much as possible is obviously the logical things to do. If you have adequate supplies and your basic needs are met, then the best advice I can give you is to stay put and avoid dangerous situations altogether.

However, if we take things one step further and start being even more pessimistic, in other words if we're talking about societal deterioration that is unlikely to end anytime soon, then relocating, either temporarily or permanently, is the smart thing to do. The next section you're about to read will focus precisely on the relocation dimension and for now, it's time for a brief conclusion.

I believe that at the very least, every person needs to have preparations in place which enable him to cope with let's call them "light" disasters. For example, brief periods of time during which the financial system isn't functioning properly or brief periods of time during which the supply chain is broken and you have difficulties acquiring the basic necessities of life. I think that at the bare minimum, each and every one of my readers should prepare for such situations. If you're busy, find the time. If you're barely making ends meet as it is, then I'm sorry but you're going to have to figure something out. There's just no way to avoid the necessity of making at least basic preparations.

Now I don't know about you but personally, I really dislike the idea of only doing the bare minimum. On the other hand though, as I'm sure you've realized by now, I'm not what you would call a prepper either. As such, investing most of my net worth in things that are in the realm of prepping isn't exactly something I consider a good idea. As usual in life, I firmly believe the truth is somewhere in the middle in this case. I would highly recommend doing more than just the bare minimum but at the same time, don't make the mistake of becoming a prepper. I understand preppers and firmly believe their hearts are in the right place but for the most part, the economist in me cannot help but realize that financially speaking, most of the decisions preppers make are wrong. Don't be brainlessly optimistic of course but then again, don't embrace prepping either.

Chapter 5.3.4.2: What If You Have to Bug Out or Relocate?

Some people find great comfort in considering themselves adequately prepared for disasters but much (or even all) of their preparedness is strictly tied to their home. They have lots of supplies. Perhaps even a great deal of independence (from the power grid, for example). As great as all of this sounds, such people need to realize that in some cases, they will be forced to leave the comfort of their home, either temporarily or permanently.

If you're interested in a highly detailed perspective on bugging out and relocating, grab a copy of Fernando Aguirre's *Bugging Out and Relocating*[64] book. The author is a prepper but one of the few I can listen to without rolling my eyes. He usually puts a reasonable (even if sometimes excessive) perspective on prepping on the table and while reading his book is probably overkill for most people, I feel it's worth mentioning.

Through this section, I'll offer a much more simplified (justifiably so, in my opinion) perspective on bugging out and relocating. Realistically speaking, you most likely don't need more information than what I'm about to give you in order to put together a coherent strategy and before starting, I want to explain that there are two main dimensions I'll be referring to:

1. Bugging out or in other words, temporarily leaving your home. For example, a short-term conflict or bout of civil unrest might force you do decide you'd be safer away from home for a while
2. Relocating or in other words, permanently leaving your home. The conflict in Syria is a good example. Nobody wants to leave everything behind but when you see that your country or region is in a conflict with no end in sight, relocating is the smart thing to do in my opinion

Let's start with the first dimension, with situations which force you to bug out. Now I for one consider that an "ideal" (as strange as it may sound) bug

---

[64] Fernando Aguirre. *Bugging Out and Relocating: When Staying Put Is Not an Option.* North Charleston: CreateSpace Independent Publishing Platform, 2014.

out scenario involves you leaving your home based on a pre-established plan or arrangement with someone who lives far enough away from whichever calamity you're trying to escape from. Most people think bugging out has to involve them temporarily moving to the wilderness but I for one would only advise this in absolute worst-case scenarios. I'd much rather temporarily move in with friends or family members with whom I've made plans earlier on than go live in the woods, a situation over which I have much less control.

That being stated, here's what I'd recommend:

1. As soon as possible, make a list of family members and highly trustworthy friends with whom you could temporarily move in should disaster strike. Some of them might just live a few miles away (but far enough to get you out of harm's way!), whereas others might live in another country. I like to have all bases covered and consider that the more options I have, the better.

    After you've compiled the list, get in touch with these people and ask if they'd be willing to help, should the need arise. Of course, right from the beginning, make it clear that you're always happy to return the favor. It works both ways and who knows, they might end up being the ones who need help rather than the other way around. You're basically making "gentlemen's agreements" with these people and again, make it clear how things are supposed to work and iron out the details when everything is calm. In each case, it should be clear how many people are to be housed, what (if any) kind of compensation you'd offer, how/when you'd arrive and so on

2. I firmly believe that if you do end up having to leave your home, a scenario such as the previously mentioned one (living with family members or friends for a while) is much more likely than one which requires you to live in the wilderness and hunt pigeons. However, I'm not going to rule out such scenarios either (minus the hunting of pigeons) and as such, it makes sense to be reasonably prepared for them as well.

    This brings us to the necessity of the so-called bug out bag that's quite famous in the world of prepping. The idea is logically sound.

Having a bag with basic supplies that you can simply take with you if necessary makes perfect sense and it's important to be selective because it's not a bug out cargo container. I think you should have two types of bug out bags ready at all times:

- o A lightweight bug out bag for when you're on foot
- o A heavyweight bug out bag for when you're traveling by car (preferably) or at least not on foot

Needless to say, you should exercise maximum restraint when deciding what to place in the lightweight bug out bag. Focus on the bare and I mean bare necessities. First of all, water but perhaps even more importantly, water filtration options because you can only carry so much water with you. Calorie and if possible also nutrient-dense food represents the second aspect that should be on your mind. Next, don't forget about cash because... well, you never know. Also, do keep in mind that at least some very basic medical supplies like bandages would be prudent to have. Other than that, a few blatantly obvious miscellaneous items such as a flashlight as well as a multifunctional knife and that's it. Again, a lightweight bug out bag needs to be just that, lightweight.

When it comes to the heavyweight bug out bag, it all depends on how you'll be traveling. If you're traveling by car, it can obviously be a very generous one and as such, you can first and foremost "afford" to carry more food and water. Furthermore, aside from the actual bug out bag, you can and should keep items in the car on a semi-permanent basis as well, from items that keep you warm to things which enhance your safety and independence on the road: a good spare tire, some fuel and so on. If you're traveling by let's say bike instead of car or something else, simply adjust the size/scope of your bug out bag accordingly. Hardly rocket science, as I'm sure you'll agree

3. Arm yourself with some basic survivalism knowledge. You don't have to become Bear Grylls but then again, you'd be in pretty bad shape in adverse scenarios if you don't at the very least know how to set a fire, how to keep yourself warm properly, what to avoid

hygiene-wise and so on. You might already have more than enough knowledge, it all depends.

If you've grown up on the countryside, surrounded by animals and maybe a big garden, you survivalism knowledge level is most likely adequate. A "city boy" like me on the other hand should definitely start learning a thing or two. Not spend an entire month watching survival videos or reading survival books but still, enough time to at least understand some basic concepts

4. Understand that what started out as bugging out can turn into a permanent relocation scenario. In other words, you might go to your bug out location thinking it's only a temporary situation but what if things unfold in a manner which makes it impossible for you to return to your home? This is one of the toughest scenarios you could end up dealing with.

    As such, having at least some forms of portable wealth with you might be a good idea. Precious metals, especially gold, represent a good example. If let's say 5% of your net worth is in gold and you take that with you, then even if you end up being forced to relocate, you'll have "something" to work it. Not an ideal scenario by any means but at least enough to get you started

I believe I've adequately covered the topic of bug out scenarios. But what if the issue you're running away from is so serious that you realize there's just no way to avoid a complete relocation? Again, the conflict in Syria is a good example. Please understand that a lot of wealthy individuals have been forced to leave almost everything behind. People who several years ago led perfectly normal lives and who never thought they'd end up dealing with such a situation. Yet it happened.

Some of the refugees who are currently living in awful conditions used to lead prosperous lives in Syria. Engineers. Doctors. Architects. Yet once it was clear there was no end to the conflict in sight, an excruciatingly difficult choice had to be made: stay in Syria and risk your life as well as the life of your loved ones or leave everything behind and seek shelter elsewhere? I for one would choose the latter.

Having to leave your home behind is traumatic as it is but to make matters even worse, most people have to do it without a plan in place. Without knowing where to go, with almost no portable wealth and so on. In such situations, you can literally go from being wealthy to becoming dirt-poor just like that. Words can't begin to describe how important having a plan is and you're probably expecting me to start enumerating things to do, just like when bugging out.

I'll do the exact opposite.

I will focus on one aspect and one aspect only: portable wealth. Why? Simply because it's so important that everything else pales in comparison. If you have enough portable wealth to buy you a fresh start, your life will be multiple orders of magnitude easier when relocating permanently. Money doesn't buy happiness but it sure is good at ensuring a smooth transition to happiness!

As you know from the financial resilience section, there are lots and lots of assets you can invest in. Many of them portable. But does this mean all portable assets represent good choices for relocation scenarios? No, not really. Let's just say that if you own lots of paintings, you can definitely say they're portable. You just pick them up. But when moving to a different country, you might realize that due to the fragility of the paintings, they're not exactly the best choice for a relocation strategy. The same can be said about let's say expensive wine, I'm sure you get the point.

For a portable asset to be considered desirable from a relocation perspective, two conditions have to be met. On the one hand, they shouldn't be too fragile, as mentioned previously. On the other hand, they shouldn't occupy too much volume and a good example would be silver for a very wealthy individual. You might be tempted to say that since silver isn't fragile and since it's portable as well, it's always a good choice. But it isn't.

If you only have $7,000 in wealth to transport then sure, go for it. But if you need to relocate and have to take $5,000,000 in silver with you, then, well... good luck with that. Again, remember the two conditions: not too fragile on the one hand and not too bulky on the other. It ultimately depends on your situation and on how much wealth you have to transport.

The two options I for one love when it comes to their relocation use are:

- 100% digital assets such as domain names and cryptocurrencies. There's little point in referring to them in detail again, there's more than enough information about these assets in the financial resilience section. Their #1 selling point is the fact that we can consider them the perfect assets in terms of portability for the simple reason that you can have access to them without carrying anything on your person.

Let's assume you own ten great domains and they're registered at GoDaddy. All you have to do is remember your username and password to have access to them. You don't even have to write them down on a piece of paper. The same principle is valid when it comes to cryptocurrencies. If you have an online wallet account, it can be as easy as with domain names. It tends to be more complicated if you prefer other types of wallets but still, it's possible to do it without even having a piece of paper on your person

- Gold. Not precious metals in general but simply gold, preferably gold jewelry because it tends to be easier to justify if there are let's say controls at the border than gold coins. If you don't have all that much wealth to transport, silver is fine as well but for relatively high amounts, it's hard to beat gold when it comes to portable assets that are also tangible.

Do keep in mind however that since times change, gold can definitely not be considered as portable as it once was. With today's technology, tracking it down tends to be a lot easier and therefore, crossing the border might prove to be a challenge. As such, from a portability perspective, the asset which was for not centuries but millennia the undisputed champion of portability has to bow before the new champions, 100% digital assets.

However, it complements them rather nicely because it's not all sunshine and rainbows in the world of digital assets either for one simple reason, the fact that without Internet access, they're pretty much useless. A good relocation strategy needs to involve exposure to both asset types. Never in the history of mankind has there been such an amazing combination for relocation purposes!

Now sure, I'm in no way saying transporting your wealth is the only aspect you should pay attention to. But again, it's so ridiculously important that absolutely everything else pales in comparison. Also, it's a lot more straightforward for me to give tips about transporting your wealth, whereas when it comes to other choices, it's almost impossible for me to provide one-size-fits-all answers.

For example, I'd love to talk to you in detail about deciding where you should move to but this decision is in such a large part driven by personal issues that it's impossible for me to guide you. For example, I could go on and on about how great Country X is but if you have a close relative living in Country Y, it makes a lot more sense to choose the latter. Let's not even talk about the fact that in a volatile environment, Country X (which seems great right now) may very well become a conflict zone.

I've therefore decided to keep things simple and believe it's time to end this section by telling you something very, very simple with respect to relocation: by investing the time and energy it takes to ensure you have enough portable wealth for a fresh start, it would be the understatement of the century to state that you're among the top 1% of the world's population when it comes to preparedness.

I like to think about being resilient as a complex endeavor which fortunately involves very simple steps. Yes, the resilience dimension of your life tends to be quite complex but fortunately, the individual aspects you have to tend to if you're serious about getting there are embarrassingly simple. After reading this chapter, you have all of the "ingredients" you need at your disposal to put together a coherent strategy. Use them wisely.

Chapter 5.3.4.3: Can You Prepare for Everything?

If you watch some of the videos published during the Cold War about how for example schoolchildren should protect themselves by hiding under their desks in the event of a nuclear blast, you cannot help but realize it's obviously a futile effort. If a nuclear bomb is to detonate near you, it's obvious that hiding under your desk isn't going to fundamentally do that much good.

The same principle is valid today, when watching various prepping videos about what you can do to survive a nuclear war. You have people going on and on about their bunkers, about the various measures they've employed and so on. They don't realize that the nuclear technology is currently so developed that there are bombs in existence that are a lot stronger than those used in Hiroshima and Nagasaki. Perhaps it would be a good idea to give some examples.

To make a long story short, let's just say you can simply not prepare for nuclear war if you live in the northern hemisphere. The main reason why two nuclear superpowers are unlikely to engage in a nuclear confrontation is represented by the "Mutually Assured Destruction" principle, according to which both combatants would be devastated. Let's not even talk about the effects on other countries, the long-term implications and so on. I'd highly recommend Irwin Redlener's TED talk[65] for a very balanced perspective on such scenarios.

The same way, you need to understand that no matter how responsible you are and no matter how much energy you expend to try to cover all bases and prepare for absolutely everything, that's just not possible. At the end of the day, there's always the likelihood that something unexpected is going to dramatically disrupt our day-to-day living and some of these events are so humbling that we are, plain and simple, powerless against them.

Whether it's a nuclear war, a natural disaster of epic proportions or perhaps something else, you need to accept the fact that human beings are very fragile.

---

[65] Irwin Redlener. "How to Survive a Nuclear Attack." *TED*. September 9, 2008. https://www.ted.com/talks/irwin_redlener_warns_of_nuclear_terrorism/transcript.

There is absolutely nothing wrong with accepting our fragility and understanding that some scenarios are simply too overwhelming for us.

Being resilient ultimately involves, to a fairly large degree, a healthy attitude toward life. Prepare for what you can and when it comes to everything else, accept your limitations. I assume the nuclear blast preparation drills they held during the Cold War were meant to make people feel safe rather than actually be effective and to a certain degree, I understand this.

However, I refuse to do this and prefer to just be frank with my readers. I could've easily written a few pages about how to prepare for truly devastating events such as a nuclear war but I don't want to do it simply so that those who read *The Age of Anomaly* develop a false sense of safety.

I believe it's better for you to have a firm grasp on reality than a false sense of security. Through this book in general and this chapter in particular, I believe I've helped with the former.

Chapter 5.4: Conclusions

In my opinion, being resilient and therefore able to withstand almost any financial storm thrown your way is just as important as being good at spotting financial storms before they affect you. This is especially valid in light of the fact that no matter how much of an economic history buff you are and no matter how good you may be at seeing the big picture, it is definitely impossible to reach a point when you can say about yourself that you always predict financial storms ahead of time with 100% accuracy and consistency.

That's just not going to happen.

You're deluding yourself if you think that by becoming better at spotting financial storms, there is no longer a need to become more resilient because after all, you will be spotting financial calamities from now on before they affect you, so why does it even matter? Please don't give in to the temptation of doing this. Just don't.

I've started this chapter with the obvious, with tips you would've expected from an economist. In other words, with the issue of financial resilience. It is, of course, the topic I have paid the most attention to in this chapter and I believe I've covered everything in a very thorough manner. By analyzing asset classes and putting them in perspective with respect to the scope of this book, I believe I've given you all of the ingredients you need to put together a portfolio and a financial strategy that best suit your situation and goals.

Here are a few final thoughts about financial resilience:

- Always and I mean always create your own portfolio based on your specific situation and needs. The job of a good economist is to give you the tools you need to do just that and I genuinely hope this book represents just what the doctor ordered. Stay away from economists who claim to have miracle one-size-fits-all solutions. As good as the idea of a quick fix may seem, I'm afraid such an approach is nothing more than a trap

- Don't invest by trying to predict the future, humans tend to be terrible at that. Instead, do your best to put together a strategy which enables you to land on your feet in a wide range of scenarios

- Status quo assets and trailblazer assets complement one another nicely in my opinion, I honestly hope everyone who reads this book ends up having exposure to both

- The status quo assets I for one prefer are stocks (for maximizing returns), real estate (for combining business with pleasure), cash and cash equivalents (so that I have firepower at hand when buying opportunities present themselves) and precious metals (as an insurance policy).

  On the other end of the spectrum, there are two status quo asset classes I for one avoid. I consider bonds overpriced and am not passionate enough about art and antiques to put in the effort it takes to invest properly, so I've decided to stay away

- The trailblazer assets I'd recommend to literally everyone are domain names (just like stocks, for return maximization during times of prosperity) and cryptocurrencies, especially bitcoin (for protection as well as return maximization when things are gloomy). In my opinion, they complement one another nicely.

  I'm also willing to invest in websites but only because I'm an online entrepreneur who knows what he's doing, I wouldn't recommend them to my readers. Also, I stay away from peer-to-peer lending because I live in a country that doesn't have a proper infrastructure for this asset class, I would have definitely tried this option if I lived in let's say the United States

… I could've just stopped there.

When you as an economist venture outside your comfort zone with a book, you risk being ridiculed. Narrow-minded people will be laughing at you, at the fact that an economist is giving advice about mental resilience or about staying in shape and preparing for other types of disasters. This book would have been extremely useful even if I would, in fact, have limited myself to just financial resilience. However, I would have done readers a huge disservice because at the end of the day, the intellectually honest thing for me to do is put what I consider to be all of the information you need and that I can provide at your disposal.

Do I believe other types of resilience are important? Yes, I do. Do I have something of value to add when it comes to each? Yes, I believe that is the case. As such, I've decided to bite the bullet and refer to things outside the world of economics as well. Specifically, I've referred to mental resilience, physical resilience and also SHTF resilience.

In the mental resilience section, I've given my perspective on things which make or break your strategy such as being able to make decisions under pressure, coping with financial losses and so on. These are things you probably won't hear other economists mention all that much but they definitely do enhance your strategy and even more so, I'd even go so as far to say as they're indispensable.

I'm sure it felt even stranger to see an economist give you advice about physical resilience but please understand that in an age of anomaly such as the one we are in, you need every edge you can get. I'm obviously not here to help you win a Miss World pageant or a Mr. Universe competition, my goal has simply been explaining which health and wellness principles I believe those who want to become more resilient should adhere to. Fair enough?

In the final section, I've made it clear that we live in a deeply interconnected world and as such, financial storms frequently degenerate and turn into disasters of other natures as well. By understanding this possibility and what you need to do to protect yourself, you will of course become much more resilient. The advice you've received in the final section is basically the perspective on disaster preparedness of an economist who is definitely not a prepper but who firmly believes in preparedness.

That's it, congratulations on making it so far! Everything you could possibly need to become more resilient is, I hope, deeply entrenched in your brain by now. However, reading and learning about these things isn't enough. If you don't develop the habit of actually incorporating the tips I've mentioned in your day to day existence, it's all in vain.

Chapter 6: How I See Things

I want to start by making it clear that this section is definitely not about me telling you what you should do. It's the exact opposite, in fact. After reading the sixth chapter of *The Age of Anomaly*, you will basically understand my way of thinking. By doing that, you will be in a much better position to create a strategy of your own. Think of this chapter as one big example. I'm going to tell you what I think about the world economy at this point, what I for one do to protect myself and so on.

Perhaps my approach will be the best solution for you as well. But that is for you to decide. A strategy that works great for a 40-year-old doctor from Norway might not be the best choice for a 65-year-old farmer from Albania. As much as I'd like to be able to simply spoon-feed you some conclusions, I just can't do that. I can however give you a glimpse into my own mind in the hope that you'll extract value not necessarily from my exact strategy but rather by understanding my way of thinking.

I don't consider myself a status quo economist. Then again, I do not consider myself non-mainstream either. Should my books and YouTube videos be considered mainstream economics? I certainly hope not, my work actually comes as a result of my conviction that economics isn't being taught properly.

Okay, then can my work be considered let's say alternative economics? I don't think so, at least not in the way that alternative economics is currently perceived. I'm not exactly your textbook conspiracy theorist or anything along those lines. I believe my "neutrality" if you'd like to call it that is a major advantage, primarily because I always try to take the best of both worlds and put it on the table.

I therefore hope you will find my thought process interesting. Am I telling you to always agree with it? Of course not, I actually encourage you to challenge everything you don't agree with. I'm not writing this book from a position of superiority, from the position of an expert that should be put on a pedestal. I always do my best to embrace a down-to-earth way of thinking and ultimately writing. Think of me as a friend who is trying to help you figure out what works best for you, not an arrogant university professor who's here to make your life miserable and hear himself speak.

Chapter 6.1: Why So Serious?

The most important thing to me as a writer is understanding my audience. Who will this book end up being read by? Well, it's a complex question with a complex answer but there are without a doubt common denominators. The main one being the fact that those who read *The Age of Anomaly* are concerned.

Some of you may have specific concerns like too much debt being accumulated by your country. Or unsustainable demographics. Perhaps inflation fears... or deflation fears. Maybe geopolitical concerns and the list could go on and one. Other readers might not necessarily have one specific scenario about which they're worried. Instead, a lingering sense that "something" is just not right might have motivated them to buy this book.

Regardless, I'm reasonably confident most of my readers are concerned.

On the one hand, this is truly great. Because if you're concerned, it means you're at least thinking about your financial future, about the financial security of your family. On the other hand though, I've found out that a lot of people like you (and me, for that matter) respond well to pitches which involve "doom and gloom" scenarios. Yes, pitches because make no mistake: the people who make money by selling books/information about catastrophic scenarios are marketers. Very talented marketers.

So talented, in fact, that even people like you and me who are quite Internet-savvy and should know better "fall" for it. Can you honestly tell me you've never watched videos about how the world as we know it will end, about economic collapse scenarios and so on? I thought so. To add to my previous question, can you tell me you've never "fallen" for fear-based marketing tactics (yes, fear sells[66])? I rest my case.

Look, the global financial crisis of 2007-2008 (among many other things) made it clear our current system will collapse at one point or another. Therefore,

---

[66] Kaylene C. Williams. "Fear Appeal Theory." *Research in Business and Economics Journal.* March 01, 2012. http://connection.ebscohost.com/c/articles/78390346/fear-appeal-theory.

protecting yourself makes perfect sense. But what most people don't understand is that by taking the idea of protecting yourself to the extreme, you will inevitably end up losing money.

The onset of the previously mentioned global financial crisis gave birth to what I like to refer to as the fearmongering industry. The industry in question has probably always existed in one way or another but as of 2007-2008, it became extremely profitable. Ridiculously profitable. Insanely profitable, one might say. What is this industry all about, you ask?

The name "fearmongering" says it all, selling fear is one of the world's most profitable business models. In fact, selling to people who are afraid is arguably easier than selling to people who are euphoric. In both cases, individuals stop thinking rationally. They let their emotions take over and you can be certain there will always be people who make money by exploiting those emotions.

On the surface, it all makes perfect sense for a person who starts being afraid after witnessing a financial crisis such as the 2007 – 2008 one. You see just how flawed our current economic system is, you become "enlightened" and naturally start asking yourself what you can do to protect your wealth. Again, there's nothing fundamentally wrong with that. Unfortunately though, some individuals end up taking things too far and becoming obsessed with anything involving disasters, economic collapse and so on.

Their judgment becomes clouded, they lose touch with reality and most importantly (this is something you'll read about rather frequently throughout this book), they lose their ability to make rational as opposed to emotional decisions. Therefore, they become easy prey for so-called "fear mongers" and ultimately end up losing money. As ironic as it may seem, you can indeed end up losing money when trying to "protect your wealth" and a lot of people did just that.

One of the most eloquent examples is represented by those who invested in precious metals back in 2011, when gold was priced at about $1,900/oz and silver was priced at almost $50/oz. At that point, a huge number of gold promoters were all over the place, explaining how you had to invest in gold and/or silver before it's too late to protect your purchasing power. They were on TV, they were all over YouTube, they had websites, blogs, newsletters and the list could go on and on.

Well, what happened?

Basically, the exact opposite of what one would expect. Someone who bought silver at almost $50 back in 2011 and sold two years later had to take a 60%+ loss in some cases and this is not a typo. The person in question "protected" his wealth so well that he lost more than half of it. Gold investors ended up having to deal with a similar scenario and the bottom line is those who trusted the various gold/silver gurus ended up losing most of their money.

This is just one example.

Let's not even start talking about those who invested their life savings in canned goods, so-called "prepper" tools and so on, let's not even go there because in some cases, those people ended up losing pretty much all of their money. Let's not even talk about those who threw their money out the window by going to overpriced seminars or paying for all sorts of courses. By now, it should be clear why a lot of those who let fear get the best of them ended up losing most or even all of their money.

Isn't this somewhat of a paradox?

Yes, it is. All of these people have something in common. Fundamentally speaking, their concerns make perfect sense. For the most part, their heart is in the right place and their purpose is noble. They simply wanted to protect themselves and the ones they love from financial calamities. These people are anything but compulsive risk takers. In fact, they're the exact opposite. This begs the question: why did people who simply wanted to engage in responsible behavior and protect their wealth lose money?

The answer isn't complicated.

They lost money because they took things too far. Think of it this way. Let's assume 70% of your wealth is represented by your house. Since a lot of bad things can happen (maybe a fire, perhaps a flood and so on), it makes sense to buy insurance. Everyone should buy insurance to protect a house and the same way, everyone should buy "insurance" to protect their wealth.

It's the responsible thing to do… within reason.

And that's exactly what makes the difference between a person who is genuinely protecting his wealth and someone who is taking things to the extreme. Yes, you should buy insurance for your home but you shouldn't spend all of your money on insurance. The same way, you should own some precious metals and even canned goods in case you'll end up dealing with a calamity.

But again, within reason.

The "gloom and doom" industry encouraged people to go overboard and a lot of bright individuals actually fell for it. Instead of just buying "some" gold and silver or "some" canned goods in case something disastrous happens, they ended up investing their entire wealth in "insurance policies" and that's just plain wrong. If you only buy gold and silver every now and then, you can afford to keep these assets somewhere safe and never touch them unless you'll actually need to cash in that proverbial insurance policy. The same way, buying some canned goods every once in a while won't break the bank.

But what if you invest all of your savings this way?

That, unfortunately, is an entirely different situation. You see, few things ever happen as planned. Maybe you need some emergency cash, perhaps you will need a lot of money due to an illness and the list could go on and on. If your entire wealth is tied up in let's say gold and silver, you'll often end up having to sell at a loss. For example, I can pretty much assure you a lot of the people who backed up the truck and bought way too much silver in 2011 at almost $50 had to sell at least some of it in 2013 for all sorts of reasons.

They didn't diversify and therefore had to liquidate some silver inventory as a "last resort" measure. Unfortunately for them, some had to take a 60% loss and this brings us to the purpose of this chapter: helping you avoid such situations, helping you get the best of both worlds. As a short recap, I hope I helped you understand that:

1. Yes, the global financial system will probably collapse eventually but this doesn't mean you have to spend every dollar and waking moment preparing

2. As ironic as it may seem, a lot of people (the gold and silver investors I've referred to previously, for example) lost outrageous amounts of money by trying to "protect" themselves

3. Being prepared makes perfect sense… within reason

4. The fearmongering industry is considerably more dangerous than you might have thought and people like us (for the reasons outlined at the beginning of this chapter) are more prone to "falling" for fear-based marketing tactics than a lot of "average Joe" individuals

Chapter 6.2: We're Doomed

I hope the title of this subchapter didn't make you spill your tea or coffee, especially if you've just read the previous subchapter and found it somewhat reassuring. Unfortunately, I do have to say that despite me not being a fear monger, we (as in society as a whole, as we currently perceive it and relate to it) are doomed.

Again, this doesn't mean you need to crawl under a rock as of this point. It may very well take a long time until the "big one" hits (but more on the "big reset" toward the end of this chapter), you might even die before it ends up happening. So while I don't believe panicking is the best approach, I do think we need to meaningfully understand the predicament society is in.

Whenever an economic crisis rears its ugly head, fear mongers have yet another opportunity to make everyone think the current calamity is "the big one" and you should protect yourself while you still can. How? Why, of course, by signing up for their newsletter for a small fee of just $99.99/month. Leaving sarcasm aside, the picture I've painted is actually painfully accurate. Panics/recessions/depressions[67] are simply components of the business cycle and thinking the world will end whenever there's a panic or whenever some of the stocks you own end up dropping in value is a surefire way to lose your sanity.

Does this mean the economy is perfectly fine? Actually, no, it doesn't. Maybe some of you made the mistake of assuming that just because I sometimes explain why doom and gloomers usually lose money, I'm automatically a perma-bull who thinks there's absolutely nothing wrong with the economy and who is 100% certain it's all sunshine and rainbows. I'm not and I don't.

Think of a doomsday scenario, just pick a random one. Chances are the scenario in question will materialize at one point or another. What I'm trying to explain is that by not factoring in timing, you'll spend your entire life worrying about events which will happen long after your death. Yes, pretty

---

[67] Todd A. Knoop. *Recessions and Depressions: Understanding Business Cycles.* Westport, CT: Praeger Publishers, 2004.

much all "end of the world" scenarios will eventually materialize but it will most likely happen within decades if not centuries.

For example, will the dollar or the euro eventually disappear?

Probably. Since the overwhelming majority of fiat currencies ended up disappearing[68], I don't see why the current ones would be any different. The same way, there's no historical precedent of hyperinflation affecting a country with a strong economy. Therefore, thinking that the United States or Japan, for example, could end up dealing with hyperinflation soon is pretty ridiculous.

However, maybe let's say 100-200 years from now, those two countries might be significantly weaker than they are at the moment of writing. As such, once their economies are severely weakened, hyperinflation might be one of the threats they will have to deal with. But this will take time, a lot of time. First, the economies of the countries in question would have to decline significantly, it cannot happen overnight. Right now, countries such as the United States and Japan have huge economies and thinking everything could implode in a few months or years is, again, pretty ridiculous. Even if their economies were to deteriorate, it would take many years for it to happen and for such a country to become weak enough to be a "candidate" for hyperinflation.

Sam Ewing summed it up quite nicely:

Inflation is when you pay fifteen dollars for the ten-dollar haircut you used to get for five dollars when you had hair.

Yes, your currency will gradually lose purchasing power but thinking it will become worthless overnight is a huge mistake if you're living in a country which currently has an economy one can consider at least decent. But hey, if you want to spend your entire life preparing for an event not even your grandchildren will witness, go right ahead. I'm not forcing anyone to do anything. Through my book and this chapter in particular, I'm simply sharing my perspective. How you use the information I'm providing is entirely up to you.

---

[68] Mike Hewitt. "The Fate of Paper Money." *DollarDaze*. January 7, 2009. http://dollardaze.org/blog/?post_id=00405.

Does this mean you shouldn't prepare at all? Of course not. Once again, I'd like to use the insurance policy analogy. Maybe your house will burn down, so an insurance policy certainly has its merits. A person who chooses a good insurance policy is being wise and responsible, can't argue with that. But a person who is spending all of his money on an insurance policy is acting foolishly, plain and simple.

Let's assume you're in the agriculture business and want to insure your crop against a bad harvest. I don't have a problem with this at all, in fact it's something I'd encourage. But most doom and gloomers end up taking things to the extreme by spending so much money on their insurance policy that there's nothing left to buy seeds with. It's all a matter of calibrating your strategy.

While I encourage people to be responsible and have nothing against insurance policies, I want to make it perfectly clear that if you're dedicating more than a small percentage of your time, money and energy to protecting yourself, you're making a huge mistake and the time/money/energy in question would be better spent becoming better at what you do for a living, helping those you love or even complete strangers, following your dreams and so on. It sure beats hiding in the woods and stocking up on guns/ammo, wouldn't you agree?

Perhaps the most dangerous aspect about fearmongering is that it affects all areas of your life in a negative manner. I've been guilty of this very thing unfortunately. Once you embrace the doom and gloom mentality, everything will be affected: your business, your relationships with others, absolutely everything. What good does excessive worrying do? Can it stop certain events from unfolding? Can it somehow make bad things go away? No. All worrying does is make you feel miserable and you deserve better.

I'd like to also briefly refer to debt because a lot of people are worried their country will collapse any minute now given the fact that its debt to GDP ratio isn't exactly great. Yes, debt is a huge problem and I'd never deny that. Throughout history, pretty much all countries ultimately ended up on an unsustainable economic trajectory. Japan isn't an exception, the European Union isn't an exception and the US isn't an exception either.

Humans aren't perfect and as such, it's highly unlikely there will ever be a civilization which will remain the number one economic player forever.

Instead, we're taken right back to cycles. Certain civilizations will rise while others will fall, it's the way it has always been. History offers quite a few examples. Athens was, at a certain point, doing extremely well but a combination between their war with the Spartans and bad economic choices eventually generated economic problems which ultimately turned them into easy prey for Rome. Speaking of Rome, they ended up dealing with their own share of economic turbulences and eventually went bankrupt. The list could go on and on.

If you grab a good history book and analyze the evolution of certain civilizations, you can't help but notice just how eerily similar their problems are to the ones countries are currently dealing with. Disregard the technological differences and you'll undoubtedly come to the conclusion that fundamentally speaking, the problems our society is currently dealing with aren't new.

Yet guess what: despite the fact that economic turbulences have been anything but a rarity, the human species evolved quite nicely when it comes to pretty much all metrics. Compare our current life expectancy to that of our ancestors and you'll come to the conclusion we are living a lot longer. Compare our quality of life to the quality of life our ancestors had and you will come to the conclusion that those who are currently in the lower class socio-economically speaking are enjoying a higher standard of living than let's say the Queen of England was enjoying not a thousand years ago but less than a hundred years ago.

The progress of the human race is remarkable.

Unfortunately, human nature makes it impossible for this progress to occur in a linear manner. Instead, there have been and always will be economic cycles but in the long run, make no mistake, humans will not only survive but thrive. Fear mongers are always trying to explain how the world will end for all sorts of reasons. Food shortages, energy shortages, population growth, you name it. Let's refer to the population growth argument for a moment because a lot of the previously mentioned doom and gloom scenarios are basically Malthusian theories which stem from the pessimistic views of Thomas Malthus when it comes to the sustainability of population growth.

In the first chapter of *An Essay on The Principle of Population*, he stated the population tends to increase in a geometrical ratio, whereas subsistence tends to only increase in an arithmetical one. Now please keep in mind this was in 1798 and I'm not undermining the merits of Thomas Malthus in any way. He was ultimately proven wrong time and time again but all in all, his arguments did help society as a whole by generating a lot of productive debates. What puzzles me is how more than 200 years later, a lot of fear mongers are referring to such arguments despite the fact that as mentioned previously, they were invalidated time and time again.

While humans are definitely not perfect, let's give our species at least some credit. For the most part, it's fairly safe to assume we will ultimately find a way to at least tend to our basic needs, even during severe economic downturns. Central banking policies, high debt to GDP ratios, issues such as resource scarcity and so on: those are all real threats but again, let's give humans some credit.

If history is any indicator, we can be pretty much certain that despite the temporary hiccups we will be dealing with, we have all of the reasons in the world to be bullish on the human race in the long run. But before ending this subchapter, I'd like to also refer to extreme scenarios and their potential impact. On the one hand, I agree you can never be 100% certain extreme scenarios won't occur. This is precisely why I actually recommend "insurance policies" because sure, I can't promise you that during your lifetime, we won't have to deal with something similar to the Dark Ages (an extended period of economic and social problems).

However, what I don't recommend is turning your life into one huge insurance policy. In other words, I'd strongly advise against becoming a "prepper" and spending your entire life protecting yourself from something which has a one in a million chance of happening. By all means, invest some money in various "insurance policies" (I'm not referring to insurance policies as in working with an insurance company but rather to assets which would be desirable if something dramatic were to occur) but be reasonable and understand that investing more than a fraction of your net worth in such a manner just doesn't make sense.

And there's one more issue I'd like to address.

A lot of people have been discussing Nassim Taleb's Black Swan Theory[69] and I don't want to move on to the next subchapter before addressing it as well. For those of you who aren't familiar with the theory in question, it basically tells us there are certain events which could render everything we thought we knew about the world we live in useless. To illustrate this, he used the turkey example:

"A turkey is fed for 1,000 days by a butcher, and every day confirms to the turkey and the turkey's economics department and the turkey's risk management department and the turkey's analytical department that the butcher loves turkeys, and every day brings more confidence to the statement. But on day 1,001, there will be a surprise for the turkey…"

Are we turkeys?

Unlike fear mongers who think they know everything and can see the future through their crystal ball, I don't like making predictions because nobody knows what the future will bring. Can we be 100% certain a world-altering event won't occur next year? No, we cannot, we can't be 100% certain of anything. Maybe such an event will occur tomorrow, maybe next week, maybe next month. Then again, perhaps it will occur 100 years from now or possibly never.

I don't know and neither do you or any of the gurus who constantly claim they can see the future through their crystal ball. Don't ask me to guarantee something will or won't happen because I won't do it. Why? Because by doing something of this nature, I'd be nothing more than a liar and I don't want to be unfair toward the people who gave me their vote of confidence by buying my book.

In a perfect world, there would never be a financial crisis. But since humans aren't perfect, we have the business cycle which unfortunately has its downs as well. Some downturns are easier to cope with than others and at a certain point in the future, there may very well be "black swan events" such as the ones Nassim Taleb refers to. This however brings us right back to one of my previous arguments. Should black swan events or let's call them catastrophic events occur then sure, those who are prepared to cope with them will do

---

[69] Nassim N. Taleb. *The Black Swan: The Impact of the Highly Improbable.* London: Penguin Books, 2007.

considerably better than everyone else. Can't argue with that and in fact, I want to make one thing clear again:

I have nothing against insurance policies.

Protecting yourself within reason makes perfect sense. Maybe a natural disaster will occur. Maybe a severe economic crisis will appear. Maybe you'll have to deal with a personal crisis. Those scenarios are all within the realm of possibility. Therefore yes, "insurance policies" as I call them throughout this section do have their merits… within reason.

But should you spend your entire life preparing for a natural disaster? Or a huge economic crisis? Or a crisis in your personal life? No, you should not. Why? Simply because if you spend every waking hour preparing for black swan events, there won't be any time left to… you know, enjoy life for example. Or focus on making more money as opposed to preserving what you currently have. The list could go on and on.

This is one of the main reasons I've decided to write this section in the first place. I hate seeing people live their life as if everything revolves around the importance of preparing for catastrophic events. It doesn't, despite what fear mongers would like you to believe. It saddens me deeply whenever I hear someone has become a "prepper" or in other words whenever I hear someone decided to dedicate his life to preparing for all sorts of disasters.

Most of the "doom and gloom" economists you see on TV or read about on the Internet are nothing more than salesmen who make money by triggering fear. Even if a catastrophic event were to occur, I'm reasonably confident it would take them by surprise as well because as Jean-Paul Kauffmann put it, an economy *"depends about as much on economists as the weather does on weather forecasters."*

As a final conclusion, I'd say that the answer to the "Are we doomed?" question is yes because human beings are anything but perfect and as such, it would be foolish to believe they are able to come up with 100% foolproof systems. At one point or another, a lot of "doom and gloom" scenarios may very well materialize. Our current economic system has been "in trouble" right from day one. Currencies will eventually disappear, once powerful economies will become irrelevant and the list could go on and on. But (and therein lies the key) you have to understand you may very well not even be alive when the inevitable does indeed occur.

Therefore, by dedicating your life to preparing for an event you most likely won't witness, you would be making a huge mistake. I'm not saying you shouldn't prepare for catastrophic events, I'm saying something else: you should but within reason. Don't spend more than a fraction of your net worth on such "insurance policies" and don't spend more than a fraction of your time on them either. Sounds reasonable, wouldn't you agree?

Chapter 6.3: Keynesian? Libertarian? Socialist? Capitalist?

In the previous subchapter, I've explained that yes, the worldwide economy is indeed in trouble but this doesn't mean you should start hoarding food, guns and ammunition. Why is it in trouble? It would be overly simplistic to assume there's just one problem and that's it. Unfortunately, things are a bit more complicated. The problems we are dealing with are political as well to a large degree politico-economic, if you will. Whenever discussions about politico-economic issues emerge, heated debates are right around the corner. For various strange reasons, people quickly get angry whenever they are involved in debates such as capitalism vs. socialism, Austrian economics vs. Keynesianism[70] and so on.

Do I have politico-economic beliefs?

Most definitely.

Will I share them with you through this book?

No.

Let me explain why. Far too many investors make the mistakes of relying on other people's opinions/predictions and throughout this book, I've made this clear on more than one occasion. In other words, I've constantly reminded you that blindly adopting another person's beliefs would be a huge mistake. Under such circumstances, I will refrain from sharing mine because otherwise, I would be nothing more than a hypocrite.

I don't write "here's what you have to do" books, I do the exact opposite. Instead of telling you what I believe and encouraging you to adopt my way of thinking, I'd rather help you figure out what the best approach for your specific situation is. Through this book, I don't want to convince you to adopt

---

[70] Paul Krugman. "The State of Macro, Six Years Later." *The New York Times.* October 14, 2014. http://krugman.blogs.nytimes.com/2014/10/14/the-state-of-macro-six-years-later/?_r=0.

my politico-economic belief system and therefore, I won't even tell you anything about it. This book is about giving you all of the tools you need to think for yourself, to make your own informed decisions.

After reading it, you will (I hope) stop blindly accepting facts, opinions, beliefs and so on. You will start questioning each and every "expert" who appears on TV, on the radio, in the newspaper or on the Internet. You will analyze facts, interpret them yourself and ultimately corroborate them in order to make the best possible decision for your specific situation. I don't want my readers to become followers, fanboys or anything along those lines. I'll take the exact opposite, thank you very much.

Chapter 6.4: [Insert Prefix Here] + Flation

One of the most remarkably ironic aspects associated with the fearmongering industry is the fact that as mentioned on more than one occasion throughout this book, fears/predictions are literally all over the place. Some analysts are afraid we'll end up dealing with another period of severe deflation such as the Great Depression of 1929, whereas others are afraid of the exact opposite and assert we will most likely end up dealing with hyperinflation.

I won't bore you with all sorts of complex definitions and terminologies, I'll try to keep things simple and use quotes as well as analogies to get the message across. My #1 goal with this book isn't sounding smart or pretentious, it's giving you the tools you need to think for yourself. I simply want my readers to not only understand but also remember the things I am trying to explain.

This subchapter will have three sections.

Through the first one, I will focus on inflation and go through everything from the basics to extreme scenarios such as hyperinflation. Through the second section, I will focus on the exact opposite of inflation, in other words deflation. Once again, I'll cover the basics but also refer to extreme scenarios such as the Great Depression of 1929. In section number three, I will also mention a thing or two about stagflation[71] because understanding the particularities of each concept is in my opinion of the utmost importance.

---

[71] Bradford J. DeLong. "Supply Shocks: The Dilemma of Stagflation." *University of California at Berkeley*. October 3, 1998. http://econ161.berkeley.edu/multimedia/ASAD1.html.

Chapter 6.4.1: Inflation

As Milton Friedman[72] put it, inflation is simply *"too much money chasing too few goods."* Let's (over)simplify things and assume you live in a city which only has two stores: one which sells bottled water and one which sells a single food product. Therefore, if you live there, you can only buy two things: bottled water and the food product in question. Let's also assume you make $x per month and have no other expenses as well as no investment opportunities.

If the government were to double everyone's salary, you'd be making two times more. But the thing is, so would everyone else. Therefore, you'd have two times more money chasing the exact same number of goods. As a result, it should come as no surprise that the price of bottled water as well as the price of the food product in question would go up.

Would it go up exactly two times? That's impossible to predict. Maybe some people will choose to hoard currency, so the price would go up less than two times. Or perhaps the exact opposite will happen, maybe people will lose faith in the currency and hoard food or bottled water instead of dollars, making the prices go up more than two times. The bottom line is this: if more money is chasing the same number of goods, the price of those goods will go up. Now an important question arises: why hasn't there been all that much inflation (at least not yet) in the United States for example, despite the fact that the Federal Reserve "printed" a lot of money?

The answer brings us right back to Milton Friedman's definition. There isn't all that much inflation because the money printed by the Federal Reserve hasn't ended up in the "real" economy yet and is therefore not chasing goods. Again, at least not yet. Where is it, you might ask? Before answering, it's important to point out the Federal Reserve cannot control what happens once it floods the market with liquidity. In our case, multiple things happened: some of that money is being hoarded by financial institutions, some of that money ended up in the stock market and so on. Nobody can guarantee that whenever a central bank prints money, the prices of everyday goods will go

---

[72] Milton Friedman. *Unemployment versus Inflation.* London: Institute of Economic Affairs, 1975.

up. Maybe the money will be hoarded, maybe that money will inflate asset bubbles such as stock market bubbles or real estate bubbles. The list could go on and on.

For a central bank, the inflation issue is a fine balancing act because every government tends to be tempted by the central bank's printing press. Normally, central banks should be 100% independent but in reality, let's face it: this is hardly true. Politicians declare themselves against inflationary policies whenever it suits them, yet end up re-considering their position toward them once they decide those policies can bring about political gains.

People unfortunately tend to often vote for the politicians who agree to give them more "stuff" in one way or another. To do it, politicians need money. Money doesn't grow on trees. One plus one equals two and therefore, we can conclude the money has to come from somewhere. Sure, governments make a lot of money through taxation but even that has its limits, so inflation is yet another tool in their arsenal. Once again, Milton Friedman is spot on by telling us *"inflation is taxation without legislation."*

Let's assume the government needs more money to fund another project. If it were to raise taxes, there would be a huge public backlash. So what do they do? They "convince" the central bank to print money. For psychological reasons, people accept the idea of losing money through the loss of their purchasing power more than the idea of losing money through taxation so again, inflation is yet another tool in the political arsenal.

Now that it's clear what inflation is, let's analyze it through the perspective which constitutes the purpose of this section: is inflation a huge risk, should you stock up on precious metals, guns and ammunition just because central banks are pumping money into the system? Well… no. So, am I saying inflation isn't a risk then? Well… no. It may sound like a contradiction but it isn't.

The Federal Reserve for example appeared back in 1913. Since 1913, the dollar lost almost 100%[73] of its purchasing power. This is not a typo, it lost almost 100%. But (and this is what people have to understand) it happened

---

[73] Rob Viglione. "The Consequences of Perpetual Inflation." *Seeking Alpha.* March 9, 2009. http://seekingalpha.com/article/124867-the-consequences-of-perpetual-inflation.

over a period of about 100 years and as Bill Vaughn eloquently said, the *"idea of inflation comes from seeing a youngster get his first job at a salary you dreamed of as the culmination of your career."*

As the quote above tells us, it takes time for these things to unfold. A lot of time. If you live in let's say the United States, worrying you'll wake up tomorrow and realize your dollars are now worthless just doesn't make sense. Yes, your dollars will ultimately be worth a lot less than they are today but this will happen gradually, over a period of many years.

Sure, if you're 30 years old today and keep your money under the mattress with the intention of giving it to your grandchildren, they won't be very happy because 50 years from now, you'll be giving them some pieces of paper which won't buy them all that much. But how many people do this? Almost nobody. Even the most conservative individuals at least keep their money in the bank and receive returns. Some invest in the stock market. Most buy real estate as in at least the house they are living in. Some acquire other desirable assets which appreciate in value such as art and the list could go on and on.

If you have a few dollars set aside, you shouldn't be in a hurry to spend or invest them right away. Instead, do some research in order to make informed decisions because you don't have to worry that a few months from now, your money will be worth 90% less. If you live in a developed country or keep your savings in currencies issued by a developed country, worrying about something like this doesn't make sense.

If you live in a country which isn't as developed as the United States then as a general rule, the less developed your country is, the higher the loss of your purchasing power will be if you keep your savings in the currency issued by the country in question. If your country is extremely vulnerable like for example Zimbabwe then yes, even hyperinflation becomes a concern.

As the name suggests, hyperinflation represents extremely high inflation. If your country goes through hyperinflation then you could find yourself paying billions or even trillions of currency units for something as trivial as a loaf of bread. It sounds and actually is scary but realistically speaking, most if not all of the people who are reading this book don't have to worry about something like that because their country isn't vulnerable enough to see hyperinflation as a real threat.

Fear mongers however love to use hyperinflation as an argument in favor of the fact that their doomsday scenario will materialize. This isn't just wrong, it's downright ridiculous because there is no historical precedent for something like this whatsoever. Throughout history, I'd like to challenge my readers to show me even one example of a strong economy which has been brought to its knees by hyperinflation.

Quick hint: there aren't any. Now a lot of people will be tempted to refer to Germany after the First World War but as explained previously, it's hardly an accurate example. Their economy was, at that point, anything but robust. It was the exact opposite. Nobody wanted to invest there, their own citizens hoarded wealth and in such an environment sure, printing money results in hyperinflation because nobody wants your currency. In other words, their economy wasn't weakened by hyperinflation, it was already extremely weak at that point, which is precisely why hyperinflation appeared in the first place. All in all, there are only two situations in which hyperinflation is genuinely a threat you need to pay close attention to:

1. The country in question was always extremely poor and unstable (Zimbabwe, for example)
2. The country in question used to have a strong economy but things deteriorated in a dramatic manner (Germany after World War 1, for example)

Those are pretty much the only two situations in which hyperinflation is a real threat. I'm reasonably confident almost none of my readers are living in such a country and therefore, hyperinflation is nothing more than a boogeyman fear mongers use to trick you into believing whatever doomsday scenario they are "pitching" at a certain point in time. Don't fall for it.

Chapter 6.4.2: Deflation

When you're dealing with inflation, there's too much money in the system, whereas when you're dealing with deflation, there is a shortage of money. Therefore, during periods of deflation, the desirability of cash rises exponentially. Money ends up being so desirable, in fact, that you are often better off hoarding cash. Why? Because if you invest it in certain assets, there's a high likelihood those assets will go down in value. Consequently, you'd be better off keeping your money in the bank, despite the fact that savings accounts are traditionally frowned upon by most investors.

Under normal circumstances, it's perfectly understandable why investors look down upon the concept of keeping your money in the bank as opposed to investing it. After all, the returns your bank can offer will be considerably lower than what you would be able to make by investing your capital. In fact, a lot of times, the returns won't even help you keep up with inflation and are de facto negative. However, since inflation isn't a threat when the economy is going through deflation, the purchasing power loss argument loses its luster.

Deflation can end up being quite dangerous because people become so afraid they find themselves doing the exact thing I've mentioned earlier, hoarding money. The velocity of money can decrease dramatically and under such circumstances, it should come as no surprise that the economy can end up in a downward spiral: on the one hand, money has to circulate in order for the economy to grow but on the other hand, people are too afraid to let their cash circulate and prefer hoarding it.

When it comes to severe deflation such as what the United States went through back in 1929, it may seem there's no way out in sight. The average Joe becomes extremely risk-averse, unemployment is high and the list could go on and on. This explains why the US government and the Federal Reserve are willing to adopt aggressive policies. The fear of another Great Depression is so entrenched in the subconscious of US policymakers that they are often willing to do whatever it takes to fight deflation.

Ironically, the exact opposite is true when it comes to Germany because unlike the United States, a completely different financial event is entrenched in their subconscious: the German hyperinflation after World War 1. Therefore, German policymakers will do whatever it takes to fight against such a scenario. These two historical events explain why the United States tends to be quicker to take aggressive monetary action than Germany.

A lot of ECB economists including the chairman, most likely, would love to print money as promptly and aggressively as the Federal Reserve. In fact, most mainstream economists agree the policy of the Federal Reserve was a better choice than that of the ECB and refer to examples such as Greece and Spain, two countries where the unemployment rate and the youth unemployment rate are downright horrible.

So why does the ECB tend to be late to react, you might ask?

Simply because Germany isn't willing to give them their blessing due to the fact that as mentioned previously, the German hyperinflation after WW1 is deeply entrenched in their subconscious and they perceive inflation as the #1 threat. For this reason, more than a few economists believe Europe may be heading toward something like the US Great Depression of 1929. Yes, the ECB did eventually start printing as well but again, their reaction time tends to be less than impressive.

Naturally, a lot of fear mongers use this argument as well but is the risk of a Great Depression in Europe real? Well yes, it is. If you were to ask me if I can guarantee there will never be a Great Depression in Europe, there's no way I'd be willing or able to do it because nobody knows what will happen in the future. As someone who was born in Europe and who lives in Europe, I can certainly say a lot of things aren't the way they should be. Real estate is overpriced in certain countries/cities, the Euro is still too strong for certain countries to be competitive and so on. Therefore, a scenario which involves deflation is plausible in the weaker EU countries.

Why? Primarily because the weaker EU countries aren't as competitive as they should be and a strong-ish currency certainly isn't helping. Therefore, the deflation argument is plausible for certain European countries. Prices may very well go down and wages as well so that these countries can once again become competitive through internal devaluation. But will all of these countries have to go through something as severe as the Great Depression? In my opinion, it's possible but highly unlikely.

A lot of people seem to think the European countries in question are kind of like a person who owes a lot of money and doesn't have any assets left. This is not an accurate description. Even the poorest EU countries have a lot of assets they could liquidate if need be. Most of them own quite a bit of gold[74], for example. And what about real estate? In most cases, the country in question owns some of the best real estate assets[75]. From quality farmland to buildings in the best neighborhoods of most cities, the state is anything but poor. Visit any important European city and you'll notice state institutions tend to be located in great neighborhoods.

Should they decide to sell some of their assets at a price which makes sense, there would undoubtedly be buyers. Lots of buyers, in fact. Now again, I can't guarantee the European Union will never deal with extreme deflationary problems. Nobody can predict the future, so nobody can guarantee anything. I'm simply trying to explain that such an EU-wide scenario is highly unlikely, leaving individual examples such as Greece aside of course.

Pretty much all EU countries have excellent infrastructure. They have lots of assets, geopolitical advantages and the list could go on and on. Some of them are undoubtedly dealing with economic problems which have to be taken seriously though, so things aren't looking great right now. However, there's a huge difference between dealing with let's say stagnation or a gradual deterioration and dealing with a sudden onset of an extreme depression. At a certain point, things might deteriorate so much that the risk of an extreme depression becomes real but again, it's highly unlikely something like this can happen overnight given the arguments I have referred to through this subchapter.

[74] World Gold Council. "World Official Gold Holdings." *Gold.org*. Retrieved July 20, 2015. http://gold.org.
[75] Elena Moya. "Greece Starts Putting Island Land Up for Sale to Save Economy." *The Guardian*. June 24, 2010. http://www.theguardian.com/world/2010/jun/24/greece-islands-sale-save-economy.

Chapter 6.4.3: Stagflation

What is stagflation? As the name suggests, it's basically a combination between the stagnation of a country's economy and inflation. Most economists think of Milton Friedman whenever someone mentions stagflation since his work on stagflation is quite popular, the term itself however most likely appeared back in 1965, when a British politician called Iain Macleod[76] used it to describe Great Britain's situation at that point.

I wanted to refer to stagflation as well because unlike scenarios such as hyperinflation or Great Depressions, the chances of something like this happening in the relatively near future are considerably higher. Overcoming stagflation can be quite difficult and it isn't a pleasant situation by any means but what I'm trying to explain is it's not exactly something which can bring about the end of the world as we know it from an economic standpoint.

Realistically speaking, we should for the most part be expecting outcomes of pretty much this nature in terms of severity for the most part. Not necessarily stagflation but rather scenarios which would have a similar score on the "how serious is it?" scale, in other words scenarios which aren't pleasant but which aren't disastrous either.

On the one hand yes, a lot of things are wrong with the worldwide economy and yes, we will most likely go through economic difficulties every once in a while. It would be great if we could somehow eliminate economic downturns altogether but the likelihood of something like this happening during our lifetime is unfortunately very low. On the other hand though, it doesn't mean we'll enter the Dark Ages once every ten years either.

Maybe we'll deal with one "big reset" (again, more on this toward the end of this chapter) throughout our lifetime, fair enough, but don't make the mistake of thinking financial calamities of such proportions are extremely common. They definitely aren't. By all means, prepare for such a scenario as well but

---

[76] Iain Macleod. "Economic Affairs." *Millbank Systems*. Retrieved 10 November 2015. http://hansard.millbanksystems.com/commons/1965/nov/17/economic-affairs#column_1165.

remember what I've been saying throughout this book: spending more than a fraction of your time, money or energy worrying about and preparing for events which are highly unlikely isn't a rational way to organize your life and allocate capital. Through the previous two sections, I've tried to analyze inflation as well as deflation from the perspective of a person who wants to figure out how likely certain events are in order to allocate capital effectively and, ultimately, make rational decisions as opposed to emotional ones. Balance is the operative word.

Chapter 6.5: Central Banking Shenanigans

A lot of people believe the aggressiveness of central banks will ultimately generate hyperinflation. Through this subchapter, I will explain that while monetary policy strategies have indeed been aggressive over the past decade, things are a bit more complicated than a simple correlation. Before doing this though, it is imperative to understand how central banks operate, what their role is, what their tools are and what the implications of their actions can be. Normally, central banks are supposed to be 100% independent. As a former Federal Reserve chairman (Ben Bernanke) mentioned, a central bank *"needs to be able to make policy without short term political concerns."*

Yes, this is the way things were supposed to work. Central bankers should have simply been technocrats who don't care about popularity or about the political implications of their actions. As the quote above illustrates, they should simply make the right policy choices without worrying about the political consequences. Unfortunately, in the real world, things don't exactly work like that. It's hard to believe even one central bank out there operates strictly based on technical factors and doesn't take political aspects into consideration. In fact, the exact opposite is true in many cases and central banks often end up being subordinated to the political interests of the individuals who are running a country at a certain point.

I assume most of my readers are adults and as such, let's not hide behind words. Pretty much everyone with half a brain understands central banks aren't and never will be 100% independent. We don't live in a perfect world, I never said we did. In an imperfect society built by imperfect humans, you can't expect perfect institutions. However, this doesn't mean the economy will collapse tomorrow. This is actually one of the most common types of intellectual dishonesty fear mongers often engage in. First of all, they make a common-sense statement which is obviously true such as "central banks aren't independent" but then, they take things to the extreme by drawing conclusions in the realm of "the economy will collapse next year because central banks aren't independent" which are severely lacking in the logic department.

Let me elaborate.

What I'm trying to explain is that it's intellectually dishonest to draw dramatic and potentially society-altering conclusions such as "the economy will collapse next year" from nothing more than a few simplistic arguments such as "central banks aren't independent" and similar ones. If you want to be taken seriously when drawing such dramatic conclusions, then I'm sorry but the burden of proof lies with you. In other words, given the severity of the things you are implying, the intellectually honest thing to do would be providing mountains of arguments and not just limiting yourself to triggering fear by stating a few obvious facts and leaving it at that.

Alright then, so what is the role of a central bank? I personally like Alice Rivlin's description, that *"the job of the Central Bank is to worry"* because this is ultimately what the role of a central bank should be. Some of the world's most talented economists work in the central banking system in one way or another and yes, this is what their role should be. Some people do indeed think the only role of central banks should be worrying about the inflation dimension but in modern central banking, that way of thinking has changed and this is illustrated by one of Janet Yellen's statements, for example:

"I'm just opposed to a pure inflation-only mandate in which the only thing a central bank cares about is inflation and not employment."

Now some of you might think I'm a die-hard Keynesian because I've quoted Ben Bernanke and Janet Yellen. I'm not. Am I an Austrian economics enthusiast? No, wrong again. In fact, I don't believe in defining my way of thinking in such a simplistic manner. I firmly believe in listening to all arguments and deciding which one makes more sense on a case by case basis.

I'm not a cheerleader and I'd strongly encourage all of you to stay away from "black or white" ways of thinking as well. The world is extremely complex and blindly following one thought current or another is a surefire way to gradually lose your ability to make rational decisions. Now that we have established we live in a complex world where, naturally, institutions such as central banks have complex roles, let's try to go through some of the most important ones. First of all, central banks have to obviously worry about inflation because as James Surowiecki[77] pointed out, investors panic when they believe inflation might get out of control and a vicious capital flight circle ensues.

If the inflation rate is high, investors will expect higher returns because otherwise, they'd risk ending up with "real" returns which are negative. For example, if you generated a return of 4% last year but the inflation rate was 5%, you basically lost purchasing power. Naturally, in this case, you'd expect a higher interest rate so as to at least break even. Aside from that, you would also be worried and move at least some money to a currency you perceive as safer than the one issued by the country with the previously mentioned high inflation rate. Again, an obvious vicious circle.

This is precisely why savers don't like our current low interest rate environment. From their perspective, the situation is straightforward: the capital they've managed to set aside is the result of their hard work and determination, therefore as far as they are concerned, the current central banking policies are an insult. As Ray Dalio[78] explained, investors/savers are basically *"putting up a lump-sum payment for a future cash flow."*

When you see central banks acting in a manner which might put your future purchasing power at risk, you naturally end up feeling frustrated as a saver. On the other hand though, it would be a mistake to assume low interest rates are bad for everyone. They're not. At the end of the day, David Axelrod[79] has a reasonably valid "other side" argument, that *"the millions of people who had been able to renegotiate their mortgages so they are paying lower interest rates are better off."*

For savers, a low interest rate environment is definitely not desirable but for borrowers, it's a blessing. For the sake of this argument, let's assume the world is simply divided into two groups: savers and borrowers. What happens

[77] James Surowiecki. *The Wisdom of Crowds*. New York City: Doubleday, 2004.
[78] Ray Dalio. "How the Economic Machine Works." *Bridgewater Associates*. October 31, 2008. http://bwater.com/Uploads/FileManager/research/how-the-economic-machine-works/ray_dalio__how_the_economic_machine_works__leveragings_and_deleveragings.pdf.
[79] Chris Wallace. "David Axelrod and Mayor Antonio Villaraigosa Defend President Obama's Economic Record." *Fox News Sunday*. September 2, 2012. http://www.foxnews.com/on-air/fox-news-sunday-chris-wallace/2012/09/2/david-axelrod-and-mayor-antonio-villaraigosa-defend-president-obamas-economic-record.

if due to all sorts of reasons, borrowers end up no longer being able to keep up with the monthly payments? If things continue in this manner, they will default, so wouldn't it make sense to find a compromise which makes their monthly payments more affordable? Now I'm not saying only borrowers need to be helped, I'm simply trying to explain why things aren't always black or white. No matter what you think about Ben Bernanke, the following statement makes sense:

"The crisis and recession have led to very low interest rates, it is true, but these events have also destroyed jobs, hamstrung economic growth and led to sharp declines in the values of many homes and businesses."

What he's trying to say is that yes, central banks have been pumping money into the system but at the same time, a lot of wealth has disappeared. Once again, let's try to imagine an overly simplified example which illustrates this state of affairs and assume you live in an imaginary country with just 1,000 citizens. Let's also assume that for most people, the price of their house represents most of their net worth and the average price of a home is $200,000.

In other words, everyone's combined net worth is $200,000,000. Alright, now let's assume that for some strange reason, an economic crisis appears and home prices collapse by 50%. As a result, everyone's combined wealth/net worth is only $100,000,000. Finally, what if the country's central bank were to pump let's say $30,000,000 into the system? For a country with only 1,000 citizens, $30,000,000 is definitely a lot of money and some of those citizens would without a doubt assume hyperinflation is just around the corner after such an aggressive move by the central bank. What they're forgetting however is that while $30,000,000 is indeed a lot of money, the combined net worth of all citizens collapsed by over 3 times more, it collapsed by $100,000,000.

Again, this is an oversimplified example through which I've tried to illustrate one aspect: despite the fact that the central bank in question flooded the market with high and unprecedented levels of liquidity, the inflationary effect of such a move has been offset by the deflationary effect of the real estate market collapse. This leads me to another question: given the fact that the United States engaged in a more timely and aggressive monetary policy than let's say Europe, why is the world considerably more worried about Europe than about the United States? Why is there record high unemployment in countries such as Greece and Spain, whereas things aren't nearly as bad in the US?

It ultimately all boils down to this: investors have considerably more confidence in the long-term solvency of the US than in the long-term solvency of Europe. Please remember one of my previous statements about monetary policy: if calibrated properly, it can help borrowers ultimately find a way to cope with their monthly payments rather than default.

This was most likely the fundamental difference between the United States and Europe. The fundamental difference between stimulating the economy when doing so makes sense and austerity. It all boils down to seeing things from the perspective of the borrower as well. If you lent money to someone and the person in question is having a hard time making the monthly payments, what would you do?

1. Find a way to lower that person's monthly payments so that he or she can ultimately manage to afford them?
2. Do nothing, sit back and watch that person come closer and closer to a default?

The United States decided to choose the first option, whereas Europe chose the second, only to realize it made a mistake and ultimately follow the example of the US. Your problem as a lender is simple. If you choose the first method, at least the person in question is making payments again and might eventually afford to pay you back in full, interest included. If you choose the second one, the person in question might default and therefore stop making payments altogether.

This is the #1 risk when it comes to countries such as Spain or Greece. Think about it. They owe a lot of money. The unemployment rate is huge, people are desperate. Instead of helping them, creditors are being aggressive by putting pressure on borrowers. Wouldn't you agree that under these circumstances, the risk of a default or even Euro Zone dissolution is high?

What creditor nations such as Germany don't understand is that by putting too much pressure on the borrowers, you risk turning them into a proverbial dead horse which can no longer be beaten. ECB economists such as Mario Draghi understand this but without support from creditor nations, there is only so much they can do. Austerity risks ultimately representing something like the gold standard. Just like European creditor nations are defending austerity today, certain countries defended the gold standard and it's precisely those countries which were the last to recover from the economic mess they were in[80].

Can we be 100% confident things will unfold this way? Of course not but the arguments I have been repeating throughout this section should at least make it clear the current situation cannot be painted in black and white. Our economic system is extremely complex and as a conclusion to this subchapter, I hope you will accept the fact that low interest rates and quantitative easing might not be as evil as everyone thinks they are.

Again, might.

My main goal isn't telling you what will happen. As you can confirm if you've read the book thus far, I'm the exact opposite of someone who claims he can predict the future. I embrace the fact that I have no way of knowing what will happen in the future and therefore question absolutely everything related to the way our economy works.

This is actually one of the main purposes of this book: making you question some of the things you thought were obvious. Most people are too quick to make the "low interest rates + quantitative easing = hyperinflation" correlation and as I've tried to explain throughout this section, our economy is considerably more complex than meets the eye.

---

[80] Ben Bernanke and Harold James. *The Gold Standard, Deflation, and Financial Crisis in the Great Depression: An International Comparison.* Chicago: University of Chicago Press, 1991.

Chapter 6.6: Facts vs. Opinions vs. Conclusions

I don't know about everyone else but I for one am tempted to simply tune out or at the very least raise an eyebrow whenever someone tries to tell me what to think, whenever someone tries to "sell" a certain conclusion. Selling conclusions is definitely a big no-no as far as I'm concerned but what about opinions?

When it comes to opinions, I'm not as strict because there's at least a certain degree of honesty involved whenever someone starts a phrase using terms such as "I think," "in my opinion" or something along those lines. In this case, we're at least not dealing with someone who puts himself on a pedestal as the absolute holder of truth and this is a good thing.

At the same time though, opinions are not information. Furthermore, they're nothing but noise a lot of times and I'm sure all of you know what they say about opinions. Everyone has one. As someone who watches TV, listens to the radio, reads newspapers/magazines or visits various websites, you will without a doubt be exposed to numerous opinions.

What should our attitude toward them be?

In my opinion (see what I did there?), you should exercise extreme caution/selectivity but at the same time, not disregard opinions altogether. Let me elaborate and assume Brian spends 10 hours each week exposed to mainstream media opinions. He watches a talk show or two, follows a few pundits and sometimes listens to the radio. The average mainstream media consumption scenario, if you will.

10 hours per week may not seem like much but they are more than enough for him to be exposed to numerous opinions: some of them articulated by the talk show hosts, some of them articulated by talk show guests, some of them articulated by pundits and the list could go on and on. Should all of these opinions be treated in the same manner, you might ask?

Well, yes and no.

On the one hand, there are certain things you should do whenever you are exposed to an opinion. No matter who articulates the opinion in question and how much credibility the person in question puts on the table, a few general guidelines should be pretty much always followed. I don't want to over-complicate things, so I'll limit myself to sharing two questions you should always ask yourself:

1. Is this opinion backed by data/information or mostly drivel?

There's a huge difference between someone who shares an opinion backed by nothing more than the weird sensation he had in his stomach after eating breakfast this morning and an opinion backed by lots of useful/interesting information. What constitutes useful information? Pretty much anything, really. Numbers, statistics, historical facts, you name it.

For example, let's assume Brian is watching a talk show and listens to two opinions related to whether or not you should invest in stocks. Person A says that yes, you should invest in stocks because they have done better than other asset classes over the past x years, whereas Person B says that no, you shouldn't because stocks are dangerous.

What should you do in this case?

I'd recommend disregarding Person B's opinion altogether because it isn't backed by anything other than a broad "they're dangerous" statement. I'm sorry but if this is all you've got, I'm not going to take your opinion seriously. Does this mean you should trust Person A instead? No, of course not because as all of those who have taken the time to read this book thus far already know, I always advise against blindly trusting people.

Therefore no, Person A hasn't earned the right to be trusted. However, due to the fact that his opinion (people should invest in stocks) is at least backed by verifiable facts (anyone can perform a few Internet searches and easily determine whether stocks have indeed outperformed other asset classes over the past x years or not), he earned the right to be taken seriously.

This would be my advice: if a person at the very least respects you enough to back up opinions with verifiable facts, he earned the right to be taken seriously. Maybe you'll end up accepting his opinions, maybe not but this much is certain: you at least have valid reasons not to disregard the opinions of the person in question right off the bat, he earned his chance to be heard.

2. Is he interpreting the previously mentioned data/information logically?

A lot of shrewd opinion formers know people trust opinions more when it seems they're backed by real data, so they resort to a little trick. On the one hand yes, they start by presenting facts/information but on the other hand, they interpret things in a manipulative manner that no matter how you spin it, has nothing whatsoever to do with logic.

Yes, referring to facts/data is good but not enough. The manner in which the person in question interprets those facts or the data in question is equally important. In other words, the person who is articulating a certain opinion needs to use easy-to-follow logic to make the connection between the data he's using to back up his opinion and the actual opinion.

For example, let's assume Brian is watching another talk show, once again with two guests. This time, it's Person C and Person D. The topic is the same as last time, whether or not people should invest in stocks. One of the guests, Person C, formulates an opinion using the same fact Person A used in the previous example, the fact that stocks have outperformed other asset classes over the past let's say 50 years. Fair enough, right?

But what if, unlike Person A, his opinion is more specific? Instead of saying people should invest in stocks because they outperformed other asset classes over the past 50 years, he says that since stocks outperformed other asset classes over the past 50 years, everyone who invested over the past 15 years is a happy camper at this point compared to those who invested in other asset classes.

I'm sorry but the second statement is just not true.

Those who invested in stocks back in let's say 2000 are less happy than those who invested in gold because while stocks outperformed gold over the past 50 years, gold outperformed stocks over the past 15-20 years. Therefore, the logic used by Person C is fundamentally flawed and in this case, it's extremely easy to figure out his second claim is false.

In other cases, it's not as easy, which is why prudence is the operative word. Yes, referring to facts/information is a good thing but if your opinion isn't derived from that data using sound logic, then absolutely everything is in vain. Maybe Person C did it to manipulate others or maybe it's just a case of incompetence. Regardless, we have more than enough reasons to disregard Person C's opinion.

These two questions should be asked no matter who is articulating an opinion. If the answer to both of them is "yes" then sure, the person who articulated the argument in question earned the right to be heard. Not the right to be trusted mind you (nobody should have this right unless we're talking about close friends or family members who have actually proven themselves) but simply the right to be heard.

On the other hand though, there are situations in which you can decide whether or not you should take an opinion seriously based exclusively on the person who is articulating it. To put it differently, there are situations in which you can make that decision without even hearing the opinion in question. It might seem weird but it all boils down to the track record of the person who is articulating an opinion.

For this subchapter's final example, let's assume that Brian is watching yet another talk show, this time with Person E and Person F as the guests. The topic? You've guessed it, whether or not people should invest in stocks. Believe it or not, Brian will be able to decide whether or not to accept the opinion of one of those two people based on this simple aspect: his track record.

We'll assume Person E is someone who has an absolutely horrible track record when it comes to financial advice. He made prediction after prediction and all of them ended up being proven wrong. All of them, no exceptions. Based on this terrible track record, I'd recommend disregarding absolutely everything that person says right off the bat, it's just not worth it.

Yes, it's true that even if someone made 99 inaccurate predictions, it doesn't necessarily mean the 100th one will be inaccurate as well. Fair enough, I agree with this completely, past performance is not necessarily indicative of future results. It's just that when it comes to people with horrible track records, the investment of time it takes to always listen to what they have to say is just not appealing enough.

When you have countless TV stations, radio stations and so on (just to limit myself to mainstream media outlets), each with lots and lots of individuals formulating opinions, is it really a good idea to listen to the guy who always got it wrong up until this point? I for one think a bad track record is a more than reasonable argument to disregard a person's opinions in today's world.

What about Person F?

We'll assume Person F is the exact opposite of Person E. He has an amazing track record and we'll even go so far as to assume he always got everything right up until this point. This *has* to mean you should trust him, right? Well no, it doesn't. Just like with the other examples, it simply means the person in question earned the right to be heard. Again, heard as opposed to trusted.

Nothing more, nothing less! If someone with an amazing track record is invited to let's say a TV show about a topic relevant to my interests, I'm willing to make time in my schedule to find out what he has to say. Not to trust him mind you but simply to listen to his opinions. Since he has such a good track record, he earned the right to have access to my most prized resource: time. If on the other hand a person with a horrible track record were to be invited in his place, there's no way I'd invest an hour (or however long the TV show in question is) of my time to tune in. I'm sorry but it's just not going to happen.

It should now be clear what my attitude toward opinions and conclusions is. Whether or not you agree with me is entirely up to you. I for one consider that this attitude is backed by reason and common sense. The day only has 24 hours and our time is therefore severely limited to say the least, so being extremely picky when it comes to the people you listen to is a must.

Chapter 6.7: The Big Reset

I don't make predictions for the simple fact that just like all other humans, I'm incapable of predicting the future. However, when saying that humanity is in for a significant reset, I'm sharing something that is so obvious to me and I believe others that it would be an exaggeration to call it a prediction.

Do I think it will happen tomorrow? Nope.

Do I think it will happen cyclically or if you will, that each financial crisis will be of a "big reset" nature? No and on the contrary, I'm convinced most of the financial calamities you'll deal with throughout your existence will be much milder than a "big reset" financial storm. However, I do believe a big reset is inevitable.

Let me illustrate this through an extreme example and assume that your best friend has a hobby of drunk driving. Each night, he consumes vast quantities of alcohol and then goes for a 30-mile drive. It's obvious that this just cannot end well. One day, you have a friend to friend to chat with him and tell him that if he doesn't stop, he's going to get into an accident.

Your friend however doesn't stop. He goes drunk driving the next day, then again the day after and continues doing his thing. Twenty days after your conversation, the friend in question has a car accident. So, does this mean you're a brilliant forecaster? Because after all, you told him he's going to have an accident if he continues and lo and behold, he actually had one.

Of course not!

What you told your friend was so obvious that it would be downright ridiculous to call it a prediction. The same way, if somebody is thinking about jumping off a skyscraper and you tell him not to do it because he will die then again, you cannot call that a prediction. You're simply sharing some information with him that is blatantly obvious.

I feel the exact same way but about my idea of a big reset.

After reading this book, but I'm sure you realize that we are indeed in an age of anomaly, surrounded by the ridiculous and the unsustainable.

Start by taking a look at your let's call it inner circle: your friends and family members. Most or perhaps all of them are loaded with debt and the exact opposite of the person you would call financially resilient. Now take it one step further and look at your community. Your local community itself is most likely highly indebted as well and most of the nice parks or amenities you see around you have been bought on credit. You will then take things even further and take a look at your country. A country, which just like your local community and your friends as well as family members, is deeply, deeply indebted. Finally, venture outside your own country and you will notice that pretty much all other countries are in the same situation, on an unsustainable path dominated by debt and excesses of various types.

You don't even have to be an economist to acknowledge this shockingly sad reality. Everyone knows it. The next question that arises should be obvious: what needs to be done? If you notice something isn't working properly with your car, you take it to a mechanic. If you notice that a bunch of documents on your desk are burning, you put out that fire as soon as possible. The same way, in our debt-burdened society, the logical question to ask is what are people doing about it?

As referred to my previous analogy, if a single piece of paper catches fire in your home then you can easily put that fire out yourself. But if you don't do that and wait, the fire might become so serious that you end up having to call the fire department. And if you call your fire department too late or not at all, your home will burn down and obviously, your life will be in for a major reset.

First and foremost, a reset is undisputable proof that you have screwed up royally.

That you've failed to take action when it could have been done with minimal damage and instead, have gotten to a point at which a reset is unavoidable. If you're driving your car at 100 km/h, then under normal conditions, you would be able to stop about 100 meters after hitting the brake pedal.

Let's assume there is a huge brick wall in front of you, located let's say 300 meters away from where you are. If you hit the brake pedal now, when you're

300 meters away, nothing bad could possibly happen and even more so, perhaps you're being too prudent. There are still going to be 200 meters separating you from the wall, a more than reasonable safety margin.

If you hit the brake pedal when you are 200 meters away from the wall, you're playing it safe. There will ultimately probably be 100 meters separating you from the wall but it's a good margin to have because you never know. Perhaps your tires are not in the best of shape and as such, your braking distance will be greater, perhaps the weather conditions aren't ideal either and because it rained and so on. A hundred meters is a decent margin to have.

If however you hit the brake pedal when you are just but 100 meters away from the wall, then I'm sorry but you should have been more prudent. You'll most likely be able to avoid an accident but again, what if your tires are not in the best of shape or what if something else makes the braking distance become greater than anticipated? So while I think you should have been more prudent, you're probably going to be safe enough. After all, even if an accident were to take place, it wouldn't be much of an impact because by the time you'd hit the wall, you'd do so at a greatly reduced speed and as such, you should be okay other than some minor damage.

If you hit the brake pedal only 75 meters away from the wall, I'm sorry but an accident is unavoidable. It's probably going to be a relatively mild accident but still, you should've taken action sooner but didn't. As such, you will face the consequences. Fortunately though, the accident will probably not result in you getting hurt.

If you hit the brake pedal only 50 meters away from the wall, not only are you going to be involved in an accident which results in vehicle damage, but you and your passengers if you have any will suffer injuries as well. Your lack of prudence will cost you dearly. Extensive car damage and also injuries.

If you wait until you're only 25 meters away, you're going to be in a serious accident and might even die. Finally, if you wait until you're only 5 meters away from the wall, then you can have the best co-pilot in the world by your side and you can be the best driver in the history of mankind, yet it will make no difference. You will, without a doubt, die.

It is my firm belief that this is the manner in which we should be seeing the economic fate of humanity at this point. The not million, not billion, not even trillion but downright quadrillion dollar question is this: where do we stand? How far away is the previously mentioned wall in our case?

It's very hard for me to answer this because while I'm not able to pinpoint the exact distance from the wall that we are currently at, I firmly believe that on the one hand, we are definitely way past the point at which we can take action without there being dire consequences but on the other hand, I do believe we have not yet reached the point when regardless of what we do, our demise is inevitable.

My best guess is that we are somewhere in the 50-75 meter region. There's just no way to avoid a car crash and injuries but fortunately, we are not yet at the point when the injuries in question would be fatal. I'm sure all of this sounds grim because it actually is a grim situation. Why didn't governments and central banks take action sooner, why did we wait until we've reached such a point?

What people have to understand is that the answer to this question is more in the realm of politics than economics. Once you've gotten elected, one of your top priorities and perhaps the top priority is not having something crash on your watch. Nobody wants to be the president or prime minister or central bank governor under whom the system crashed, this much is certain. If we see things from this paradigm, it becomes obvious why the powers that be would much rather prolong things as much as possible, in the hope that nothing will crash while they're in charge, so that the leaders who are next in line will be the ones holding the hot potato.

I cannot help but notice that as of certain point, the fate of the world's financial system has become a game of hot potato. You make promises, get elected, then try to kick the can down the road. Rinse and repeat until, well, until it's no longer possible. The "until that is no longer possible" part is the key here in my opinion because when the inevitable big reset does eventually occur, I for one am convinced it's going to simply occur because it was no longer possible to prolong the inevitable.

It won't occur because politicians thought it's time to actually face facts but simply because prolonging the inevitable was no longer possible. I for one think this is terrible news for humanity because let's face it, a controlled reset is much but easier to cope with than an uncontrolled one. For a controlled reset to take place, there needs to be what I would call political goodwill and it is clear to me at this point that we will never have such a thing.

This is why, in this book, I've focused just as much on being prepared for the unexpected in general and being resilient as I have on the idea of spotting financial storms before they occur. Since I for one expect an unplanned and unpredictable reset, I believe it makes sense to have all bases covered.

But what exactly will the big reset involve?

I'd like to start by saying that in all honesty, I'm not sure. However, since this section is about my opinions specifically, I'll do my best to articulate some thoughts. A lot of people believe currencies will crash and that a hyperinflationary scenario is inevitable. It's fairly easy to understand why in light of the fact that authorities always love the idea of printing their way out of problems. But up until this point, huge injections into the system have been possible without extremely inflationary effects.

However, you can only print your way out of problems as long as the market allows you to do that. Can this go on a lot longer than most people predict? It already has, look at Japan. However, as of a certain point and for reasons which remain to be seen, the market will say that it had enough. Once that happens, good luck!

There's no metric which tells you when the market is ready to say that it had enough, your guess is as good as mine. My baseline scenario however is that before currencies depreciate dramatically, there will be some kind of a deflationary cataclysm. Up until this point, this is how it worked: a deflationary event such as a significant financial crash took place and the authorities responded by injecting money into the system, lowering interest rates and so on.

It's a dream come true for politicians at the end of the day. Instead of dealing with the big reset themselves, they can try buying some time this way and it has been proven that the market is a lot more lenient than a lot of analysts gave it credit for. From politicians, I tend to expect more of the same. In other words, each time a financial crisis rears its ugly head, they're

THE AGE OF ANOMALY

going to try to print themselves out of it. Until that no longer works, of course.

Despite the fact that like Jon Snow, I know nothing (for sure), my best guess is that the big reset will unfold in a "deflation followed by inflation" pattern. In other words, I think politicians will continue with the current modus operandi, that we're going to keep having deflationary crashes and each time, the authorities will try to print themselves out of the mess… until the market has enough.

Perhaps we're going to have a crash relatively soon and when politicians try to once again fire up the printing presses, the market will say no. Then again, perhaps it won't and politicians will get away with that yet again. Then after a few more years, we're going to have another deflationary event and once again, we'll just have to see if the market accepts the response of politicians or not.

I for one expect something like a significant market crash, followed by the usual reaction of politicians and central bankers, which is trying to print themselves out of the mess. However, the big reset will occur when the market will say that it had enough and when confidence in currencies will collapse.

Make no mistake, everything related to currencies is dictated by confidence.

Even if we were on a 100% gold standard, it's still confidence that dictates everything because if for some reason people would lose confidence in gold, currencies would go down the drain even if they're backed 100% by something tangible and scarce. The gold standard is by no means a miracle solution.

This is what you have to watch out for in my opinion, confidence is what makes or breaks any man-made system. From currencies to the very structure of society. When confidence crumbles, that's when things get ugly and that is when I expect the big reset to take place. Do keep in mind however that these are just my thoughts with respect to how the big reset will unfold and I for one want to make it very clear that they should not be considered predictions. At the end of the day, the best piece of advice I can give you is to keep your eyes open and be ready to react quickly.

I'm not like most economists, I don't care all that much about getting it right and about my predictions being 100% spot on. I really don't. I'd much prefer being prepared than being right. What I've done with this particular book reflects that. You didn't read *The Age of Anomaly* so you can be prepared for whichever scenarios I envision. You read it because you want to be better at spotting financial storms in general and because you want to become resilient so that when some kind of a big reset eventually occurs, you're able to land on your feet.

Chapter 6.8: What Happens After the Big Reset?

It wouldn't make sense to discuss the big reset without thinking about what is likely to happen after it. Could we end up living in a perpetual Mad Max world? Perhaps, nothing is impossible but I for one seriously doubt it. At the end of the day, we need to understand that the world around us won't stop functioning just because man-made systems like the financial system go belly-up.

Crops will keep growing. The sun will keep shining. The moon will continue taking its place during the night and so on but. I for one tend to believe that no matter how disruptive the cataclysm may be, some kind of a balance will end up being reached, with of course notable exceptions such as nuking ourselves to death.

However, I hope as well as ultimately believe that in the end, humanity will always remain at least one step away from its total annihilation. Therefore, I think a good baseline scenario is that sure, things will initially be awful, there will be a lot of disruption but balance will ultimately be reached in one way or another.

As someone who is preparing for financial storms, you also have to put together a plan for their aftermath. At the end of the day, your main objective should not only be surviving the storm. It's just as important what happens next and how you as well as your family can resume your day-to-day existence.

Even though I sometimes sound like a broken record, I always remind people to focus on sustainability, no matter what it is that they're doing. There's more to life than just hunkering down in your home and living on canned goods. What happens next? That's the million-dollar question.

The answer to this question depends on the type of crisis we are dealing with.

If we're talking about a simple financial crisis with no meaningful repercussions on our day-to-day living, then after it is over, it's simply a matter of people licking their wounds no matter what they may be and moving on with their lives. These wounds include of course any financial losses they have suffered during the crisis in question.

However, the more serious the financial storm is, the more complicated it is for us to recover from it. And since we are now talking about the big reset, it should be obvious that you won't be able to merely dust off your jacket and move on. How people will be moving on primarily depends on which systems will be affected by the big reset.

Right now, due to the current banking system mechanism which is called fractional reserve banking, banks keep a very low amount of cash at hand and therefore, if even one out of three people demands his money back, there is no such thing as a bank which can withstand something like that. Why, you might ask? Mainly because when times are good, people have complete confidence in the banking system and even the idea of 5% of a bank's depositors demanding their money in the form of cash seems downright ridiculous.

Needless to say, confidence in systems in general will be lost to a large degree after the big reset. As such, I fully expect banking business models to change and banks to keep more cash, whatever form that cash may take, at hand. Perhaps the most straightforward direct effect of the big reset will be the fact that the banking system as a whole will change fundamentally and since our lives depend more than we realize on the banking system, things will probably get complicated. Not as complicated for the average individual, most likely, as for people who are running businesses and depend on financing from banks. Needless to say, the way in which you do business will be significantly disrupted after the big reset.

Secondly, speaking of banks holding more cash, what we need to realize is that there's no telling what cash might ultimately be if currencies themselves end up collapsing. The scenario I envision as the most likely outcome is one that's similar to what happened in Weimar Germany after their hyperinflation. Specifically, the most probable scenario in my view is that of currencies being relaunched but since confidence in currencies that aren't backed by anything tangible will be minimal, the authorities will have no choice but to link the currencies to something.

A lot of gold enthusiasts will be quick to say that of course, what better solution could there possibly be than precious metals? And while I do agree that gold could be a decent fit, let's not forget that currencies can be linked to absolutely anything. For example, in Germany, real estate was initially chosen instead of gold. The name of the game will not be linking occurrences to one specific thing because nothing else can possibly work but rather linking currencies to whatever it is people are more likely to have confidence in.

However, given the significant loss of confidence that will probably occur, I'm not ruling out scenarios which also involve parallel currencies circulating. Perhaps parallel currencies that are not backed by the government. It wouldn't surprise me one bit if, at least for a considerable amount of time after the big reset, something like bitcoin ends up being used right alongside the state-issued currencies.

But I would also like to address the idea of barter. A lot of people consider bartering the primary scenario they're working with but I for one have trouble seeing how barter can end up becoming the status quo rather than simply something people use for a short amount of time after a big reset. In the section about SHTF resilience, I have explained that having highly tradable and highly portable items is definitely not a bad idea. But to expect barter to be a long-term replacement rather than a short-term solution but would be taking it too far in my view.

Now that we've covered banks as well as currencies, let's see how else our day-to-day lives are like to be affected. First and foremost, just like before, the main driving force of the changes we will be witnessing will be represented by the fact that people will lose confidence in the state in general. After the big reset, I fully expect people's loss of confidence in state-run systems to manifest itself through things like increased civil disobedience, higher black market activity and so on. It will probably take a lot of time for the wounds of the big resets to heal and we all need to prepare for that.

Fortunately, this book's section about resilience tells you everything you need to know and that needs to be done in order to cope with not just the actual financial storm but its aftermath as well. Someone who is genuinely resilient will have no problems coping with whatever short as well as long-term effects the big reset will have.

Therefore, the best piece of advice I can give you is to re-read the section about resilience as frequently as necessary. Becoming genuinely resilient is a

Herculean task and not everyone can pull it off spectacularly. But by reading the chapter in question and actually implementing the tips I've provided, then even if your resilience level won't be perfect, it will be multiple orders of magnitude better than it is today and a gazillion orders of magnitude better compared to that of the average individual.

.

Conclusions?

I don't exactly have the habit of writing short books. Make no mistake, it would be far more profitable for me to do so, editors would think it's a good idea and my schedule would be a lot more reasonable. But if I feel that I need 400 pages to get the message across properly, then 400 pages it is.

First and foremost, what's my main goal with this book?

Simply put, it's helping people understand anomalies and protect themselves against financial storms. Quite a few authors try to do the same but in my opinion, there was a clear demand on the market for a reasonable, coherent approach to dealing with financial calamities. Not books written by charlatans who claim they can predict the future, not books written by people who are driven by either excessive doom and gloom or irrational optimism.

I believe the value I bring to the table revolves around my ability to offer a balanced perspective.

Through the first two chapters, I've introduced this book and told readers a thing or two about my way of seeing the world as well as about what I hope to accomplish through *The Age of Anomaly*. I believe in being frank (and occasionally brutally honest) with people, so I was upfront about my limitations right off the bat.

Embarking on a journey with realistic expectations is in my opinion 25% of the battle, so I resisted the temptation of surrounding myself with an aura of infallibility and instead, did the exact opposite by embracing my limitations "publicly" and even more so, making them a core element of my strategy.

I'm not one to waste time with introductions, so we went right down to business as of chapter 3.

The third chapter of this book revolved around analyzing case studies and had two sections: then and now. My main goal wasn't covering as many case studies as possible but rather, through careful selection, exposing readers to a wide range of financial storms so that in the end, appropriate conclusions can be drawn.

I started by analyzing what I consider to be the most interesting case studies of the relatively distant past (the "Then" section):

1. The tulip mania, which experienced its peak from very late 1636 to very early 1637, a fascinating tale about human nature and more specifically, a more than generous source of examples when it comes to the things we're willing to do when greed gets the best of us.

   Many readers will without a doubt consider the tulip mania subchapter an eye-opener from the perspective of human behavior when there's ample financial incentive involved. It might initially be hard to comprehend that investors sometimes pick the craziest assets (tulips, in this case) but you'll get used to it and the fact that the final case study of chapter 3 is about the short domain mania of 2015-2016 makes it clear that even in the present, humans are willing to try "exotic" assets on for size if the potential rewards seem juicy enough

2. The South Sea bubble, which peaked in June of 1720 or the first recorded example of government manipulation for financial gain. A remarkable case study about how something that seems to have or even actually has the state's "seal of approval" doesn't necessarily have to be the best thing since sliced bread.

   Once again, I expect this case study to be a bit of an eye-opener but this time when it comes to the faith (or lack thereof) you should have in the state. As you're about to find out, the government is frequently involved in its share of let's call them shenanigans. So as always, proceed with caution and be skeptical, even when dealing with the state!

3. The Mississippi bubble, which also peaked in 1720 but unlike the
    South Sea bubble, it actually has two dimensions. The first dimension
    is of course the state manipulation one (creating a state company with
    a monopoly on trade and pitching it to investors so as to alleviate
    France's debt burden), whereas dimension number two is of
    monetary nature.

    John Law (the Mississippi bubble mastermind) had an even deadlier
    mix of ingredients than John Blunt (the South Sea bubble
    mastermind) in his arsenal and what resulted was a downright
    spectacular display of (in our case evil) financial ingenuity. Strangely
    enough, you'll most likely have a "this might have actually worked"
    sense toward the end because indeed, it would have been interesting
    to observe how things would have unfolded if John Law and those
    surrounding him had been more prudent

4. The panic of 1825, which tends to be considered the world's first
    international crisis, the world's first emerging market crisis as well as
    the start of modern economic cycles. It's remarkable how when the
    perfect conditions present themselves, anomalies are just around the
    corner.

    On the one hand, you had people who were optimistic about the
    future and ready to spend in a risk-on manner on the Old Continent
    and on the other hand, you had several newly-formed states over in
    South America who were eager to relieve investors of their excess
    liquidity

5. The British railway manias, especially the bubble which took place in
    the 1840s, events at the end of which investors lost a fair bit of
    money (to put it mildly) but the state itself actually benefited from
    the newly built infrastructure, even if things went overboard toward
    the end and too much was built.

    It's refreshing and intellectually stimulating to also see the silver
    lining when it comes to financial storms because in a lot of cases,
    there is indeed a silver lining. Whenever revolutionary technology
    emerges, we do have this tendency of speculating recklessly and it

doesn't always end well in the short run. After the dust settles however, it's not always all doom and gloom

6. The Weimar Republic hyperinflation, at the height of which (November of 1923) one US dollar was worth 4.2 trillion marks. This is one of the most popular economic case studies out there but unfortunately, misunderstandings abound because economists frequently present (or even distort) the facts in a manner which confirms their existing beliefs, which isn't exactly intellectually honest.

I did my best not to make the same mistake and tried to explain things in a fact-based, coherent but at the same time easy-to-understand manner. From causes to manifestation and of course conclusions, I tried not to let my own belief system influence the manner in which I painted the Weimar Republic hyperinflation picture

7. The Florida real estate boom of the 1920s, as a result of which the roaring 20s ended sooner in Florida than in the rest of the United States. Throughout this book, I've tried to find the right balance between case study popularity (case studies people at least kind of, sort of heard about and can therefore relate to more easily) and my desire to sprinkle in nuggets of economic knowledge which aren't as common.

The Florida real estate boom of the 1920s is a good example of a frequently overlooked case study where the value lies in the details. In understanding the way of thinking people were characterized by back then, in seeing things from their perspective and ultimately drawing the appropriate parallels

8. The infamous Great Depression of 1929, which most people consider a benchmark when it comes to financial calamities. It would have been downright ridiculous not to cover this case study. Therefore, I have of course included it and even more so, have done my best to help people get their facts straight about what actually happened.

> The most dangerous aspect about (in)famous calamities such as the Great Depression is the fact that with so much information about them being readily available, there's also a great deal of misinformation circulating. While there aren't as many misunderstandings/myths as with the Weimar hyperinflation floating around the Internet, it still makes sense to be fact-oriented rather than willing to accept anything you read online

… so there we have it, the "Then" dimension of chapter number three!

I've then (see what I did there?) moved on to the second half of the third chapter and referred to events closer to the present, starting with the gold and silver bubble of 1977 to 1980. People tend to find it easier to relate to events that are closer to the present and therefore, writing this half has been easier for me for the simple reason that I didn't have to go through so much trouble in order to put readers in the proper mindset.

When referring to situations that took place hundreds of years ago such as the tulip mania, South Sea bubble or Mississippi bubble, it's always important to dedicate at least a bit of time to helping people understand what the life of the average person was in the Dutch Republic, Great Britain and respectively France back then. Frankly, it was half the battle when it comes to the first half of chapter 3. While providing the proper context was of course also necessary in the second half, it was a much more straightforward endeavor.

Also, may I just add that finding trustworthy data that didn't make me raise an eyebrow was a lot easier as we got closer to the present. From the perspective of accuracy, I do have to point out that once again, my life was a lot easier with the "Now" dimension of my case study analysis efforts.

Finally, it's worth noting that while one might have expected there to be fewer and fewer anomalies as time passes and investors become more educated/sophisticated, the exact opposite happened. As technology evolves, so does "financial ingenuity" and this tends to give birth to quite a few monsters.

Just imagining what the John Blunts and John Laws of today are capable of doing with their (far) more impressive arsenal of tools gives me goosebumps. The risk this state of affairs poses cannot be overstated and there's no hiding from in. Frankly, the abundance of anomalies in the 21st century thus far is what ultimately made me decide to write *The Age of Anomaly* in the first place.

That being stated, here are the case studies I've chosen for the "Now" section of chapter 3:

1. The end of Bretton Woods and the gold/silver bubble of 1977 to 1980. I realize some people are going to hate me for calling it a bubble but before jumping to conclusions, I would strongly recommend reading the subchapter in question. There's method to my madness, I promise!

   While I frequently recommend precious metals and consider them worthwhile assets, I do my best not to be a gold/silver "cheerleader" like a lot of other economists, just like I try to never cheer for any of the other asset classes either. Falling in love with assets is never a good idea

2. The "Black Monday" stock market crash which took place on the 19th of October 1987, when stocks went down by a whopping 22.6% in just one day, the most impressive (and at the same time devastating) single-day market crash in history. By far, I might add!

   Now sure, pretty much everyone tends to think about the Great Depression of 1929 when someone mentions market crashes and sure, the long-term implications of the Great Depression make the 1987 situation look like a joke. In the (very) short run however, the 1929 Great Depression doesn't even come close to beating Black Monday of 1987 (12.8% vs. 22.6%)

3. The Japanese bubble of the 1980s which, after it burst, gave birth to Japan's lost not decade but actually decades from which the country has yet to recover. It's nothing short of shocking how anomalies can even affect downright impressive countries like Japan. Impressive from an economic perspective, from a work ethic perspective and pretty much any other perspective one can think of.

   Yet as you were able to find out, the bubble of the 1980s made it crystal-clear that not even a country like Japan is truly immune. Even the most responsible people in the world are prone to making capital allocation mistakes and the Japan case study can be considered a "poster boy" in that respect

4. The Asian financial crisis of 1997, similar when it comes to certain perspectives to what happened in Japan but with a lot more let's call them "Wild West" elements such as rudimentary corruption, blatantly obvious displays of nepotism (something quite common in my country as well, nepotism as in hiring people not based on competence but because they're friends or relatives).

    All in all, this crisis definitely deserves a case study of its own and represents a more than generous source of anomalies. Observing how anomalies manifest themselves in an emerging market framework broadens our horizons and enables us to spot similarities as well as notice differences

5. The 1998 collapse of what was once the spoiled child of the financial industry, Long-Term Capital Management. A case study which proves that even a dream team that consists of rock star experts and even two Nobel Prize winners (Myron S. Scholes and Robert C. Merton) is not above failure.

    On the contrary, it can fail in a spectacular manner and turn the entire endeavor into a nightmare for all parties involved. Such a nightmare, in fact, that Wall Street ended up ultimately bailing them out, yet another interesting particularity of the Long-Term Capital Management case study

6. The dot-com bubble which peaked back in the year 2000 and represents a remarkable example of creative destruction. At its core, the bubble did have solid fundamentals because let's face it, the Internet dramatically altered pretty much all sectors of society. You wouldn't have heard about my book without it, among a gazillion other things.

    However, this doesn't mean you should blindly "invest" in anything that has a Dot Com suffix, thinking you can't go wrong. You most definitely can, as examples such as the Pets.com fiasco (with

Pets.com going from a market valuation of $300,000,000 at its peak all the way down to zero) illustrate

7. The 2007-2008 Great Recession about which people are still talking to this day and even more so, its effects are still being felt. Just think about our ultra-low interest rate environment or about the fact that central banks are still easing over in for example Europe and Japan.

    Make no mistake, we haven't "recovered" from the Great Recession, far from it. Even more so, it remains to be seen what the long-term consequences of the post-recession measures will end up being. As tempted as we might be to assume central bankers saved the day by lowering interest rates and "printing" money, it remains to be seen just what the long-term ramifications (if any, of course) will look like

8. The short domain mania of 2015 to 2016 which was nowhere near as popular as the Great Recession, nor did it produce devastating effects when it comes to the economy as a whole but which does a splendid job of showing us a thing or two about human nature or more specifically, about what humans tend to do when spectacular returns are on the table and irrational greed takes over.

    In my opinion, we have more than enough reasons to remember the very first case study of chapter 3 (the tulip mania) and draw parallels. A lot of things have changed since then, we're now communicating with people from all corners of the world through smartphones for example. A totally different world, right? Well, no, not necessarily. Technology evolved, things changed politically as well as socially but let me ask you, has human nature changed in an equally dramatic manner?

So, now that you understand all of these case studies and hopefully managed to internalize a few core concepts, will you be able to accurately predict the next financial storm and all of the ones that are going to follow? To put it differently, does *The Age of Anomaly* come with a complimentary crystal ball?

No, I'm afraid it doesn't.

As mentioned right from the beginning of this book, it was never my intention to turn *The Age of Anomaly* into a tool that's somehow supposed to enable you to predict the future. I'm sorry but that's the kind of thing you'd buy after watching a late-night infomercial and you will most certainly not buy something like that from me.

On the contrary, I've explained time and time again as well as provided meaningful arguments which support the idea that humans cannot predict the future, not even Nobel Prize winners like the two members of the Long-Term Capital Management dream (turned nightmare) team.

To those of you who were accustomed to listening to all sorts of self-proclaimed gurus who claim to hold all of the answers, I hope this book represented a much-needed wake-up call. Fortunately however, I'm not just here to destroy and walk away, I'm here to replace.

More specifically, I'm here to replace a childish approach to preparedness with something argument-based, rational and coherent. The manner in which I've structured this book hopefully speaks for itself. I firmly believe in taking things one step at a time, in structure if you will.

My main goal with chapter number three has been giving people a proper historical context. By choosing case studies that complement one another, I did my best to expose readers to a wide range of human nature manifestations. Even more so, I've identified several common denominators and have drawn conclusions which will undoubtedly help you become better at spotting financial storms.

Will you be able to do it every time? Of course not, there's a more than reasonable likelihood that even yours truly will be caught off-guard when the next financial storm hits. Regardless, knowledge is power and somebody who possesses a proper and fact-based supply of knowledge ammunition is in a much, much better position to be prepared for future financial storms than the average individual.

Through chapter 4, I took things one step further by providing information that will make you multiple orders of magnitude better at spotting future financial storms. I never really understood why people placed so much importance on the idea that there is this guru out there who can tell you precisely on which day and at what hour disaster will strike. That's just ridiculous and even more so, even if it were possible, it wouldn't be as useful as you might think.

I believe there's more than enough value in a far more reasonable approach which revolves around the idea of understanding financial storms and becoming better at spotting warning signals, reacting quickly and so on. A lot of times in life, it's a few simple common-sense measures that make all the difference in the world.

There's no need to be a financial genius, nor should it be your intention to become a fortune teller. Just do your best to get better and better at spotting financial storms in a reasonable manner and chapter number four will enable you to do just that… or at least I certainly hope so!

The fourth chapter started with general "evergreen" information and toward the end, I have of course also processed the data I've shared in the third chapter in order to draw conclusions. These conclusions have been packaged into something I've chosen to call the 11 storm-causing deadly sins:

1. Ignorance
2. Indebtedness
3. Imprudence
4. Wrath
5. Incompetence
6. Delirium
7. Foolhardiness
8. Thoughtlessness
9. Greed-induced delusion
10. Sentimentalism
11. Disregard

… however, I didn't stop there!

I took things one step further by sharing what I've decided to call "Polgar's Prudence Principles" (I do apologize for the corniness but I just couldn't help myself!), which are basically 25 common-sense tips based on my knowledge as well as experience/vision.

CONCLUSIONS?

Do these tips involve rocket science in any way?

Of course not but I can pretty much guarantee that if we follow two almost identical people (similar jobs, income levels, family situations and so on) over the course of several years, with one of them having internalized my 25 principles and one of them refusing to do so, the former will be in much, much better financial shape.

I can't stress this enough: a healthy dose of common sense can and will get you far!

Keeping it logical is the name of the game and chapter number five should therefore surprise nobody. Since we've already analyzed case studies, interpreted that information and found out how to become better at spotting financial storms, I believe it makes sense to also be prepared for situations in which we do not manage to spot a certain financial calamity and it hits us.

Chapter number five is therefore dedicated to something that should be the number one priority of the modern-day consumer in my opinion, becoming more resilient in general. Maybe the next storm is going to be deflationary in nature. Or perhaps inflationary. Then again, what if it's deflationary first and then inflationary? Or geopolitical?

The list could go on and on.

The problem with trying to predict the future is that you end up being the prisoner of your own pride and consequently not preparing enough for scenarios that differ from the one you are predicting. For example, a lot of self-proclaimed gurus are afraid of imminent hyperinflation and therefore tell everyone to stock up on gold.

That ultimately makes them sound like a broken record because they give the same advice time and time again. Now if their hyperinflationary scenarios end up manifesting themselves then sure, they as well as the people who followed them will be more than happy. But I would argue that there are far more scenarios than that to worry about and by not worrying about alternative scenarios, you're becoming ridiculously vulnerable.

Instead of letting pride be your number one enemy, let humility become your top ally.

Let's assume John is afraid of hyperinflation and ends up selling everything he has aside from the apartment he lives in so as to buy precious metals. He backs up the truck, as they say in the world of investing. He however does something else as well, something that's commonly referred to in the investing industry as putting all of your eggs in the same basket.

Oddly enough, people like John can lose money even if they are ultimately right. For example sure, maybe there will be hyperinflation 10 years from now but what if that hyperinflationary event is preceded by an extended period of annoyingly persistent deflation?

Deflation which can make John lose his job, deflation that can cause him to lose access to various other income sources and, you've guessed it, deflation which might take its toll on precious metal prices as well. John, just like everyone else, needs to... you know, eat, and therefore, people like him are very likely to end up having to liquidate at least an important part of their position in precious metals by selling their gold or silver at whatever the market price is when they are in dire need of capital.

So yes, we'll assume 10 years go by and John is finally proven right.

But what good does it do him if by the time the scenario he's been preparing for actually materializes, his net worth has all but evaporated? There's not as much financial value as you might think in telling people "I told you so" and bragging rights can't be traded for food.

Therefore, you have all the reasons in the world to consider the idea of putting all of your eggs in the same basket unappealing. The same way however, I'm not encouraging people to spread themselves too thin and chapter number five represents my attempt at showing readers how you can be smart about becoming more resilient.

I've even analyzed a wide range of asset classes, one at a time, in order to help people make informed decisions. Being resilient if you live in the United States is not the same as being resilient if you live in China. Or Egypt. Or Australia. It's ultimately all a matter of making the best possible decision(s) for your specific needs.

It won't do you much good to stock up on precious metals if there was never much of a gold/silver culture in your country and as such, should the proverbial you know what actually hit the fan, people are likely to choose something else as a medium of exchange and store of value.

The same principle is valid when it comes to your exposure to other asset classes as well and the most important thing to remember is this: decisions related to becoming more resilient are not something I would recommend people outsource, as appealing as it may seem.

Should you accept information from others? Sure, by all means!

Should you however delegate the final decision-making process? No!

But how exactly have I analyzed assets one at a time? I'm sure people expect some kind of structure as well as coherence from me and I did my best not to disappoint. I've basically started by dividing asset classes into two (very) broad categories as follows:

1. Status Quo Assets or in other words, assets pretty much everyone (including those who aren't exactly financially literate) has heard about. Assets such as stocks, real estate and so on. Their main advantage is the fact that for better or for worse, you at least "kind of, sort of" know what to expect. You're not venturing into unchartered territory and are instead, walking on a beaten path.

    However, the main drawback is represented by the fact that the return potential isn't amazingly high in a lot of cases. It's basically a trade-off, in that you're willing to accept the previously mentioned lower return potential in exchange for a higher degree of predictability

2. Trailblazer assets or assets that are so new and at the same time "hot" that profit potential abounds. Instead of walking down a beaten path, you're willing to blaze trails yourself and venture into the unknown. As such, it shouldn't come as a surprise that if you get it right, you'll be rewarded with impressive returns

However (there has to be a "however" in this case as well I'm afraid), the risks are considerably higher as well. If you're not willing to accept not just the possibility but actually the likelihood of eventually losing even absolutely everything you've invested, I'm afraid trailblazer assets aren't for you

Did I stop there, are two categories enough?

No!

For each of the two categories, there are in my opinion three asset subtypes:

1. Fair-weather assets or assets that do well when the economy as a whole is in good shape. Of course, this also means they perform poorly when sentiment is down and investors are not exactly thrilled about the future. A good example of a fair-weather status quo asset is represented by stocks, whereas an example of a fair-weather trailblazer asset would be investment grade one-word Dot Com domains

2. Life jacket assets, in other words the exact opposite of fair-weather assets. They tend to underperform when everything seems to be going well with the economy but when the proverbial you know what hits the fan, they frequently skyrocket in value. A good example of a life jacket status quo asset would be precious metals, whereas an example of a life jacket trailblazer asset would be… you've guessed it, bitcoin

3. Sentiment-neutral assets, which are assets that don't necessarily fluctuate based on how market participants are "feeling" at one point or another, even if only because not all assets of this subtype behave in the same manner. A good example of a sentiment-neutral status quo assets would be bonds, whereas investment grade websites represent an example of a sentiment-neutral trailblazer asset. In each case, there are several different bond/website types and as such, it's impossible to simply slap a label on them based on market sentiment

I am of course an economist and needless to say, this means I've focused quite a bit on the financial dimension but make no mistake, I'm not a hermit.

I know that not everything in this world revolves around economics, so I did my best to cover all sorts of other dimensions, more specifically:

1. Professional resilience or simply put, investing in yourself and becoming better at whatever it is you currently do for a living. Investments in education, equipment and so on can be remarkably efficient from the perspective of returns as well as resilience in general

2. Mental resilience or if you will, not letting negative outcomes mess with your head. This is of course easier said than done but there's just no way to meaningfully become more resilient without working on the mental dimension as well. By learning to become better at things like coping with losses or dealing with high-pressure situations, you'll be multiple orders of magnitude stronger as a person

3. Physical resilience because yes, even though this is a book written by an economist and which you'd expect to focus on anything but getting in shape, I have to be intellectually honest and venture outside my comfort zone. My main goal wasn't helping you get the perfect beach body but rather explaining why physical resilience is important and what some common-sense measures that could help you in this respect would be

4. SHTF resilience or being prepared not just for financial calamities but for disasters of other nature as well. Whether we're talking about natural disasters such as earthquakes or floods, socio-political calamities or anything else, it makes sense to be prepared. Now does this mean I'm encouraging you to become a prepper and move to the mountains? Of course not but make no mistake, SHTF resilience (within reason) can get you far

Despite the fact that I'm not too thrilled about it, there are people who consider me an opinion former and this does tend to put a little bit of pressure on a person to articulate his own thoughts when it comes to the world we live in. It's not that I want to, it's that everyone expects me to and the people pleaser in me feels a strong urge to deliver.

Chapter 6 has been dedicated to just that.

In other words, I've presented my perspective on how things currently stand in the world around us but right from the beginning, have made it abundantly clear that I may very well be wrong. You shouldn't read the sixth chapter with the intention of simply copying my ideas or mimicking what I do. My approach may very well not represent a suitable solution for you and even more so, it might even be completely wrong. Instead, you should read it in order to have access to my thought process and extract whatever value from it you see fit.

If you believe I'm a person worth listening to then thank you. And by all means, listen to what I have to say but always draw your own conclusions and more importantly, always make your own decisions. Never lose sight of my recommendation when it comes to delegating the decision-making process.

Well, that's pretty much it!

I firmly believe that if you take the time to properly digest *The Age of Anomaly*, you'll be in very good shape even if it's the only book about preparedness you read. I weigh my words very carefully, as you undoubtedly know by now, but I feel very confident in that statement because by making it, I'm not showing confidence in myself but rather in you, in my readers.

My goal with this book hasn't been creating a following and branding myself as a guru.

In fact, I wanted to do the exact opposite.

I've continuously tried my best to demystify the idea of financial gurus in general and write a book that enables people to make their own decisions. I for one am convinced I've given you the proper tools you need for just that, where you take it from here is entirely up to you.

Bibliography

Aguirre, Fernando. Bugging Out and Relocating: When Staying Put Is Not an Option. North Charleston: CreateSpace Independent Publishing Platform, 2014.

Auret, Christo and Robert Vivian. "A Comparative Analysis of Returns of Various Financial Asset Classes in South Africa: A Triumph of Bonds?" Southern African Business Review. December 9, 2014. http://www.unisa.ac.za/contents/faculties/service_dept/docs/Sabview_18 _3_Chap%208.pdf.

Aytoun, William E. "How We Got Up the Glenmutchkin Railway, and How We Got Out of It." Blackwood's Edinburgh Magazine. October 1, 1845. http://www.dtc.umn.edu/~odlyzko/rrsources/glen6.pdf.

Barro, Robert J. and Sanjay P. Misra. "Gold Returns." National Bureau of Economic Research. February 1, 2003. http://www.nber.org/papers/w18759.pdf.

Bell, Claes. "Budgets Can Crumble in Times of Trouble." Bankrate. January 7, 2015. http://www.bankrate.com/finance/smart-spending/money-pulse-0115.aspx.

Bernanke, Ben and Harold James. The Gold Standard, Deflation, and Financial Crisis in the Great Depression: An International Comparison. Chicago: University of Chicago Press, 1991.

BlackRock. "Asset Class Returns. A 20-Year Snapshot." BlackRock.com. Retrieved July 1, 2015. https://www.blackrock.com/investing/literature/investor-education/asset-class-returns-one-pager-va-us.pdf.

Chalmers, George. A Collection of Treaties Between Great Britain and Other Powers. London: John Stockdale, 1790.

Cheetham, RJ. "Asia Crisis." School of Advanced International Studies at Johns Hopkins University. June 7, 1998. https://www.sais-jhu.edu.

Clark, Gregory. "The Long March of History: Farm Wages, Population, and Economic Growth, England 1209-1869." Economic History Review. February 10, 2007. http://faculty.econ.ucdavis.edu/faculty/gclark/papers/farm_wages_&_living_standards.pdf.

Cuban, Mark. "The Stock Market." Blog Maverick: The Mark Cuban Weblog. January 10, 2013.

Curl, Donald W. "Boca Raton and the Florida Land Book of the 1920s." Tequesta. March 01, 1986. http://digitalcollections.fiu.edu/tequesta/files/1986/86_1_02.pdf.

Dalio, Ray. "How the Economic Machine Works." Bridgewater Associates. October 31, 2008. http://bwater.com/Uploads/FileManager/research/how-the-economic-machine-works/ray_dalio__how_the_economic_machine_works__leveragings_and_deleveragings.pdf.

Dash, Mike. Tulipomania. New York City: Broadway Books, 2001.

Defoe, Daniel. An Essay on the South-Sea Trade. London: J. Baker, 1712.

DeLong, Bradford J. "Supply Shocks: The Dilemma of Stagflation." University of California at Berkeley. October 3, 1998. http://econ161.berkeley.edu/multimedia/ASAD1.html.

Dimson, Elroy, Paul Marsh and Mike Staunton. Triumph of the Optimists: 101 Years of Global Investment Returns. Princeton, New Yersey: Princeton University Press, 2002.

Dunn, Alan. "Why $10,000 For A Domain Name Is Still Cheap." Business Insider. April 11, 2011. http://www.businessinsider.com.au/why-10000-for-a-domain-name-is-still-cheap-2011-4.

Federal Deposit Insurance Corporation. "Failed Bank List." FDIC.gov. Retrieved June 11, 2015. https://www.fdic.gov/bank/individual/failed/banklist.html.

Ferreira, Miguel A., Aneel Keswani, António F. Miguel and Sofia B. Ramos. "The Determinants of Mutual Fund Performance: A Cross-Country Study." Oxford University Press. April 18, 2012. http://rof.oxfordjournals.org/content/early/2012/04/18/rof.rfs013.

Friedman, Milton. Unemployment versus Inflation. London: Institute of Economic Affairs, 1975.

Garber, Peter M. "The Collapse of the Bretton Woods Fixed Exchange Rate System." National Bureau of Economic Research. January 15, 1993. http://www.nber.org/chapters/c6876.pdf.

Gibbons, Whit. "The Legend of the Boiling Frog Is Just a Legend." Ecoviews. November 18, 2002. http://srel.uga.edu/outreach/ecoviews/ecoview021118.htm.

Grout, James. "Tulipmania." Encyclopaedia Romana. April 17, 1997. http://penelope.uchicago.edu/~grout/encyclopaedia_romana/aconite/tulipomania.html.

Hasanov, Fuad and Douglas C. Dacy. "Yet Another View on Why a Home Is One's Castle." Real Estate Economics. March 1, 2009. http://papers.ssrn.com/sol3/papers.cfm?abstract_id=1395426.

Hewitt, Mike. "The Fate of Paper Money." DollarDaze. January 7, 2009. http://dollardaze.org/blog/?post_id=00405.

Holley, Joe. "Beloved Radio Broadcaster Paul Harvey Dies at 90." The Washington Post. March 1, 2009. http://www.washingtonpost.com/wp-dyn/content/article/2009/02/28/AR2009022802096_2.html.

Kesmodel, David. The Domain Game: How People Get Rich From Internet Domain Names. Bloomington, Indiana: Xlibris Corporation, 2008.

Keyser, Hannah. "Why Do Ostriches Stick Their Heads in the Sand?" Mental Floss. April 15, 2014. http://mentalfloss.com/article/56176/why-do-ostriches-stick-their-heads-sand.

Knoop, Todd A. Recessions and Depressions: Understanding Business Cycles. Westport, CT: Praeger Publishers, 2004.

Korteweg, Arthur, Roman Kräussl, and Patrick Verwijmeren. "Does It Pay to Invest in Art? A Selection-corrected Returns Perspective." Review of Financial Studies, Forthcoming. October 15, 2013. http://som.yale.edu/sites/default/files/files/Roman%20paper.pdf.

Krugman, Paul. "The State of Macro, Six Years Later." The New York Times. October 14, 2014. http://krugman.blogs.nytimes.com/2014/10/14/the-state-of-macro-six-years-later/?_r=0.

Laplamwanit, Narisa. "A Good Look at the Thai Financial Crisis in 1997-1998." Columbia University. September 1, 1999. http://www.columbia.edu/cu/thai/html/financial97_98.html.

Law, John. Money and Trade Considered, with a Proposal for Supplying the Nation with Money. Edinburgh: Heirs and Successors of Andrew Anderson, 1705.

Lievrouw, Leah. Alternative and Activist New Media. Cambridge: Polity Press, 2011.

Lowenstein, Roger. When Genius Failed. New York City: Random House, 2000.

Mackay, Charles. Extraordinary Popular Delusions and the Madness of Crowds. London: Richard Bentley, 1841.

Mackay, Charles. Extraordinary Popular Delusions and the Madness of Crowds. London: Richard Bentley, 1841.

Macleod, Iain. "Economic Affairs." Millbank Systems. Retrieved 10 November 2015. http://hansard.millbanksystems.com/commons/1965/nov/17/economic-affairs#column_1165.

Madrick, Jeff. Age of Greed: The Triumph of Finance and the Decline of America. New York City: Vintage Books, 2011.

Malkiel, Burton G. A Random Walk Down Wall Street. New York City: W. W. Norton & Company, 2007.

Markham, Jerry W. A Financial History of the United States, Volume II. Armonk, New York: M.E. Sharpe, 2002.

Merton, Robert C. "Theory of Rational Option Pricing." The Bell Journal of Economics and Management Science. May 10, 1973. https://www.jstor.org/stable/3003143?seq=1#page_scan_tab_contents.

Mitchell, Amy. "State of the News Media 2015." Pew Research Center. April 29, 2015. http://www.journalism.org/files/2015/04/FINAL-STATE-OF-THE-NEWS-MEDIA1.pdf.

Moen, Jon. "John Law and the Mississippi Bubble: 1718-1720." Mississippi History Now. October 01, 2001. http://mshistorynow.mdah.state.ms.us/index.php?id=70.

Morgan, Don and James Narron. "Crisis Chronicles: The Panic of 1825 and the Most Fantastic Financial Swindle of All Time." Liberty Street Economics, Federal Reserve Bank of New York. April 10, 2015. http://libertystreeteconomics.newyorkfed.org/2015/04/crisis-chronicles-the-panic-of-1825-and-the-most-fantastic-financial-swindle-of-all-time-.html.

Moya, Elena. "Greece Starts Putting Island Land Up for Sale to Save Economy." The Guardian. June 24, 2010. http://www.theguardian.com/world/2010/jun/24/greece-islands-sale-save-economy.

Nakamoto, Satoshi. "Bitcoin: A Peer-to-Peer Electronic Cash System."
Bitcoin.org. November 1, 2008. https://bitcoin.org/bitcoin.pdf.

Narron, James and David Skeie. "Crisis Chronicles: The Mississippi Bubble
of 1720 and the European Debt Crisis." Federal Reserve Bank of New
York. January 10, 2014.
http://libertystreeteconomics.newyorkfed.org/2014/01/crisis-chronicles-
the-mississippi-bubble-of-1720-and-the-european-debt-crisis.html.

Neal, Larry. "The Financial Crisis of 1825 and the Restructuring of the
British Financial System." Federal Reserve Bank of St. Louis Review. May
01, 1998.
https://files.stlouisfed.org/files/htdocs/publications/review/98/05/9805ln
.pdf.

Odlyzko, Andrew. "Collective Hallucinations and Inefficient Markets: The
British Railway Mania of the 1840s." School of Mathematics and Digital
Technology Center, University of Minnesota. January 15, 2010.
http://www.dtc.umn.edu/~odlyzko/doc/hallucinations.pdf.

Ostrofsky, Mark. Get Rich Click!: The Ultimate Guide to Making Money on
the Internet. New York City: Free Press, 2013.

Pareto, Vilfredo. Manual of Political Economy. Augustus M. Kelley. New
York City: Augustus M. Kelley, 1971.

Philips, Cristopher B. "Considerations for Investing in Non-US Equities."
Vanguard. March 1, 2012. https://personal.vanguard.com/pdf/icriecr.pdf.

Redlener, Irwin. "How to Survive a Nuclear Attack." TED. September 9,
2008.
https://www.ted.com/talks/irwin_redlener_warns_of_nuclear_terrorism/tr
anscript.

Reinert, Hugo and Erik S. Reinert. "Creative Destruction in Economics:
Nietzsche, Sombart, Schumpeter." Springer US. October 1, 2006.
https://link.springer.com/chapter/10.1007%2F978-0-387-32980-2_4.

Reinhart, Carmen M. and Kenneth S. Rogoff. "Financial and Sovereign Debt Crises: Some Lessons Learned and Those Forgotten." International Monetary Fund. December 24, 2013. https://www.imf.org/external/pubs/ft/wp/2013/wp13266.pdf.

Reinhart, Carmen M. and Kenneth S. Rogoff. "The Forgotten History of Domestic Debt." National Bureau of Economic Research. April 15, 2008. http://www.nber.org/papers/w13946.

Richardson, Gary. "Bank Distress During the Great Depression: The Illiquidity-Insolvency Debate Revisited." NBER Working Paper. December 1, 2006. http://www.nber.org/papers/w12717.pdf.

Rubey, Tom. "Computer Ownership Up Sharply in the 1990s." U.S. Department of Labor. March 4, 1999. https://www.bls.gov/opub/btn/archive/computer-ownership-up-sharply-in-the-1990s.pdf.

Sandrock, John E. "John Law's Banque Royale and the Mississippi Bubble." The Currency Collector. August 28, 2008. http://www.thecurrencycollector.com/pdfs/John_Laws_Banque_Royale.pdf.

Scholes, Myron S. and Fisher Black. "The Pricing of Options and Corporate Liabilities." Journal of Political Economy. May 02, 1973. http://www.journals.uchicago.edu/doi/abs/10.1086/260062.

Sée, Henri Eugène. Economic and Social Conditions in France During the Eighteenth Century. New York City: A. A. Kopf, 1927.

Shiller, Robert J. Irrational Exuberance. Princeton, New Yersey: Princeton University Press, 2005.

Siegel, Jeremy J. Stocks for the Long Run. New York City: McGraw-Hill Companies, 1994.

Sohl, Jeffrey. "UNH Center for Venture Research: Angel Investor Market on Solid Path of Recovery in 2011." Peter T. Paul College of Business and

Economics. April 4, 2012.
http://www.unh.edu/news/cj_nr/2012/apr/lw03angel.cfm.

Sommer, Kyle. "The Art of Investing in Art." J.P. Morgan. August 22, 2012.
https://www.jpmorgan.com/pages/jpmorgan/is/thought/magazine/3Q20
13/art.

Steinisch, Monica. "Peer-to-Peer Lending Survey." Consumer Action. June
21, 2012. http://www.consumer-action.org/downloads/english/CA_News-
Summer_2012.pdf.

Surowiecki, James. The Wisdom of Crowds. New York City: Doubleday,
2004.

Suzman, Richard and John Beard. "Global Health and Aging." National
Institute on Aging. October 1, 2011.
https://www.nia.nih.gov/research/publication/global-health-and-
aging/living-longer.

Taleb, Nassim N. Antifragile: Things That Gain From Disorder. New York
City: Random House, 2012.

Taleb, Nassim N. The Black Swan: The Impact of the Highly Improbable.
London: Penguin Books, 2007.

Taleb, Nassim N. The Black Swan: The Impact of the Highly Improbable.
London: Penguin Books, 2007.

Viglione, Rob. "The Consequences of Perpetual Inflation." Seeking Alpha.
March 9, 2009. http://seekingalpha.com/article/124867-the-consequences-
of-perpetual-inflation.

Wallace, Chris. "David Axelrod and Mayor Antonio Villaraigosa Defend
President Obama's Economic Record." Fox News Sunday. September 2,
2012. http://www.foxnews.com/on-air/fox-news-sunday-chris-
wallace/2012/09/2/david-axelrod-and-mayor-antonio-villaraigosa-defend-
president-obamas-economic-record.

Williams, Kaylene C. "Fear Appeal Theory." Research in Business and Economics Journal. March 01, 2012. http://connection.ebscohost.com/c/articles/78390346/fear-appeal-theory.

Wiltbank, Robert E. "Siding With the Angels: Business Angel Investing – Promising Outcomes and Effective Strategies." Nesta.org.uk. May 15, 2009.https://www.nesta.org.uk/sites/default/files/siding_with_the_angels.pdf.

Wiltbank, Robert E. and Warren Boeker. "Returns to Angel Investors in Groups." SSRN. November 14, 2007. http://papers.ssrn.com/sol3/papers.cfm?abstract_id=1028592.

World Gold Council. "World Official Gold Holdings." Gold.org. Retrieved July 20, 2015. http://gold.org.

Yang, YC, Courtney Boen, Karen Gerken, Ting Li, Kristen Schorpp and Kathleen Mullan Harris. "Social Relationships and Physiological Determinants of Longevity Across the Human Life Span." Proceedings of the National Academy of Sciences of the United States of America. January 19, 2016. https://www.ncbi.nlm.nih.gov/pmc/articles/PMC4725506.

CPSIA information can be obtained
at www.ICGtesting.com
Printed in the USA
LVHW081503160119
604146LV00017B/637/P

9 781976 406171